ACCOUNTING THOUGHT AND PRACTICE THROUGH THE YEARS

Edited by Richard P. Brief

A Garland Series

TOWARDS A THEORY AND PRACTICE OF CASH FLOW ACCOUNTING

T. A. Lee

Garland Publishing, Inc.
New York and London
1986

For a complete list of Garland's publications in accounting,
please see the final pages of this volume.

Articles in this book are reprinted by permission of the following:
Pitman Books Ltd., 'Cash Flow Accounting and Corporate Financial Reporting'.
Accounting and Business Research, 'Goodwill—An Example of Will-O'-The Wisp
Accounting'. 'Enterprise Income: Survival or Decline and Fall?', 'Reporting
Cash Flows and Net Realisable Values', 'A Note on Users and Uses of Cash Flow
Information', 'Cash Flow Accounting, Profit and Performance Measurement: A
Response to a Challenge'. *The Accountants Magazine*, 'The Relevance of
Accounting Information Including Cash Flows', 'The Nature and Purpose of Cash
Flow Reporting', 'SSAP 10 and Cash Flow Analysis', 'Further News on Barrett',
'Cash Flow Decomposition and Business Failure'. *Journal of Business Finance
and Accounting*, 'A Case for Cash Flow Reporting', 'The Contribution of Fisher
to Cash Flow Accounting—A Resolution of the Accounting Entity Dilemma',
'A Cash Flow Disclosure of Government-Supported Enterprises' Results', 'Cash Flow
Accounting and the Allocation Problem'. Martinus Nijhoff, 'The Cash
Flow Accounting Alternative for Corporate Financial Reporting'. Scholars
Book Co., 'The Simplicity and Complexity of Accounting'. *Maanblad Voor
Accountancy en Bedrijfshuishoudkunde*, 'Reporting Cash Flows and Net
Realisable Values'. Philip Allan Publishers Ltd., 'Cash Flow Accounting and
Reporting'. *The Investment Analyst*, 'Funds Statements and Cash Flow
Analysis'. *Financial Times*, 'What Cash Flow Analysis Says about BL's
Finances'. *Accountancy*, 'Laker Airways—the Cash Flow Truth'
The Accountant, 'The Lonrho Phenomenon'. Athlone Press Ltd., 'The Financial
Statements of the HongKong and Shanghai Banking Corporation, 1865–1980'.
Abacus, 'A Survey of Accountants' Opinions on Cash Flow Reporting', 'Cash
Flows and Net Realisable Values: Further Evidence of the Intuitive Concepts'.

Copyright © 1986 by T. A. Lee

Library of Congress Cataloging-in-Publication Data

Lee, T. A. (Thomas Alexander)
Towards a theory and practice of cash flow accounting.

(Accounting thought and practice through the years)
Includes index.
1. Cash flow—Accounting. I. Title. II. Series.
HF5681.C28L433 1986 657'.48 86-9957
ISBN 0-8240-7868-3

Design by Bonnie Goldsmith

The volumes in this series are printed on acid-free, 250-year-life paper.

Printed in the United States of America

LIBRARY
The University of Texas
At San Antonio

CONTENTS

Introduction

Review and History
"Cash Flow Accounting and Corporate Financial Reporting,"   3
in M. Bromwich and A. Hopwood (eds.), *Essays in British Accounting Research*, Pitman, 1981, pp. 63–78.

Initial Ideas
"Goodwill: An Example of Will-o'-the-Wisp Accounting,"   20
Accounting and Business Research, Autumn 1971, pp. 318–28.

"The Relevance of Accounting Information Including Cash   32
Flows," *The Accountant's Magazine*, January 1972, pp. 30–34.

Early Argument
"The Nature and Purpose of Cash Flow Accounting," *The*   38
Accountant's Magazine, April 1972, pp. 198–200.

"A Case for Cash Flow Reporting," *Journal of Business Finance*,   41
Summer 1972, pp. 27–36.

"Enterprise Income: Survival or Decline and Fall?" *Accounting*   52
and Business Research, Summer 1974, pp. 178–92.

Extending the Argument
"The Cash Flow Accounting Alternative for Corporate Finan-   69
cial Reporting," in C. van Dam (ed.), *Trends in Managerial and Financial Accounting*, Volume 1, Martinus Nijhoff, 1978, pp. 63–84.

"The Simplicity and the Complexity of Accounting," in   91
R. R. Sterling and A. L. Thomas (eds.), *Accounting for a*

Simplified Firm Owning Depreciable Assets, Scholars Book Co., 1979, pp. 35–55.

"The Contribution of Fisher to Cash Flow Accounting,"   113
Journal of Business Finance and Accounting, Autumn 1979, pp. 321–30.

A Major Extension

"Reporting Cash Flows and Net Realizable Values," *Maanblad*   124
Voor Accountancy en Bedrijfshuishoudkunde, February/March 1981, pp. 82–100.

"Reporting Cash Flows and Net Realisable Values," *Accounting*   143
and Business Research, Spring 1981, pp. 163–70.

Obtaining the Data

"Cash Flow Accounting and Reporting," in T. A. Lee (ed.),   152
Developments in Financial Reporting, Philip Allan, 1981, pp. 148–70.

"Funds Statements and Cash Flow Analysis," *The Investment*   175
Analyst, July 1983, pp. 13–21.

"SSAP 10 and Cash Flow Analysis," *The Accountant's Maga-*   184
zine, June 1984, pp. 232–33.

"Further News on Barratt," *The Accountant's Magazine*, April   186
1985, p. 170.

Analysis of Entities

"What Cash Flow Analysis Says About BL's Finances," *Finan-*   189
cial Times, 23 October 1981, p. 15.

"Laker Airways—The Cash Flow Truth," *Accountancy*, June   190
1982, pp. 115–16.

"The Lonrho Phenomenon," *The Accountant*, 19 May 1983,   193
pp. 11–12.

[with A. W. Stark], "A Cash Flow Disclosure of Government-   195
Supported Enterprises' Results," *Journal of Business Finance and Accounting*, Spring 1984, pp. 1–11.

"The Financial Statements of the Hongkong and Shanghai   207
Banking Corporation, 1865–1980," in F.H.H. King (ed.),
*Eastern Banking: Essays in the History of the Hongkong and
Shanghai Banking Corporation*, Athlone Press, 1983,
pp. 77–92.

Empirical Findings

"A Survey of Accountants' Opinions on Cash Flow Reporting,"   224
Abacus, December 1981, pp. 130–44.

"A Note on Users and Uses of Cash Flow Information,"   239
Accounting and Business Research, Spring 1983, pp. 103–106.

"Cash Flows and Net Realizable Values: Further Evidence of   243
the Intuitive Concepts," *Abacus*, December 1984, pp. 125–37.

"Cash Flow Decomposition and Business Failure," *Research*   256
Supplement to The Accountant's Magazine, 1985, pp. 42–51.

Criticisms

"Cash Flow Accounting and the Allocation Problem," *Journal*   269
of Business Finance and Accounting, Autumn 1982, pp. 341–52.

"Cash Flow Accounting, Profit and Performance Measure-   281
ment: A Response to a Challenge," *Accounting and Business
Research*, Spring 1985, pp. 93–7.

INTRODUCTION

In a recent review of accounting history texts, the following statement was made in conclusion (Lee, 1979, pp. 298–99):

> All four texts covered in this review article reveal clearly a relative lack of progress in financial accounting thought and practice over the last one hundred years or so. Most of the problems identified by practitioners at the beginning of this period are still problems to the practitioners of today. Accounting is gradually maturing as a profession and a discipline. As such its theory and practice are evolving over the years. On the evidence briefly presented in this review, however, they are also revolving—as if on a spinning wheel. Perhaps this more than any other comment should be of most concern to today's accounting policy makers. For how many of these same problems will remain unresolved at the end of the next one hundred years?

Events in the accounting world since 1979 have done nothing to falsify the above comments nor to dispel the pessimism of the final question. The reader has only to review developments in the UK debate on alternatives to historic cost accounting. The almost inevitable result of numerous attempts at current cost accounting and current purchasing power accounting has been confusion, bitterness, and a general loss of credibility in the work of the accountancy profession. In addition, the present diminishing interest in current cost accounting by practitioners and businessmen, despite considerable earlier support, gives credence to Tinker's observation of agency theory-based arguments (1985, p. 111):

> . . . public interest arguments are always a sham to mask self-interest.

When put in less emotive terms, what is being argued is that the stated need to protect investors and other report users from misleading historic cost information during periods of high inflation may not be the real reason for advocating an alternative such as current cost accounting. The truth may be more related to a desire to protect businesses from, say, over-taxation and to justify price increases, and that, when inflation rates diminish, these latter needs subside, and the current cost argument disappears.

Accounting ideas may therefore appear and disappear according to self-interest, and this may explain the aforementioned revolution of accounting problems—that is, what Sterling (1979, p. 4) describes as the "recycling" of accounting issues. However, as previously asserted, there is also an evolution of ideas despite their revolution—each successive generation of accountants revealing a deeper and more detailed understanding of the problem. This can be evidenced, for example, when comparing the debate on financial and physical capital maintenance in the 1920s and 1930s (Lee, 1983) with that in the 1970s (Sterling and Lemke, 1982). The later arguments are much more sophisticated, but the principles discussed remain the same. The lack of a generally acceptable solution is also consistently lacking.

Relevance of Ideas

The above comments lead to two observations on the development of accounting ideas and practices. First, the repeated incidence of specific accounting problems prompts the important question of whether the proposed solutions are relevant. The fact that an accounting problem such as coping with the instability of the monetary measurement unit has been under discussion by theorists and practitioners since the early 1900s, and numerous solutions have been advocated and practiced recently without the debate subsiding, would indicate that either the problem is misspecified or the solutions are inadequate. That this has occurred despite a wealth of available literature (details of which can be found in Lee [1985] and Tweedie and Whittington [1985]) does not give grounds for optimism regarding the eventual resolution of the problem.

Second, the history of accounting is replete of ideas. Some are new and some are extensions of others. Within the context of the evolution and revolution of these ideas, it is of considerable interest to accounting historians to discover what has influenced them. Such knowledge enhances an understanding of why the ideas were advanced in the first place and, more important, provides clues as to whether they have a continuing relevance. This might prevent any unnecessary "recycling" of accounting ideas and ensure that past ideas were applied relevantly and developed appropriately. Certainly the quality of the UK current cost accounting debate would have been improved considerably by such an understanding.

Cash Flow Accounting

This book concerns developments in the history of one accounting idea. It discusses cash flow accounting and, as such, relates what can only be described as a "recycled" accounting problem. Cash flow accounting is the oldest form of monetary accounting, preceding the now conventional accrual and allocation-based accounting (Winjum, 1972). Specifically in terms of external financial reporting, cash flow accounting has been ignored for many decades except, occasionally, in small and noncommercial organizations such as charities and churches. However, it has been discussed infrequently in the literature since the early 1950s (for a review, see Paper 1). But its most consistent development is attributable in the 1970s and 1980s to Lawson and Lee in the UK. This text concentrates on the work of the latter writer and aims to provide the reader not only with a relevant selection of his writings on the subject since 1971, but also with a structured collection that attempts to explain the way in which his thinking has developed on the subject. In particular, it will focus on relevant influences.

Cash flow accounting can be described in the following way (Lee, 1981, p. 63):

> [Cash flow accounting] is the term used to denote a system of financial reporting which describes the financial performance of an entity in cash terms. It is based on a matching of periodic cash inflows and outflows, free of credit transactions and arbitrary accounting allocations . . . as such, it is a measurement and reporting system which avoids time lags and distortions. It concentrates on the liquidity and financial management of the reporting entity. . . .

This definition suggests a deceptively simple form of accounting and reporting. As the writings reproduced in this text will indicate, it is far more complex than casual observation would suggest. Indeed, it follows in the tradition of numerous financial accounting theorists—that is, a fairly detailed argument and structure at the beginning and a considerable fine tuning and adjustment subsequently due to a combination of further thinking and responses to criticism.

Progress of Ideas

Few accounting theorists have attempted to explain the progress of their ideas over time and the influences that have shaped these ideas. With some theories, it is possible to deduce the main influences. For example, in the 1920s and 1930s, the work of the economist Fisher had a considerable effect on accounting theorists such as Canning (1929), and the work of Sweeney (1936) owed much to the thinking of European writers such as Mahlberg and Schmalenbach. Other writings are more difficult to assess—for example, Paton (1918) advocated initially the use of replacement costs for reporting purposes, but, by 1920, he was arguing for their use for management purposes only (Paton, 1920) and, finally, with Littleton, supported firmly the production of historic cost reports (Paton and Littleton, 1940). No conclusive evidence is available to explain these changes (Zeff, 1979), and given the considerable influence of Paton on accounting matters from the 1920s onwards, it is an important omission.

When the work of the accounting theorists of the 1960s and 1970s is examined, the influences and changes are even more intangible. In what Nelson (1973) has described rather extravagantly as the "golden age" of a priori theory in accounting and Wells (1976) has termed more realistically a revolution in accounting thinking, the theorists of the 1960s are usually silent on the evolution of their thinking. Edwards and Bell (1961), for example, appear to rely on conventional marginalist economic analysis, revealing little obvious dependence on prior accounting theorists advocating replacement costs such as Paton (1918) and Rorem (1929). Likewise, Sterling (1970) uses his background (in his case as a philosopher of science) and, despite a recognition of accounting theorists in his analyses, appears not to have been influenced in his advocation of sale values by other theorists such as Daines (1929), Canning (1929), and MacNeal (1931). Chambers (1979b), on the other hand, has attempted to outline the development of his arguments for continuously contemporary accounting. But, in doing so, his explanations appear mainly as descriptions of events and responses to individual critics, and there is little evidence in any of his work of influencing by other accounting theorists. Indeed, in his main work (Chambers, 1966) the influences appear to be those of nonaccounting theorists such as Cherry, Margenau, and Simon. With ideas in accounting arguably being part of the same evolutionary process, coupled with the considerable importance of writers such as Edwards and Bell, Sterling, and Chambers in accounting thought in the 1960s and 1970s, a complete understanding of their work in the context of the history of such thought unfortunately is not possible. It is hoped that developments in cash flow accounting can avoid these omissions. Such is the purpose of this introduction, although it must be noted that it is the work of one theorist (Lee) that is being examined.

The Lee Case for Cash Flow

As previously indicated, the idea of cash flow accounting for purposes of external financial reporting can hardly be described as new. However, in its modern form of interrelated financial statements, it is very different from its antecedents in terms of both purpose and structure. Thus, this review of its modern development by Lee will be concerned mainly with contemporary influences.

Lee commenced his interest in cash flow accounting as part of a study of the nature of goodwill for accounting purposes (Paper 2). Originating in a classroom analysis of goodwill in takeover and merger situations, Lee's paper is devoted largely to a detailed examination of the nature of goodwill and the problems associated with its accounting for financial reporting purposes. However, Lee's analysis reveals his unhappiness at leaving an accounting problem unanswered merely because of its enormity, and his paper concludes with a detailed postscript in which he suggests the reporting of forecast and past cash flows to enable the use of financial statements to determine entity (and capital) valuations based on a possible discounting of these cash flows (and thereby recognizing and taking into account all resources of the entity). As such, the paper is merely a glimpse into the complex function of cash flow accounting, and much work had yet to be done to flesh out the rather over-simplified recommendations. The major influence on Lee's thinking at this stage was undoubtedly Chambers (1966) and particularly the latter's advocation of "correspondence" as a major concept of accounting and reporting—that is, the need to reflect economic reality as objectively as possible in financial statements. Lee's insistence on the need for accountants to recognize adequately the existence of goodwill is an example of his acknowledgement of the importance of Chambers's concept of "correspondence" in accounting thought—financial statements being a substitute for direct observation of business events and resources.

The 1971 goodwill paper was supported by a short paper written at about the same time for a professional journal in which the relevance of cash flow information to investors and others is argued (Paper 3). The arguments for cash flow accounting are spelt out in more detail than in Paper 2, but remain in outline only—that is, particularly, the need for relevant financial information and the wisdom of avoiding subjective accounting allocations in financial reports. The major impetus for the relevance argument had been derived from a paper by Shwayder (1968), and the work of Thomas (1969) was helping Lee formulate ideas on the judgmental aspects of accounting.

Due to a considerable interest by academics and practitioners in the initial ideas, a much fuller argument for cash flow accounting was written in 1972 (Paper 5). Arguing, inter alia, that cash flow information reflecting past and forecast performance is suited to the needs of a variety of decision makers, Lee also provides in this paper a detailed reporting format of linking financial statements and supporting explanations. At this stage in his thinking, Lee saw a system of reported cash flows as the focal point of financial reporting, with other information (such as historical cost data) supplementary to it. As such, his ideas were compatible with those being argued by another UK academic, Lawson (1971). Remarkably, although the early work of Lawson and Lee was similar, both were relatively unaware of each other's work at the time of writing. In the case of Lee, the matter of fundamental importance in cash flow accounting was (and is) the need to develop a relevant system of financial reporting for a variety of users, whereas Lawson's ideas were (and are) directed at important issues concerning taxation, distribution, wage claims, and pricing. Lee's most basic argument is the reporting need to reflect the cash flow of the reporting entity as the single most important feature of its attempt to survive. This reporting characteristic has been the focal point in all his writings on cash flow accounting. But it should also be noted that his early arguments in this context predated the liquidity crisis of the mid 1970s in the UK and elsewhere, and thus cash flow accounting should not be seen as a short-term response to such events and thus likely to disappear when the crisis goes. Cash flow is seen by Lee as fundamental to every business at any time.

Paper 5 was supported by a simplified version for students (Paper 4), following Lee's belief that it is students of accounting who should be influenced more than practitioners. The latter tend to be set in their ways and attitudes—partly due to education and training and partly because of time pressures. Changes in accounting are most likely to come from students exposed to new ideas rather than from practitioners who have to give up old and often cherished habits. Paper 5 was also followed up by a detailed critique of the income concept (Paper 6), which appears to Lee to be the root cause of much of the subjectiveness and arbitrariness in financial accounting and reporting. The nature and problems associated with periodic income are explored at length in this paper, with the general conclusion that other relevant forms of reporting (including cash flows) ought to be considered. The work of Solomons (1961) was a considerable influence on Lee in this respect, and it is interesting in 1985 to reflect on Solomons's concluding remarks (p. 383):

> Each of us sees the future differently, no doubt. But my own guess is that, so far as the history of accounting is concerned, the next twenty-five years may subsequently be seen to have been the twilight of income measurement.

The twenty-five-year period speculated by Solomons is nearly complete, and given the almost universal problems associated with programs of accounting standardization, the rebellions, criticisms, and doubts over alternatives to historic cost accounting, and the apparent upsurge in interest in cash flow accounting in the US and UK, there is too little evidence to suggest that Solomons was wrong in his prediction. Certainly, the idea of cash flow accounting has received remarkably little challenge or criticism during the same period.

Gap and Extension

Lee did not write on cash flow accounting between 1974 and 1978. This was partly in order to allow his initial ideas and arguments to "bed down" in the literature (typically, it appears to take four or five years for such writings to have some influence—if they are likely to influence at all) and partly because a related issue required researching. Accounting theorists normally present their arguments on the implicit assumptions that the financial statements they advocate for reporting purposes will, if relevant to the needs of report users, be used and understood by them. In 1974 it appeared to Lee to be important to determine whether or not existing reports were used and, if so, if they were likely to be understood. For, if cash flow accounting statements were believed by accounting policymakers to be relevant to report users, they could have utility in that respect only if they were likely to be used *and* understood. No matter how relevant an accounting statement is, it is useless unless both used and understood.

In conjunction with Tweedie, Lee commenced a series of research studies covering almost a decade, in which shareholder use and understanding of historic cost, current cost, and current purchasing power accounting information was questioned (Lee and Tweedie, 1975a, 1975b, 1976, 1977, 1978, and 1981). The overall conclusion from these studies was that only a very few suitably educated and experienced investors use and are capable of using accounting information based on accruals and allocations. In addition, Tweedie (1977) had provided some initial but related evidence that nonaccountants tend to interpret such information in cash flow terms, thereby leading to potential misunderstanding regarding the nature and meaning of traditional financial statements.

The above shareholder evidence was important in its own right, but has since been largely ignored in the UK by accounting policymakers and standard-setters except for a rather weak attempt to propose simplifying financial statements (Hammill, 1979). But it was also important to Lee as a strengthening of his arguments for cash flow accounting. The evidence suggested that not only were there measurement problems in conventional accounting but also communication issues. Cash flow accounting appeared to Lee to be a solution to both measurement and communication problems, and this argument was contained by him in a 1978 paper to a European conference (Paper 7). The paper had two other important objectives—it was an opportunity to pull together Lee's previous arguments for cash flow accounting (which had been influenced further by the writings of Thomas [1974], Chambers [1975], and Sterling [1975]). What each of these writers had convinced Lee about was the need to state clearly the cash flow argument in logical terms, using simple examples, and to challenge forthrightly the conventional wisdoms of accounting. In addition, they suggested through their writings the need to argue their case regularly. Lee's case for cash flow accounting has been made continuously since 1978.

Regular Argument

The opportunity for a further approach to presenting the case for cash flow accounting came in 1979 in an invitation from Sterling and Thomas to examine a simple business situation and recommend an appropriate financial accounting system (Paper 8). Several accounting theorists were presented with this situation, and in the form of a scientific experiment, it was the hope of Sterling and Thomas that this would provide a common solution (and, if not, at least a means of examining why there were differences in the solutions presented). In the event, what was achieved was what Whittington (1981) later described as an accounting Tower of Babel. Each theorist, perhaps inevitably, presented a solution in terms that represented the reporting model with which he was usually identified. A form of functional fixation had been discovered by Sterling and Thomas. Lee presented a simple cash flow and net realizable value combination based on a "real life" business situation. In Paper 7, he advocates net realizable value balance sheets, and this theme is continued in Paper 8—although cash flows and realizable values are kept separate in both formats.

At this stage of his thinking, the impact of the net realizable value accounting theorists on Lee was becoming very apparent—particularly through the work of Sterling. In fact, arguably the single most influential piece of work was Sterling (1979). In this text, Sterling argues for a scientific approach to accounting theory with the acceptance that accounting cannot be treated totally in the same way as a more obvious science such as physics or chemistry. Nevertheless, it is a subject that is capable of being governed by scientifically derived rules of measurement. Cash flow accounting appears to Lee to fall into such a category. An elementary example of this way of thinking is seen in the work of the economist Fisher (Paper 9) in which the business entity is regarded as a clearing house for business transactions and accounting allocations are not regarded as suitable means of recording the latter. This straightforward, logical thinking about an issue such as a relevant identification of an appropriate form of accounting for the business entity has been sadly lacking in accounting standard-setting (Lee, 1980).

A Combined System

For Lee, the idea of combining cash flows and net realizable values was born in Papers 7 and 8—particularly in the latter. In Papers 10 and 11 Lee argues that net realizable values are essentially potential cash flows (what Chambers has described in numerous writings as current cash equivalents) and, as such, are suited to be combined with realized cash flows in a total cash flow accounting system. Such a suggestion has a number of advantages. The main ones are, first, the ability to provide a complete system of cash flow information (realized and unrealized; income measures and balance sheet positions) without abandoning the principal objection to conventional accounting allocations and, second, the bringing together of two apparently separate schools of accounting theorists—the cash flow school and the net realizable value school. Papers 10 and 11 must also be seen as a deliberate response by Lee to the challenge of critics such as Egginton (1984) that his cash flow proposals lack an income measure of performance and a related statement of financial position.

Deriving and Analyzing Data

Prior to 1981, Lee's work in the literature on cash flow accounting had been concerned mainly with a priori argument. However, two further matters had impinged on his thinking. The first related to his teaching business and bank managers at the Manchester Business School and elsewhere, which had convinced him of the need to instruct them on how to derive cash flow data if it were not immediately available in the form of the financial statements he was advocating. The second matter was, again, the influence of Chambers (1973), who, by practical illustration, had demonstrated the frailties of conventional accounting practices and the already considerable use of net realizable values in the latter. Papers 12, 13, 14, and 15 develop this theme in relation to cash flow accounting by revealing the ease with which realized cash flows can be derived from conventional funds statements.

These papers, through the examples that Lee uses, reveal also a further development in his thinking—that is, the formatting of the derived cash flow data in terms of inflow and outflow and in such a way as to provide an objective reporting for analysis purposes. The detailed form of analysis of realized and unrealized cash flows is contained in Lee (1984), but the most immediate concern is with liquidity performance in realized terms.

Papers 16 to 20, inclusive, are further examples of the potential utility of cash flow data; in each case, the subject being a well-known entity (and usually one in which there have been or are severe liquidity problems). Paper 16 examines a failed private enterprise entity subsequently supported financially by government. Paper 17 examines the Laker Airways collapse and reveals how obvious the cash flow signs were prior to failure. The high-risk nature of Lonrho is observable in cash flow terms in Paper 18. The cash flow problems of government-supported entities are outlined in Paper 19. Paper 20 is of specific interest to the accounting historian, as it applies the ideas and techniques of cash flow accounting and analysis to a historical review of the development of a major international banking corporation. It is an example of Lee's desire to link the past to the present and use history as a means of understanding the current position.

Producing Evidence

It is remarkable how little empirical research has been undertaken by a priori accounting theorists. Some have undertaken none, relying on the force and logic of their arguments to win the day (for example, Edwards and Bell). Others, such as Sterling (1969) and Chambers (1980) have completed a little, again depending largely on their argumentative skills. Lee, on the other hand, sees a need for a balanced approach—some a priori reasoning and some empirical support. In this respect, his output is not prolific, although his "use and understanding" work with Tweedie is extensive. Nevertheless, a number of studies have been undertaken—Paper 21 provides evidence of a considerable support for cash flow accounting in practice by accountants; Paper 22 discovers the alarming finding that little or no attention is paid to cash flow and liquidity matters by investors and others; Paper 23 extends the previous work of Tweedie (1977) and concludes that the cash flow intuitions of nonaccountants can be removed by an educational process based on accruals and allocations; and Paper 24 describes some exploratory work involving the decomposition of cash flows as a means of detecting signs of business failure. Each of these papers attempts to support the reasoning in Lee's earlier work—that there is a case and support for cash flow accounting; that nonaccountants do think in cash flow terms but reveal a distinct bias in their use of financial reports for noncash data; and that there are cash flow signs of business failure to be detected and thus, again, a need for cash flow reporting.

Answering the Critics

Arguably the most difficult task for the accounting theorist is answering the challenges made by critics of his arguments. A priori reasoning is inevitably followed by such challenges, and the theorist must be willing to listen to the critic and, where relevant, use the counter arguments to improve the original theorizing. Chambers (1970 and 1974) has been an outstanding example of the theorist answering his critics—although his strict attention to argumentative rigor has made his responses appear at times unbending to the weight of the criticism.

Cash flow accounting thoughts are no strangers to detailed criticism—for example, Rutherford (1982) and Egginton (1984). In the main, the criticism has concerned, first, the argument that cash flow accounting is an allocation-free system and, second, the lack of an income measure and a statment of financial position in cash flow accounting theory. These criticisms had a validity in terms of the original arguments of Lee (for example, as in Paper 5) but have less merit as the original arguments have been amended and developed. Paper 25 answers specifically the allocation challenge—Lee acknowledging that only time-period accounting allocations are avoided by cash flow accounting. Paper 26 covers the income and financial position criticisms—these having already been incorporated in earlier writings (Papers 10 and 11).

Conclusions

Lee's arguments for cash flow accounting have attempted to be a response to a need to provide financial reports that reflect the liquidity performance of the reporting entity. They adopt a commonsense approach to theorizing and have included practical illustrations and empirical evidence in support of the basic a priori reasoning. The ideas have been at least partially shaped by a variety of influences, the most important of which have been Chambers and Sterling. This debt is openly acknowledged by Lee. But it is one that concerns their means of argument rather more than the end product. It should be of interest to accounting historians and policymakers alike that the arguments of Lee, challenging conventional accounting thinking from a different direction from that adopted by Chambers and Sterling, have arrived at a proposed system of financial reporting that utilizes net realizable values.

One final matter, Chambers, particularly, has evidenced a considerable working interest in the history and development of accounting ideas—witness his work on such writers as Bonbright (1971) and Canning (1979a). This review of Lee's contribution to the history of the cash flow accounting idea is in that tradition—however pale the imitation.

REFERENCES

J. B. Canning, *The Economics of Accountancy: A Critical Analysis of Accounting Theory*, Ronald Press, 1929.

R. J. Chambers, *Accounting, Evaluation and Economic Behaviour*, Prentice Hall, 1966.

―――, "Second Thoughts on Contemporary Accounting," *Abacus*, September 1970, pp. 39–55.

―――, "Value to the Owner," *Abacus*, June 1971, pp. 62–72.

―――, *Securities and Obscurities*, Gower Press, 1973.

―――, "Third Thoughts," *Abacus*, December 1974, pp. 129–37.

―――, "Accounting for Inflation," *Exposure Draft*, University of Sydney, 1975.

―――, "Canning's *The Economics of Accountancy*—After 50 Years," *Accounting Review*, October 1979, pp. 764–75.

―――, "The Development of the Theory of Continuously Contemporary Accounting," *Working Paper 13*, Academy of Accounting Historians, 1979.

―――, "The Design of Accounting Standards," *Monograph 1*, University of Sydney Accounting Research Centre, 1980.

H. C. Daines, "The Changing Objectives of Accounting," *Accounting Review*, June 1929, pp. 94–110.

E. O. Edwards and P. W. Bell, *The Theory and Measurement of Business Income*, University of California Press, 1961.

D. A. Egginton, "In Defence of Profit Measurement: Some Limitations of Cash Flow and Value Added as Performance Measures for External Reporting," *Accounting and Business Research*, Spring 1984, pp. 99–112.

A. E. Hammill, *Simplified Financial Statements*, Institute of Chartered Accountants in England and Wales, 1979.

G. H. Lawson, "Cash-Flow Accounting," *The Accountant*, 28 October 1971 and 4 November 1971, pp. 386–89 and 620–22.

T. A. Lee, "The Evolution and Revolution of Financial Accounting: A Review Article," *Accounting and Business Research*, Autumn 1979, pp. 292–99.

―――, "The Accounting Entity Concept, Accounting Standards and Inflation Accounting," *Accounting and Business Research*, Spring 1980, pp. 176–86.

―――, "Cash Flow Accounting and Corporate Financial Reporting," in M. Bromwich and A. Hopwood (eds.), *Essays in British Accounting Research*, Pitman, 1981, pp. 63–78.

———, "The Early Debate on Financial and Physical Capital," *Accounting Historians Journal*, Spring 1983, pp. 25–50.

———, *Cash Flow Accounting*, Van Nostrand, 1984.

———, *Income and Value Measurement: Theory and Practice*, Van Nostrand, Third Edition, 1985.

——— and D. P. Tweedie, "Accounting Information: An Investigation of Shareholder Usage," *Accounting and Business Research*, Autumn 1975, pp. 280–91.

———, "Accounting Information: An Investigation of Shareholder Understanding," *Accounting and Business Research*, Winter 1975, pp. 3–17.

———, "The Private Shareholder: His Sources of Financial Information and His Understanding of Reporting Practices," *Accounting and Business Research*, Autumn 1976, pp. 304–14.

———, *The Private Shareholder and the Corporate Report*, Institute of Chartered Accountants in England and Wales, 1977.

———, "Subjectivity in Research in Shareholder Behaviour," *The Accountant's Magazine*, July 1978, pp. 295–98.

———, *The Institutional Investor and Financial Information*, Institute of Chartered Accountants in England and Wales, 1981.

K. MacNeal, *Truth in Accounting*, Ronald Press, 1939.

C. L. Nelson, "A Priori Research in Accounting," in N. Dopuch and L. Revsine (eds.), *Accounting Research 1960–1970: A Critical Evaluation*, Centre for International Education and Research in Accounting, 1973.

W. A. Paton, "The Significance and Treatment of Appreciation in the Accounts," *Twentieth Annual Report*, Michigan Academy of Science, 1918, pp. 35–49.

———, "Depreciation, Appreciation and Productive Capacity," *Journal of Accountancy*, July 1920, pp. 1–11.

——— and A. C. Littleton, *An Introduction to Corporate Accounting*, American Accounting Association, 1940.

C. R. Rorem, "Replacement Cost in Accounting Valuation," *Accounting Review*, September 1929, pp. 167–74.

B. A. Rutherford, "The Interpretation of Cash Flow Reports and the Other Allocation Problem," *Abacus*, June 1982, pp. 40–49.

K. Shwayder, "Relevance," *Journal of Accounting Research*, Spring 1968, pp. 86–97.

D. Solomons, "Economic and Accounting Concepts of Income," *Accounting Review*, July 1961, pp. 374–83.

R. R. Sterling, "A Test of the Uniformity Hypothesis," *Abacus*, September 1969, pp. 39–47.

————, *Theory of the Measurement of Enterprise Income*, University Press of Kansas, 1970.

————, "Relevant Financial Reporting in an Age of Price Changes," *Journal of Accountancy*, February 1975, pp. 42–51.

————, *Toward a Science of Accounting*, Scholars Book Co., 1979.

———— and K. W. Lemke, *Maintenance of Capital: Financial Versus Physical*, Scholars Book Co., 1982.

H. W. Sweeney, *Stabilized Accounting*, Harper, 1936.

A. L. Thomas, "The Allocation Problem in Financial Accounting Theory," *Studies in Accounting Research 3*, American Accounting Association, 1969.

————, "The Allocation Problem: Part Two," *Studies in Accounting Research 9*, American Accounting Association, 1974.

T. Tinker, *Paper Prophets: A Social Critique of Accounting*, Holt, Rinehart and Winston, 1985.

D. P. Tweedie, "Cash Flows and Realisable Values: The Intuitive Concepts? An Empirical Test," *Accounting and Business Research*, Winter 1977, pp. 2–13.

D. Tweedie and G. Whittington, *The Debate on Inflation Accounting*, Cambridge University Press, 1985.

M. C. Wells, "A Revolution in Accounting Thought?" *Accounting Review*, July 1976, pp. 471–82.

G. Whittington, "A Tower of Babel?" *Accounting and Business Research*, Summer 1981, pp. 249–52.

J. O. Winjum, *The Role of Accounting in the Economic Development of England: 1500 to 1750*, Centre for International Education and Research in Accounting, 1972.

S. A. Zeff, "Paton on the Effects of Changing Prices," in S. A. Zeff, J. Demski, and N. Dopuch (eds.), *Essays in Honour of William A. Paton*, University of Michigan, 1979.

Review and History

3 Cash flow accounting and corporate financial reporting

T A Lee
Professor of Accountancy and Finance, University of Edinburgh

Approximately 50 writings have been read as preparation for this essay. Three-quarters of them were U.K.-based, and in excess of one-half could be attributed to two U.K. writers—Professors Lawson and Lee. Furthermore, three-quarters of the writings were published in the 1970s. Thus, the subject of cash flow accounting (CFA) is a relatively new one, not attracting many writers to its cause, and being of mainly U.K. interest (at least within the context of corporate financial reporting). However, despite this lack of apparent support in the literature, CFA remains potentially as a serious and viable addition to the corporate financial reporting function, and it is the aim of this essay to review it in order to assess its importance in this context. Inevitably, because of the volume of their contribution to CFA, the work of Lawson and Lee will form the substance of this review. But the work of other accountants will be examined, and a full bibliography is given at the end of the essay.

Nature and Role of CFA

CFA is the term used to denote a system of financial reporting which describes the financial performance of an entity in cash terms. It is based on a matching of periodic cash inflows and outflows, free of credit transactions and arbitrary accounting allocations. Inflows include cash from trading operations and providers of long-term finance; and outflows include payments for replacement and growth investment, taxation, interest, and distributions. As such, it is a measurement and reporting system which avoids time lags and distortions. It concentrates on the liquidity and financial management of the reporting entity, and can be conceived in terms both of actual and forecast cash transactions.

History of CFA

CFA is not a new concept. In fact, as Winjum (1972) has demonstrated, it was the main system of accounting up to the beginning of the 18th century.

Prior to that time, accounting allocations and profit measurements were relatively unimportant; the profit and loss account being used to close off ledger accounts at each period end. However, with the advent of the concept and practice of business continuity, the need grew to produce periodic measures of profit and statements of financial position (Littleton and Zimmerman, 1963). Thus, the basic cash transactions became the foundation for the allocation-based systems of accounting of today.

Although there has been a reasonably sustained interest in funds flow statements (based on allocated accounting data) since the beginning of the 20th century (see Käfer and Zimmerman, 1979), CFA appears to have received little or no support from accountants until the early 1960s. At that time, there was concern over the use of 'cash flow' data in financial analysis—cash flow being interpreted as 'profit plus depreciation' (see Paton, 1963 and Drebin, 1964).[1] The major worry was that such data were being used for decision-making purposes as a substitute for income, and that the cost of durable assets was not being taken into account. Also, at this time, two writers advocated the reporting of pure cash flow data (i.e. CFA)—in the U.S., Coughlan (1960; 1962; 1964) and, in the U.K., Edey (1963).

Coughlan's recommendations were based on a capital budgeting approach involving the reporting of past and expected cash flows as a basis for producing discounted cash flow balance sheets from which measures of income could be derived as a form of internal rate of return. He described these computations of economic income and value as 'industrial accounting', and argued for them because of the distortions caused by conventional accounting allocations, and the need, therefore, to account properly for the influence of time. His pioneering work which, however, appeared to be aimed at internal reporting functions, was apparently not developed further by him.

Edey, on the other hand, advocated the reporting of forecast cash flows because of the difficulties associated with the measurement of profit. He believed such predictive data to be more relevant than profits for the purposes of estimating future dividend levels, evaluating management, and assessing corporate liquidity. Mainly concerned with the provision of relevant information for investors, and with the lack of precision in the meaning of profit, Edey also recommended that investors should be provided with net realizable value-based balance sheets in order to assess potential corporate liquidity, chargeable capacity,[2] and the minimum return to be earned on investment. Edey repeated his recommendations later (1970) but has not developed them since in the literature.

Staubus (1961; 1966) also provided a relatively early contribution to the contemporary CFA debate when reviewing the nature and role of the

---

[1] Confusing CFA with 'cash flow' data which are allocation-based is a common mistake in the accountancy literature—particularly that of the U.S. in the 1960s.

[2] Defined as the value of the assets available to act as security for potential borrowings.

funds flow statement for investors. Identifying the importance of assessing corporate liquidity for investment or managerial decisions, he rejected the use of net realizable value data for this purpose and, instead, advocated the reporting of funds statements based on cash or near-cash resources (i.e. including debtors and creditors). In his early work (1961), he envisaged such statements as being of use only to short-term creditors, but in his later writing (1966), he appeared to have widened his views on the relevance of such statements. He particularly emphasized the opinion that cash flow statements ought to distinguish recurrent from non-recurrent flows in order to aid their users in assessing corporate liquidity. Staubus does not appear to have developed his work on CFA since 1966.

Contemporary Contributions

In 1968, Lawson (1968) published his first paper on CFA. Since then he has continued to develop his ideas both conceptually and empirically. Lee (1971) published his first CFA contribution some time later but, together, these writers have provided most of the CFA literature of the 1970s, and this will be examined in detail in later sections. However, Lawson and Lee have not been alone in their support of CFA. In the U.S., the main contributors (other than Coughlan and Staubus) have been Thomas (1969; 1974; 1979), Ijiri (1977; 1978; 1979) and Heath (1978).[3] Briston and Fawthrop (1971), Jones (1975), Climo (1976), and Waldron (1980), have also provided contributions to the CFA debate and literature in the U.K. (in addition to Edey). Their work will be discussed prior to that of Lawson and Lee but, meantime, the U.S. contribution will be reviewed briefly.

U.S. Contributions

Thomas' pioneering work on the frailties of the allocation system in conventional accounting led him to recommend the abandonment of income measurement by accountants, concentrating instead on funds statements using a notion of funds defined in terms of cash plus debtors minus creditors (1969). These net quick asset statements were recommended in addition to statements of monetary and non-monetary assets (1974).

---

3 The idea of combining CFA and NRVA ought not to be confused with the suggestion by Ronen and Sorter of merging a market rate-determined economic value of the reporting entity with the exit values of its conventionally classified assets and liabilities—see Ronen and Sorter (1972) and Ronen (1974). The Ronen and Sorter proposal was intended to provide investors with (a) means of comparing market values with economic values of the reporting entity and its equity; (b) managerially forecasted cash flows (but in the form of reporting one discounted measure of value); and (c) measurement of the conversion of entity asset economic values into exit values, and vice versa. Nowhere in their system was there a recommendation to specifically disclose either past or forecast CFA data.

However, his relative vagueness with regard to what precise form these statements should take, leaves Thomas' work in a somewhat indeterminate state; he is strongly in favour of reporting allocation-free data (especially related to flow statements) but is less than clear with regard to position statements.[4]

Historic cost accounting is the area for which Ijiri is best known (1967). However, he has recently advocated the use of CFA (1977; 1978; 1979) as a means of enabling the results of managerial decisions to be evaluated on the same basis as they were taken. Ijiri's CFA system, however, is an extension of historic cost, allocation-based accounting. He recommends the reporting of statements reflecting investment flows (changes in historic cost-based assets) and financing flows (changes in sources of finance). The former flows are to be stated before deduction of fixed asset depreciation, and the latter flows are to include such aggregate provisions. Historic costs in this sense are used not to value assets but to describe the entity's investment in them. Ijiri concentrates on what he describes as cash flow recovery (usually profit plus depreciation, interest, and fixed asset sales) and relates this to the total gross investment in assets (before depreciation) in order to determine corporate recovery rates. He recommends these rates as surrogates for discounted cash flow returns in situations where *ex post* measurements of the latter are not possible due to the continuity of the entity concerned. It is not, however, a system which can be regarded as pure CFA; rather, it should be looked upon as an extension of historic cost accounting.

The final U.S. contributor to CFA has been Heath (1978). Writing of the need to provide relevant financial information for investors, creditors and other persons interested in evaluating corporate solvency and liquidity, he has advocated the presentation of a statement of cash receipts and payments (giving a listing of the various sources of cash matched with an equivalent listing of the various uses to which these were put), coupled with a further two statements—one describing the various changes on the assets side of the historic cost-based balance sheet, and the other dealing with the equivalent changes on the liabilities side of the same report. As such, Heath's recommendations do contain an element of CFA but they cannot be taken as advocations of a complete system of financial reporting based on CFA.

U.K. Contributions

A consistent feature of the U.K. accounting literature over the last 10 years or so has been the development of a detailed argument and structure for CFA as a major part of the corporate financial reporting function. Spearheaded by Lawson (1968; 1969; 1970; 1971a; 1971b; 1971c; 1972;

---

[4] In his most recent work, Thomas (1979) advocates cash flow statements coupled with virtually unspecified allocation-free balance sheets.

1973; 1975a; 1975b; 1976; 1978a; 1978b; 1978c; 1979) and Lee (1971; 1972a; 1972b; 1972c; 1974; 1978; 1979a; 1979b; 1979c; 1980a; 1980b), the main argument has been for a logical and coherent reporting framework including statements of past and forecast cash flows, and supported by additional statements concerning, *inter alia*, explanations of variances between actual and forecast data, descriptions of the major assumptions underlying forecast results, audit opinions, and explanations of non-cash transactions. In these respects, the work of Lawson and Lee are reasonably similar, although Lee (1980b) has extended it to include net realizable value-based position statements which relate to the recommended CFA statements.[5]

There have been other contributions to the U.K. debate on CFA. Edey (1963; 1970), as mentioned earlier, provided the initial impetus with his suggestion for the reporting of forecast cash flows. Briston and Fawthrop (1971) also suggested the reporting of such forecasts, supplemented by an audited statement of variances between actual and previously forecast results. Jones (1975) supported the idea of past and forecast cash flow statements as a feasible alternative to the problem of standardizing accounting allocations. The Sandilands Committee on Inflation Accounting (1975), whilst appearing to receive the idea of CFA for corporate financial reporting purposes with some enthusiasm, rejected it on the practical ground that it would not comply with existing company law because of its lack of adherence to statements of profit and financial position.[6] In contrast, Climo (1976) felt that the reporting of CFA data (past and future) would be exceedingly relevant to investors, particularly if the flows concerned were divisionalized, segregated between recurrent and non-recurrent items, and supported by some form of (unspecified) net realizable value-based balance sheet. Waldron (1980) also felt that past CFA reports ought to be supported by forecast data and financial position data—in this case, the former was recommended to be contained in a statement of needs and resources (describing the next 12 months cash receipts and payments), and the latter to take the form of a balance sheet based on (undefined) economic values. On the whole, therefore, these contributions have lent support and added weight to the CFA argument and debate without having the degree of depth and consistency to be evidenced in the work of Lawson and Lee.

The Lawson/Lee Case for CFA

The remainder of this essay is concerned with CFA as advocated by Lawson and Lee. This review will be a general one, examining, first, the

---
5 The early work on CFA by Lawson and Lee has been reviewed by Ashton (1976), and various similarities and dissimilarities at that time have been examined by him.
6 This appeared to ignore the fact that CFA is usually advocated by its supporters as an addition to the traditional and long-standing system of financial reporting.

structure of the system and, secondly, the considerable advantages which have been claimed for it. References will be made to specific papers when necessary.

Suggested CFA System—Users

The suggestion of a corporate financial reporting system based on cash flows has been underpinned by the fundamental concepts of utility and relevance (Lee, 1971; 1972a; 1972c). This general theoretical base has been operationalized in terms of specific report user groups. Lawson, for example, has been concerned mainly with the use of cash data by investors, CFA containing all the determinants of distributable cash flows—this has characterized most of his writings (as in, for example, 1969; 1971a; 1971b; 1971c; 1972; 1975a; 1978a). However, he has recognized other uses—wage negotiation (1975a; and Lawson and Stark, 1977); bank lending (1978c); and governmental policy-making in relation to corporate taxation (e.g. 1971b; 1973; 1975a; 1975b; 1976; 1978a; 1978c; 1979).

Lee, too, has emphasized the importance of CFA in relation to specific user groups—at first in relation to shareholders (1971; 1972c) but, increasingly, his recommendations for CFA have been given in relation to the needs of a number of specific groups—for example, lenders and creditors, bankers, employees, managers, government agencies, etc. (1974; 1978; 1979b). He has also more recently argued for its general purpose nature in a corporate financial reporting context—i.e. CFA is capable of satisfying a number of different user groups rather than being specifically relevant to a particular group (1980b).

In light of the above comments, as well as a review of the other U.K. papers on CFA, it is clear that such recommendations have been made within the context of an increasing awareness in the 1970s of the need to satisfy the informational needs of corporate report users. Not only is the suggested CFA system seen as being relevant to specific users but is also regarded as having a general relevance. In other words, cash flow data are believed to impinge on most users' behaviour. In this sense, the Lawson and Lee proposals are definitely aimed at aiding user decisions. This underlies all their work, and is made most explicit in their consistent suggestion for the reporting of both past and forecast cash flows. This is not to say that either writer has ignored the use of CFA as a means of making entity management accountable to ownership—the stewardship function (e.g. Lawson, 1975a; and Lee, 1974; 1978). CFA is therefore conceived as a multi-purpose reporting system, compatible with the decision and accountability aims usually associated with the conventional allocation-based reporting systems.

Suggested CFA System—Structure

The system of CFA advocated by Lawson and Lee is all-embracing, containing data related to both actual and predicted business activity, supported (as mentioned previously) by a number of explanatory statements pertaining, *inter alia*, to forecasting assumptions, variances, non-cash transactions, and relevant audit opinions. As his earlier writings indicate (e.g. 1969; 1971a), Lawson has described the reporting entity as a total financial system. Accordingly, his consistent recommendation has been that CFA is an explicit statement of such a system—i.e. the entity receives a net cash flow from its various operational activities (O), and uses this to pay for replacement and growth investment (R), taxation (T), interest on borrowings (I), and distributions to its owners (D). By including new equity receipts (E) and borrowings (B), Lawson's simple tabulated CFA presentation can be reconciled to the periodic change in cash resources of the entity (C). Thus:

$$O - R - T - I + E + B - C = D$$

In other words, the major emphasis is on disclosing the distributed, or distributable, cash flow to the entity's owners and, by deducting E from D, producing a measure of the latter's cash flow which can be used for purposes of discounting to derive a present value of equity. Except for a supplementary statement describing the composition of the operational cash flow, Lawson's system is a relatively simple tabulated one involving 10 years of past data, and between 12 and 18 months of forecast data (1975a). It is also divisionalized, where relevant (1971a).

As will be shown in later sections, the essence of the CFA system described by Lawson is to provide relevant data for a number of measurable tasks—e.g. for determining effective rates of tax, and interest and dividend covers. In other words, he has concentrated on the uses to which CFA could be put rather than on the detail and structure of CFA as a corporate financial reporting system. In contrast, Lee has been mainly concerned with the detail of CFA as a reporting system. Like Lawson, his general recommendations have consistently included the reporting of 10 years of past data, and at least 1 year of forecast data—all suitably audited and supported by a statement of explained variances between actual and forecast results (distinguishing between controllable and uncontrollable differences). However, Lee has also extended this broad framework in a number of ways—first, in relation to statements to support the main CFA data (Lee, 1972c) and secondly, in relation to financial statement data which are compatible with CFA (Lee, 1980b).

Using the above notation, Lee's main CFA statements originally (e.g. 1972c) used the following pattern:

$$O - R - I - T - D + E + B = C$$

This was reasonably similar to that of Lawson above. It assumed that operational cash flows were available to pay, in order of priority, replacement and growth investment (to ensure continuity of the entity), interest on borrowings (deducted before tax as it is allowable for taxation purposes), taxation, and distributions to the entity owners. This would leave a surplus or deficit of cash to be augmented or supplemented by new equity and borrowing receipts. However, as a reporting system, it provided matchings of cash inflows and outflows which suggested new long-term finance was being raised by the reporting entity to pay for dividends (and even taxation) in circumstances where operating cash flows were inadequate to cover these payments in addition to replacement and growth investment. In order to provide a more neutral reporting statement, Lee has recently suggested the formulation (1980b):

$$O - I - T - D + E + B - R = C$$

This effectively leaves the deduction of payments for replacement and growth investment until all available cash resources have been utilized to cover deductions for payments for which some prior commitment or obligation has been recognized by management.

The above basic data in Lee's system are each recommended to be supported by a detailed supplementary statement enabling the report user to comprehend how each figure is composed—e.g. the taxation measure could comprise payments for U.K. and non-U.K. tax; and the replacement and growth investment figure, as well as being derived after making the basic distinction of replacement and growth, could be shown along with receipts for asset disposals and government grants. Furthermore, the operational cash flow statement could be suitably segmented, and all reported statements would require to be audited. A unique feature of Lee's system is the inclusion of a statement to disclose entity transactions which have not involved a cash flow (e.g. the acquisition of assets for equity or loan stock).

Lee (1980b) has extended his CFA system to include statements of financial position based on net realizable values. By combining these potential cash flows with realized cash flows, a measure of total cash flow can be computed. This complete system of CFA can then be tied in with a statement of financial position which describes (in order of realizability) a minimum future cash inflow to be matched against (in order of date of settlement) the various obligations due by the reporting entity. This suggestion is intended as a reasoned answer to the charge that CFA is an incomplete reporting system because it concentrates solely on 'flows' rather than 'stocks'. The combined system appears to provide both, and is, therefore, a practical implementation of the original idea of Edey (1963).

To summarize on the suggested structure of CFA reports, it is clear that there is reasonable agreement in the U.K.—actual and forecast data should be disclosed (segmented where relevant); supplementary disclosure can come from a variety of supporting statements; particular attention ought to be paid to explained forecasting assumptions, and explained variances between actual and forecast results; and auditing of these statements appears to be a priority. Finally, Edey, Climo and Lee (in the U.K.) and Thomas (in the U.S.) have recommended net realizable value position statements in support of CFA. Lee has attempted to implement this suggestion.

However, despite the agreement, there appear to be fundamental differences in the Lawson and Lee proposals. First, Lee conceives of the structure of CFA as an interlocking series of statements for a variety of users. Lawson, on the other hand, is mainly concerned with the provision of cash flow data to improve the information base of investors and financial managers. Secondly, Lawson's system is largely proprietorial in nature because of its attention to distributable flows and investors; Lee's system is enterprise-orientated, intended for a variety of user groups, and concentrating on a reporting of the various cash flows of the entity. The latter approach owes much to the work of Fisher who regarded the entity as a clearing house for various cash flows to creditors, employees, lenders, bankers, government, and owners (Lee, 1979a). This is not to say that Lawson's work has lacked an enterprise approach—his earliest work (e.g. 1969) described CFA as a means of portraying the reporting entity as a total financial system. His later work, however, has concentrated particularly on the needs of investors.

Suggested CFA System—Computation

The computation of CFA data ought to be uncomplicated in an accounting sense. After all, part of its *raison d'etre* is to avoid the complexities and subjectiveness of accounting allocations. Thus, preparing CFA statements from cash transactions should only involve the complications of presentation and disclosure.[7] However, due to the conventional structuring of the credit and allocation-based accounting system, it may not be possible to produce CFA statements directly. In these cases, it should be feasible to take allocated data and, by reversing the effect of the credit transactions and accounting allocations, derive the underlying cash flows. This is particularly feasible when funds statements are available.

Much of the work on adjusting conventional data to their cash flow equivalents is due to the efforts of Lawson (e.g. 1971c; 1976; 1978a; and Lawson and Stark, 1975). By unveiling the hidden cash flows in allocated data, Lawson has been able to highlight the two major shortcomings of the latter, particularly during a period of inflation—i.e. the working capital and depreciation shortfalls in measuring periodic surpluses (e.g. 1975a; 1975b). In conventional accounting, the full cost of working capital is not (and may never be) matched against revenues—e.g. under FIFO systems of stock accounting, there is a base level of stock which will never be

---

[7] There will, of course, also be the problem of forecasting judgements when preparing predicted CFA data.

matched against sales unless the stock is completely consumed (Lawson, 1975b). The same is true of fixed asset costs, assuming continuity of the reporting entity.

Thus, although Lawson's cash flow adjustments to allocated data are, in themselves, relatively obvious and straightforward, his use of them to demonstrate the consistent overstatement of reported entity earnings has been a considerable advance in accounting thinking. In particular, his demonstration that, during periods of inflation, these overstatements become more material, has highlighted the inadequacies of systems of current cost accounting to bridge the gap between the partial costs which are conventionally matched against revenues, and the total costs which, because they have been committed, ought to be so matched (Lawson, 1976; 1978a).

12 Suggested CFA System—Main Features

CFA has a considerable number of identifiable features which suggest its reporting potential in terms of improving the utility of financial reports. Again, these owe much to the work of Lawson and Lee for their identification. They are given below in no particular order of importance.

1. CFA avoids dubious accounting allocations and thus, unlike periodic income measurements, cash flows provide relatively unambiguous measures of entity financial performance (e.g. Lawson, 1968; 1969; 1970; 1971b; 1971c; and Lee, 1971; 1972c).

2. CFA captures the vital factor in decision-making and valuation of the time value of money; conventional accounting ignores this by allocating data in order to 'smooth' income trends (e.g. Lawson, 1968; 1970; 1971b; 1971c; and Lee, 1971; 1972b).

3. CFA can therefore avoid dubious measures of periodic income which have a variety of meanings depending on the particular measurement contexts and uses to which they are being applied. CFA has a relatively unambiguous meaning, no matter what the measurement context or use is (e.g. Lee, 1974).

4. CFA emphasizes some of the most fundamental and vital features of business activity (cash is the key factor in this long-term issue); the ability of the enterprise to pay its obligations, make distributions, and provide for its future continuity (cash is needed to reinvest, to expand, and to pay for taxation, interest, and distribution commitments, as well as to repay credit and borrowings previously received) (e.g. Lee, 1972c; 1974; 1978).

5. CFA does not require price-level adjustments due to specific inflation as it expresses the cash flow data concerned in the purchasing power of the period in which they were transacted and accounted. However, it may be necessary to convert CFA data of different periods to a base year (by some

form of general price restatement) (e.g. Lawson, 1970; 1971c; 1972; and Lee, 1971; 1978).

6. CFA is capable of producing data which are needed for a variety of decision and control activities both within and without the reporting entity. It, therefore, ought to improve the quality of these matters—e.g. by providing report users with management's views of the future, and data on working capital and depreciation shortfalls, and fiscal drag,[8] there is an argument that the stock market (at least in aggregate) would be more efficient and derive more accurate share values as a consequence (Lawson, 1970; 1971c; 1975a); bankers and lenders would be provided with data relevant to their assessment of the reporting entity's quality of financial (and, particularly, cash) management (Lee, 1980b); and government would learn of the lack of neutrality[9] in its corporate taxation system (Lawson, 1978c; 1979).

7. CFA is the only proper basis for measuring the value of entities as going concerns because of its attention to the time value of money. It is thus capable of providing not only present values of investments but also rates of return which conform with economic principles. CFA is also compatible with Hicksian notions of periodic income and capital valuation (Lawson, 1968; 1969; 1971a; 1978a; and Lee, 1971).

8. CFA as a system of financial reporting is objective, understandable, and simple. It avoids the subjectiveness and language of accounting allocations, and presents the data in a way that is potentially recognizable to its users (Lawson, 1970; and Lee, 1972c; 1974; 1978).[10] It also provides comparable data which are not rendered incomparable because of measurements of different purchasing powers, and subjective allocations (Lee, 1974).

9. CFA conforms to a number of non-accounting theories which, nevertheless, have strong associations with the accounting and reporting function—for example, CFA (as mentioned above) is compatible with economic theories of the time value of money and interest, and of income and capital valuation; it is also consistent with modern capital market theory (Lawson, 1978a).

These are merely a few of the various arguments for, and main features of, CFA which have been highlighted by Lawson and Lee. They cannot really do justice to the case for CFA in financial reporting due to the brevity of description given to each point. Nevertheless, when taken as a whole, they

[8] Fiscal drag in this context is the term used by Lawson (1979) to denote the time lag between providing for corporate tax on high levels of accounting profit, and paying for this tax out of considerably smaller cash surpluses in later years (assuming a period of inflation).

[9] Tax neutrality is the term used to denote a system of tax which bears equally upon all taxpayers—i.e. it does not favour or discriminate against individual taxpayers.

[10] Tweedie (1977), in a pilot study, has produced evidence to suggest that non-accountants may intuitively think of periodic income and financial position in terms of, respectively, cash flows and net realizable values.

provide a formidable case for CFA which is not to be evidenced to such an extent in other systems of financial reporting which have received favour by accountants.

Suggested CFA System—Empirical Evidence

As well as giving conceptual arguments for the introduction of CFA to financial reporting, Lawson and Lee have provided empirical evidence of its utility. In a number of research studies over recent years, both writers have been concerned to back up their assertions with proof of CFA's reporting potential.

In a preliminary study of CFA utility, Lee (1979c) invited shareholders in two medium-sized companies to rank five brewing companies in order of investment preference in accordance with the type of information supplied to them. CFA data comprised one of the information sets provided, and it was found that the companies were ranked considerably differently by shareholders who received CFA data only, compared with those who received historic cost, allocation-based equivalents or a mixture of both. CFA data did not appear to cause any difficulties to its investor-users despite their lack of familiarity with it.

Lee (1980a) has also examined accountants' attitudes towards CFA reporting to external user groups. He evidenced considerable support for the idea—more so for actual cash flow results than for forecast results. CFA data were believed to be useful to most external user groups interested in companies, but especially to bankers and lenders concerned with assessing corporate liquidity. No particular problems were foreseen in preparing past data—several years of audited data being envisaged as the typical reporting format. Forecast statements were not believed to be worthwhile beyond more than one or two years of predicted activity. Most of the respondents' companies utilized CFA systems to a considerable extent for internal management purposes.

Using, alternatively, hypothetical and live data (for individual companies as well as in aggregate), Lawson has documented extensive evidence concerning the utility of CFA data. He has shown that the working capital and depreciation shortfalls for manufacturing companies can be considerable, and can increase substantially as the rate of inflation increases (1975a)—thus, conventional accounting consistently overstates corporate earnings during periods of inflation. He has demonstrated the misleading effects this overstatement may have—e.g. the wisdom of wage claims based on reported income when the effective rates of tax based on CFA are well in excess of the notional rate (Lawson and Stark, 1977).

In more recent times, Lawson has further demonstrated the utility of cash flow data for purposes of economic and financial management. He has revealed (1978c) that, using aggregate data for 1954 to 1976, inclusive, real cash flow returns (net of tax) to shareholders and lenders have typically been negative (particularly between 1964 and 1976). In the same study, Lawson evidences that the market, as a whole, uncovers the cash flows underlying conventional earnings, and impounds these into share prices. His overall conclusions from this data are (a) the market is efficient with regard to cash flow; (b) U.K. companies are consistently paying dividends in excess of cash flow earnings and financing the deficit by borrowings; and (c) company tax rates on a cash flow basis are confiscatory and lack neutrality. These results were further confirmed in a more recent study (Lawson, 1979), although it is not clear that the market is as efficient in unveiling underlying cash flows of individual companies. Suffice to say, however, that Lawson's evidence in the U.K. is of overtaxation, over-distribution, and crisis levels of borrowing to finance this. In this respect, the utility of CFA in the area of corporate taxation has recently been recognized in the report of the Meade Committee (1978), in which it is recommended that company tax in the U.K. be based on measured cash flows. This is the first tangible evidence, other than from the advocates of CFA, of its practical utility and importance.

Conclusions

Although CFA is not as yet a formal part of financial reporting, cash flow data can be derived from conventional allocation-based figures. This can be done relatively easily, and CFA's utility can be reasonably demonstrated at a conceptual level and, increasingly, at an empirical level. A relatively few accountants have achieved this position and, as such, CFA has been argued for at least as consistently as any other system of accounting. Unlike other systems, however, it has not so far suffered from any significant criticism in the published literature.

The argument for CFA has progressed at two levels: conceptually (both in relation to what CFA attempts to describe, and for whom it is addressed); and, more recently, empirically (in terms of utility and feasibility). In other words, CFA is a system which already has a sound theoretical underpinning, a developed measurement and presentation framework, and growing empirical support. Obviously, a great deal of work remains to be undertaken—e.g. in relation to improving the structure and detail of CFA reports (particularly with regard to position statements), forecasting, and avoidance of managerial manipulation of cash flows. Also, there is the very real 'political' problem to be overcome of convincing accounting policy-makers that CFA is a valid, useful and complete reporting system worthy of inclusion in the overall financial reporting package.

That much of this work has been achieved in the U.K. in recent years by so few accountants is a unique contribution to financial reporting. It is to be hoped that their effort will continue to a successful outcome whereby the U.K. can be seen to be the birthplace of the practice of modern CFA for external reporting purposes.

References

Ashton, R., 'Cash Flow Accounting: A Review and Critique,' *Journal of Business Finance and Accounting* (Winter 1976), pp. 63–81.

Briston, R. J. and Fawthrop, R. A., 'Accounting Principles and Investor Protection', *Journal of Business Finance* (Summer 1971), pp. 10–19.

Climo, T. A., 'Cash Flow Statements for Investors', *Journal of Business Finance and Accounting* (Autumn 1976), pp. 3–14.

Coughlan, J. W., 'Contrast Between Financial-Statement and Discounted-Cash-Flow Methods of Comparing Projects', *NAA Bulletin* (June 1960), pp. 5–17.

Coughlan, J. W., 'Accounting and Capital Budgeting', *The Business Quarterly* (Fall 1962), pp. 39–48.

Coughlan, J. W., 'Funds and Income', *NAA Bulletin* (September 1964), pp. 23–34.

Drebin, A. R., ' "Cash-Flowitis": Malady or Syndrome?', *Journal of Accounting Research* (Spring 1964), pp. 25–34.

Edey, H. C., 'Accounting Principles and Business Reality', *Accountancy* (November 1963), pp. 998–1002; (December 1963), pp. 1083–8.

Edey, H. C., 'The Nature of Profit', *Accounting and Business Research* (Winter 1970), pp. 50–5.

Heath, L. C., 'Financial Reporting and the Evaluation of Solvency', *Accounting Research Monograph 3*. American Institute of Certified Public Accountants (1978).

Ijiri, Y., *The Foundations of Accounting Measurement*. Prentice Hall (1967).

Ijiri, Y., 'Corporate Recovery Rate and Cash Flow Accounting', *GSIA Working Paper*. Carnegie-Mellon University (1977).

Ijiri, Y., 'Cash Flow Accounting and Its Structure', *Journal of Accounting, Auditing and Finance* (May 1978), pp. 331–48.

Ijiri, Y., 'A Simple System of Cash Flow Accounting', in R. R. Sterling and A. L. Thomas (eds.), *Accounting for a Simplified Firm*. Scholars Book Co. (1979), pp. 57–71.

Inflation Accounting Committee, 'Inflation Accounting', *Report of the Inflation Accounting Committee*, Cmd 6225 (HMSO, 1975), pp. 156–8.

Jones, C. J., 'Accounting Standards: A Blind Alley?', *Accounting and Business Research* (Autumn 1975), pp. 273–9.

Käfer, K. and Zimmerman, V. K., 'Notes on the Evolution of the Statement of Sources and Applications of Funds', in T. A. Lee and R. H. Parker (eds.), *The Evolution of Corporate Financial Reporting*. Nelson (1979), pp. 133–52.

Lawson, G. H., *Applications of a Business Theory*. University of Liverpool Press (1968).

Lawson, G. H., 'Profit Maximisation Via Financial Management', *Management Decision* (Winter 1969), pp. 6–12.

Lawson, G. H., 'Radical Change in Financial Reports', *Financial Times* (15 July 1970).

Lawson, G. H., 'Measuring Divisional Performance', *Management Accountant* (May 1971a), pp. 147–52.

Lawson, G. H., 'Accounting for Financial Management—Some Tentative Proposals for a New Blueprint', in R. Shone (ed.), *Problems of Investment*. Blackwell (1971b), pp. 36–64.
Lawson, G. H., 'Cash-flow Accounting', *The Accountant* (28 October 1971), pp. 586–9; (4 November 1971c), pp. 620–2.
Lawson, G. H., 'Distributable Profits and Dividends', *Management International Review* (Vol 12 (2–3), 1972), pp. 113–19.
Lawson, G. H., 'Financial Objectives and Annual Financial Targets in the Imputation Tax System', *Journal of Business Finance* (Summer 1973), pp. 1–18.
Lawson, G. H., 'Memorandum Submitted to the Inflation Accounting Committee in July 1974', *Working Paper Series 12* (Manchester Business School, 1975a).
Lawson, G. H., 'The Rationale for Measuring the Cost of Working Capital', *Working Paper Series 15*. (Manchester Business School, 1975b).
Lawson, G. H., 'Initial Reactions to ED18', *Certified Accountant* (December 1976), pp. 357–65 and p. 422.
Lawson, G. H. 'The Rationale of Cash Flow Accounting', in C. van Dam (ed.), *Trends in Managerial and Financial Accounting*. Martinus Nijhoff (1978a), pp. 85–104.
Lawson, G. H., 'The Valuation of a Going Concern on a Cash Flow Basis', *Managerial Finance* (August 1980), forthcoming (1978b).
Lawson, G. H., *Company Profitability and the U.K. Stock Market—An Exercise in Cash Flow Accounting*. Manchester Business School (1978c).
Lawson, G. H., 'The Cash Flow Performance of U.K. Companies: Preliminary Analysis', *paper* to SSRC Conference on Accounting Research (1979).
Lawson, G. H. and Stark, A. W., 'The Concept of Profit for Fund Raising', *Accounting and Business Research* (Winter 1975), pp. 21–41.
Lawson, G. H. and Stark, A. W., 'Does Ford Cash Really Flow?', *Accountancy Age* (12 August 1977), pp. 8–9.
Lee, T. A., 'Goodwill—an Example of Will-o'-the-Wisp Accounting', *Accounting and Business Research* (Autumn 1971), pp. 318–28.
Lee, T. A., 'The Relevance of Accounting Information Including Cash Flows', *The Accountant's Magazine* (January 1972a), pp. 30–4.
Lee, T. A., 'The Nature and Purpose of Cash Flow Accounting', *The Accountant's Magazine* (April 1972b), pp. 198–200.
Lee, T. A., 'A Case for Cash Flow Reporting', *Journal of Business Finance* (Summer 1972), pp. 27–36.
Lee, T. A., 'Enterprise Income: Survival or Decline and Fall?', *Accounting and Business Research* (Summer 1974), pp. 178–92.
Lee, T. A., 'The Cash Flow Accounting Alternative for Corporate Financial Reporting', in C. van Dam (ed.), *Trends in Managerial and Financial Accounting*. Martinus Nijhoff (1978), pp. 63–84.
Lee, T. A., 'The Contribution of Fisher to Cash Flow Accounting', *Journal of Business Finance and Accounting* (Autumn 1979a), pp. 321–30.
Lee, T. A., 'The Simplicity and the Complexity of Accounting', in R. R. Sterling and A. L. Thomas (eds.), *Accounting for a Simplified Firm*. Scholars Book Co. (1979b), pp. 35–55.
Lee, T. A., 'A Test of the Use of Cash Flow Reporting', *Discussion Paper 2*. University of Edinburgh (1979c).

Lee, T. A., 'A Survey of Accountants' Opinions on Cash Flow Reporting', *Discussion Paper 3* (University of Edinbrugh, 1980a).
Lee, T. A., 'Reporting Cash Flows and Net Realizable Values', *Discussion Paper 5*. University of Edinburgh (1980b).
Littleton, A. C. and V. K. Zimmerman, *Accounting Theory: Continuity and Change*. Prentice Hall (1963), pp. 49–71.
Meade Committee, *Structure and Reform of Direct Taxation*. George Allen & Unwin (1978).
Paton, W. A., 'The Cash-Flow Illusion', *The Accounting Review* (April 1963), pp. 243–51.
Ronen, J., 'Discounted Cash Flow Accounting', in J. J. Cramer Jr. (ed.), *Objectives of Financial Statements*. American Institute of Certified Public Accountants (1974), pp. 143–60.
Ronen, J. and Sorter, G. H., 'Relevant Accounting', *Journal of Business* (April 1972), pp. 258–82.
Staubus, G. J., *A Theory of Accounting for Investors*. University of California Press (1961), pp. 134–6.
Staubus, G. J., 'Alternative Asset Flow Concepts', *The Accounting Review* (July 1966), pp. 397–412.
Thomas, A. L., 'The Allocation Problem', *Studies in Accounting Research 3*. American Accounting Association (1969), p. 101 and pp. 108–9.
Thomas, A. L., 'The Allocation Problem: Part Two', *Studies in Accounting Research 9*. American Accounting Association (1974), pp. 119–22.
Thomas, A. L., 'Matching: Up from Our Black Hole', in R. R. Sterling and A. L. Thomas (eds.), *Accounting for a Simplified Firm*. Scholars Book Co. (1979), pp. 11–33.
Tweedie, D. P., 'Cash Flows and Realizable Values: the Intuitive Concepts? An Empirical Test', *Accounting and Business Research* (Winter 1977), pp. 2–13.
Waldron, R., 'Reporting Cash Flow Measurement of Business Achievement and the Statement of Needs and Resources', *Accountancy*, forthcoming.
Winjum, J. O., *The Role of Accounting in the Economic Development of England 1500–1750*. Centre for International Education and Research (1972).

Initial Ideas

Goodwill
An Example of Will-o'-the-Wisp Accounting
T. A. Lee

Introduction
Over the last eighty years or so, goodwill has been the subject of a controversial debate which has failed to produce a consensus of opinion regarding its accounting treatment. The debate was started by a Scottish Chartered Accountant, Francis More, in 1891 (when he defined goodwill as the present value of business profits in excess of a normal rate of return), and it has been continued over the years by such eminent accountants as Lawrence R. Dicksee, Henry Rand Hatfield, P. D. Leake, William A. Paton, George O. May, and more recently, by Leonard Spacek.[1]

To date in this country, despite the obvious interest of individual practitioners in the subject, there has been no definitive statement on goodwill as such from the professional bodies. By way of contrast, the American Institute of Certified Public Accountants has commented on the treatment of goodwill in its Accounting Research Bulletin No. 43 (1962 revision), *Intangible Assets*, and through its Accounting Principles Board, it has also published Accounting Research Study No. 10 (1968), *Accounting for Goodwill*, and Accounting Principles Board Opinion No. 17 (1970), *Intangible Assets*.

The purpose of this paper is to examine the main characteristics of goodwill which affect its accounting treatment, and hopefully, to offer some suggestions which may help to bring greater uniformity to present practices.

Goodwill and business combinations
The problem of accounting for goodwill normally arises in practice at the present time, only when there is a combining of two or more business enterprises by means of takeover or merger. As Spacek[2] has observed:

'Goodwill exists in every business, but it becomes an accounting issue only when we have an acquisition of one business by another.'

Because goodwill is frequently part of the total valuation placed on a business for takeover or merger purposes, accountants have the task of accounting for that part of the total purchase cost which is attributable to goodwill. The Companies Act 1967 (Schedule 2, paragraph 8(1)*b*) provides for the disclosure of the allocated cost of goodwill in company balance sheets — goodwill, patents and trade marks being aggregable for disclosure purposes at their net book value. The Act, however, gives no indication of where goodwill should be presented in the balance sheet (that is, whether it should be treated as a fixed, current or 'other' asset). The effect of this lack of definition can be seen from a scrutiny of current company accounts. For example, in six recently published reports of public companies, the following differing treatments and descriptions of goodwill were given:

1. Goodwill shown as a fixed asset; original cost and aggregate depreciation to date being disclosed separately, giving a net book value of £1.
2. Goodwill, representing 2½ per cent of total assets, shown as a separate asset between fixed and current assets, with the following note attached:

   'Goodwill arises where, on the acquisition of a business, the price exceeds the value attributed to the net assets taken over. Except for that which arose on the acquisition of XY Ltd, all goodwill has been charged against reserves.'

3. Goodwill, representing over 20 per cent of other assets, shown as a deduction from capital reserves.
4. Goodwill, representing 17 per cent of net assets, shown as a separate asset, and described as representing

   'the excess of the cost of shares in subsidiary companies over the book value of their net tangible assets at the dates of acquisition.'

5. Goodwill, representing 30 per cent of net assets, shown as a separate asset, and described in the

---
[1] For a discussion of the earliest writings on goodwill, readers are referred to Bryan V. Carsberg, 'The Contribution of P. D. Leake to the Theory of Goodwill Valuation', *Journal of Accounting Research*, Spring 1966, pp. 1–15.
[2] Leonard Spacek, 'The Treatment of Goodwill in the Corporate Balance Sheet', *The Journal of Accountancy*, February 1964, p. 35.

following manner:

> 'Goodwill is stated at cost, having arisen mainly from the excess of the cost of shares in subsidiaries over the value attributed to their net tangible assets at the dates on which the subsidiaries were acquired.'

6. Goodwill, representing 8 per cent of net assets, shown as a separate asset, no supporting description or explanation being offered.

In Britain, business combinations are generally accounted for at a 'fair' valuation – that is, the acquired assets, etc., are recorded at their agreed takeover or merger values. This means that goodwill is accounted for as representing the excess amount paid for a business over and above the fair value of all its separable assets, less any liabilities also assumed. In America, on the other hand, the problem of accounting for goodwill is one of the reasons for the development of 'pooling of interests' accounting. This method states that where there is no substantial change in ownership following a business combination, the takeover or merger is accounted for entirely at the existing book values, irrespective of the valuations agreed upon in arriving at the purchase consideration. This results in goodwill, and the problem of its accounting treatment, being ignored completely.[3] At present, there is considerable debate going on in America concerning the validity of pooling accounting, and the need for more acceptable guidelines governing its application in practice.[4] As pooling accounting does not appear to be as widely adopted in this country, it follows that the question of accounting for goodwill is not one which is being ignored by British accountants. It follows, therefore, that the goodwill problem is one which should be looked at a little more closely than hitherto.

Goodwill and profits

There appears to be a general acceptance by writers on goodwill that, in some way, its existence is directly related to the profit level of the business entity it is being attributed to – that is, that the value of goodwill is dependent on the level of profit earned, or about to be earned, by the business. This appears to be a rational supposition for the value of the business as a whole is clearly acknowledged as being dependent on its profitability. A general criterion has been established which stipulates that goodwill exists only if the earning power or profitability of the business is above an accepted normal level. From this basis, phrases such as 'superior earnings', 'excess profits', and 'super profits' have evolved. Spacek has summarised this relationship between goodwill and profits as follows:

> 'Goodwill is the present value placed on anticipated future earnings in excess of a reasonable return on producing assets. Thus, it is the cost to the buyer of earnings over and above the cost of the assets required to produce these earnings.'[5]

Originally, goodwill was regarded by accountants as an asset in its own right, and it was valued accordingly. Total business profits were divided between normal profits and super profits, and goodwill was valued at so many years' purchase of allotted super profits. This approach totally ignored the fact that the value of goodwill is entirely dependent on the business as a going concern, with all of its assets interacting and combining with one another to earn the overall profits. As a refinement to this early conception of goodwill, several accountants, including Leake, advocated the treatment of each annual super profit as an annuity, with the discounting of each such segment of profit at a reasonable rate of interest, in order to arrive at the present value of several years' super profits. The summation of these present values was regarded as the value of goodwill. However, this again ignored the concept of a business as a going concern.

Gradually, however, it was realised that the division of total business profits between one group of assets and another was too artificial and too subjective, with the result that goodwill is now valued as part of the business as a whole. As Hendriksen has pointed out:

> 'Tangible assets may have value in their specific use because of imperfect competition and changes in demand for the products as well as efficient utilisation. All factors interact in the production of the final service or product and in permitting cash distributions to stockholders. Any attempt to allocate a portion of the total value of a firm on the basis of the capitalisation of superior earnings is, therefore, artificial.'[6]

Anticipated profits are calculated, and are either capitalised, or discounted to present values, at a reasonable rate of return. Fair valuations are given to the tangible, and if possible, certain of the intangible assets being acquired. Goodwill is then the difference between the total purchase consideration and the total of the fair values attributed to the net assets taken over. To quote Spacek again:

---

[3] For a further discussion of the merits of purchase v. pooling accounting, see Arthur Wyatt, 'A Critical Study of Accounting for Business Combinations', *Accounting Research Study No. 5*, 1965, AICPA.

[4] The most recent statement on pooling guidelines is contained in 'Business Combinations', *APB Opinion No. 16*, reproduced in *The Journal of Accountancy*, October 1970, pp. 69–84.

[5] Leonard Spacek, 'The Treatment of Goodwill in the Balance Sheet', in *A Search for Fairness in Financial Reporting to the Public*, Arthur Andersen & Co, 1969, p. 297.

[6] Eldon S. Hendriksen, *Accounting Theory*, Irwin, revised edition 1970, p. 434.

'In simple language, goodwill is the valuation placed on the earning power of the going concern as a whole over the amounts paid for the net assets necessary to produce, market, sell and administer its products and services.'[7]

Nevertheless, this having been said, the first roadblock concerning goodwill is met – the basic confusion between the nature of goodwill and its valuation. Goodwill is not simply a valuation, no more than land or plant or cash can be regarded as valuations. The earning power, or profitability, of the going concern is the means by which goodwill is evaluated, but it is not a reasonable description of what goodwill is. Spacek and many other writers, past and present, have fallen into this conceptual trap. The point was adequately made by Gynther when emphasising the fact that the *existence* of goodwill depends on certain factors which contribute to the overall profitability of the business.[8] The *value* of goodwill depends on the level of this profitability.

Factors contributing to goodwill

Goodwill has normally been thought of as an intangible asset. For example, Sprouse and Moonitz described it as an intangible, as did the AICPA in its *Accounting Research and Terminology Bulletins*.[9] Catlett and Olson similarly described the 'individual intangible factors contributing to goodwill'.[10] However, in addition, several factors thought to be capable of contributing to the existence of goodwill have been occasionally put forward. Originally, the main factor was considered to be the business's customers and location. For example, a judge in 1810 (in *Cruttwell* v. *Lye*) stipulated that

'The goodwill which has been the subject of sale, is nothing more than the probability that the old customer will resort to the old place.'

Subsequently, other factors have gradually been recognised as contributing to goodwill, and now the list is long; it includes development costs such as advertising; secret processes; franchises; licences; patents, trade marks and copyrights; good management; an efficient labour force; weaknesses in competitors; good industrial relations; a favourable credit rating with suppliers; sound training schemes; a high community standing; good relations with other companies; and favourable government regulations. No doubt this list could be added to. The main points to evolve from it are as follows:

1. Goodwill, as such, does not exist. It is simply a word used to conveniently describe a number of business resources contributing to the overall profitability of the business.

2. Certain of these resources are within the direct control and administration of the business, others are not, being more directly attributable to customers, competitors, suppliers and government. It is conceded, however, that even these resources can be regarded as being under the 'control' of the business – that is, in the loosest sense of the term. For example, weaknesses in a competitor may exist because of corresponding strengths in the business; customers' favour has to be worked for and won; and a favourable credit rating requires a great deal of effort and control from the business and its management.

3. Contrary to the usual description of goodwill, certain of the factors contributing to its existence have a definite tangible quality – for example, management, secret processes, licences and training schemes. On the other hand, there are others which are definitely intangible by nature – for example, weaknesses in competitors and a high community standing.

Summarising, therefore, it appears logical to adopt the approach of Gynther and regard goodwill as an aggregate valuation of several business resources. This means that it should not be regarded as an intangible asset, for it is not an asset in its own right, nor are the resources it represents exclusively intangible. In any case certain of these resources benefit the business without being directly controlled by it.

Purchased and created goodwill

As previously mentioned, goodwill is acknowledged for accounting purposes only when it is purchased as part of a takeover or merger acquisition. The widespread adoption of this procedure appears illogical, for goodwill is recognisable at times other than when a business combination takes place. As pointed out in the previous section, goodwill has a value because of resources contributing to the overall profitability of the business. So long as these resources exist with a value to that business, goodwill must be recognisable. In addition, it should be accepted that its nature and valuation are bound to change whenever the contributing resources it represents change. A great deal of expenditure can be incurred by a business to maintain and augment its goodwill resources – for example, money and time spent on research, on advertising, on industrial relations, and on public relations. There-

---

[7] Spacek, *op. cit.*
[8] Reg. S. Gynther, 'Some "Conceptualising" on Goodwill', *The Accounting Review*, April 1969, pp. 247–255.
[9] Robert T. Sprouse and Maurice Moonitz, 'A tentative set of broad accounting principles for business enterprises', *Accounting Research Study No. 3*, AICPA, 1962, p. 58; and *Accounting Research and Terminology Bulletins*, AICPA, revised edition, 1961, p. 37.
[10] George R. Catlett and Norman O. Olson, 'Accounting for Goodwill', *Accounting Research Study No. 10*, AICPA, 1968, p. 20.

fore, why not account for non-purchased or created goodwill, in addition to accounting for that which is included in the purchase price for a takeover or merger? Not to account for created goodwill raises an additional question of whether or not the balance sheet gives a fair representation of the business resources which have contributed to the profits reported in the accompanying profit and loss account. To date in this country, no attempt has been made to account for anything other than purchased goodwill. The reasons are understandable, but sometimes difficult to justify. The following are a few such reasons:

1. The acquired conservatism of accountants, combined with a fear that created goodwill may well be a fictitious asset introduced to improve the financial position of the business described in its balance sheet.
2. Certain generally accepted concepts of accounting which are extremely difficult to apply in practice to goodwill – that is, historic cost, objectivity, and verifiability.
3. The difficulty of annually revaluing goodwill, such an exercise having to be based on several assumptions, including estimations of future profits and of what is a reasonable rate of return for the particular business.
4. The difficulty of capitalising the business costs which are contributing to the value of goodwill – for example, the cost of research or advertising expenditure. Which part of the total advertising expenditure of the business contributed to the sales which generated the profits related to goodwill? Such an allocation exercise would be, at best, artificial.

There is no major difference between purchased and created goodwill, except that the former is bought as part of a purchase consideration, whilst the latter is developed from within the business; however, being purchased in the sense that money and other resources are expended to create and maintain it. The main difference arises when the question of accounting for the two types is considered. Purchased goodwill, because it has a known money value established for it at one particular point in time, is by far the easier to account for. It should be noted, however, that once it is accounted for, and disclosed in the balance sheet, it merely represents the agreed valuation placed on certain resources, expected to contribute to future profits, at the *date of purchase*. It does not necessarily represent either the goodwill resources, or their reasonable valuation, at the *date of disclosure*. The nature of such resources can radically alter after the date of purchase, and their value is equally liable to fluctuations. It appears, therefore, to be wrong in principle to disclose the purchased goodwill figure as an asset, when it does not conclusively represent the resources which contribute to its existence at the *date of disclosure*. Every other asset in the balance sheet, despite a probably conservative valuation, can be said at least to describe business resources which existed at the balance sheet date. This is not so with goodwill. There appear, however, to be two alternative solutions to this problem:

1. 'The amount assigned to purchased goodwill should be accounted for as a reduction of stockholders' equity.'[11] In other words, goodwill should be immediately written off, *in toto*, to reserves and surplus. This, of course, gets rid of the immediate problem, but tends to ignore the problems it creates in turn. For example, it ignores the fact that goodwill can represent a great many tangible and intangible business resources, each with a different value. Not to account for and disclose these resources in the balance sheet, under the heading of goodwill, could result in misleading financial accounts for either of the undernoted reasons:

   (*a*) Not all resources contributing to the overall profitability of the business would be represented in the balance sheet; and

   (*b*) there would be a consequent creation of secret reserves, universally condemned since the *Rex* v. *Kylsant* case in 1931.

2. Alternatively, despite the acknowledged difficulties, goodwill should be reviewed annually to reappraise its value, and thus, to ensure that the resources contributing to its valuation at the date of disclosure are realistically represented in the balance sheet.

These alternatives will be discussed further in other parts of this paper.

Goodwill as an asset

Goodwill is generally treated for accounting purposes as an asset, despite its composition of several resources contributing to business profits. The essential distinction which must be made in this respect is between the nature of goodwill, and the means by which it should be accounted for. The former factor logically precludes the description of goodwill as an asset in its own right, because there is in fact no such thing as goodwill, *per se*. On the other hand, the fact that goodwill is not an asset should not preclude an accounting for it as one. What have to be looked at are the resources represented by the term goodwill. If *they* can be regarded as business assets, then there appears to be no reason why they should not be treated as such for accounting purposes. Chambers, however, has

---

[11] A view expressed in *Accounting and Reporting Problems of the Accounting Profession*, Arthur Andersen & Co, 1969, p. 160, and supported in the conclusions of Catlett and Olson, *op. cit.*, p. 112.

taken an opposite viewpoint when declaring

'Goodwill is not an asset of a firm, being neither severable or measurable.'[12]

The characteristic of severability, advocated by him, requires that a would-be asset should be capable of being separated from the other assets of the business, thereby being capable of exchange or conversion. He regards goodwill as lacking this quality, despite being capable of evaluation but not of measurement in physical terms. It is true that many of the factors contributing to the existence of goodwill are neither severable nor measurable, but not to treat goodwill as a business asset for accounting purposes on these grounds appears to take too narrow a view of the nature of an asset. After all, many items of 'special purpose' plant could be defined as non-severable.

Hendriksen has laid down more reasonable conditions for resources qualifying as assets:

'There must exist some specific right to future benefits or service potentials.'

'The rights must accrue to a specific individual or firm.'

'There must be a legally enforceable claim to the rights or services.'[13]

So far as the contributing goodwill resources are under the direct control of the business and its management, these conditions appear to support the treatment of at least the 'controllable' elements of goodwill as assets for accounting purposes – that is, those representing such factors as secret processes, franchises, advertising campaigns, etc. However, there are other contributing resources which fail to satisfy the second and third conditions of Hendriksen, either because an individual business cannot have an exclusive right to benefits from them (for example, a favourable trading location or government regulations), or because it has no legal claim to them (for example, its labour force or its management, after allowing for any contractual commitments).

The treatment of goodwill as an asset, if the above conditions are taken as reasonable criteria, therefore appears to be only partially justifiable because of the nature of many of its contributing resources. Nevertheless, it appears unfair to ignore goodwill as an accountable asset, merely on the grounds that other businesses can benefit from the contributing factors, or that the business has no legally enforceable claim to the latter. Hendriksen's conditions are reasonable when taken in the context of resources which can be separately identified, valued, and exchanged or converted – for example, those such as plant, inventory, debtors or cash. But they do not apply to many of the resources represented by goodwill which lack the general quality of separability for identification or valuation or exchange purposes. This conceptual difficulty has precipitated what appears to be the rather illogical approach advocated by Arthur Andersen and Co and its partners (including Spacek, Catlett and Olson), of removing the goodwill problem by eliminating it from the financial accounts whenever it arises in a purchase consideration. They argue that goodwill is not an asset of the business, rather that it is an evaluation of the business's future by the investor, and as such should not appear in the financial accounts of the business. Spacek has summarised this viewpoint in the following manner:

'Goodwill value reflects a state of mind of the investor based on his expectations or anticipations.'[14]

He and his partners believe that it is the investor who determines the value of goodwill, this being based on what he expects will be the future profitability of the business. Goodwill, therefore, is put forward as nothing more than a statement of value describing what the business's owners expect to be its future profits. This original, if somewhat startling conclusion is, however, at variance with the accounting concept of goodwill as an asset, for the following reasons:

1. It ignores the various resources contributing to the existence of goodwill, and thus, to the overall profitability of the business.

2. It confuses the nature of goodwill with the means of valuing it.

It therefore fails on the grounds of logic, for if such an approach was adopted with all the resources of the business, the entity would, by definition, have no assets to account for.

The valuation of goodwill[15]

The valuation of business assets should subsist in the expectation of benefits which can be derived from their use or existence within the business, measured in terms of expected profitability. This view of asset valuation, supportable for no other reason than common-sense, is at variance with certain of the concepts of traditional historic cost accounting, mainly because of its weakness in terms of objectivity and verifiability. Initially, purchased goodwill is valued according to future expectations – that is, those which exist at the time of its acquisition. Forming part of a business combination, its value is determined by reference to the anticipated future profitability of the business – capitalisation or discounting methods being used for this purpose. However, having been pur-

---

[12] Raymond J. Chambers, *Accounting, Evaluation and Economic Behaviour*, Prentice-Hall, 1966, p. 218.
[13] Hendriksen, *op. cit.*, p. 253.
[14] Spacek, *op. cit.*, p. 362.
[15] This paper is essentially devoted to the accounting treatment of goodwill, and for this reason, a detailed exposition of how goodwill is evaluated is not given.

chased, the agreed valuation for goodwill is accounted for in the traditional manner. It becomes merely another past capital cost, possibly to be allocated in some arbitrary manner against future sales revenue. It no longer remains a figure representative of *current* expectations of the future. Instead it is representative only of past expectations of the future. It would therefore appear to be not only unrepresentative of the resources contributing to the profits which give grounds for its existence (as previously pointed out, it is only purchased goodwill which is recognised for accounting purposes), but also, unrepresentative of the value of the future benefits to be derived from these resources. To be fair, however, the latter point is also true of the traditional accounting for many of the other resources portrayed in the business balance sheet, which are valued on the basis of their original cost. The problem of accounting for the value of goodwill reflects, therefore, a much greater valuation problem, involving all the resources contributing to business profits.

The disposition of goodwill

Probably the most discussed goodwill topic of all has been the problem of its treatment in the financial accounts, once it has been recorded as a purchase cost. The solutions advocated have been various, yet no generally acceptable treatment has emerged. The reason for this lack of agreement appears to be the lack of a corresponding agreement on the nature of goodwill itself.

The earliest writers on goodwill (for example, Dicksee) thought that it should be excluded from financial accounts, mainly because of the fear that existed at the time that the introduction of goodwill into the balance sheet could produce misleading information. The intangible quality of goodwill was regarded at the time with a great deal of suspicion, a figure often being introduced to the accounts in order to create reserves which could be used to pay dividends to shareholders. Because of this abuse, goodwill, when it was purchased, was written off immediately to capital reserves (including any share premium account). Gradually, however, with the recognition of goodwill's relationship to the overall profitability of the business, the idea evolved that the purchased cost could be amortised over an estimated life, and effectively charged against profits. Indeed, the AICPA advocated this procedure in 1944 in *Accounting Research Bulletin No. 24*, and has continued to do so since in its subsequent publications.[16] However, despite this official guidance, a controversy has arisen over the accounting disposal of goodwill, involving three different viewpoints – (*a*) goodwill should be written off completely as soon as it is purchased,[17] (*b*) it should be amortised systematically over a reasonable period of time,[18] or (*c*) it should not be written off at all, unless there is strong evidence to support this procedure.[19]

Some of the arguments for writing off the purchased cost have been as follows:

1. Goodwill is constantly changing, in nature and value, because of corresponding changes in the underlying contributing resources. The goodwill that exists at one particular point in time is not necessarily the same goodwill that was originally purchased. Therefore, the latter figure should be eliminated from the accounts in order to avoid misrepresenting the contributing resources at the date of disclosure.

2. Purchased goodwill is a 'momentum' – that is, a promotional push which the buyer is willing to pay for rather than build up himself. It gives him the platform upon which he can maintain and increase the existing profitability of the business.

'The Momentum Theory is the hypothesis that a businessman purchases a promotional push instead of an annuity and that "push" dissipates like momentum.'[20]

Writing off goodwill therefore represents the dissipation of this momentum.

3. Goodwill is a depreciable asset, and therefore, its cost should be written off as a depreciation charge to profit.

4. The resources contributing to goodwill also contribute to the profits which are the basis of its valuation. The cost of these resources is part of the total cost of earning such profits, and consequently, should be treated as such.

5. The so-called 'superior earnings' or 'excess profits' which evidence the value of goodwill cannot last forever. Therefore, goodwill cannot 'exist' forever.

The main arguments against writing off goodwill include:

1. The danger of unnecessarily creating a secret reserve in the financial accounts when the value of goodwill is not falling.

2. The difficulty of determining any change in the value of goodwill.

3. When profits of the business are rising, over and above any general expansion in the business, the

---

[16] See 'APB Opinion No. 17: Intangible Assets', *The Journal of Accountancy*, October 1970, pp. 85–89.

[17] See Spacek, *op. cit.*, and Catlett and Olson, *op. cit.*

[18] George T. Walker, 'Why Purchased Goodwill Should be Amortised on a Systematic Basis', *The Journal of Accountancy*, February 1953, pp. 210–16.

[19] See Gynther, *op. cit.*

[20] Robert H. Nelson, 'The Momentum Theory of Goodwill', *The Accounting Review*, October 1953, p. 492.

indications are that the value of goodwill is also rising. It would therefore appear illogical to write off goodwill in these circumstances.

4. In a successful business goodwill should be being maintained and increased in value.

If any consensus has been achieved, at least amongst writers on goodwill, it is that its purchased cost should be amortised over an estimated life, and charged against current profits. Such an approach recognises the gradual diminution in the value of the contributing goodwill resources which existed at the original date of purchase, but it completely ignores the replacement value of such factors, which have been created since that point in time. The accounting disposition of goodwill, as with any other aspect of the topic, should be viewed in terms of the existence and profit contribution of the contributing resources. All too often, goodwill is regarded as a complete asset in its own right, with a consumable cost to be matched against sales revenues. It is therefore advocated that the purchased cost of goodwill should not be written off unless there is firm evidence of a diminution in the profit contribution of the supporting goodwill resources.[21] How such an approach can be practised will be looked at in the following sections.

Summary and conclusions

The following summary and conclusions are offered for comment and discussion:

1. Accounting for goodwill normally arises when there is a payment for such an item as part of a business combination. It is usually treated, for accounting purposes, as an intangible asset, and disclosed as a separate asset in business balance sheets. Its eventual accounting disposition varies from one business to another, some amortising it, some writing it off immediately, and others not writing it off at all.

2. The problem of goodwill, and especially its disposition for accounting purposes, can be avoided, by the technique of pooling accounting, if certain conditions are satisfied.

3. There is general acceptance of the direct relationship between goodwill and profits, and this has given rise to a basic misunderstanding – that is, the nature of goodwill, as described in the profit-contributing resources it represents, being consistently confused with the means of valuing it on the basis of anticipated profits.

4. Goodwill represents several tangible and intangible resources which contribute to its overall profitability, but which cannot be separately valued.

5. Goodwill 'exists' in a business at any time so long as the resources it represents exist. The business continually incurs expenditure to maintain, replace and augment existing goodwill. Basically, therefore, there is little to distinguish purchased and created goodwill. But, because traditional accounting does not recognise the latter aspect of goodwill, there is a danger of disclosing a figure in the balance sheet which is not representative of the nature or the valuation of the resources it is intended to describe.

6. Goodwill has been generally regarded in the past as an intangible asset. In fact, no such asset exists, goodwill representing several resources contributing to overall profitability. Many of these resources would be hard to classify as business assets in the conventional sense, but this should not prevent their accounting treatment as such, for all are potentially profit earning.

7. Goodwill is part of the business, and should not be attributed to investors in terms of their expectations.

8. Purchased goodwill is valued on the basis of future expectations of profit, but once accounted for as purchased, it becomes merely a record of *past* expectations of the *future*.

9. There is no generally accepted method for the accounting disposition of goodwill. The most reasonable approach appears to be to write it off only when there is evidence of a decline in its value.

10. The easiest way of dealing with the goodwill problem appears to be to adopt the 'ArthurAndersen and Co.' approach of recording goodwill only when it is purchased, and then, writing it off totally to reserves and surplus. This ignores the very nature of goodwill, and is liable to produce misleading financial accounts.

11. A totally different approach to accounting for goodwill appears to be necessary, in which the nature and existence of the underlying resources which goodwill represents are adequately recognised. To recognise and account only for purchased goodwill ignores the continuing presence of these resources in a business. To amortise goodwill on an arbitrary, albeit systematic, basis equally ignores the changing nature and valuation of the resources. To immediately write off goodwill as soon as it is purchased is to provide misleading information.

What the previous discussion has attempted to highlight are the gross inadequacies in the present accounting treatment of the business resources represented by the term goodwill. These resources are recognised only when there is a commercial exchange between parties, with an agreed purchase price. Their continuing existence is not recognised, and this means that possibly the most valuable resources of the business (value being measured in terms of profit potential)

---

[21] This is similar to the conclusion of Gynther, *op. cit.*

are being ignored for accounting purposes. There appear to be three alternative approaches to this problem: Either

1. a 'head in the sand' approach is adopted, in which the problem of the accounting creation of continuing goodwill is ignored, as at present. This would leave the separate problem of accounting for any purchased goodwill along the alternative lines previously discussed. The lack of logic in this approach has already been stated; or
2. the existence of continuing goodwill is acknowledged without formally accounting for it. This could be done in the manner suggested by Gynther of not writing off goodwill so long as there are reasonable grounds for not doing so. However, it appears to be a rather casual way of accounting for business resources; or
3. some formal attempt is made to acknowledge the continuing existence of the underlying resources contributing to goodwill. As most of these resources have not formed part of a historical cost exchange transaction, the most important accounting criterion appears to be their 'service potential' or future profitability. But in order to separately value continuing goodwill for accounting purposes, the future profits to be anticipated from the underlying resources would require to be estimated for capitalisation or discounting purposes. As it is somewhat unrealistic to divide total anticipated business profits between individual resources (to do so would be a necessarily artificial and subjective exercise), the logical conclusion is that it would be an equally artificial exercise to attempt to value continuing goodwill in a situation where there is no willing buyer or seller to place an exchange value on it.

The above remarks, together with earlier ones in this paper, reflect one of the main drawbacks of traditional historical cost accrual accounting, which relies so heavily on the firm foundation of past business transactions – resources only being accounted for if they are part of a transaction of some sort or another. The result is that not all the business resources contributing to overall profitability are accounted for and reported in the periodic financial statements. In addition, if there was to be a departure from traditional accounting methods in order to account for these hitherto undisclosed resources, the valuation process could very well prove to be an extremely unreliable one. The inevitable conclusion is that to account and report on business resources, as part of a stewardship function, tends to give unreliable information, whether continuing goodwill is acknowledged or not. The answer may very well be to place less emphasis on the provision of 'stewardship' information, and instead, to produce information of greater use and relevance to the investor in his decision-making function. This, as the next section attempts to show, could result in business resources not being accounted for at all, the emphasis switching to the contribution of these resources to the *future* success and continuance of the business as a whole. In this way, it is hoped, goodwill resources could be acknowledged without having to be formally accounted for.

Postscript—a possible solution

The most pressing requirement for formal financial information describing business activity comes from investors making continual assessments of the desirability of investing in individual entities. The requirement is for information of use and relevance in such an exercise – that is, information which helps the investor to decide which of the following alternative actions is likely to be the most beneficial:

1. Whether to maintain an existing investment in a business; or
2. to increase such an existing investment; or
3. to dispose of it, either partially or totally; or possibly,
4. to acquire, for the first time, an investment in the business.

With each of these alternatives, the investor is comparing the desirability of investing in the business with the desirability of investing in others.

It is therefore suggested that the most valuable information for this type of investment appraisal is that which describes future business activity, including information regarding the financial rewards to be anticipated from it. It is submitted that it is *future* business performance which is most relevant and useful in this respect, and not past activity. The present form of stewardship financial statements merely tend to support or contradict the *past* desirability of investing in a business.

If it is accepted that anticipated business activity is both relevant and useful to the investor, then it is a logical extension of the argument to suggest that profit forecasts might be the basic type of information required. However, profit forecasts tend to be accrued historic cost measurements of projected activity, subject to all the problems of traditional accounting and superimposed upon the subjectiveness and uncertainty inherent in any forecast about a business's future. The only type of financial information which effectively minimises the effects of present-day accounting practices is that relating to cash flow projections. It is therefore suggested that, in the first instance, quoted companies should publish cash transaction forecasts (incorporating both revenue and capital items) for, say, the next three to five years, depending on the nature of the business and the degree of uncertainty about its future, together with (a) a statement detailing the various commercial, economic and political assumptions on which the forecasts have been based, and (b) a statement describing the effect on these forecasts due to possible variations in the assumptions.[22] The disclosed forecasts should be supported by statements of past cash flows achieved by the company, and should be subject to annual re-assessment for disclosure purposes. They would *not* be supplemental to the existing profit and loss accounts and balance sheets, although the latter statements could still be published for stewardship purposes. In addition to publishing past and future cash flows, management should also be required to disclose its explanations of any material differences between forecast and actual figures, as well as of differences due to revisions to original forecasts. The advantages of this type of financial information are as follows:

1. Management's view of the future of its business is projected for the benefit of investors who are basically concerned with evaluating the desirability of being part of that future.

2. An estimation of the present value of the disclosed cash flows can be made, *by investors,* and used as a basis to their decisions concerning alternative investments. By discounting back the projected cash flows to present values at a rate of interest regarded by him as reasonable for that type of company, business or industry, the investor can calculate the discounted cash flow per share for the company, apply it to the current market value of the shares, and calculate a 'price/discounted flow' ratio for comparison with similarly calculated ratios for other companies. Ideally, the projected cash flows should be split into monthly or three monthly streams for discounting purposes, rather than assume the entire flow is achieved on the last day of each annual period. This analysis could certainly be done for the first one or two years of the disclosed forecasts. With the less sophisticated investor, the 'price/flow' ratio could be calculated without the discounting procedures.

The 'price/flow' ratio appears to be a somewhat more reliable investment indicator than the present 'price/anticipated earnings' ratio, which is subject to the problems of present accrual accounting practice. However, like all financial or accounting indicators, it is only reliable so long as it is computed on a comparable basis.

3. Future business activity would be quantified on a cash basis, thereby avoiding the allocation problems met with in traditional accounting, including the depreciation of fixed assets, valuing inventory, writing off research and development costs, and so on.

4. The effects of any changes in the purchasing power of money due to inflation or deflation, for so long a recurrent problem in historical cost accounting (with its assumption of a stable monetary unit), are avoided. Price-level adjustments, which are no more than amendments to historical costs, would no longer be necessary.

5. The somewhat artificial distinction between capital and revenue transactions, and the development of criteria to classify business assets, would be equally unnecessary.

6. A present value of anticipated cash flows can be calculated, thereby acknowledging the existence of *all* the resources of the company contributing to its overall financial success or failure, including those resources represented by the term goodwill. In this way, there would be no need to separately account for goodwill, or indeed any of the other so-called business assets. They would be recognised and accounted for in a manner which accepts the fundamental interrelationship of all business resources in a going concern – their contribution to the total business cash flow. There would therefore be no artificial distinction between purchased and created goodwill.

7. Should business profitability be regarded as relevant financial information for investors, then periodic profits could be computed by comparing the present values of anticipated cash flows at the beginning and end of each accounting period, along the lines suggested by Hicks in his concept of 'well-offness'.[23]

8. Most important, investors could see from the projected cash flows the anticipated ability of the company to pay its way in the future in terms of cash, and in particular, its planned financial policy. The importance of generating sufficient cash resources, and of cash forecasting, should be more than obvious at a time which has witnessed the crash of Rolls-Royce Ltd.

The disadvantages of this solution must also be stated:

---

[22] Such a suggestion goes further than the recent views of Gerald Lawson on cash flow accounting (*See Accountancy Age,* 6/11/70, pp. 10–11). He advocated disclosure of past cash flows, but so far as disclosing anticipated flows, he had this to say:
'From a managerial standpoint the budgetary requirement is eminently desirable but as regards the implications for disclosure in published accounts, it is at present perhaps too *avant garde.* In the longer run though, I would have thought it desirable that companies should be required to disclose more details of corporate plans in numerical terms'.

[23] J. R. Hicks, *Value and Capital,* Clarendon Press, 1946, pp. 171–81.

1. It is extremely difficult to project business cash flows, particularly in times of inevitable change, both economically and technologically. However, management should be making these projections as part of its procedures for planning, decision making and control. Internal information would therefore be made available to external sources.

2. There are also difficulties to be faced when assuming a reasonable rate of interest for discounting purposes. It is suggested that in order to retain objectivity in this matter, management should be required to disclose a rate of interest necessary to at least maintain its anticipated financial position. For this reason, the rate used would approximate with the anticipated deterioration in the general purchasing power of money. The known current deterioration rate would be used as a basis to this exercise. This evaluation could then be used by investors in a separate evaluation of *their* expectations of the business's potential, over and above the minimum necessary to maintain its anticipated activity (see also 4(*b*) below).

3. There is a danger of giving competitors information concerning the future plans of the company. However, if such information was generally disclosed by quoted companies, then all would to some extent be aware of each other's plans. This could have the added advantage of improving the forward-thinking of management as a whole, to the benefit of the community at large.

4. There is a danger that management could take advantage of the inevitably hypothetical nature of the exercise, to over or underestimate the cash flow of the business in order to alter its market rating. However, two means of controlling this situation exist:

(*a*) those companies disclosing anticipated cash transactions would also be required to disclose the actual transactions which took place, giving investors the opportunity to examine for any material differences;

(*b*) any existing or would-be investor, would have to use his own rate of interest in the present value calculation, which may or may not agree with the 'minimum' one supplied by management. The investor rate would depend on an evaluation of several factors, including the degree of risk and uncertainty in the type of business activity undertaken; and in general, economic and political conditions and regulations. For purposes of making personal evaluations of present values, investors could be supplied with appropriate annuity tables in the financial statements. This would help to counter a major criticism made by Hendriksen of these exercises:

'Expectations regarding future cash flows cannot be converted into single values or certainty equivalents without knowing the risk preferences of the users of the information.'[24]; and

(*c*) both the anticipated cash flows, and the reasonable discounting rate, should be subject to audit, the result of which would be an opinion on their reasonableness. The purpose of this audit would be to lend *credibility* to the forecasts. Who would conduct this function must be determined by the subject-matter being verified. Accountants are experts at verifying accounting matters, but cash forecasting involves assumptions and calculations which are mainly non-accounting in nature. It is therefore suggested that the audit be divided into two distinct parts:

(i) the non-accounting part, involving verification work which can only be conducted by management experts, such as those presently employed by consultancy firms and merchant banks. Their report would contain an opinion on the reasonableness of the main economic, political and commercial assumptions underlying the cash forecasts, the minimum rate of interest for discounting purposes, the probabilities linked with any disclosed forecast variations, and the consequences of forecasting errors; and

(ii) the accounting part, conducted by professional accountants, who would comment on any accounting methods and calculations used by the business when computing the forecasts, as well as reporting on their verification of the disclosed cash flows actually achieved. This would introduce a greater degree of objectivity and verifiability to auditing than is at present being experienced in accrual accounting audits. However, the latter audits would presumably continue as at present.

The above division of auditing duties is similar to that required with current profit forecasting for takeover and merger purposes.

5. There are problems in using this type of financial information to assess managerial efficiency – that is, when determining whether the cash flows are due to managerial action or fortuitous circumstances.[25] This point is conceded with the reservation that

---

[24] Hendriksen, *op. cit.*, p. 137. Readers are recommended to read his conceptual objections, most of which are answerable by the suggestions in this paper.

[25] Indeed, one recent writer, Harold Edey, in 'The Nature of Profit', *Accounting and Business Research*, Winter 1970, pp. 50–55, although apparently supporting the theoretical justification of present value calculations of this type, concluded that they 'probably cannot be more than rough and generally speaking unreliable gauges of management efficiency'.

good management should be taking full advantage of fortuitous circumstances; and in any case, it is extremely difficult to produce *any* quantified information which is likely to completely satisfy such an assessment.

The above solution goes far beyond the problem of accounting for goodwill. It is radical and of necessity, tentative; yet it appears to provide financial information which satisfies the criteria of relevance and utility to the investor. The problem of goodwill highlights the fact that traditional historical cost accrual accounting does not provide information with the necessary degree of these qualities. It is therefore hoped that this possible solution may at least open a discussion and debate on the inadequacies of both goodwill accounting and financial reporting, which is long overdue.

Note: I would like to record my appreciation of the efforts of two of my colleagues, Peter Forbes and Tom Robertson, who over a relatively long period of time have helped me over many of the conceptual and practical hurdles in this paper.

The Relevance of Accounting Information Including Cash Flows

T. A. LEE, M.SC., C.A., A.T.I.I.

Lecturer, Department of Accounting and Business Method, University of Edinburgh

This article has been based on comments made by the writer and made in debate, firstly, at a meeting of the Edinburgh Accounting and Finance Seminar Group, when discussing his paper on goodwill accounting; and secondly, during an address to staff and students in the Faculty of Humanities, Heriot-Watt University (both in April 1971).

The Edinburgh Accounting and Finance Group, originally formed in 1968 under the aegis of Professor Edward Stamp and now renamed the Wednesday Forum, was re-formed in 1971 to encourage the presentation and discussion of original and controversial ideas; debates on contentious problems of the day; and the presentation of group viewpoints and opinions on these matters to a wider audience through formal publication. The group meets monthly for dinner, usually to discuss a paper presented by a group member. At the present time, membership (now 25) is by invitation, but is not restricted solely to the accountancy profession. The topics discussed are concerned, however, mainly with accounting or related financial and business matters. (A report of the group's last meeting appears at page 59 of this issue.)

The Relevance Problem

" Accounting information must be useful to people acting in various capacities both inside and outside of the entity concerned. It must be useful in the formulation of objectives, the making of decisions, or the direction and control of resources to accomplish objectives. The utility of information lies in its ability to reduce uncertainty about the actual state of affairs of concern to the user."[1] This basic criterion for accounting theory and practice—*information utility*—appears to be so obvious as not to require stating. But, strangely, it has been stated explicitly in recent years only. Its undoubted importance to accounting theory and practice is that it immediately focuses attention on the information *user* and the *uses* to which he applies accounting information. Traditionally, however, in the area of external financial reporting, the importance of knowing something about information users and uses has been largely ignored. This has created the somewhat belated research task to find the type of accounting information which satisfies user needs best by adhering to the criterion of utility. Utility, however, introduces another equally important yet ignored information criterion—*relevance*.

" Relevance is the primary standard and requires that the information must bear upon or be usefully associated with actions it is designed to facilitate or results desired to be produced. Known or assumed informational needs of potential users are of paramount importance in applying this standard."[2] Once again, this is apparently an obvious statement to make in relation to accounting information. But, as with utility, relevance has only recently been made explicit in accounting thought. However, linking the two, it appears to be perfectly reasonable to state that reportable accounting information should be relevant to its users' needs—in other words, useful. Unfortunately, it is doubtful whether

---

[1] Committee to Prepare a Statement of Basic Accounting Theory, *A Statement of Basic Accounting Theory*, American Accounting Association, 1966, page 8.
[2] A.A.A. Committee, *op. cit.* page 7.

present-day accounting information which is reported outside the business entity has ever had its relevance and utility tested and analysed.

Today, taking corporate activity as the example, companies are legally required to publish annual financial reports representing the accounting for stewardship of their managements to their shareholders. The object of the statutory profit and loss account and balance sheet is to make management accountable to ownership for the funds entrusted to it, and for the use it makes of these funds. They are financial statements which have not changed much *in purpose* since the early days of the company balance sheet which was intended to reflect the solvency of the company and the honesty and integrity of its management. Today, however, company accounts are known to be used by a variety of persons, all having one thing in common—the need for financial information of use in making *decisions* concerning their relationships with companies. Basically, these decisions concern some evaluation or other of a business's *future*. Despite this, however, the information which is currently used in this process is mainly descriptive of the *past* (sometimes being many months, if not years, out of date). The question that must therefore be asked is whether historical information of this type is relevant, and thus useful, to the type of decisions commonly made by investors and others. The answer must surely be that no one really knows because no one has bothered to prove or disprove the point. Company law *assumes* that present-day company accounts are both relevant and useful to the shareholders for whom they are intended. It is to be *assumed* that shareholders are satisfied with this type of information. Likewise, it is to be *assumed* that the same information is equally of relevance and use to creditors, lenders, government agencies, and so on. But is it? There appear to be a great many assumptions in this exercise, and for this reason it is strongly recommended that their validity must be tested.

The Uniformity Problem

In addition to the large question-mark surrounding the relevance of stewardship accounting information for decision making purposes, there is an equally large doubt about the way in which it is being measured—the so-called " uniformity v. flexibility " problem brought about by *accrual* accounting. The availability of so many individual accounting treatments for particular items of information has created the present storm of criticism of accounting practice. The possibility of a wide range of " true and fair " views of company profitability and financial position has given the financial journalist a field day and, incidentally, probably created a loss of confidence in the credibility of accountants and accounting information so far as the consumer is concerned.

The popular cry of the moment is for greater uniformity in accounting practice in order to reduce the alternative treatments to a minimum, and the mandatory Statements of Standard Accounting Practice of the three Chartered Institutes are intended to do just that. However, even with greater uniformity of accounting principles and practices, are the number of possible " true and fair " views going to be reduced? To the extent that they involve established principles and practices, the answer is yes. But to the extent that they involve individual personal judgments, the answer must be that a wide range of alternative financial results must always remain a possibility. However, this having been said, one other aspect of the problem should be looked at, and that is whether a greater uniformity in practice makes historical cost accrual information in stewardship reports any more relevant or useful to the decision maker than it is with the present flexibility. Unfortunately, the quest for standardisation of accounting practices has been started without the relevance and utility of the basic information being questioned. It would appear to be a potentially pointless exercise to spend so much time and resources in the production of uniformly prepared but totally irrelevant information. Such a position is possible.

The Measuring Unit Problem

One other current accounting problem should be mentioned which is pertinent to this discussion—that is, the problem of producing accounting measurements in terms of the unstable measurement unit of money. At present, accounting stewardship reports are expressed in terms of historical costs which assume that the monetary measuring unit has a stable value. However, it is a well-known economic fact of life that the purchasing power of money varies, thus invalidating this basic accounting assumption. Over a great many years, a debate has existed concerning the need to make some adjustments to historic data to eliminate the effects of a variable monetary measuring unit. Agreement, at least within the professional bodies, has eventually been achieved regarding the necessity to make price-level adjustments. But how this is to be done is at present still under debate. All well and good. But is historical accounting information, adjusted for price-level changes, a relevant and useful form of information for external reporting purposes? The answer at present is unknown, for the relevance of this type of information does not appear to have been seriously questioned in the past. It does seem somewhat illogical, therefore, to proceed with the inevitable extensive and complicated exercise of price-level accounting without first asking " is this information going to be relevant and useful? "; or indeed, " is price-level adjusted information any more relevant and useful than that which is unadjusted? "

Who can say what is relevant?

What the previous paragraphs have briefly attempted to highlight is that reportable accounting information is an economic commodity which should be capable of satisfying the informational needs and requirements of its potential consumer. If it does not do this, it is meaningless to produce and communicate it. Unfortunately, the meaningfulness of reportable accounting information—*whatever its nature*—is a totally unknown factor. Today, no one can realistically say whether stewardship information of the present type is more *or* less relevant and useful than any other type of information which is capable of being reported. It therefore appears to be pointless to condemn the production of one particular type of accounting information, whilst advocating the use of another. All that can be said at the present time is that certain types of accounting information *appear* to be more relevant than others to potential users. The state of reportable accounting information is at a watershed. Criticism has brought the present type of information into disrepute—more often than not on perfectly reasonable grounds. Improvements in external accounting reports must be sought, but this will not come from haphazard amendments to existing information. The only sensible approach is, firstly, to determine who are the potential information users, and in particular, what are their various informational needs and requirements (that is, an extremely involved investigation and analysis of a variety of differing decision models upon which accounting information can come to bear. This work should ideally be done by those who are experienced observers of information usage); secondly, to develop alternative types of reportable accounting information which may or may not be relevant and useful to the defined decision making groups (this is primarily the concern of accountants); and thirdly, to test for the relevance and utility of each type of alternative information so far as concerns each defined user group (this is primarily the concern of behavioural scientists, such as psychologists). It is only when there has been an adequate testing of all the alternatives that the most relevant and useful information will be found. However, such an exercise, so briefly described above, is an extremely long-term affair, involving a great deal of expertise which any accountants researching in this area will have to acquire.

Alternative Types of Information

Neither having the knowledge nor the expertise with which to comment realistically on information users and their various information needs, all that is left for accountants to discuss at the present time are the alternative types of information which could be of possible relevance and use to the user. Basically, there are four main types:—

(*a*) information about *past* business activity, measured on an *accrual* basis;

(*b*) information about *past* business activity, measured on a *cash* basis;

(*c*) information about *future* business activity, measured on an *accrual* basis; and

(*d*) information about *future* business activity, measured on a *cash* basis.

With (*a*), there are additional alternatives to the stated basis in the sense that it can be expressed in terms of either historic, current, or price-level adjusted historic costs.

Accounting information about past activity describes what has happened in a business—it is a historical record and, to that extent, is apparently appropriate to the stewardship function involving management and owners, where the former is accounting to the latter for the work it has conducted on their behalf, and for the resources it has been entrusted with. For this reason, historic accounting information *appears* to be of limited relevance and utility to the decision maker who is primarily concerned with evaluating the future. However, it is being used at present by investors and others making decisions, and it must be presumed that a description of a business's past is of some relevance to someone basically concerned with the future. It would therefore be unjustifiable to recommend the abandonment of stewardship information on the grounds that it was of no relevance to the decision maker. Clearly, it has some relevance, otherwise it would not be used (and there is no evidence whatsoever of this situation having been reached).

Accounting information describing future activity is a reflection of what the management of the business considers will happen to the business in the future. Thus, there is an attempt to quantify and measure the effects of the potential use of its resources. In an ideal sense, this type of information *appears* to be extremely relevant and useful to the decision maker concerned with anticipating future business activity. It *appears* to give him greater guidance and assistance in this matter than does historic accounting information.

Accrual accounting is concerned with the allocation of accumulated data between specified accounting periods, and this inevitably leads to the injection of a great deal of highly personal and subjective judgment into the process. The result is that it is possible to have a wide range of financial results evolving from the same basic data. On the other hand, *cash* accounting avoids the problems brought about by accruals, tending to reduce considerably the amount of personal judgment involved in accounting measurement. Because of this latter factor, *cash* accounting *appears* to be preferable to *accrual* accounting, reducing as it does the degree of doubt and uncertainty the information user may have about the reliability of accrued information.

Summing up this section, a tentative, and as yet untested, statement can be made that accounting information about future activity, when measured on a cash basis, may eventually prove to be the most relevant and useful to the decision maker because it offers guidance for the future, whilst at the same time using a relatively easy to understand measurement basis. For those potential users of accounting information requiring a stewardship report, historic accounting information on a cash basis *appears* to be the most useful and relevant because of the high degree of objectivity in its measurement, and also because of its potential for comparison with any disclosed forecast cash information.

The Relevance of Cash Flow Information

In 1970, Professor Lawson of the Manchester Business School suggested that conventional financial statements, produced on an accrual basis, should be scrapped, and that cash flow statements should be substituted instead.[3] He advocated the disclosure of up to fifteen years of *past* cash flows in order to give the decision maker more reliable information concerning company performance, whilst at the same time trying to eliminate many of the problems commonly associated with accounting for profitability (including, for example, the flexibility of accrual accounting practice, the effects of inflation, and the difficulty of distinguishing capital and revenue expenditure). Lawson's suggestion has so far met with a relatively unfavourable public response, ranging from uninformed comments about "cash book" or "receipts and payments" accounting to milder comments about cash flow statements being useful supplements to conventional financial statements. In a relatively recent paper, Lawson's ideas have been taken one step further with the suggestion that *forecast* cash flows should also be communicated to external users concerned with decision making.[4] Some of the main advantages of this type of information are as follows:—

(1) It reflects the business's ability to "pay its way" in the future. In an age when the ability of a firm to stay in business is of paramount importance to investors, lenders, creditors, employees and consumers alike, the availability of cash for this purpose is critical. Accrual accounting, whilst reflecting apparent profitability, can mask a potentially critical cash position;

(2) management's view of the business's future is projected for the benefit of external decision makers who are vitally concerned with that future. A progressive management should be making cash flow forecasts for purposes of internal planning and decision making. It would appear to be *socially* beneficial to publish them (so long as users were fully aware of their tentative and subjective nature);

(3) the problems of accrual accounting and of inflation are avoided, and the artifical distinction between capital and revenue transactions rendered meaningless; and

(4) the contribution of all the resources of the

---
[3] *See* ACCOUNTANCY AGE, 24.7.1970 and 6.11.1970.
[4] T. A. LEE: "Goodwill—an Example of Will-o'-the-Wisp Accounting," ACCOUNTING AND BUSINESS RESEARCH, Autumn 1971, at page 318.

---

business towards its maintenance and expansion is recognised (including the human resources which are at present not accounted for at all). The underemployment or inefficient use of all resources would be reflected in their contribution to cash flow.

The main difficulties should also be made explicit:—

(1) There are enormous difficulties to be faced in projecting the future of a business in quantitative terms. The future of many businesses is necessarily full of doubt and uncertainty. The further into the future the projections go, the more uncertain will be the quantifications. However, all good businessmen should be doing this as a matter of routine. Their *attitude* towards the certainty and reliability of such information is very different from that concerning the reliability of historic information. So it must also be with external users of forecast information. They must understand that it cannot be objectively determined in the same way as traditional stewardship information. To help them in the use of the information, it is suggested that the various commercial economic, political and social assumptions which underlie it should also be disclosed. It may also be expedient to publish a range of forecasts, based on a range of assumptions;

(2) there is the danger of giving competitors information about the plans of the business, which may prejudice its market position. This point is recognised although in mitigation it should be said that the detail of the information supplied in forecasts would not be sufficient to reveal any commercial, scientific or technical "secrets". There is also the added advantage that a greater market competitiveness could arise due to the disclosure of this type of information on a widespread scale; and

(3) there is the possibility of forecast information being drastically affected by the natural or contrived optimism or pessimism of management. However, two safeguards to this situation could exist. Firstly, actual cash flows could be published, and management could be required to comment on any material variances between forecast and actual figures; and secondly, an independent audit function could be required where outside management experts were required to examine and report on the reasonableness of the forecasts. Actual cash flows could be audited by professional accountants.

The Road to Forecast Cash Flows

Before any reader "explodes" at the implications of the above ideas, two comments are pertinent:—

(1) Cash flow information is *not* being advocated—either in historic or forecast terms—as *the* most

relevant and useful information to a decision maker, such as an investor. It is simply suggested as one type of information which appears on the surface to have greater relevance and utility than other types—including historic cost accrual information. It will only be after considerable research effort that the relative relevance and utility of one type of information over another can be authoritatively determined and stated; and

(2) there is some evidence available to trace a movement away from historical accrual accounting towards forecast cash accounting—witness the development of " flow of funds " statements, the increasingly quantitative look forward to the future by company chairmen in their reports to shareholders, the disclosure by very large companies of detailed reports on capital projects (for example, Unilever and ICI), and the provision for mandatory profit forecasts when there is an acquisition or merger of companies. Information being disclosed to the public by companies in particular is showing clear signs of becoming more forward-looking as time goes on.

In conclusion, one fact is abundantly clear—it is an act of some irresponsibility to criticise dogmatically or to defend the preparation and use of one type of accounting information to the complete exclusion of another, until such time as the relevance and utility of each has been adequately tested, analysed and proved.

© T. A. Lee, 1972.

Early Argument

STUDENTS' SECTION
(PAGES 198 TO 200)

The Nature and Purpose of Cash Flow Accounting

T. A. LEE, M.SC., C.A., A.T.I.I.

Lecturer, Department of Accounting and Business Method, University of Edinburgh

Introduction

During the last year or so, there has been a not insignificant amount of attention paid to the possibility of accounting for and reporting on, for the benefit of investors, the numerous *cash* transactions of companies. Although Lawson has attracted the greatest proportion of this attention,[1] other writers have also made public their views on the matter.[2] Their reason for developing the concept of reporting in detail on the cash position of a business has been the prevailing economic climate, which has resulted in a number of well-known businesses each being confronted with a cash crisis. It has served to highlight the key factor of cash in business, which exists whether or not the economic climate is favourable or unfavourable. Indeed, what the critics of cash flow accounting forget, when they suggest that such a concept is merely a passing gimmick whose relevance will disappear when inflation is checked, is that cash is central to the survival of any business, in good times *as well as* in bad. In other words, there is always a case for accounting for cash flows. However, this paper is not concerned with the case for cash flow accounting for

[1] *See* GERALD LAWSON: comments in ACCOUNTANCY AGE, 24.7.70, pages 1-2; and 6.11.70, pages 10-11; and " Cash-flow Accounting ", THE ACCOUNTANT, 28.10.71, pages 386-389.

[2] *See* H. C. EDEY: " Accounting Principles and Business Reality ", ACCOUNTANCY, November 1963, pages 998-1002, and December 1963, pages 1083-1088; T. A. LEE: " Goodwill—An Example of Will-o'-the-Wisp Accounting "; ACCOUNTING AND BUSINESS RESEARCH, Autumn 1971, at page 318; " The Relevance of Accounting Information Including Cash Flows ": THE ACCOUNTANT'S MAGAZINE, January 1972, pages 30-34; " A Case for Cash Flow Reporting "; JOURNAL OF BUSINESS FINANCE, Summer 1972 (forthcoming); and GEORGE J. STAUBUS: " The Relevance of Evidence of Cash Flows " in Asset Valuation and Income Determination, (ed.) Robert R. Sterling; *Scholars Book Co., Kansas*, 1971, pages 42-69.

external interests, as this has been adequately covered in the writings already referred to. Instead, the purpose of the paper is to give a simple explanation of what is meant by cash flow accounting. Confusion has arisen as to what it means exactly—ideas range from " a summary of the cash book " to " the external reporting of discounted cash flow evaluations ". The sections which follow will attempt to show that, although these are extreme viewpoints, the proposals currently being made contain an element of each.

Cash in Business

It is a self-evident fact that all developed economies have based their business activity on money, which is used as the main means of exchange of goods and services. Therefore, it follows from this premise, most of the economic activity of a business entity is in some way reflected in cash terms. In other words, the typical " cash to cash " nature of the business can be shown as follows:—

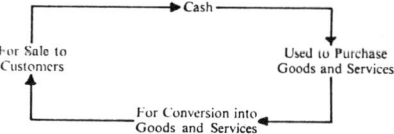

The above simplistic diagram ignores the intermediate stages which are created by credit purchase and sale transactions. (However, they ultimately will require to be settled by cash.) It also assumes the purchase of raw materials, labour, and overhead services, as well as the purchase of " service potential " in the form of capital goods (conventionally described for accounting purposes as fixed assets). Nevertheless, it ignores the outflow of cash from the business in the form of taxation and distributions representing returns on loan and ownership capital. An amended diagram can therefore be presented as follows:—

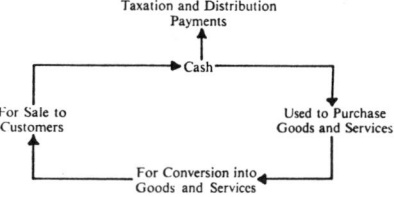

It is the above flow of cash, in and out of the business,

which cash flow accounting attempts to measure and describe. It ignores, therefore, the traditional "accruals" of debtors and creditors, and cost allocations represented in inventories and fixed assets. Cash flow descriptions can reflect both—

(1) cash transactions which have actually occurred; in which case they must evolve from a detailed analysis of the " cash book " records of the business; and

(2) cash transactions which it is forecast will occur; in which case these bear a great deal of similarity to capital investment evaluations on a DCF basis.

The Development of Cash Flow Accounting

The idea of cash flow accounting is not a new one. Indeed, it is probably in part as old as accounting itself—the earliest accountants recording and reporting business transactions in terms of cash or the equivalent means of exchange. However, particularly during the trading revolution of the 15th and 16th centuries and the industrial revolution of the 18th and 19th centuries, the idea of the business entity as a going concern of indefinite life, and the importance of business profitability (particularly when related to capital employed), resulted in the introduction of " accrual " accounting techniques, which are now accepted as a major part of the measurement and communication of financial accounting information to external interests. Nevertheless, the basis of this form of accounting is still to a very large extent determined by the cash transactions of the business. Apart from its use as a basis for " accrual " accounting, cash flow data can be seen to be used for other purposes at the present time, for example—

(1) in the day to day control of a business's cash resources and requirements;

(2) in the production of income and expenditure statements for non-profit making organisations; and

(3) in the evaluation of the relative " profitability " of alternative capital projects.

The current advocation of cash flow accounting merely reflects, therefore, an extension of the use made of cash data—that is, from its main use as a management decision-making and control aid towards its use as a means of reporting actual and forecast business activity for the benefit of those persons located outwith the business (for example, its owners, lenders and creditors).

Objectives of Cash Flow Accounting

As previously mentioned, the aim of this paper is to explain rather than to justify cash flow accounting. However, in order to produce a balanced portrayal of the topic, the following are given briefly as the main reasons for its existence: [3]

(1) as an *alternative* reporting form to " accrual " accounting—the latter emphasising profitability, whereas cash flow accounting emphasises the business's capability and potential to *survive* in terms of cash; and

(2) following on from (1), as an aid to help external interests to make *decisions* concerning their existing or potential investment or involvement in the business.

The Nature of Cash Flow Accounting

It follows from what has been stated in the previous sections that cash flow accounting (as recently advocated) is intended to describe past *and* projected business activity for control and decision making purposes. Its main advantage over " accrual " accounting is that it avoids, in both its historic and forecast forms, the subjectiveness introduced into accounting by the accrual methodology, which contains a great deal of personal opinion and judgment (for example, in cost allocations, stock valuations, provisions and depreciation). It introduces, however, an additional element to financial reporting to external interests—that of reporting forecast information about projected business activity. Therefore, its basic elements are:

Cash Flows	Historic	Projected

In order to obtain the greatest use from cash flow information, it is recommended that a pattern of flows must be reported reflecting several years' activity. This is done in order to minimise the effect of exceptional inflows or outflows of cash in one particular year, which can distort the cash position of the business when looked at in isolation. The inherent uncertainty in forecasting business activity will, however, limit the number of years of projected information for reporting purposes. Taking into account, therefore, the need to report several years' activity, the elements of a cash flow report could be as follows:

		Historic				Projected		
Cash Flows	Year	1	2	3	4	5	6	7	8

So far, the specific nature of reportable cash flow in-

[3] For a more detailed account, *see* Lee: " A Case for Cash Flow Reporting "; *op cit*.

formation has not been mentioned. It is recommended that it should contain the following elements: the cash *inflows* generated from—

(a) operational (trading or manufacturing) transactions;
(b) non-recurrent, exceptional, operational transactions; and possibly
(c) financial (capital and loan) transactions;

together with the cash *outflows* caused by—

(d) capital expenditure;
(e) research and development expenditure;
(f) taxation;
(g) distributions; and possibly
(h) financial (capital and loan) repayments.

The overall cash flow statement could, therefore, take the following form:

Cash Flows Year	Historic					Projected		
	1	2	3	4	5	6	7	8
Cash Balances brought forward	±	±	±	±	±	±	±	±
Operational Transactions Flow	±	±	±	±	±	±	±	±
Exceptional Transactions Flow	±	±	±	±	±	±	±	±
Financial Transactions Flow	±	±	±	±	±	±	±	±
Capital Transactions Flow	±	±	±	±	±	±	±	±
Research and Development Flow	−	−	−	−	−	−	−	−
Taxation Transactions Flow	−	−	−	−	−	−	−	−
Cash available for Distribution	±	±	±	±	±	±	±	±
Distribution Flow	−	−	−	−	−	−	−	−
Cash Balances carried forward	±	±	±	±	±	±	±	±

[NOTE: + *is a net cash inflow, and* − *is a net cash outflow.*]

The above is not intended to be representative of a *pro forma* cash flow statement; it is simply used to describe the main elements of such a statement. In practice, however, as well as a total " sources and uses " statement, there could also be subsidiary statements analysing each of its main elements.[4]

What the total statement, therefore, aims to describe is—

(1) how much cash has been *generated* within the business;
(2) how much has been *injected* into it from external sources; and
(3) how the cash has been *applied*
 (a) to maintain and expand the business, and
 (b) to satisfy government for tax due, and owners and lenders *re* a return on their investments.

[4] For detailed *pro forma* statements, *see* Lee, *ibid.*

A Word of Warning

Before finishing, a word of warning appears appropriate. The phrase " cash flow " is often used nowadays, either in conversation or in writing, without any deliberate regard to its real meaning. When a financial headline appears stating " XY Ltd. has an improved cash flow in 1971 ", the impression, following the descriptions of the previous sections, is that the company has generated more cash than in previous periods. However, what is really meant is that the company has improved its flow of funds through an increase in undistributed net profits, together with an increase in the fixed assets depreciation provisions. In other words, the phrase " cash flow " is being used instead of the more appropriate " funds flow ". The two concepts of flow are entirely different—funds relating to profits measured on the accruals basis, and cash referring to pure cash transactions. A cash flow statement, therefore, should be what it states it is—a statement of cash flowing in and out of the business. On the other hand, a funds flow statement should always be regarded as a statement of sources and application of funds (including profits retained).

© T. A. Lee, 1972.

A case for cash flow reporting

by T. A. Lee
Department of Accounting and Business Method
University of Edinburgh

A RELUCTANCE TO CHANGE?

INVARIABLY, over the years, whenever there has been a sustained demand for better accounting information[1] for investors, the traditional response has been an increased disclosure of items of the existing type of reported information—that is, stewardship information.[2] This somewhat illogical principle of attempting to equate quantity with quality has failed to combat (at least in this writer's opinion) the increasing doubt with regard to the relevance and utility of stewardship accounting information for investors who are concerned mainly with making decisions.[3] It is a problem which has caused numerous writers to look for alternative types of reportable accounting information, hopefully more relevant to the decision-making investor. The main effort to date in this area has been concerned with expressing the traditional stewardship information in contemporary terms, by adjustment of its original monetary value measurements [1]. However, what has either been forgotten or ignored in this drive for improvement in financial reporting is the question of whether stewardship information (adjusted or unadjusted) is the most relevant and, therefore, the most useful type available for reporting to persons primarily concerned with making investment decisions. Surprisingly, despite a mounting debate about the needs of information users, those who have advocated monetarily adjusted stewardship statements have rarely, if indeed ever, questioned their fundamental relevance to the user. The implication to be drawn from this is that those who seek to make such technical adjustments are quite satisfied with the information's basic relevance and utility. They therefore do not advocate a major change in the *nature* of the accounting information being supplied to investors. Instead they look for refinements in the *technical* process of valuation. This gives an impression that there is a deep-seated, if unwitting, reluctance to change the nature of reported information when there appears to be a pressing need for change.

THE NEED FOR CHANGE

Utility and relevance are, in the opinion of the writer, *the* primary concepts of accounting. They should govern the measurement and communication of all types of accounting information; the logic being that information can be useful to its user only if it is likely to influence or have a bearing on his decisions and actions. If utility and relevance are accepted as such important parts of accounting thought, it follows that all accounting information, whatever its nature or measurement process, should be capable of satisfying the informational needs of its potential user. Those persons who support the production of stewardship accounting information for what are basically decision-making activities, either consciously or unwittingly are assuming that the needs of the investor are thereby satisfied. A study of the available literature reveals that they appear to think it unnecessary even to argue in support of this assumption, despite the conflicting fact that stewardship accounting information, in either its monetarily adjusted or unadjusted form, looks back in time, whereas the investor is predominantly interested in the future. In contrast to this school of thought there is another, much more recent and very much smaller, which has suggested the measurement and communication of past and forecast cash flow information as relevant sources of knowledge about the

---

[1] Accounting information, in the sense it is used throughout this paper, refers to that which is communicated by companies to their shareholders.

[2] For an authoritative acknowledgment of stewardship as the main purpose of present-day company financial statements, see "Accountants' liability to third parties", *Statement S8*, ICAEW, p. 2.

[3] For purposes of this paper, the term "investors" is intended to include both the "average prudent investor" and the "investment manager", although it is recognized that detailed accounting information is probably more extensively and intensively used by the latter person than by the former.

A case for cash flow reporting

company for the investor [2]. Advocacy of this type of information for decision-makers has so far appeared to meet with little support, despite the fact that the arguments both for and against such a proposal have been put forward in detail by those concerned. So far as can be seen, only Lawson has advocated the complete abolition of conventional stewardship financial statements, the other writers advocating cash flow statements as supplements to them. In this connection it should not be forgotten that stewardship accounting information is extremely useful for accountability purposes and, consequently, should be available to fulfil such a role—that is, as a means of making management accountable for the custodianship of the resources entrusted to it by the shareholders. In addition, so far as profit is a measure of the use made of these resources, then the reporting of such a measure is an important part of any stewardship function. However, when it comes to the question of decision-making, stewardship information *appears* less relevant and less useful to the investor than cash flow information in either its historic or projected form. The following sections attempt to support this observation.

THE KEY FACTOR OF CASH

The proposition being made in this section is that cash is *the* key resource of a company and, consequently, it is suggested that investors should have a much better knowledge about company cash than they do at present by means of the conventional profit statements, balance sheets and funds statements. As Hendriksen has stated (italics added), "In the final analysis, cash flows into and out of the business enterprise are *the most fundamental events* upon which accounting measurements are based and upon which investors and creditors base their decisions" [3].

The business activity of a company is normally on a "cash to cash" basis, most transactions involving some cash movement either in the short or in the long term. Without cash the company could not survive in the economic world today, no matter how good its products, no matter how bright its public image, no matter how skilled its managers and workers. Cash, at the end of the day, determines its fate; indeed, cash may be likened to the life blood of the company. This raises the question that if cash is so important to corporate economic survival, then why should not investors (and, consequently, interested creditors and lenders) be given detailed accounting information about it? After all, they should be concerned with the vital question of the company's survival, for the value (both present and future) of their existing or potential interest in the company is quite definitely linked with this factor.

In addition, looking at the company's cash position specifically from the point of view of the interested investor, it is reasonable to suggest that cash is also the key factor so far as his expectations of dividends are concerned. The company's ability to provide the shareholder with a return on his investment is obviously geared to its cash position, both present and future. If there is no cash, there can be no dividends, and so far as can be reasonably observed, investment values are at least partly influenced by the dividend factor. As well as the question of dividends, the investor's expectations of recovering his investment are equally geared to the survival and, thus, to the cash position of the company, for if the company fails he may very well lose part or all of his investment in it.

Summarizing, therefore, it appears that the investor's interest in the survival of the company, together with its ability to provide a stream of dividends for him, demands far more accounting information about its current and anticipated cash positions than is required to be communicated at present.

DECISIONS CONCERN THE FUTURE

Investors who are interested in the business activities and affairs of companies should be regarded first and foremost as decision-makers, for they periodically have to make decisions affecting their existing or potential interests in the company. These decisions, by definition, require consideration of alternative courses of action, and the main factor in this process is the future. Questions about the future of the company, and of investments in it, must be asked and to some extent answered by the investor if he is to take investment action in a rational and reasonable manner. Thus it can be safely said that in almost every decision he has to make, the investor must inevitably take cognizance of forecasts—whether these are his own or someone else's. These forecasts should be as formal and credible as possible, and avoidance of uninformed guesswork must be aimed for at all times. It therefore appears to be very important that the investor should have some form of information relating to the future of the company. In the opinion of the writer, it is extremely doubtful whether historic accounting information, of the type contained in either monetarily adjusted or unadjusted stewardship financial statements, is the most relevant and useful for purposes of helping the investor to predict (a) future dividends and other benefits receivable by him from the company; (b) its future survival, maintenance or expansion; and (c) the degree of risk and uncertainty connected with his existing or potential investment in it. This, however, should not be taken as a statement of absolute denial of the relevance and usefulness of historic accounting information for decision-making purposes. Such information is *known* to be used by investors (exact research will have to be carried out to determine the extent of this usage), and it is also accepted that historic data is an essential ingredient in the techniques of quantitative forecasting, including time series analysis and causal models [4]. Nevertheless, it appears to be reasonable to suggest that forecast accounting information, projecting the activity of the company into the future, should prove to be more beneficial than historic data to the investor when he makes decisions. It relates to the future, and it is that dimension of time, despite its inherent uncertainty, which corresponds most with the investor's needs and requirements in the decision-making process. In addition, if cash is such an important key factor to the investor (as explained in the previous section), it would seem logical to provide forecast information relating to the cash flows and cash position of the company. The further into the future these forecasts go, the better equipped the investor should be to make his decisions. However, it must be remembered that the usefulness of forecasts undoubtedly diminishes the more they extend into the future, until such time as they have little relevance because of the degree of uncertainty attached to them. In other words, forecasts should not reflect time periods which are unrealistic to predict. Despite this constraint, which effectively is acknowledging the constantly and rapidly changing society of which the company is a part, it appears that the general propositions being put forward in this section hold true in business investing today—that is (a) the existence of a future creates a need to make decisions concerning that future; (b) these decisions require some formal information about the expected future; and (c) accountants should be concerned with satisfying this informational need (despite the possible high degree of uncertainty, and despite the views of those who, like Chambers, are concerned solely with accountants measuring and reporting factual information about business activity which has already taken place [5]).

THE IMPORTANCE OF OBJECTIVITY

It has long been recognized by accountants that one of the main concepts of accounting is objectivity —that is, whenever possible, bias or lack of objectivity should be avoided in the accounting process by those persons responsible for it. Chambers has summed it up well in his concept of neutrality where he states that accounting information should be relevant to its user, no matter what decision or action he takes related to it [6]. In other words, the processor of the information[4] should not bias it toward any one potential decision or action of the decision-maker. This is quite clearly a fundamental aspect of accounting thought, and one which should underlie all accounting practice. It is therefore not surprising

---

[4] The term "processor" will be used from now on throughout the remainder of this paper to cover collectively all those persons in company management who are in some way involved in or responsible for the production of accounting information.

to learn that critics of published forecast accounting information find it largely unacceptable because of its supposed lack of objectivity. Objectivity however, in the sense they are using the term, concerns not so much the attitude of mind of the information processor but more the availability of verifiable evidence to support the information. What is being forgotten in this apparent conflict between objectiveness and subjectiveness in accounting is that there are two distinct, albeit related, concepts of objectivity. The first concerns the neutrality of the processor—his attitude of mind to the information and its potential user. The second concerns a technical characteristic of the information. Mental objectivity is an essential aspect of *all* accounting and should be adhered to at all times, whatever the nature of the information being produced. On the other hand, technical objectivity cannot possibly be achieved in all areas of accounting and this fact should be recognized and accepted. Personal judgment and opinion is a fundamental part of the accounting process. It applies just as much to stewardship accounting information on the accrual basis (because of the underlying allocation and valuation procedures involved) as it does to forecast accounting information on a cash basis (because this is based on an uncertain future). It is therefore suggested that so long as mental objectivity is being adhered to by the information processor, technical objectivity (or the lack of it) should not be used as an excuse for not producing forecast accounting information when this is *technically feasible*—the overriding criteria should always be the relative relevance and usefulness of the information to the investor. If there is any doubt about mental objectivity on the part of the processor, then the audit function goes some way towards establishing the credibility of the accounting process and, indirectly, of the processor. A 1966 American Accounting Association Committee supported this view that accounting information (whether past or future) should be verified whenever possible, in order to retain the confidence in it of its potential user [7]. The same Committee, however, also acknowledged the fact that there are varying degrees of verifiability, depending on the type of accounting information concerned. Both the writer [8] and Tomkins [9] have acknowledged the importance of information verification and have suggested that forecast accounting information should be independently audited and reported on. Edey, on the other hand, has stated that the audit of such information is not necessary [10], whilst Briston and Fawthrop have elaborated on this latter opinion, seeing little point in verification when there is such uncertainty underlying the information [11]. What these "no audit" writers appear to neglect is the fact that the audit function can be regarded as a behavioural study of the information processor as well as a technical exercise to prove the validity of certain accounting procedures.

Taking the above points collectively, it is proposed in this section that, if objectivity is accepted as an important criterion of accounting, production of the type of accounting information which appears to present the most reasonable balance of relevance *and* objectivity should be aimed for at all times— because of its overall utility to the user. Cash flow information appears to the writer to satisfy these conditions best. Firstly, in its historic form, it is perhaps the most objective information possible, avoiding most of the subjectiveness which enters into the technical adjustments involved in the traditional accrual accounting; it is also the most relevant information for purposes of comparison with forecast information should this be measured on a cash basis. Secondly, forecast cash flows, although involving a great deal of uncertainty (however, no more so than budgeted profits on the accrual basis), clearly avoid the necessary subjectiveness of accrual judgments and opinions. Therefore, they appear to be far less subjective in a *total* sense than profit forecasts.

CASH FLOW STATEMENTS

The above points appear to the writer to be several of the main arguments in favour of preparing and presenting past and forecast cash flows for investors. The main advantages and disadvantages of such a reporting system have already been discussed by him in a previous paper [12], and therefore it is not intended to repeat them here. What will be looked at in greater detail at this stage are the nature and content of the proposed cash flow statements. This is done in order to give interested readers an opportunity of seeing what these reports could look like in practice. It is hoped that their presentation may generate further suggestions for amendment and improvement.

One or two general points about the statements should be noted before going any further: (a) It is recommended by the writer that conventional stewardship financial statements, portraying past business activity, measured on the accrual basis and described in contemporary money terms, should be published in addition to the cash flow statements, not so much for decision-making but more as information for an entirely different purpose—that of stewardship; (b) The forecast cash flows ideally should reflect several years' anticipated activity within the company—say, four or five years at the most. The earlier years, because of their proximity to the present, would naturally tend to be more accurate than the later years. But each forecast year would be subject to continuous reassessment, and this process should ensure that account is being taken of significant events likely to alter an original forecast. For the purposes of the following illustrations, only three years of forecasts are shown, as this is thought to represent the maximum which companies should be asked to disclose, at least until such time as management becomes more skilled and experienced with available forecasting techniques. As Chambers *et al.* have stated, "The need today, we believe, is not for better forecasting methods, but for better application of the techniques at hand" [13]; (c) Both past and forecast cash flow information published for the benefit of investors should be subject to independent audit. Past cash flows should reasonably be expected to be audited by professional accountants, but as far as future cash flows are concerned, these would in all probability require to be verified and reported on by experts in specialist management fields, including business forecasting.

The composition of both past and future cash flows for external reporting purposes should be made up of the following elements:

a) Manufacturing and/or Trading Transactions Flow—giving details of revenues received and expenditure paid for, both relating to the operational activity of the company. This data would be analysed according to significant economic unit groupings, and would exclude any exceptional or relatively non-recurrent items.

b) Exceptional or Non-recurrent Transactions Flow—giving details of those cash transactions, connected with the company's operational activity, which can reasonably be described as either exceptional or relatively non-recurrent.

c) Financial Transactions Flow—giving details of monies received and repaid by the company to its shareholders, lenders and bankers, but excluding interest and dividend payments.

d) Capital Transactions Flow—giving details of the cash movements resulting from the purchase and sale of "profit-contributing" resources by the company, including land, buildings, plant, equipment, investments and sums expended in the area of research and development.

e) Taxation Transactions Flow—giving details of taxation payments made by the company, as well as the receipt of any refunds from the tax authorities.[5]

f) Interest and Dividend Transactions Flow—giving details of interim and final dividends paid by the company to its shareholders, as well as interest payments to lenders.

In addition to the above statements, it is also suggested that the following supplementary statements should be published for use by investors:

g) Non-cash Transactions Statement—giving details of those transactions incurred by the company which in themselves will not cause any immediate move-

---

[5] It should be noted that, unless the government of the day changed the basis of computing company taxation liabilities, the payment of these liabilities would continue to be arrived at with reference to accounting profits measured on the accrual basis. This, obviously, is one very good reason for retaining stewardship statements until such time as government can be convinced of the merits of measuring tax on a cash basis.

A case for cash flow reporting

ment of cash, but which should have a significant bearing on cash flows in the future. Examples include the purchase of shares in another company when satisfied in part or in whole by the issue of shares or loan stock in the acquiring company; the purchase and sale of goods and services between companies which are settled by contra accounting entry in the respective books of account; and the issue of bonus shares to shareholders. Failure to include this type of data in cash reports (because it does not directly affect cash) would, in the opinion of the writer, fail to provide all the information required by the investor to assess the survival prospects of the company, his dividend expectations, etc.

h) Statement of Basic Assumptions—giving details, at least in relatively general terms, of the main assumptions which management has had to make in order to compute the figures contained in the forecast cash flow information mentioned above. Such assumptions could be classified as follows:

1) *Business Assumptions*—that is, assumptions specifically connected with the operational and related activity of the company. These would include those relating to estimations of sales demand (including consumer behaviour), production levels, pricing, capital projects, financing schemes, etc, over which the company and its management should have some degree of control and influence.

2) *Economic, Political and Social Assumptions*—that is, assumptions, unlike those in (1) above, which mainly reflect matters completely outside the control and direction of the company and its management. Examples include governmental policy regarding industrial development; the general economic and social climate, including rates of inflation and interest, unemployment levels, the state of the Balance of Payments, and so on.

In a fully developed system of reported cash forecasts it is possible to envisage the publication of a range of expectations reflecting possible variations in the underlying assumptions. At first, however, the forecasts should reflect "reasonable" expectations rather than the extremes of optimism or pessimism.

i) Statement of Material Variations—giving details, again in relatively general terms, of the major variations between actual and forecast cash flows. This would help to give the investor some idea of differences due to (1) factors within the control of the company's management; and (2) factors outside such control. It would also provide him with some knowledge of the dependability of forecast information in the type of business activity the company is in. This would be helpful in assessing the degree of uncertainty and risk applicable to an investment in such a company. It also satisfies the stewardship function between management and ownership in a relatively obvious and meaningful way.

DRAFT CASH FLOW STATEMENTS

The main statement, outlined below, reflects the overall cash flow of the company (both actual and forecast), and follows the pattern of a related form of stewardship financial statement—the source and application of funds statement. In the case of cash flow statements, the "funds" are described in terms of cash. In the case of funds statements, the "funds" are measured in terms of accounting accruals.

From the above type of statement, the investor could obtain the following specific information, *inter alia*, about the company he was assessing for investment purposes, and which he could then compare with similar data for other companies. (Each comment is applicable to both actual and forecast information.)

a) The company's ability to generate sufficient cash resources to survive in the long term is conveyed in the overall picture portrayed in the statement, particularly in the individual and total figures in items 1, 7 and 9.

b) The company's ability to generate sufficient cash resources to distribute satisfactory dividends, as well as to pay its interest obligations to lenders, is also conveyed in the statement as a whole, but

TABLE 1: Statement of total cash flow of company
Statement of total cash flow—year to 31 July 1971

Cash Flows	Appen-dix	1967 F A	1968 F A	1969 F A	1970 F A	1971 F A	Total F A	1972 F	1973 F	1974 F	Total F
1) Bank and Cash Balances Brought Forward		+ + − −	+ + − −	+ + − −	+ + − −	+ + − −	+ + − −	+ −	+ −	+ −	+ −
2) Operational Transactions Flow	A	+ + − −	+ + − −	+ + − −	+ + − −	+ + − −	+ + − −	+ −	+ −	+ −	+ −
3) Exceptional Transactions Flow	B	+ + − −	+ + − −	+ + − −	+ + − −	+ + − −	+ + − −	+ −	+ −	+ −	+ −
4) Financial Transactions Flow	C	+ + − −	+ + − −	+ + − −	+ + − −	+ + − −	+ + − −	+ −	+ −	+ −	+ −
5) Capital Transactions Flow	D	+ + − −	+ + − −	+ + − −	+ + − −	+ + − −	+ + − −	+ −	+ −	+ −	+ −
6) Taxation Transactions Flow	E	+ + − −	+ + − −	+ + − −	+ + − −	+ + − −	+ + − −	+ −	+ −	+ −	+ −
7) *Net Distributable Flow*		+ + − −	+ + − −	+ + − −	+ + − −	+ + − −	+ + − −	+ −	+ −	+ −	+ −
8) Interest and Dividends	F	− −	− −	− −	− −	− −	− −	−	−	−	−
9) Undistributed Bank and Cash Balances		+ + − −	+ + − −	+ + − −	+ + − −	+ + − −	+ + − −	+ −	+ −	+ −	+ −

Note: In this and subsequent Tables column "F" contains forecast data, and column "A" contains actual data; + is a cash inflow and − is a cash outflow.

with particular reference to the figures given in items 7 and 8.

c) The investor should be interested in the dividend *and* interest "covers" applicable to the company, and these can be obtained from the above statement by comparing the related figures in items 7, 8 and 9.

d) Following the comments made in (b) and (c), it is possible to calculate figures for *distributable* cash per share, as well as for *distributed* cash per share, both being measures of the worth of the shares compared with other alternative investments. It should be noted, however, that as individual annual figures for cash flows can be materially affected by periodic movements in cash due to financial or capital transactions, then it would perhaps be more reasonable to use five-yearly averages for this purpose to eliminate the "ups and downs" of individual years.

e) The cash available and used for capital transactions, which are designed to ensure the company continues as a going concern, should be considered by the investor, and items 1 to 4 inclusive, when related to item 5, should be of assistance to him in this respect.

f) The relative contribution of cash generated from operational activity and from external finance, in order to meet capital, tax and dividend requirements, can be gained from the individual and total figures.

The appendices A to F in the above statement are intended to refer the investor to additional statements which contain the detail of the total figures given in the overall statement. B, E and F are relatively self-explanatory, but the remainder merit some further explanation and illustration. Table 2 (below) outlines the Statement of Operational Transactions Flow, and supports the figures in item 2 in the overall statement in Table 1.

The main advantage of this supporting cash flow statement appears to be that it supplies the investor

A case for cash flow reporting

TABLE 2: Appendix A to total cash flow statement
Statement of operational transactions flow—year to 31 July 1971

Cash Movements	1967 F A	1968 F A	1969 F A	1970 F A	1971 F A	Total F A	1972 F	1973 F	1974 F	Total F
Economic Unit A										
1) Sales Revenues	+ +	+ +	+ +	+ +	+ +	+ +	+	+	+	+
2) Materials Costs	− −	− −	− −	− −	− −	− −	−	−	−	−
3) Labour Costs	− −	− −	− −	− −	− −	− −	−	−	−	−
4) Allocable Overhead Costs	− −	− −	− −	− −	− −	− −	−	−	−	−
5) *Net Cash Contribution* 1−(2+3+4)	+ + − −	+ + − −	+ + − −	+ + − −	+ + − −	+ + − −	+ −	+ −	+ −	+ −
Economic Unit B										
6) Sales Revenues	+ +	+ +	+ +	+ +	+ +	+ +	+	+	+	+
7) Materials Costs	− −	− −	− −	− −	− −	− −	−	−	−	−
8) Labour Costs	− −	− −	− −	.. −	− −	− −	−	−	−	−
9) Allocable Overhead Costs	− −	− −	− −	− −	− −	− −	−	−	−	−
10) *Net Cash Contribution* 6−(7+8+9)	+ + − −	+ + − −	+ + − −	+ + − −	+ + − −	+ + − −	+ −	+ −	+ −	+ −
11) Non-allocable Overhead Costs	− −	− −	− −	− −	− −	− −	−	−	−	−
12) *Net Operational Cash Flow* 5+10−11	+ + − −	+ + − −	+ + − −	+ + − −	+ + − −	+ + −	+ −	+ −	+ −	+ −

with information concerning the contribution to total cash flow of each of the company's economic units. It does so without revealing individual profit margins, a point which is often put forward as the reason for not disclosing detailed costs of production in conventional stewardship financial statements. The emphasis of the statement, therefore, is not on the relative profit contribution of each unit, but on the relative contribution each makes to the continuing survival of the company as a whole—a much more fundamental, and in many ways, more important issue to the investor.[6]

Table 3 outlines the Statement of Financial Transactions Flow, reflecting the movements of cash to and from persons outside the company who are partly financing the activity.

The last illustration, Table 4, outlines the Statement of Capital Transactions Flow, which is perhaps the most vital of all as far as the future continuance of the company is concerned. It depicts the "sunk"

[6] The extreme difficulty of convincing management of the need to disclose this analysis is recognized by the writer.

costs which the company has paid for in order to maintain and expand its business activity. It includes purchases of profit-contributing resources such as land, buildings, plant and investments in other companies paid for by cash. These latter investments would include any controlling interests in subsidiary companies, purchased wholly or partly for cash. If the purchase has been wholly in cash then a full analysis of the resources and liabilities taken over should be made in this statement. If, on the other hand, only part of the investment is paid for in cash, then the statement should contain the payment, and a footnote should refer the reader to the Statement of Non-cash Transactions which should contain details of the full transaction. One further heading to be included in this statement warrants additional explanation at this stage, and that is the cost of research and development expenditure. This mainly reflects the company's commitment to the future, and gives some indication of the anticipated revenues which must flow into the company in the long term if it is to recover these "sunk" costs

TABLE 3: Appendix C to total cash flow statement
Statement of financial transactions flow—year to 31 July 1971

	Year to 31 July									
Cash Movements	1967 F A	1968 F A	1969 F A	1970 F A	1971 F A	Total F A	1972 F	1973 F	1974 F	Total F
1) Loans Received	+ +	+ +	+ +	+ +	+ +	+ +	+	+	+	+
2) Loan Repayments	− −	− −	− −	− −	− −	− −	−	−	−	−
3) Share Issue Receipts	+ +	+ +	+ +	+ +	+ +	+ +	+	+	+	+
4) Total Net Contribution 1−2+3	+ + / − −	+ + / − −	+ + / − −	+ + / − −	+ + / − −	+ + / − −	+ / −	+ / −	+ / −	+ / −

49

TABLE 4: Appendix D to total cash flow statement
Statement of capital transactions flow—year to 31 July 1971

	Year to 31 July									
Cash Movements	1967 F A	1968 F A	1969 F A	1970 F A	1971 F A	Total F A	1972 F	1973 F	1974 F	Total F
1) Outright Purchase of Physical Resources:										
Land and Buildings	− −	− −	− −	− −	− −	− −	−	−	−	−
Plant and Vehicles	− −	− −	− −	− −	− −	− −	−	−	−	−
2) Instalment Purchasing of Physical Resources:										
Plant and Vehicles	− −	− −	− −	− −	− −	− −	−	−	−	−
3) Hire Rental of Plant	− −	− −	− −	− −	− −	− −	−	−	−	−
4) Sale of Physical Resources:										
Land and Buildings	+ +	+ +	+ +	+ +	+ +	+ +	+	+	+	+
Plant and Vehicles	+ +	+ +	+ +	+ +	+ +	+ +	+	+	+	+
5) Net Cost of Acquiring Physical Resources 1+2+3−4	+ + / − −	+ + / − −	+ + / − −	+ + / − −	+ + / − −	+ + / − −	+ / −	+ / −	+ / −	+ / −
6) Purchase of Investments:										
In Subsidiary Companies	− −	− −	− −	− −	− −	− −	−	−	−	−
In Associated Companies	− −	− −	− −	− −	− −	− −	−	−	−	−
In Quoted Companies	− −	− −	− −	− −	− −	− −	−	−	−	−
7) Sale of Investments:										
In Quoted Companies	+ +	+ +	+ +	+ +	+ +	+ +	+	+	+	+
8) Net Cost of Acquiring Investments 6−7	+ + / − −	+ + / − −	+ + / − −	+ + / − −	+ + / − −	+ + / − −	+ / −	+ / −	+ / −	+ / −
9) Research and Development Costs	− −	− −	− −	− −	− −	− −	−	−	−	−
10) Net Capital Transactions Flow 5+8+9	+ + / − −	+ + / − −	+ + / − −	+ + / − −	+ + / − −	+ + / − −	+ / −	+ / −	+ / −	+ / −

35

A case for cash flow reporting

and survive. The delay between incurring the expenditure and later recovering it through sales is of vital interest to the investor.

These, then, are some suggestions put forward by the writer in support of cash flow reporting. The next stage is to test their acceptability in the "market-place". It is hoped to be able to report the results of such research in the near future.

REFERENCES

[1] For example, see *Accounting for Stewardship in a Period of Inflation*, ICAEW, 1968 (for general adjustments): and E.O. Edwards and P.W. Bell, *The Theory and Measurement of Business Income*, California University Press, 1961 (for specific adjustments). For a detailed account of this extremely complex problem, see Edward Stamp, "Income and Value Determination and Changing Price-Levels: An Essay Towards a Theory", *The Accountant's Magazine*, June 1971, pp. 277-92.

[2] See for example, H.C. Edey, "Accounting Principles and Business Reality", *Accountancy*, November 1963, pp. 998-1002 and December 1963, pp. 1083-88; Gerald Lawson, comments in *Accountancy Age*, 24 July 1970, pp. 1-2 and 6 November 1970, pp. 10-11; and in "Cash-Flow Accounting", *The Accountant*, 28 October 1971, pp. 386-89; and T.A. Lee, "Goodwill—An Example of Will-O-the-Wisp Accounting", *Accounting and Business Research*, Autumn 1971, pp. 318-28; and in "The Relevance of Accounting Information Including Cash Flows", *The Accountant's Magazine*, January 1972, pp. 30-4.

[3] Hendriksen, Eldon S., *Accounting Theory*, Irwin, 1970 (revised edition), p. 237.

[4] See for example, John C. Chambers, Satinder K. Mullick and Donald D. Smith, "How to choose the right forecasting technique", *Harvard Business Review*, July-August 1971, pp. 45-74.

[5] See his views on this matter in Raymond J. Chambers, "The Role of Accounting", *The Accountant*, 22 February 1969, pp. 255-60; and in *Accounting, Evaluation and Economic Behaviour*, Prentice Hall, 1966, p. 98.

[6] Raymond J. Chambers, *Accounting, Evaluation and Economic Behaviour*, Prentice Hall, 1966, pp. 154-56 and 164.

[7] The Committee to Prepare a Statement of Basic Accounting Theory, *A Statement of Basic Accounting Theory*, American Accounting Association, 1966, pp. 10-11 and 53.

[8] Lee, "Goodwill—An Example of Will-O-the-Wisp Accounting", *op. cit.*, p. 327.

[9] Tomkins, C.R., "The Development of Relevant Published Accounting Reports", *Accountancy*, November 1969, pp. 817-18.

[10] Edey, *op. cit.*, p. 1088.

[11] Briston, R.J. and Fawthrop, R.A. "Accounting principles and investor protection", *Journal of Business Finance*, Summer 1971, pp. 15-17.

[12] Lee, *op. cit.*, pp. 326-28.

[13] Chambers, Mullick and Smith, *op. cit.*, p. 74.

Enterprise Income: Survival or Decline and Fall?
T. A. Lee

Introduction

'... it is possible for individual income calculations to have an important influence on individual economic conduct; for calculations of social income to play such an important part in social statistics, and in welfare economics; and yet, at the same time, for the concept of income to be one which the positive theoretical economist only employs in his arguments at his peril. For him, income is a very dangerous term, and it can be avoided; a whole general theory of economic dynamics can be worked out without using it'.

This warning to economists was argued and demonstrated by Hicks[1] within the context of his analysis of income as a useful theoretical tool for examining personal economic behaviour. Some years later, Frankel added further weight to the argument when he stated that income is no more than a conventional symbol which has relevance only in certain well-defined circumstances related to developed societies.[2]

'There is no harm... in conventional ways of looking at certain things. The danger arises when we forget what is convention and what is reality, and when merely conventional symbolism determines unduly the goals of public policy'.

The caution and concern related to the use of the concept of personal income in economic analysis remains of no more than academic interest to accountants until it is noted that similar remarks have been made about enterprise income, and by an accountant.[3]

'Just as Hicks was led to the conclusion that income was not an effective tool of economic analysis, so it seems to me that we are led to the conclusion that periodic income is not an effective tool of financial planning or control. This conclusion seems to accord ill with the fact that income measurement has long been a central theme of accounting and the main preoccupation of the accounting profession. Yet this fact need not impress us. The practice of medicine once consisted largely of blood-letting. It may be that we are already witnessing a decline in the importance of income measurement'.

Solomons developed his argument in even stronger terms:[4]

'The fact is that for several important purposes periodic income, either historical or perspective, has already been or is being superseded. For decision-making purposes the idea of 'contribution' has taken over from net income. In the field of taxation, we depart from income as the tax base every time we introduce special allowances for depletion, or provide for accelerated depreciation, or permit an anomalous treatment of capital gains. Even for reporting to stockholders, just as in the first half of this century we saw the income statement displace the balance-sheet in importance, so we may now be de-emphasising the income statement in favour of a statement of fund flows or cash flows. Each of us sees the future differently, no doubt. But my own guess is that, so far as the history of accounting is concerned, the next twenty-five years may subsequently be seen to have been the twilight of income measurement'.

This viewpoint of Solomons, perhaps not surprisingly, has remained a minority one since it was

---

[1] J. R. Hicks, *Value and Capital*, Second Edition, Clarendon Press, 1946, pp. 180–181.

[2] S. H. Frankel, *Economic Impact on Underdeveloped Societies*, Basil Blackwell, 1953, p. 55.

[3] D. Solomons, 'Economic and Accounting Concepts of Income', *The Accounting Review*, July 1961, p. 382.

[4] Solomons, op. cit., p. 383.

made originally. Certainly, as a search of the accounting literature reveals, there has been a marked lack of response to his propositions. The literature continues to concentrate on writings centred around the concept of enterprise income; the implied assumption being that, at least in the opinion of numerous writers, income is of the utmost importance in economic activity. It dominates thinking in the area of financial accounting and reporting, and it is widely used in investment analysis. Its significance remains unquestioned, unchallenged.[5] Is Solomons, therefore, right or wrong? The purpose of this essay is to attempt to explore several of the major issues involved in order that the debate may be continued after more than a decade of silence. In particular, it will discuss, *inter alia*, the elusive nature and quality of reported enterprise income figures; the information requirements of investors and other interested persons; and the arguments for funds flow and cash flow reporting. The discussion will take place entirely within the context of financial reporting for corporate enterprises.

The elusive concept of reported enterprise income

The purpose of this section is to demonstrate that enterprise income is no more than a conventional financial management symbol which is capable of definition and computation in a variety of ways. In particular, the following points will be elaborated on:

1. The problem of the existence of a variety of differing income concepts for reporting purposes because of different interpretations placed on the meaning of the underlying capital computations.
2. The problem of flexibility with regard to the application of accounting principles in the process of enterprise income measurement.
3. The problem of flexibility in accounting practice due to the degree of subjective judgement which is part of the enterprise income measurement process.
4. The problem of unsatisfactory measures of enterprise income due to the exclusion of significant elements from the computation of capital, notably those relating to goodwill and other intangible resources.

Differing Concepts of Income

This essay is concerned with problems associated with the nature and measurement of income as related to the corporate business enterprise – that is, pertaining to concepts of income which are or could be reported to shareholders and other persons interested in the economic progress and affairs of the limited liability company. In this respect, a review of the relevant literature reveals that enterprise income cannot be thought of solely in terms of the traditional *ex post* periodic matchings of revenues from sales with related costs. Such may be the current concept of reported enterprise income, but it is certainly not the only one available.

The economist's view of income, for example, is entirely different from that of matching past efforts and accomplishments. Conceived originally by Fisher[6] in terms of personal consumption and psychic experiences classified as enjoyment, its current form is based upon the Hicksian model[7] of measures of periodic consumption plus periodic changes in the value of economic capital – the so-called concept of 'welloffness'; income being the maximum a person can consume in a period and still be able to expect the same level of consumption in the next period. Consumption, in this sense, is related to the expired economic benefits derived from capital, and the value of economic capital is measured on the basis of an aggregation of the present values of anticipated future economic benefits.[8]

The economist uses the Hicksian concepts of income as a means of theorising about the economic behaviour of individuals, rather than of business enterprises. Consequently, it is a concept which appears to be somewhat irrelevant to the corporate financial reporting function which is concerned primarily with aggregate measures of entity activity. However, at least in theory, the economic income concept can be adapted to the enterprise role – either as an 'equity' concept, with consumption defined in terms of realised or realisable dividends, and capital defined in terms of the present value of future dividend and investment realisation flows; or as an 'entity' concept, with consumption defined in terms of the realised or realisable aggregate entity cash flows, and capital defined in terms of the present value of future aggregate entity cash flows. Whichever interpretation

---

[5]The Companies Act 1929 was the first British enactment requiring boards of directors to provide their shareholders with an income statement, the previous feeling being that publication of such documents would stimulate competition (see The Report of the Company Law Amendment Committee, 1906).

[6]See, for example, I. Fisher, *The Theory of Interest*, Macmillan, 1930, pp. 3–35.

[7]Hicks, op. cit., pp. 171–181.

[8]For fuller details of these computations, see P. Hansen, *The Accounting Concept of Profit*, North-Holland Publishing, 1962, pp. 9–44.

is used, enormous problems would arise in practice if such adaptation took place – for example, forecasting over considerable periods of time, selecting an appropriate discount factor, the reinvestment constraint in order to maintain future 'welloffness'[9], and the treatment and attribution of 'windfall' gains or losses in the *ex ante* and *ex post* variations of the Hicksian model.[10]

Each of the above problems associated with the measurement of economic income tends to minimise the practical worth of the concept for financial reporting purposes. This is not to say that the various economic income models have no useful purpose – indeed they have, but only in the sense of helping to make rational theoretical explanations of income which aid an understanding of its nature. Certainly, capital valuations in terms of discounted future benefits, and income measures in terms of incremental capital value movements, appear to conform best with the reality of the meaning of the income symbol, particularly from the point of view of treating capital as a valuation of future income, and income as a measure of the expired portion of such capital. The rather false and misleading isolation of capital from income, as if they were two distinct and separate concepts, is thus avoided in the Hicksian philosophy. Unfortunately, the practical problems mentioned above negate completely the use of the Hicksian approach for financial reporting purposes. This inevitably leads to an analysis of the alternative approaches of the accountant.

As previously mentioned, the traditional accounting approach to income measurement is an *ex post* one, involving a comparison of sales revenues with related costs through the so-called 'matching' process. Accounting income is recognised, with certain well-defined exceptions, when revenue is realised – the so-called realisation principle. This process, whilst appearing eminently sensible, practical and objective, has several drawbacks. Firstly, the basis of measuring transactions involving historic costs, together with the related realisation principle, prevents the reporting of significant unrealised income elements, and results in the periodic reporting of a heterogeneous mixture of enterprise gains and losses; some relating to the current period and others to previous periods. If *ex post* measures of enterprise income are believed to be useful indicators of periodic business performance, both for control and predictive purposes, it can hardly be argued that the measures which are reported currently are particularly useful in these respects – income earned during the period concerned is not fully reported; contemporary values for all resources of the enterprise are not reported; and the reported income measure contains gains and losses earned in previous periods.

It is no argument to suggest that the traditional measure of accounting income is a stewardship measure and is not intended for decision making.[11] Present-day financial reports appear to be used mainly in practice for purposes of decisions and, in any case, the stewardship function implies the making of decisions in order to control the activities of management. It is doubtful if an income measure which, because of an inherent conservatism,[12] presents an incomplete and misleading mixture of income elements, can provide useful information to persons desiring knowledge of company performance during the period to which the income measure purports to relate.

The imperfections of the traditional accounting income model have given rise, over the years, to a number of pleas for alternative accounting models which attempt to minimise its most obvious faults. These arguments have been mainly for the so-called current value models; where income is derived using current price based values – that is, either buying prices in terms of current replacement costs[13] or selling prices in terms of current realisable values.[14] The income model based on replacement costs attempts to derive income when capital is maintained in terms of the physical resources underlying it. The realisable value model, on the other hand, derives income following a maintenance of capital in terms of what the company is sacrificing by keeping its resources in their existing form rather than in a next best alternative form such as cash.

Both current value based income models produce what can be radically different measures of income

---

[9]A. A. Robichek and S. C. Myers, *Optimal Financing Decisions*, Prentice-Hall, 1965, pp. 18–19.

[10]For a discussion of the *ex ante* and *ex post* models and of 'windfalls' see Hicks, op. cit., or Hansen, op. cit.

[11]See 'Accountants' Liability to Third Parties', *Statement S8*, The Institute of Chartered Accountants in England and Wales, 1965.

[12]For a discussion of the convention of conservatism, see R. R. Sterling, 'Conservatism – The Fundamental Principle of Valuation in Traditional Accounting', *Abacus*, December 1967, pp. 109–132.

[13]According to the model proposed in E. O. Edwards and P. W. Bell, *The Theory and Measurement of Business Income*, University of California Press, 1961, and practised in The Netherlands – see A. Goudeket, 'An Application of Replacement Value Theory', *The Journal of Accountancy*, July 1960, pp. 37–47.

[14]According to the model proposed by R. J. Chambers, *Accounting, Evaluation and Economic Behaviour*, Prentice-Hall, 1966; and R. R. Sterling, *Theory of the Measurement of Enterprise Income*, University of Kansas Press, 1970.

when using the same enterprise transactions. The differences arise because of the different value concepts which are applied to the measurement of capital. Nevertheless, both contain points of similarity which are worthy of note.

They both abandon the traditional accounting principle of historic cost, because of the use of current valuations, and they both ignore the restrictive realisation principle. Thus, they present the realised and unrealised gains and losses of the defined period rather than a misleading mixture of income elements, as is the normal case with the traditional model. They also incorporate gains or losses resulting from operating activity as well as from the holding of resources. This separation of income elements is believed to have merit because it may well enable the decision maker to differentiate for predictive purposes, between gains which are normally within the effective control of management and those which are not.

As the foregoing remarks have indicated, each accounting model produces what can be significantly different measures of enterprise income. This raises the questions of what exactly is the income of the enterprise, and of which model provides the best indication of it, for it can be defined and measured in a variety of ways, each measure depending on the particular definition of capital to be maintained and, thus, the valuation concept to be applied. The historic cost model attempts to maintain the original money capital subscribed and retained in the enterprise; the replacement cost model involves maintenance of the physical resources underlying capital; and the realisable value model involves maintenance of capital which could be invested in an alternative form. The problem with current value accounting, therefore, is that it adds two further concepts to that already employed in practice; further complicating the issue of how best to report on enterprise activity.

One further extension of this discussion can also be made at this stage. The foregoing paragraphs have concentrated on accounting models which are all *ex post* measures of enterprise income. The Hicksian economic approach to income, on the other hand, acknowledges that there are two time dimensions in a world of uncertainty – the past and the future. Thus, the economist uses both an *ex post* and an *ex ante* model to analyse economic behaviour. The accountant, too, can produce *ex ante* measures of income by budgeting or forecasting future enterprise activity. He can do this within the terms of any of the historic cost, replacement cost, and realisable value models, by forecasting enterprise transactions and capital movements in any of these valuation terms. The computation of an *ex ante* historic cost income measure is required presently in certain takeover or merger situations in Britain due to the provisions of the City Code on Takeovers and Mergers. It is simply a logical extension of this practice to consider similar *ex ante* computations in current value terms. However, *ex ante* accounting income, no matter what its valuation base is, will create the forecasting problems which appear to negate the practical usefulness for financial reporting purposes of the economic models of Hicks.

The elusive nature of reportable enterprise income is further complicated by the relaxation of the traditional accounting measurement assumption of a stable monetary unit.[15] If the reality of a monetary unit with a fluctuating value (in terms of its generalised purchasing power) is introduced into each of the aforementioned accounting models of income, then an equivalent number of further income models emerge – that is, for each accounting model, there exists an adjusted and an unadjusted measure of income. (Adjusted in this sense means that the income measurement process has been undertaken allowing for changes in the generalised purchasing power of the monetary unit used; in other words, the so-called inflation accounting which is being advocated presently by the Accounting Standards Steering Committee.)[16]

The concept of reportable enterprise income cannot therefore be regarded as a straightforward issue; there are just too many variations to be considered, each raising the question of what exactly is the periodic income of an enterprise given a certain set of circumstances.

Flexibility of Accounting Principles

The validity of the enterprise income concept as a useful part of the corporate financial reporting function is brought further into focus when the question of applying accounting principles in the measurement process is raised.

In each of the historic cost and current value income models, the emphasis is entirely on enterprise performance using measurements of known or forecast

---

[15] See, for example, Edwards and Bell, op. cit., pp. 12–23 and 233–269; R. S. Gynther, 'Accounting for Price Level Changes – One General Index or Several Specific Indices?', *Accountancy*, July 1962, pp. 560–564; R. L. Mathews, 'Income, Price Changes and the Valuation Controversy in Accounting', *The Accounting Review*, July 1968, pp. 509–516; K. Shwayder, 'The Capital Maintenance Rule and the Net Asset Valuation Rule', *The Accounting Review*, April 1969, pp. 304–316; and Sterling, op. cit., pp. 331–351.

[16] 'Accounting for Changes in the Purchasing Power of Money', *Provisional Statement of Standard Accounting Practice* No. 7, May, 1974.

economic transactions of the business enterprise. In order to construct these various measures, accountants have devised a series of measurement guidelines or principles which implement the so-called process of accrual accounting so necessary to the periodic matching of revenues and costs – that is, accounting principles related to such matters as the need to depreciate fixed assets; provide for inventory of unsold stocks and work in progress; amortise research and development costs; defer taxation liabilities; aggregate the financial results of a group of companies; account for the consequences of a takeover or merger; and so on. However, whereas there can be a great deal of uniformity of meaning in these general principles, there is also a great deal of flexibility in their execution in practice.[17] Consider, for example, the problem of accounting for stocks and work in progress, a matter which affects materially the computation of the periodic income figure – whether this is based on historic costs, replacement costs or realisable values. In the historic cost model, there is the problem of defining inventory cost. Each definition brings a different value and a different measure of income – even within the same conceptual definition of income. The same issue does not arise with the current value models because of their use of replacement costs or realisable values, but they are affected by related issues – for example, should replacement costs or realisable values be applied to individual items or to batches of stock; should overheads be included in the replacement cost figure, and, if so, to what extent (this issue also affects the historic cost model); what replacement costs should be used when the nature of stock items is changing due to technological developments; what realisable values should be used – should they be related to the existing or future state of the stock? In other words, within each defined accounting income model, there are a variety of possible income measures depending on the particular accounting methods used to implement the accounting principles adopted to measure income. This is no new problem; indeed, it has been recognised for a long time by accountants[18] and, recently, at least within the context of the historic cost model, the professional accountancy bodies in Britain have commenced work on trying to narrow the areas of possible differences.[19] This notwithstanding, it is inevitable that a significant degree of flexibility will remain, which raises further doubts about the validity of a concept, which is not only capable of differences in interpretation and measurement because of variations in capital and value concepts, but is also subject to differences due to an inevitable flexibility in measurement procedures.

The Problem of Subjective Judgment

The previous section dealt with that aspect of the elusive nature of the enterprise income concept relating to the flexibility of accounting practice because of the application of so-called generally accepted accounting principles. There is one further aspect of accounting practice, which arguably introduces the greatest degree of flexibility in income measurement. This relates to the application of subjective judgment by management and accountants during the income measurement process.

It is an inevitable aspect of financial accounting practice that the measurement process which is undertaken to derive periodic income contains a great deal of subjective judgment, particularly from the point of view of resource valuation. As a consequence, it is not unfair to suggest that subjective judgment, albeit of an expert and experienced kind, has a great deal of influence on the resultant capital and income measures. For example, personal opinions have to be formed regarding provisions and write-offs of bad debts; provisions for damaged or obsolete stock; the depreciable life-time of fixed assets; the amortisable life-time for research and development costs; and the provision of creditor liabilities when these are not determinable accurately at the reporting date. In addition, a great deal of subjective judgment may be required in both current value models when replacement costs and realisable values are not readily ascertained from recent market transactions, price lists, contracts, etc. The application of general price-level techniques to account for the inflationary element of value increments in income measurement also can contain a great deal of personal judgment on such matters as determining dates of acquisition of fixed assets, particularly when these are very old as in the case of land and buildings, or in choosing the appropriate type of index for adjusting capital to

---

[17]R. J. Chambers, 'Financial Information and the Securities Market', *Abacus*, September 1965, pp. 3–30; and E. Stamp, 'Reforming Accounting Principles', in E. Stamp and C. Marley, *Accounting Principles and the City Code: the Case for Reform*, Butterworths, 1970, especially pp. 129–140.

[18]The then American Institute of Accountants and the New York Stock Exchange were actively concerned with the problem in the 1930s; and the Accounting Principles Board of The American Institute of Certified Public Accountants, established in 1959, was primarily directed to combat it.

[19]Through the Statements of Standard Accounting Practice evolving from the work of the Accounting Standards Steering Committee.

segregate the effects of inflation. In addition to the foregoing comments, there are the obvious problems which face the accountant should he decide to extend his time horizon into the future in order to compute measures of *ex ante* accounting income. Not only does he have to cope with the subjective judgments mentioned above, but he also has to meet the judgmental problems of forecasting transactions, values, etc.

These personal judgments normally have to be made by experts in the appropriate area – for example, engineers and production managers. However, such opinions are sought because of a lack of verifiable, objective evidence, and the possible variations in an opinion on a particular factor may thus be immense. The effect is to accentuate the possible flexibility in income measurement to extents which may cause income measures to be wide open to question because of doubts relating to the lack of objectivity exercised in their derivation. Thus, despite the laudable efforts of the professional accountancy bodies to minimise variety in accounting practice, it still remains a fact of life that no one can regulate against flexibility due to subjective judgment. Needless to say, this is hardly a point in support of income as such an important aspect of the corporate financial reporting function.

Significant Resource Omissions

In both accounting and economics, the relationship between income and capital is well established and accepted – one of the main differences between the approaches of the two disciplines being that the economist computes capital in order to derive income, whereas the accountant traditionally computes income with capital being the residue of such an exercise.[20] Whatever the approach, however, one point of similarity emerges – periodic income can be interpreted in terms of the periodic change in the value of capital. This means that, so far as enterprise income is concerned, it is important to ensure that capital is measured fully – that is, that its value takes cognisance of all economic resources which contribute to the existence of income. However, if the historic cost and current value income models are examined, it is clearly seen that the relevant capital computations are incomplete; that in most situations enterprise capital is computed on the basis of an aggregation of resource valuations which have arisen from past transactions and events. This means that significant enterprise resources may well be omitted from the relevant capital and income computations.

This entire problem has been discussed elsewhere[21] in connection with accounting for goodwill; goodwill being the term used to cover such intangible business resources as development projects, secret processes, franchises, licences, patents, trade marks and copyrights, efficient management, efficient and skilled labour, good industrial relations, sound training schemes, a high community standing, high quality products and services, and so on. What experience shows is that goodwill becomes part of enterprise capital for accounting purposes normally when there is payment for such an item as part of a business combination. Even then, it can be avoided by techniques of so-called pooling accounting.[22] Goodwill, however, exists in any business enterprise at any time in its lifetime, and sums of money are expended constantly to maintain or augment a positive value for it. Nevertheless, the traditional practice of accountants is to ignore the existence of goodwill unless this is unavoidable due to a business combination, in which case indications are that the majority of companies prefer to write off the relevant acquisition costs against income or capital (that is, by writing it off to reserves).[23]

Any expenditures incurred on augmenting the resources underlying goodwill are treated as costs in determining periodic accounting income. The question of ignoring goodwill, which certainly is the case with the historic cost income model, would almost certainly arise with both the current value based models, in either their *ex post* or *ex ante* forms.

The above comments lead to the apparent conclusion that the accounting models for determining periodic enterprise income are somewhat less than adequate because capital computations are incomplete. In addition, matchings of related sales and costs may result in overstated costs due to expenses incurred on the creation of goodwill being written off rather than capitalised.

The meaning of enterprise income

If, as the evidence clearly suggests, income is a major part of the present corporate financial reporting system, it is also clear that it should have some

---

[20]For such a comparison, see Solomons, op. cit., pp. 374-383 and Hansen, op. cit. pp. 57-63.

[21]T. A. Lee, 'Goodwill: an Example of Will-o'-the-Wisp Accounting', *Accounting and Business Research*, Autumn 1971, pp. 318-328.

[22]See A. T. McLean, *Accounting for Business Combinations and Goodwill*, The Institute of Chartered Accountants of Scotland, 1972.

[23]For evidence of this point, see T. A. Lee, 'Accounting for Goodwill: An empirical study of company practices in the United Kingdom – 1962 to 1971', *Accounting and Business Research*, Summer 1973, pp. 175-196.

precise meaning; particularly from the point of view of those persons using it as part of their investment activities. Surprisingly, despite its long history and the extent of its current use, the concept of enterprise income has remained ill defined, if it has been defined at all. The following comments and quotes are given as brief illustrations of this assertion:

Arthur Andersen and Company[24] implied a definition of enterprise income in a recent publication:

'The purpose of the statement of income is to provide a summary analysis of the significant events and factors that give rise to an increase or decrease in the net economic resources of a business enterprise for a period of time other than those changes resulting from additional investments by, or distributions to, the owners'.

'Perhaps more than any other, the statement of income is used in an attempt to assess the future. Past performance with respect to earnings may prove to be an indicator of future performance'.

These statements suggest that income represents a periodic change in enterprise resources, and is of use as an indicator of future performance. However, this merely begs the question because the terms 'resources' and 'performance' then require to be defined. Chambers[25] appears to have used the same approach when he identifies income as one of the reasons for periodic changes in capital. But, whilst defining capital and the process of capital maintenance, he fails to provide a useful definition of income. For example, he describes it typically as follows[26]:

'Under static conditions (there being no change in the price level or in specific prices and excluding new contributions and withdrawals by constituents) income of the period (t_0, t_1) is the difference between the measures of capital at t_1 and t_0, . . .'.

This type of approach to the meaning of income is not exactly a recent one. Macneal,[27] for example, stated that:

'There is one correct definition of profits in an accounting sense. A profit is an increase in net wealth. A loss is a decrease in net wealth. This is an economist's definition. It is terse, obvious, and mathematically demonstrable'.

The question of what is meant by 'wealth' is raised, and the meaning of income remains in doubt. The situation is no better in the professional literature. For example, Sprouse and Moonitz[28] state:

'Net profit (earnings, income) or net loss for an accounting period is the increase (decrease) in owner's equity, assuming no changes in the amount of invested capital either from price-level changes or from additional investments and no distribution to the owners'.

Grady, on the other hand, failed to provide any contemporary definition, indicating[29] that:

'It is important that accountants keep in the forefront of any discussion of income, its composite nature as the resultant of positive (credit) and negative (debit) elements'.

It is obvious from even this brief look at the accounting literature that, whereas most writers are agreed that income is a derivation of the periodic change in enterprise capital, the exact meaning of the term is assumed either to be so self-evident as to require no further explanation, or to be explained adequately in terms of the way in which it is measured. By way of contrast, economists are much more particular about the definition they use. Fisher[30] described it as a series of perceived events or psychic experiences called enjoyment – that is, consisting of 'those final physical events in the outer world which give us our minor enjoyments'. Hicks[31] went further than this by adding the element of saving to consumption:

'The purpose of income calculations in practical affairs is to give people an indication of the amount which they can consume without impoverishing themselves. Following out this idea, it would seem that we ought to define a man's income as the maximum value he can consume during a week, and still expect to be as well off at the end of the week as he was at the beginning'.

This well-known definition of income does not attempt to define income simply in terms of changes in capital; it looks at income in a much more fundamental way – as the so-called 'guide to prudent economic conduct'. As such it has been accepted by economists as the basis for analysing personal economic behaviour; and it has even been stated and

---

[24]Arthur Andersen and Co., *Objectives of Financial Statements for Business Enterprises*, privately published, 1972, p. 65.

[25]R. J. Chambers, *Accounting, Evaluation and Economic Behaviour*, Prentice-Hall, 1966, pp. 103–123 and 220–226.

[26]Op. cit., p. 264.

[27]K. Macneal, *Truth in Accounting*, Scholars Book Co., 1970 reprint, p. 295.

[28]R. T. Sprouse and M. Moonitz, 'A tentative set of broad accounting principles for business enterprises', *Accounting Research Study No. 3*, American Institute of Certified Public Accountants, 1962, p. 54.

[29]P. Grady, 'Inventory of Generally Accepted Accounting Principles for Business Enterprises', *Accounting Research Study No. 7*, American Institute of Certified Public Accountants, 1965, pp. 410–412, at p. 411.

[30]Fisher, op. cit., pp. 3–4.

[31]Hicks, op. cit., p. 172.

used within the accounting context[32] as a basis of an explanation of accounting income – for example, that the income of a company is the maximum amount it can distribute whilst maintaining its capital intact. What can be said at this stage, therefore, is that the typical Hicksian economic definition of income, either in its original personal form or in its adapted entity form, reveals that income is no more than a conventional economic indicator of human or entity behaviour – such behaviour relating to prudent consumption and capital maintenance. This point is not brought out in the typical accounting definitions which concentrate mainly on the computational properties of the concept.

The concept of enterprise income is no more than a man-made conventional symbol or indicator of economic conduct. It can therefore be thought of in the familiar terms of financial prudence and the ultimate survival of the enterprise – that is, as indicating the most appropriate consumption or distribution policy to be adopted if the enterprise is to survive and its owners are to be satisfied.

However, the above having been said, it is evident that income can be interpreted in a variety of ways. (Much of the following commentary stems from the work of Hendriksen,[33] who, without doubt, is one of the few accounting writers who has attempted to look at the variety of meaning attributable to enterprise income in some detail.)

Firstly, income can be interpreted as the 'flow' of gains or benefits from a 'stock' of capital, following the Fisher tradition.[34] This view of income is commonly adopted by accountants for purposes of differentiating between income and capital, particularly when establishing rates of return on capital which can be used as indicators of the effective use made of the resources underlying capital. It arose presumably from the stewardship approach to financial reporting, where there is an evident need for management to account for the use of economic resources entrusted to it, as well as a need to determine the income and capital rights of individual or groups of owners, both when the enterprise is a going concern, and when it is ultimately realised. However, there is a significant doubt regarding the meaningfulness of interpreting income as a 'flow' from a 'stock' of capital. Much depends on the classification for accounting purposes of expenditure which has ceased to have a useful service potential from that which still has.

Secondly, following on from the above point, it is evident that enterprise income is believed to be indicative of the efficiency of management in connection with the holding and operational use made of the economic resources entrusted to it. The computation and use in investment analysis of financial relationships such as earnings per share, price earnings ratios, gross margins and net margins supports this point, and the typical interpretation of these indicators is that, comparatively, the higher the level of reported income, and the higher the resultant rates of return, etc., the more efficient and effective management may be assumed to be.

'In our complicated, changing world, it is not really possible to distill a whole year's operations of a vast business enterprise into a single, absolute figure. The public, however, doesn't always appreciate this. Thus, the annual net earnings figure tends to have a magical significance – not only for the ordinary investor but for security analysts and even for aquisition-minded managements. It becomes, in effect, what grades are for the students – a measure of excellence or lack of excellence, of progress or lack of progress.'[35]

Apart from the doubts which have already been discussed regarding the computation of the necessary income and capital measures, there must also be doubt regarding the meaning of enterprise income as an indicator of managerial performance. The term 'efficiency' is open to a variety of interpretations, depending on the enterprise attribute to which it refers – for example, does it refer to the level of operational productivity, the quality of goods or services produced, the use made of machines or labour, the effect of operations on the quality of the environment, or what? 'Efficiency' also depends on the objectives which have been set for management – for example, were these to produce a reasonable return on investment or to go all out to maximise the return? Unfortunately, there is little or no evidence to suggest that enterprise objectives are made so explicit to investors and other interested groups.[36] There is evidence to suggest that managerial effectiveness and efficiency may well be being judged in the light of enterprise objectives which do not necessarily have a direct relationship to the traditional income objective[37]

---

[32]Solomons, op. cit., p. 378.

[33]E. S. Hendriksen, *Accounting Theory*, Irwin, 1970, revised edition, pp. 124–130.

[34]Fisher, op. cit.

[35]'What are Earnings? The Growing Credibility Gap', *Forbes*, 15 May 1967, p. 29.

[36]The Companies Acts 1948 and 1967, which govern the publication of annual corporate financial reports at the present, contain no such statement of objectives.

[37]T. W. McRae, 'The Behavioural Critique of Accounting', *Accounting and Business Research*, Spring 1971, pp. 85–86.

– that is, social and economic considerations, such as the quality of life, are increasingly being regarded as important aspects of managerial behaviour.

Thirdly, reported enterprise income has, despite statements to the contrary,[38] been used by investors as an investment predictor – witness the rapid growth in Britain of the disclosure and use of 'earnings per share' and 'price-earnings' measures which are specifically designed for this purpose. In other words, it may be presumed that the investment community finds measures of past enterprise income of use in predicting future income levels in order to predict the level of future distributions of dividends which, at least in part, determine share prices. Certainly, some knowledge of the past is useful when predicting the future, as it is the past and current situations which develop into those of the future. However, the volatility of enterprise activity may well be an important factor in determining whether past income levels, and rates of change in these levels, are likely to persist in the future. The empirical findings to date are confused and conflicting – Rayner and Little[39] concluding that there is no evidence to suggest that above average growth in income levels in the past will be repeated in the future, whilst Singh and Whittington[40] found that above average income levels can persist. Whittington also concluded in a recent study[41] that average income levels tend to persist in the future, but not to the same extent as in the past. The prediction of future income levels, certainly from the point of view of individual companies, appears, therefore, to be an indeterminate factor. As Hendriksen[42] has stated:

'But just as the weatherman observes recurring and non-recurring patterns and looks for signs of change, so the investor must analyse the recurring nature of the favourable and unfavourable aspects of operations and observe other factors which are likely to cause changes in incomes. While historical net incomes are valuable in making predictions regarding future incomes, the prognosticator should analyse the favourable and unfavourable aspects, including only those items that are recurring by nature'.

In other words, it appears that, within the context of the meaning of income, income can be interpreted as a device of use in predicting future dividend levels, but that this implication has attendant disadvantages in the sense that the past need not necessarily repeat itself in the future; although the 'average' past may well persist into a similar 'average' future.

The interpretation of reported enterprise income as a significant financial indicator of enterprise and managerial performance appears to be the most usual meaning to be attributed to it. However, as the above comments have tried to indicate, there are differing interpretations within the 'financial indicator' category, each of which is open to some questioning due to either a possible lack of standards or definitive yardsticks, or a lack of conclusive empirical research findings. Because of this, it is hard to lend to enterprise income a meaning which has any general acceptance. It is therefore understandable that it is so often interpreted in terms of its measurement and computation rather than in terms of its fundamental purpose which is as a tool of financial management.

Information needs of investors and others

This section is concerned with what is arguably the most significant question to be asked of the concept of reportable enterprise income – that is, are accounting measures of enterprise income relevant to the needs and requirements of those persons using corporate financial reports? Clearly, it must be concluded that measures of historic cost based income have been, and still are, assumed to be of use to shareholders and other persons interested in the affairs of companies, simply because of the past and current emphasis which is placed upon such measures in the function of financial reporting. But are they, or the alternative current value based measures, of value to the persons who are assumed to use them?

It is a relatively self-evident observation that a variety of persons are interested, in varying degrees, in an individual company and, therefore, require periodic information of its economic activity and financial affairs. This point appears to be recognised fairly generally in the literature,[43] the main group of users usually being identified as those who have a known or potential investment commitment with the company – that is, shareholders, lenders and creditors.

---

[38] Statement S8, op. cit.

[39] A. C. Rayner and I. M. D. Little, Higgledy Piggledy Growth Again, Basil Blackwell, 1966, pp. 76–81.

[40] A. Singh and G. Whittington, Growth, Profitability and Valuation, Cambridge University Press, 1968, pp. 133–134.

[41] G. Whittington, The Prediction of Profitability and Other Studies of Company Behaviour, Cambridge University Press, 1971, pp. 82–104.

[42] Hendriksen, op. cit., pp. 129–130.

[43] For example, G. O. May, 'The Nature of the Financial Accounting Process', The Accounting Review, July 1943, pp. 189–193; and The Committee to Prepare a Statement of Basic Accounting Theory, A Statement of Basic Accounting Theory, American Accounting Association, 1966, pp. 20–23.

However, the various legislative provisions regulating company activity have, for many years, recognised solely the right of shareholders to receive regular information about the financial affairs of companies in which they have invested.

This form of statutory provision for financial information has been made in order to comply with the requirements that company management reports periodically to ownership on the way it has utilised the resources entrusted to it – the traditional stewardship accounting – an objective of corporate financial reporting which is supported by The Institute of Chartered Accountants in England and Wales.[44]

Thus, traditional corporate financial reports to shareholders are deemed to be part of the managerial stewardship function, and are apparently not intended for decision making. This notwithstanding, both existing and potential investors do make use of such reports for investment purposes and, indeed, it is hard to conceive of even the stewardship function without also thinking of decisions, for the use of stewardship orientated information must inevitably lead to some form of decision, even if this is to do nothing. Thus, it does not appear to be unfair to suggest that the use by investors and others of any financial information reported by a company must result in some decision or another. In addition, it must be stated that corporate financial reports, due to the legal requirements of registration and filing, become effectively public information and, consequently, are of use in an indefinite number of decision situations connected with the companies concerned. Thus, it appears that the validity of reportable accounting income measures must be looked at in the light of the foregoing remarks – that is, in connection with their relevance to the process of investment decision making. However, such a review is not as simple as it may look at first sight:

'A review of literature by committees of leading accounting organisations and by individuals who have given lifetimes of serious thought to accounting reveals that surprisingly little attention has been paid to the objective of providing information for investment decisions. Accounting writers frequently mention owners, stockholders, creditors, or some other sub-classification of investors as readers of financial statements, but they seem to have made no special effort to show the relation between accounting and problems facing investors. Rather they have assumed that there is a relation without having bothered to analyse the problems of investors with a view to specifying just what information can be provided by accountants and also be useful to investors'.[45]

This section is concerned, therefore, with looking at the nature of decisions made by investors in particular, and the financial information which may be required to satisfy them. (The term 'investors' is intended to cover potential and existing shareholders in a company; the question of lenders, creditors, etc. will be discussed at a later stage.)

From a study of the relevant business finance and investment literature[46] it appears that the most favoured assumption regarding the objectives of the individual investor is that he attempts to maximise the value of his command over resources, both over time and in terms of cash – cash, rather than measures of enterprise income, representing his capacity to consume and command resources.

Thus, it has been further assumed, without the existence of significant evidence to the contrary, that:
'Investors commit assets to the undertaking with the expectation of being repaid a larger amount of assets in the future'.[47]

It can then be argued that, in order to maximise the value of his consumption over time, the typical investor must assess the alternative courses of action available to him, these being centred on a choice of current or future consumption – that is, whether to consume currently available cash or to delay such consumption by investment, the value of such investment being determined according to the personal valuation model developed from the Fisher tradition; that is,

$$V = \sum_{t=1}^{n} \frac{D_t}{(1+i)^t}$$

where V is the present value of the relevant shareholding, D is the dividend expected to be received at each point in time (including the eventual realisation proceeds) and i is the investor's time-preference rate for discounting purposes.

---

[44]'Statement S8, op. cit., para 8(b).

[45]G. J. Staubus, *A Theory of Accounting to Investors*, Scholars Book Co., 1971 reprint, p. 3.

[46]For example, this is implied throughout Robichek and Myers, op. cit., and, particularly, pp. 2–4; the same implication is to be seen in R. J. Briston, *The Stock Exchange and Investment Analysis*, George Allen and Unwin, 1970, pp. 459–460; but it is made explicitly in J. Freear, *Financing Decisions in Business*, Accountancy Age Books, 1973, pp. 9–11. It should be noted that this is a typical and familiar assumption only; it has yet to be fully tested and proved in practice. It should also be noted that the term 'command over resources' represents capacity to consume and, as such, in this context includes potential dividends and realisable share values.

[47]Staubus, op. cit., p. 11.

To the existing investor, this assessment involves a consideration of the following alternatives:

(1) To continue to invest in the company concerned, thereby deferring consumption; in this case, future cash flows from the investment are crucial to the decision.

(2) To realise in total his investment and consume the proceeds, thereby opting for immediate consumption; in this case, the realisation proceeds are relevant to the decision.

(3) To realise in total his investment and reinvest the proceeds either in whole or in part; in this case, the realisation proceeds of his existing shares, the purchase prices of alternative investments, and the future cash flows from alternative investments would aid the making of the decision.

(4) To realise in part his investment and reinvest the proceeds in whole or in part; in this case, the realisation proceeds of his existing shares, the future cash flows from the continuing partial investment, the purchase prices of alternative investments, and the future cash flows from alternative investments would all impinge upon the decision.

Thus, so far as concerns the company in which the investment is held, the reportable financial information required by the investor for purposes of his decision would appear to be that related to the realisable value of its shares and to its potential dividend flow; and, in particular, a requirement for some form of financial information which aids him in determining what the potential dividend flows might be. So far as alternative investments are concerned, it would appear that the same financial information requirement also holds. Thus, the total information requirements of the existing investor relate to current purchase and realisation values (which, in the usual case, are determinable other than by the investor) and the computation of present values in terms of discounted future dividend and realisation flows (which, by definition, must be determinable by him). In other words, the existing investor's information needs mainly involve several values for comparative purposes – that is, comparisons of the present value of the existing investment with the current realisable value; possibly, of the present values of alternative investments with their current purchasing values; and, possibly, of the realisation proceeds of the existing investment with the potential acquisition costs of alternative investments. Whatever the particular value comparison and, thus, whatever the particular investment decision, it appears that the existing investor should receive reportable financial information of relevance to his perception of future dividend flows from the various enterprises, assuming he has, in addition, access to information concerning the current purchasing and realisation values of the shares being assessed.

The potential investor's decisions involve assessments of alternatives which are similar to those of the existing investor, with the exception of the alternatives related to the continuation or cessation of an existing investment. Certainly, his information needs are connected with personal computations of present values of various alternative shareholdings using estimated future dividend and realisation flows. Thus, it appears that the corporate financial reporting system should be aimed at providing information of use in estimating these flows. The question is whether or not an enterprise income-orientated reporting system satisfies this goal – that is, whether or not measures of historic cost or current value based income are useful to the investor when he is attempting to predict future dividends for purposes of computing relevant share present values.

Dividend payments appear to require an assessment of two factors – the availability of distributable enterprise income, and the availability of cash to satisfy the eventual payments. The first factor is the familiar legal one of ensuring that dividends are not repayments of subscribed capital;[48] and the second factor is the common-sense one of financial prudence, depending to a considerable extent on the need for the enterprise to retain liquid resources to maintain and expand its existing operations. So far as the legality of dividends is concerned, there does not appear to be an absolute need for income figures to ensure the appropriate maintenance of subscribed capital. Indeed, this particular point can be established by means of relatively simple statements of cash movements since the original subscription – dividends only being payable out of cash generated from sources other than share and loan issues. In addition, for purposes of financial prudence when paying dividends, statements of measured enterprise income appear to be a complete irrelevance, as the key factor is the availability of cash rather than the availability of so-called distributable income. Thus, from the point of view of assessing possible dividends, it appears that the availability of cash from operational or trading sources is the most significant matter, and that periodic income, although traditionally used in this exercise, is not as relevant as its past use in this context indicates. It therefore could be concluded

---

[48] It should be noted that the legality of dividend payments, according to the decisions of previous court cases, appears to refer to the maintenance of subscribed capital rather than to existing capital inclusive of retained income, etc.

that the investor requires financial information relevant to the prediction of future dividends, and that information concerning periodic income may not be as relevant for this purpose as is generally assumed.

Before dealing with the information needs of persons other than investors, one further point should be made in connection with the use of accounting income measures as a basis for dividend prediction. It should be remembered that the measures which have been used in practice to date have all been historically based – that is, historical not just in terms of the valuation basis, but also in terms of the economic activity which is being described. Thus, the investor, who apparently must predict dividend flows in order to make his subjective valuation of relevant shareholdings, is given measures of past income which would require to be used to predict future income levels, in order to further predict future dividend levels. The question which this point raises is, not merely whether the concept of income is relevant to investment decisions, but whether measures of past income are reasonable indicators of future income measures and of future dividend levels. As previously mentioned, the existing empirical evidence on the question of predicting future income is inconclusive.[49]

Investors are not the only persons interested in the financial progress and affairs of the company. Lenders and creditors, for example, are two groups who 'invest' funds in it and, consequently, require to manage their 'investments'. Their information needs, however, appear to centre on the cash position of the company – that is, the availability of cash resources to enable the enterprise to meet its relevant interest and repayment commitments. In this respect, enterprise income does not appear to be a significant factor in helping lenders and creditors to predict future liquidity positions. Rather, it is the cash-generating potential of the company which is likely to interest them: not its income-generating potential.

Finally in this section, the information requirements of a further group of users of corporate financial information should be noted – that is, the Inland Revenue. The entire system of corporate taxation in Britain, as in other developed countries, is based on an assessment of periodic enterprise income. Historic cost accounting income has been used for many years as the basis for computing company taxation liabilities. It would therefore appear to be the case that, subject to radical changes in the basis of computation of tax, income must remain of primary importance in this respect – despite the faults and problems associated with its use in other areas. But it must be stated that taxation of companies need not necessarily be based on their measured income. It is simply convention and habit that supports the present practice.

Summary to date

This essay has concentrated on what the writer regards as several major defects in the concept of enterprise income. Because of the length of the essay, however, it may well be useful to the reader to pause to reflect on a summary of the main points made, before proceeding further. The following comments are therefore intended as such a summary:

(1) Enterprise income is a many-sided concept. There is no such thing as *the* concept of income. Entirely different measures of periodic income are possible despite the use of the same set of economic circumstances. Thus, it is exceedingly difficult to determine precisely the periodic income of the business enterprise. Unfortunately, the concepts of income which seem the most appropriate in theory (that is, the economic models) are the least measurable in practice.

(2) The concept of enterprise income has remained a relatively ill-defined aspect of accounting, despite its prominence in the practice of financial reporting. It is defined traditionally in terms of its measurement and computation rather than in terms of its underlying meaning. However, it can be explained as a conventional symbol for enterprise (and management) success or failure, and as an investment indicator of enterprise performance in the future. There are, however, significant reasons for questioning the interpretation of income in such ways.

(3) When looking at the informational needs of investors and others, it is apparent that, in the case of investors, these centred around data of use in the process of valuation for decision making purposes and, in the case of lenders and creditors, around data of use in the process of evaluating enterprise potential for meeting its known commitments. In both these instances, accounting data reflecting the cash situation of the enterprise appears to be more valuable than that describing its periodic income.

The foregoing remarks do not reflect well on the concept of enterprise income; it is subject to a great deal of variation in both its conception and practice; its measurement is open to criticism; its meaning is imprecise and it does not appear to be entirely appropriate to the economic factors it is intended to symbolise; nor does it appear to be entirely relevant to the majority of persons who may be assumed to be using it. As the objective of accounting is to provide

---

[49]See references in footnotes [39], [40] and [41].

financial information which is relevant to the needs of its users,[50] it therefore is appropriate to look a little more closely at this point and, particularly, to see if there is an alternative form of financial report which may eventually supplant the income statement.

An alternative to income reporting

The problem with enterprise reporting systems which concentrate on measures of income is that they tend inevitably to focus accountants' attention on the very significant problems associated with income determination and asset valuation. In other words, there is the danger that other relevant forms of financial reporting may be neglected, thus placing income reporting in a place of prominence which is not fully deserved or justified. The purpose of this section, therefore, is to look at one alternative which appears to have as much, if not more, relevance to investors and others interested in the financial affairs of companies – the system of so-called cash flow reporting.[51]

In the previous section dealing with the information needs of investors and others, it was suggested that all such groups, despite their differing interests in companies, were concerned, generally, with the future development and progress of these enterprises; and, particularly, with their ability to pay dividends and interest, and repay liabilities, over what could be a considerable period of time. This would further suggest that investors, etc. require information which reflects these factors. The question posed is whether the traditional income statement, together with its supporting balance sheet, are sufficient for this purpose.

The income statement and the balance sheet, whatever the valuation basis used, cannot be expected to reveal the full picture of how the company is developing and progressing over time. The income statement portrays a periodic measure of operational activity, and the balance sheet reflects the company's resultant financial position at one point in time. The inevitable information gap which exists because of the limitations of these two statements has resulted in an increasing use in recent years of a further financial report – that is, the funds statement, which is intended to show periodic changes in the sources of finance available to the company as well as the ways in which the resultant funds have been employed by it.[52] It is this type of dynamic report which appears to have relevance to a person assessing and predicting the financial progress of an individual enterprise over time. However, funds flow reports contain one very significant limiting factor – they are based upon the concept of enterprise income and its supporting system of accrual accounting.

Thus, the flow of funds depicted in such statements contains all the measurement faults and problems associated with income determination. Despite this problem, nevertheless, the concept of reporting on the flow of enterprise funds appears to have great relevance to investors, lenders and creditors, and should be pursued further.

In the opinion of the writer, there is one economic factor which is crucial to a proper assessment of the dividend potential, etc. of the enterprise and that is its capacity to survive as an enterprise – indeed, it could be argued that survival should be the primary enterprise objective. If the enterprise does not survive over the long-term, there will be no flow of dividends, no payment of interest, and no repayment of loans and other amounts due. Therefore, it can be argued that investors and other interested parties require information which enables them to assess and predict the development and progress of the individual business enterprise over time; its capacity to survive over time; and its capacity to pay its dividend, interest, and repayment commitments over time.

Ideally, the information required should be expressed as a flow of funds in order to reflect these factors. In particular, it should also be measuring the one resource which indicates progress, survival and the ability to provide returns on investments – that is, cash. A business cannot survive, progress, repay loans and other debts, or pay dividends without cash. The ability of the enterprise to generate sufficient cash for

---

[50]For a fuller explanation of the concept of relevance, see T. A. Lee, 'Utility and Relevance: the search for reliable accounting information', *Accounting and Business Research*, Summer 1971, pp. 242-249.

[51]The writer has developed his arguments for cash flow reporting on a number of occasions, and the following comments are derived mainly from 'Goodwill: An Example of Will-o'-the-Wisp Accounting', *Accounting and Business Research*, Autumn 1971, particularly pp. 325-328; 'The Relevance of Accounting Information Including Cash Flows', *The Accountant's Magazine*, January 1972, pp. 30-34; 'The Nature and Purpose of Cash Flow Accounting', *The Accountant's Magazine*, April 1972, pp. 198-200; and 'A Case for Cash Flow Reporting', *Journal of Business Finance*, Summer 1972, pp. 27-36. These ideas have also been discussed within differing contexts – for example, H. C. Edey, 'Accounting Principles and Business Reality', *Accountancy*, November 1963, pp. 998-1002, and December 1963, pp. 1083-1088; G. Lawson, 'Cash-flow Accounting', *The Accountant*, 28.10.71, pp. 386-389; and G. J. Staubus, 'The Relevance of Evidence of Cash Flows', in *Asset Valuation and Income Determination*, ed. R. R. Sterling, Scholars Book Co., 1971, pp. 42-69.

[52]See T. A. Lee, *The Funds Statement: a review and study of its nature and use in the United Kingdom*, research report for The Research and Publications Committee of The Institute of Chartered Accountants of Scotland, 1974.

these purposes appears to be of crucial interest to investors and others, and this has been hinted at already in the previous section dealing with information needs. Thus, the writer has argued on several occasions for a system of funds flow reporting based on cash.[53]

Such a system would add a new dimension to financial reporting, showing sources and uses of cash over a period of time. The cash flows could be segregated to disclose those which evolve from trading operations, financial activities, long-term investment, and so on. The statements could be supported by other statements disclosing non-cash transactions, such as in acquisitions and mergers with other companies, which could have a significant bearing on the capacity of the enterprise to survive. They should also be subject to audit, in much the same way as for traditional financial statements, not only to verify their adequacy but also to remove any suspicion that company management may be manipulating the figures by delaying or accelerating cash movements. It is also recommended, for the above reason and because of the need to disclose a sufficient trend of figures, that several years' data be reported. It is also recommended, in order to minimise the criticism that past flows may not be repeated in the future, that forecast data should also be reported. It is felt that the relevance of this information to investors and others far outweighs its inevitable subjectiveness. The reporting of at least one year's forecast data should not present insuperable problems as it is information which management should have available in any case. The argument against forecasts of giving away vital information to competitors is a lame one because of the general nature of any externally reported information, and because there is no evidence existing to support it.

On the other hand, the arguments for a system of cash flow reporting are numerous, and appear significant enough to warrant a little more attention than they have been given hitherto.

(1) It is the generation and use of cash which enables the individual enterprise to survive; investment in companies, whatever its form, depends entirely on the capacity of companies to accumulate and apply cash in the most efficient and productive ways possible.

(2) Thus, although it may be argued that enterprise income is symbolic of company success and, therefore, of survival, it is no more than a symbol. Cash is the underlying economic success factor; income is not; and cash flow reporting therefore concentrates on the reality rather than the traditional symbol of enterprise success and survival.

(3) Cash is an economic factor which most persons in a developed society understand, through their day to day affairs. Income, on the other hand, is not, for it has developed far beyond the relatively simple surplus accounting generally associated with matching revenues and costs. Cash flow reporting, therefore, does not contain the considerable conceptual and practical measurement problems which beset income determination and asset valuation.

(4) The prediction of future dividends, loan repayments, creditor payments, and so on, *appear* to be far more strongly related to cash changes and situations than to periodic income. This further suggests a de-emphasising of income as the primary financial reporting concept.

(5) It is apparent from the literature[54] that there is a perceptive movement towards disclosure of forecast data, particularly that relating to enterprise income. Forecasting brings with it its own measurement problems,[55] and these are magnified considerably when future values and associated accruals require to be forecast in addition to the underlying economic activity. It is felt that forecast cash data at least minimises subjectivity by eliminating the requirement to forecast future accruals, etc.

(6) Cash flow reporting appears to satisfy the need to supply investors and others with stewardship-orientated information as well as with decision-orientated information. By eliminating the valuation problem from this type of financial report, management can report factually on its stewardship function, whilst at the same time disclosing data of use in the decision making process. In other words, cash flow reporting eliminates the somewhat artificial segregation of stewardship and decision making information, and emphasises properly that valuation is the concern of the investor and not of

---

[53] See references in footnote [51].

[54] 'For example, J. G. Birnberg and N. Dopuch, 'A Conceptual Approach to the Framework for Disclosure', *The Journal of Accountancy*, February 1963, pp. 56–63; W. W. Cooper, N. Dopuch and T. Keller, 'Budgetary Disclosure and Other Suggestions for Improving Accounting Reports', *The Accounting Review*, October 1968, pp. 640–648; C. R. Tomkins, 'The Development of Relevant Published Accounting Reports, *Accountancy*, November 1969, pp. 815–820; and N. Bedford, *Extensions in Accounting Disclosure*, Prentice-Hall, 1973, especially p. 36.

[55] See C. Robinson, *Business Forecasting: an economic approach*, Nelson, 1971, especially pp. 163–178.

the reporting management.⁵⁶

(7) Comparability, both inter- and intra-firm, is considerably enhanced by cash flow reporting; not only are data expressed in the same terms, free of the abuses of valuation and accrual accounting, but they can be compared with prior expectations if forecast data are also disclosed.

Conclusions

The primary intention of this essay has been to explore and analyse the complex nature of the enterprise income concept which has, and still does, dominate the present-day system of corporate financial reporting. The concept can be criticised on many grounds, sufficiently to cause the writer to believe that it does not deserve its present considerable position of importance. Nevertheless, it would be foolish to argue against it completely,⁵⁷ to do so would be to argue against the many years of constant and, presumably, successful use made of it by countless investors and others in the area of financial management. Indeed, simply because of the present tax structure, enterprise income cannot be neglected.

The defects attributable to enterprise income warrant consideration of other forms of financial report which appear more relevant to the needs of investors and others. In this respect, cash flow reports are worthy of a great deal of attention. The conclusion of the writer, therefore, is that there exist sufficient doubts about the relevance of income reporting to justify the serious comment made by Solomons that the concept may well be on the decline as other forms of financial reporting are recognised and adopted. It is the responsibility of the accountancy profession to ensure that the financial reports so recognised and adopted are the most relevant to the needs and requirements of those persons receiving and using them. Future developments in financial reporting must not be thought of solely in terms of the concept of enterprise income.

---

⁵⁶As suggested in the segregated system of funds accounting – R. A. Rayman, 'Is Conventional Accounting Obsolete?' *Accountancy*, June 1970, pp. 422–429; and by E. S. Hendriksen, *Accounting Theory*, Irwin, 1970 revised edition, pp. 136–137.

⁵⁷ As it has been suggested by Lawson, op. cit.

Extending the Argument

Reprinted from: Cees van Dam (Ed.), *Trends in Managerial and Financial Accounting*, Martinus Nijhoff Social Sciences Division, Leiden/Boston 1978.

IV. THE CASH FLOW ACCOUNTING ALTERNATIVE FOR CORPORATE FINANCIAL REPORTING

Tom A. Lee

1. Introduction

Financial accounting theory began to take its present form around the turn of the century. It crystalized into what are now the various orthodox rules and ways of perceiving things by the 1930's. Recently, signs of major change have become visible. Perhaps the majority of academic theorists now reject the historical cost rule. And many theorists are attempting far more sweeping changes than this. Many writers, especially the younger theorists, are trying to reconstruct financial accounting on entirely new foundations.[1]

Thomas thus summarises the present situation in financial accounting and reporting. Winds of change are blowing throughout the accounting world, and reporting accountants are having to cope with a seemingly endless stream of recommendations, requirements and amendments. It is reasonably clear that the greatest attention is being given to two main areas — that is, the objectives of reporting systems (in particular emphasising the various needs of different user groups); and income and value measurement systems (with specific regard to the problems arising from significant rates of price inflation). In addition, the prevailing debate has made one matter abundantly evident — historic cost accounting has a limited utility for reporting purposes, and the major problem over the next few years will be to find suitable alternatives which meet report users' known needs, adequately reflect economic reality, and can be implemented in practice.

The traditional accounting underlying corporate financial reports is based on accruals — that is, the financial data generated in the accounting system are allocated to the specific reporting periods to which they are judged to relate. The main practice adopted for this purpose is the familiar matching principle whereby revenue outputs are related to allocated inputs when measuring periodic income. Readers will very probably know of no system other than that defined above, and it is understandable that accountants react strongly against

1. A. L. Thomas, 'The Allocation Problem in Financial Accounting Theory', *Studies in Accounting Research 3*, American Accounting Association, 1969, p. 105.

any attacks on its adequacy. However, the number of attacks have been few and, consequently, the accrual basis to financial reporting has remained virtually unscathed over the years. Indeed, a review of the history of accounting thought and practice would reveal that accountants have been concerned, almost exclusively, with problems within the accrual accounting context. Unfortunately, most of these problems remain unresolved, despite attempts to standardise practice.

It is therefore my contention that accrual accounting, largely because of its dependence on subjective judgments for allocation purposes, has created a stockpile of problems which has diverted accountants' attention away from the more fundamental problem of finding the most suitable financial information to meet the needs of a variety of users of financial reports. For example, they have been far too busy with the problem of how to allocate fixed asset depreciation to bother to investigate whether depreciation is vital to the needs of report users. Even now, when the crucial question of price-level accounting is being debated, the framework for discussion remains the accrual process. The implicit assumption must therefore be that accountants, on the whole, are satisfied with this judgmental allocation system as a proper structure for their financial reports. There is no evidence to suggest otherwise.

2. Challenges to date

The validity of such an assumption deserves to be challenged. It is much too fundamental a point to be left unquestioned for so long. The number of sustainable challenges, however, have been few – the most detailed and direct outside the U.K. being that of Thomas,[2] with Chambers[3] and Sterling[4] also contributing in a somewhat different manner. The U.K. experience is similarly sparse, but will be looked at in detail in the following sections.

Thomas has concluded that the allocation or accrual process is indefensible in terms of attempting to measure information which adequately describes the real world:

Excepting rare instances where productive processes do not interact, and very high levels of input aggregation, financial accounting's allocation assertions are ambiguous and incorrigible. They may be employed to code the accountant's communication of estimates

---

2. Thomas, *op. cit.*; and 'The Allocation Problem: Part Two', *Studies in Accounting Research 9*, American Accounting Association, 1974.
3. R. J. Chambers, *Accounting, Evaluation and Economic Behaviour*, Prentice-Hall, 1966.
4. R. R. Sterling, *Theory of the Measurement of Enterprise Income*, University Press of Kansas, 1970.

about the firm, but allocation assertions do not reflect anything that exists in the external world, and do not correspond to any aspects of the firm's economic state or activities.[5]

Thomas' main argument, therefore, is that the arbitrary nature of accounting allocations leads to false descriptions of the reality of economic phenomena in reporting entities. His main solution is the production of allocation-free financial statements – in terms either of exit values or cash flows.

Chambers and Sterling, on the other hand, arrived at their exit value reports when considering the most relevant type of financial information to meet the needs of decision makers, rather than by specifically attempting to resolve the allocation problem. It can therefore be argued that their recommendations avoid the allocation problem whilst remaining within the familiar income and financial position framework. However, their work represents a significantly different approach to financial reporting as compared with other systems depending on accrual accounting.

3. The U.K. example

In the past, several U.K. writers have hinted at the possibility of a cash flow alternative to accruals – that is, a system based on cash transactions. However, to date, only Lawson[6] and myself[7] have investigated the proposal in any depth. As with Thomas, the Lawson-Lee case rests on a fundamental dissatisfaction with accrual accounting and also on doubts about the absolute utility of the income concept. The accountancy profession has remained relatively silent on these matters, but cash flow reporting has achieved a limited support in the recent Sandilands Committee report (although it was felt that it could not easily be accommodated within the present U.K. legal requirements).[8]

There are therefore grounds for hoping that a wider acceptance of cash flow reporting may eventually be forthcoming. With this in mind, the remainder of this paper will be concerned with my own arguments for such a system as they have developed over the years. In no way can they be regarded as entirely original nor, indeed, are they complete. However, at this stage, they fall into three

---

5. Thomas (Part Two), *op. cit.*, p. 156.
6. See, for example, G. H. Lawson, 'Cash-Flow Accounting', *The Accountant*, 28 October 1971, pp. 586-9, and 4 November 1971, pp. 620-22; 'Distributable Profits and Dividends', *Management International Review*, Vol. 12, No. 2/3, 1972, pp. 113-19; *Memorandum Submitted to the Inflation Accounting Committee*, Manchester Business School, 1974; and 'The Rationale of Cash Flow Accounting', *Investment Analyst*, pp. 5-12.
7. These writings will be referenced in appropriate parts of the remainder of this paper.
8. 'Inflation Accounting', *Report of the Inflation Accounting Committee*, Cmnd. 6225, HMSO, 1975, p. 156.

groupings – conceptual (being related particularly to the objectives of financial reporting); measurement (being concerned with the validity of accrual accounting, and the relevance of income reporting); and comprehension (being directed at the communications problems facing report users). Each will be discussed in the following sections, and interested readers will find in the appendix to this paper outline cash flow statements, together with exit value statements based on the same data.

4. The conceptual argument

A conceptual study of accounting for goodwill gave rise to my initial thoughts on cash flow reporting.[9] Typically, such an asset tends either to be ignored or summarily dismissed in financial reports. However, if it is to be accounted for properly, it requires to be continually recognised and valued. But market values do not exist for such a purpose – goodwill cannot be purchased in the market place in the same way as plant or inventory. Its value therefore must depend upon some form of present value calculation involving the discounting of future income benefits to be derived from it. In other words, economic principles of valuation would require to be introduced into the accounting measurement process.

My eventual recommendation was therefore for the reporting of historic and forecast flows for the entity as a whole in order to give decision makers relevant data for purposes of making their own estimates of its economic value (including its goodwill resources). I felt this would prevent the rather dubious exercise of decomposing the total flows in order to value individual assets. The reporting of historic and predicted data, together with explanations of material differences between the two, and disclosure of forecasting assumptions, were also felt to satisfy both the decision making and stewardship objectives of reporting.

These initial proposals were tentatively made but they did contain one firm recommendation – that the reported flows should be measured on a cash rather than an accrual basis, thereby avoiding the inherent problems of the latter. In addition, I believe that forecast cash flows provide a more appropriate basis for discounting purposes than do accrual-based flows. Arbitrary accounting allocations (such as for depreciation, inventory, deferred taxation, etc.) would appear to distort the timing element with which the discounting process is designed to cope in present value calculations.

9. T. A. Lee, 'Goodwill: An Example of Will-O-the-Wisp Accounting', *Accounting and Business Research*, Autumn 1971, pp. 318–28.

Initially, therefore, I saw the advantages of a cash flow reporting system as follows:

1. Financial report users would be provided with a data base which could be used by them for purposes of deriving valuations necessary for decisions – for example, for the investor estimating future dividend flows for his share price model.
2. Managerial accountability would be improved by the reporting of actual and forecast data, coupled with explanations of material differences.
3. The major problem of allocation in financial accounting would be largely avoided, although cash flows would require some temporal segregation.
4. The attendant problems of price-level variations could also be largely avoided by using money cash flows, to which a money time preference rate could be applied in discounting by decision makers.
5. All resources (tangible and intangible) of the reporting entity would be represented in its total net cash flow, thereby avoiding incomplete reporting.
6. The classical Hicksian model of income and capital could be applied by decision makers by obtaining opening and closing entity capital from a discounting of forecast cash flows.

In other words, I envisage a system of reporting entity cash flows which avoids the traditional problems of accounting, although introducing new ones – particularly in the area of forecasting. I also see it as a system which distinguishes two separate functions – that of measurement and reporting of relevant data (which I believe to be the domain of the reporting accountant) and that of *overall* valuation (which I believe to be the responsibility of the decision maker when he makes use of reported data). Far too much emphasis has been and still is given to the need to report *individual* values in financial reports. In my view, this has given the impression that the reporting accountant is attempting to give an overall valuation of the entity to decision makers. This is clearly not the case. Whilst I would take issue with the proposition that all forecasting should be left to report users, it is my belief that overall valuations of the entity, or shares in it, should be made by them, and that cash flow data are more relevant than accrual-based data for this purpose. I also believe that they should be provided with entity management's quantifications of future activity as a basis for their personal forecasts.

These conceptual arguments for cash flow reporting have been developed further in two relatively recent papers[10] and, coupled with those contained in my

---

10. T. A. Lee, 'The Relevance of Accounting Information Including Cash Flows', *The Accountant's*

goodwill paper, have been grouped into three main categories – the need for change; the key factor of cash; and maximising objectivity.

4.1. The need for change

The traditional objective of financial reporting is stewardship or managerial accountability but there now appears to be an almost universal acceptance of economic decision making as the major reason for financial reports. Thus, accountants must ensure that reported data adequately meet the latter need, either in terms of historic information with a reasonable predictive ability or in terms of forecast data with a reasonable credibility – or possibly a combination of both.

The predictive ability of historic accounting information is relatively uncertain, either in historic cost or current value terms. Surprisingly, this aspect of accounting has remained inconclusive and unproven,[11] although there is a school of thought which suggests that no form of historic information should be used for predictive purposes.[12] This approach can be summarised as follows:

> The primary goal of financial reporting should be to 'feedback' data about values of resources held by the firm as distinct from the shareholders. . . . For present and past measurements to be selected on the basis of their capacity to predict future valuations of the same (distorted) measurements . . . involves a circularity of reasoning unlikely to be of real use to investors in the end. Investors, after all, want for prediction purposes private information they can trade upon to their exclusive advantage. But accounting messages are public data and, hence, are best used for the verification of expectations.[13]

In other words, there is a very persuasive argument for treating historic information as control information, and for decision makers to use it only within such a context.[14] Additionally, there is evidence (which would apply to historic

---

Magazine, January 1972, pp. 30–34; and 'A Case for Cash Flow Reporting', *Journal of Business Finance*, Summer 1972, pp. 27–36.

11. The difficulties of assessing predictive ability can be seen in such studies as W. H. Beaver, 'Market Prices, Financial Ratios and the Prediction of Failure', *Journal of Accounting Research*, Autumn 1968, pp. 179–92; M. C. O'Connor', 'On the Usefulness of Financial Ratios to Investors in Common Stock', *Accounting Review*, April 1973, pp. 339–52. Altogether there have been little more than 20 empirical studies in this area between 1966 and 1975. All have been either restrictive in their coverage or tentative in their conclusions.

12. For example, M. N. Greenball, 'The Predictive-Ability Criterion: Its Relevance in Evaluating Accounting Data', *Abacus*, June 1971, pp. 1–7.

13. K. V. Peasnell, 'The Usefulness of Accounting Information to Investors', *Occasional Paper*, International Centre for Research in Accounting, 1973, p. 20.

14. There is evidence to suggest that, in relation to annual financial reports, investors use them for purposes of verifying information made public earlier in other sources such as interim reports – see,

cost or replacement cost systems, but not to realisable value systems) that the accrual process can introduce variations likely to affect the predictive ability of the resultant data – for example, different accounting techniques and allocations applied to the same situation can result in materially different decisions;[15] and fluctuating income series can be smoothed by companies for reporting purposes, thereby masking the true situation.[16] However, due to the limited nature of this evidence, I would be reluctant at this stage to condemn entirely the predictive ability of historic-orientated reporting systems which depend on accrual accounting. But I do believe that the frailties which appear to exist in them are sufficient to warrant investigation of reporting models which appear better suited to meet the needs of decision makers.

In particular, there appears to be merit in the argument for the formal provision of predictive data in financial reports. This recommendation has been made several times in the past and, despite doubts about its credibility, has been used for some years in the U.K. – albeit in the limited context of corporate acquisitions and mergers.[17] My doubts about forecast data concern not so much their inherent subjectiveness (which is unavoidable and can be allowed for by decision makers), but more the additional subjectivity which is created if the accrual basis is adopted as the measurement process. In my opinion, cash flow forecasts are more credible than accrual-based forecasts. They avoid the variability and manipulation which can result from the use of accrual accounting. I also feel that adequate descriptions of the assumptions underlying cash forecasts would be necessary to improve their credibility; as would explanations of material differences between actual and forecast performance (for example, distinguishing between variances due to economic circumstances and variances due to forecasting errors). This would mean ,.e provision of forecast data for predictive purposes and actual data for 'feed-back' purposes – all on a cash and, therefore, allocation-free basis.

---

for example, R. Ball and P. Brown, 'An Empirical Evaluation of Accounting Income Numbers', *Journal of Accounting Research*, Autumn 1968, pp. 159–77.
15. See, for example, N. Dopuch and J. Ronen, 'The Effects of Alternative Inventory Valuation Methods – An Experimental Study', *Journal of Accounting Research*, Autumn 1973, pp. 191–211, for evidence of effects on individual decisions. At an aggregate level, however, evidence suggests the market is not 'fooled' by these variations – see R. Ball, 'Changes in Accounting Techniques and Stock Prices', *Empirical Research in Accounting: Selected Studies*, 1972, pp. 1–44. Presumably individual decision variations are compensated at the aggregate level.
16. For example, R. M. Copeland, 'Income Smoothing', *Empirical Research in Accounting: Selected Studies*, 1968, pp. 101–16. These results as with other similar studies, were tentative only, and require replication.
17. As under the provisions of *The City Code on Take-overs and Mergers*, Issuing Houses Association, revised 1976, p. 19 and pp. 39–41.

4.2 The key factor of cash

Whereas the previous section has emphasised certain failures of the traditional reporting system which give rise to the need to examine the cash flow proposal as a suitable alternative, this next section outlines the main reasons why cash flow reporting is of value, *irrespective of the frailties of the accrual system*. My main argument in this connection is that cash is *the* key resource of most reporting enterprises. Irrespective of the vital importance of other resources in business (such as workers and managers), the cash flow of an entity is essential to its very existence. Not to recognise this is to ignore the harsh realities of the business world. Cash is the life blood of a business entity.

In other words, no business entity can survive over the long-term without an adequate and positive net cash flow from its trading operations. Profitability is not enough and reasonable liquidity is required too. However, the traditional financial reporting system, with its considerable emphasis on profitability, is not specifically geared to highlight the key resource of cash. Funds statements are a considerable help in this respect, but they are not universally produced in practice and, in any case, are based on the income-orientated, accrual-based accounting system which does not necessarily identify the stark reality of cash flows. Admittedly, income contributes to liquidity but it is not the only factor to do so, and funds statements are somewhat inadequate for the purpose of isolating pure cash inflows and outflows. Cash is such an essential ingredient in the survival of reporting entities that it is very surprising that reporting accountants have paid so little attention to it. Some emphasis has been given through the use of accrual-based funds statements which are often, and misleadingly, termed cash flow statements (cash flow being defined as reported income after deduction of tax and addition of the depreciation provision). But, as previously mentioned, funds statements are no more than imperfect substitutes for cash flow statements.

It is also equally surprising that the needs of report users in relation to cash data have been virtually ignored. For example, the generally accepted share investment decision model is based on predictions of dividend flows which, in turn, depend to a large extent on the existence of distributable cash in the future. Accrual-based historic information cannot be said to be ideally suited to meet these particular needs. Nor can it be said to meet the needs of creditors anxious to assess a reporting entity's ability to pay its way both in the near-present and future (for example, with regard to interest and capital repayment commitments). Likewise, the employee and his official representatives concerned with wage negotiations, job security, and entity investment performance would find cash flow data more directly relevant to these needs than income-orientated information. In other words, just as a business will collapse through lack of cash, report users would appear to be equally disadvantaged through lack of information relating to cash. This applies whatever the economic climate, although it is most evident in times when cash is in short supply.

4.3. Maximising objectivity

One of the most fundamental and influential guidelines in traditional financial accounting is that reported information should be as objective as possible. There has been a significant switch of emphasis by accountants in recent years – away from the rather rigid interpretation of this concept in terms of being able to verify independently the fairness of reported information in relation to available evidence, towards the increasingly accepted view of informational neutrality vis-à-vis report users. This change has evolved from a growing awareness on the part of accountants that reported information is in many ways a compromise. In particular, it must be relevant to its users but at the same time it must be credible in their eyes. The problem is therefore one of finding an optimal mixture of the essential features of financial reports. They cannot be completely relevant; nor can they be completely objective. However, they can be reasonably relevant and reasonably objective. With this in mind, I have come to the following conclusion in relation to the utility of cash flow data:

... if objectivity is accepted as an important criterion of accounting, production of the type of information which appears to present the most reasonable balance of relevance and objectivity should be aimed for at all times – because of its overall utility to the user. Cash flow information appears ... to satisfy these conditions best. Firstly, in its historic form, it is perhaps the most objective information possible, avoiding most of the subjectiveness which enters into the technical adjustments involved in the traditional accrual accounting; it is also the most relevant information for purposes of comparison with forecast information should this be measured on a cash basis. Secondly, forecast cash flows, although involving a great deal of uncertainty (however, no more so than budgeted profits on the accrual basis) clearly avoid the necessary subjectiveness of accrual judgments and opinions. Therefore, they appear to be far less subjective in a *total* sense than profit forecasts.[18]

I would therefore have thought that a cash flow reporting model would be considerably attractive to accountants, in the sense that it appears to increase the relevance of financial reports whilst also increasing the objectivity of historic data and minimising the subjectivity of forecast data. In addition, it tends to switch the burden of responsibility for reporting away from the reporting

18. Lee (A Case for), *op. cit.*, p. 30.

accountant (by eliminating the absolute necessity for accounting allocations and valuations) towards entity management which, after all, is ultimately responsible for the quality of financial reports. If cash flow reporting were implemented, the onus would be on management to produce credible forecasts and not to manipulate historic flows by accelerating or decelerating cash transactions.

5. The measurement arguments

The conceptual arguments for cash flow reports have one thread running continuously through them – that of the frailty of accrual accounting. So far in this paper the latter has been examined mainly in terms of the element of subjective judgment involved. But it also gives rise to the need to look more closely at, first, the way in which traditional accounting is conducted (particularly the flexibility of accounting practice) and, secondly, what is accounted for (with specific regard to income and value measurement). Both these areas appear to me to contain matters which should be closely questioned when considering the suitability of the cash flow alternative.

5.1. Flexibility in accounting

It almost goes without saying that the measurement of past income and financial position on the accrual basis, without any guidelines or standards, is likely to reduce financial accounting to ultimate chaos due to the inherent flexibility of practice and the lack of a suitable mechanism to remove irrelevant or obsolete practices. Nevertheless, the accountancy professions in many countries have operated under such a laissez-faire system for several decades. The result has been the predicted chaos, increasing criticism, and the eventual implementation of programmes of standardisation.

It is not the purpose of this paper to describe in detail the degree of flexibility which exists in present-day financial reporting. Evidence of this can be found in various surveys of financial reporting practices now produced by professional accountancy bodies in many countries. Additionally, as part of my argument for cash flow reports, I have conducted empirical studies of the problem in three areas (goodwill accounting, disclosure of business combinations, and funds reporting)[19] and, in each study, evidenced substantial differences of approach, both between companies and over time.

19. Respectively, 'Accounting for Goodwill', *Accounting and Business Research*, Summer 1973, pp.

THE CASH FLOW ACCOUNTING ALTERNATIVE

The various programmes of standardisation which are now in operation have helped to reduce considerably the absolute level of flexibility in accounting practice. Major problems have been identified, and suitable solutions have been made mandatory for the reporting entities to which they have been judged to apply. Despite this, several problems remain which, in many ways, are as fundamental as the original problems to which the standardisation process was directed. They appear to me to be as follows:

1. Prescribed accounting standards cannot eliminate the flexibility of accounting practice entirely. For example, a standard which states that inventory should be valued at the lower of cost or net realisable value, without stating how cost should be determined, reduces flexibility only marginally. Additionally, it may not be possible to standardise certain areas of practice which depend entirely on subjective judgment – for example, with regard to the probable life of a depreciable fixed asset or the estimation of irrecoverable debtors. Finally, standards can include provisions allowing reporting entities the right to deviate from a prescribed practice if a reasoned case can be advanced for so doing; again with the effect of perpetuating possible flexibility.

2. There is a considerable danger that prescribed standards, once stated as such, remain as the advocated practice beyond the point of time at which they become irrelevant or obsolete. In other words, unless they are constantly reviewed, and amended or abandoned where necessary, financial reporting will suffer from the 'stockpiling' effect that standardisation, in part, was designed to eliminate. This puts a considerable onus on professional bodies to police prescribed standards.

3. The question of who is ultimately responsible for producing and implementing accounting standards appears to be unclear at the present time. The obvious favourites are reporting accountants and their professional bodies and, in the U.K. and elsewhere, this appears to have been the course followed. However, this leads to problems because accountants are not usually responsible by law for financial reports (this normally being the function of entity management) and, in any case, standards may involve issues going beyond the boundaries of accounting. A possible solution may be to incorporate accounting standards into legislation, but this tends to place them within a context which is extremely difficult to amend except in the long-term.

4. The proliferation of accounting standards in recent years has resulted in a similar proliferation of standard-setting bodies. Whilst it is gratifying to find so

175–96; 'Accounting for and Disclosure of Business Combinations', *Journal of Business Finance and Accounting*, Spring 1974, pp. 1-33; and *The Funds Statement*, The Institute of Chartered Accountants of Scotland, 1974.

much interest in the problems of accounting and financial reporting, I cannot help but feel uneasy at the situation which could arise over the years whereby different bodies prescribe different solutions to the same problem. This is reasonably easy to cope with so long as the reporting entity is confined within its own national boundaries. But the same is not the case for the international or multi-national entity. In these instances, they will have to decide which of several standards they have to apply; a situation remarkably similar to the condition of flexibility which standards were aimed at minimising.

5. Finally, the development of accounting standards has resulted in an ever increasing disclosure of explanations of particular practices utilised in individual financial statements. Although it is wholly desirable for reporting accountants to make adequate disclosure of their accounting messages, I find it rather perturbing to see financial reports become more and more complex in order to improve their content. As a later section of this paper will explain more fully, a considerable number of report users are unable to use and understand the present form of financial report. Standardisation, and its related disclosure, does nothing to ease these problems.

Taken together, these various points force me to the conclusion that accrual accounting creates a problem of variability in practice which, to some extent, can be reduced by standardisation, but only by creating further problems for both the consumer and producer of financial reports. For this reason, I am not very impressed by the standardisation programme. In my view, it is simply another example of accountants looking for ways of repairing the accounting framework; ignoring the fact that it may not be capable of adequate repair and, instead, should be replaced. Unfortunately, at least in my view, the thinking which has taken place on the question of flexibility in accounting has caused accountants to ignore the possibility of alternative systems of financial reporting. Cash flow reporting would, after all, avoid many of the difficulties mentioned above in relation to accrual accounting and its standardisation.

5.2 The relevance of income

As an accountant educated in the tradition of income measurement and reporting, I find it hard, and more than a little confusing, to build my case for cash flow reporting to a large extent on the irrelevance of income measures. After all, over many decades, financial accountants have concentrated their attention almost exclusively on ways of improving income measurement – that is, in relation, first, to historic cost allocations (and standardisation thereof); secondly, to resolving the monetary purchasing power fault inherent in historic cost accounting; thirdly, to investigating current value alternatives to historic cost; and, fourthly, to examining ways of incorporating purchasing power and current value changes to derive measures of so-called real income.

I have examined these particular matters at length, sufficiently to conclude that income is akin to a very flexible piece of elastic. It can be as long or as short as its manipulator wishes; indeed, it is almost infinitely variable. In other words, there is no such thing as *the* income of a reporting entity for a defined period. Instead, there are many possible income measures, each dependent on the particular rules and judgments applied by the reporting accountant. Of course, the theoretical possibility of a large number of income measures, based on the same economic data, exists. And, of course, there is reassurance in the knowledge that reporting accountants usually operate within a fairly limited set of income rules. But there is also cause for concern in the fact that, by changing these rules, accountants are capable of describing entity income in an entirely different way to that previously entertained.

This is particularly important in relation to report users, for periodic income is a major factor in their assessment of reporting entities. It can be, and presumably is, used as a means of judging the success or failure of an entity and its management and, therefore, can be used as an indicator of future performance. Moreover, in relation to consumption and investment, it is a means of determining how much an entity can afford to distribute, and how much it must retain in order to maintain, expand, or change its existing operations.

In light of these matters, it is vital to define income in a consistent and acceptable way in order that report users can make rational judgments about the matters referred to above. Unfortunately, income does not lend itself to easy definitions, nor to any definitions likely to receive general acceptance. Much depends on the way in which a number of matters are treated. Put briefly, income cannot exist unless capital exists. But capital exists only if the resources underlying it have a value to the entity. Thus, resource valuation is one variable to be resolved before periodic income can be determined – differing values resulting in different capital measures, thereby producing different capital increments or decrements for purposes of determining income.

The next income variable with which reporting accountants have to cope concerns the decision about how much of each periodic capital increment or decrement should be treated as income – that is, the familiar capital maintenance decision. Again, the range of possible answers is wide, depending on the question of what is regarded as the appropriate capital to maintain. Subjective judgments have a considerable influence on this matter. For example, in the U.K., the Sandilands Committee has recommended that holding gains which result from its current cost variant of replacement cost accounting should not be treated as income, and, instead, should be taken to reserve.[20] If implemented as an accounting standard, this particular treatment of holding gains would eliminate the need for capital maintenance judgments. However, as seems likely, if the matter is left to the discretion of the reporting entities and their accountants, the judgmental aspect of accounting will be increased beyond present levels.[21] In other words, what is capital and income to one entity may not be the same for another entity. Indeed, what is capital and income to an entity in one period may be different in another period. Income is therefore not only variable in nature between entities, it is also temporally variable within the same entity.

In summary, periodic income can be measured and perceived in many different ways. Much of the variability exists because of the number of accounting procedures and resource valuations which can be applied to its measurement. But the judgmental aspects associated with capital maintenance decisions are likely to have an increasing impact on the potential variation of income. I would have sympathy with these problems if I felt that income was absolutely essential to the various users of financial reports. In my opinion, it may be of some use but it certainly does not appear to be of paramount importance to, for example, the investor assessing future dividend flows; the employee seeking wage increases or job security; the lender examining the ability of the entity to meet its loan commitments; and the tax authority computing entity taxation liabilities. Each of these matters can be satisfied without recourse to income measurements. Cash flow reports could provide all the necessary information for these purposes, thus avoiding the elasticity of income.

6. User comprehension

My earlier studies of the cash flow alternative to income were all in the areas described in the previous sections – that is, they were concerned exclusively either with purely conceptual points or with the measurement problems inherent in the income-orientated, accrual-based reporting system. This meant that one further matter had been largely ignored – the ability of report users both to use and understand the existing form of financial report. Even if the existing reporting system was free of the conceptual and measurement faults already mentioned, I can hardly argue for its overall utility unless I am convinced that it can be reasonably used and understood by those persons to whom it is directed. With

20. 'Inflation Accounting', op. cit., p. 162.
21. This is precisely what has happened in 'Current Cost Accounting', Exposure Draft 18, Accounting Standards Committee, 1976. pp. 5–6.

this in mind, it seemed appropriate to examine the extent to which report users make use of traditional financial reports, as well as the degree to which they appear to understand the accounting messages contained in these reports. The subjects looked at to date have been private shareholders in limited companies – typically in the U.K., they hold a substantial majority of shareholdings, without necessarily holding a majority in terms of value. In comparison with institutional investors employing a great deal of accounting and financial expertise, they appear to be at the greatest risk in relation to the complexities of financial statements prepared on an accrual basis.[22]

To date, financial reporting systems have been based on general-purpose financial statements – that is, statements designed to meet the needs of as many potential users as possible, irrespective of their abilities, background, and experience in such matters. So long as financial reports remain uncomplicated documents, no major problem of use or comprehension would appear to exist. When they become complex, technical statements, written in a specialist language, these problems are all too apparent. But, so far, no attempt has been made by reporting accountants to meet this challenge. Indeed, the reverse appears to be true, with financial reports appearing to become more complex day by day as amendments and additions are made to the existing accrual structure.

A small number of studies have revealed that accounting and financial messages are likely not to be understood by a majority of people.[23] The research with which I have been associated supports these earlier findings, the level of understanding of the private shareholders questioned being usually very low – the only exceptions being for those with an accounting background or experience. The greatest difficulty was found to exist with valuation procedures and accounting terminology used in financial reports, and with financial ratios. In particular, balance sheet terminology was very badly understood.

So far as use of financial reports was concerned, the overall finding was that the annual report was generally little used, with the chairman's report being the

22. This research has been conducted in association with Dr. D. P. Tweedie of the University of Edinburgh. The detailed findings are contained in the following list of publications, and have been summarised for purposes of this paper: T. A. Lee and D. P. Tweedie, 'Accounting Information: A Study of Private Shareholder Usage', *Accounting and Business Research*, Autumn 1975, pp. 280–91; 'Accounting Information: A Study of Private Shareholder Understanding', *Accounting and Business Research*, Winter 1975, pp. 3–17; 'The Private Shareholder: His Sources of Financial Information and His Understanding of Reporting Practices', *Accounting and Business Research*, Autumn 1976 (forthcoming), pp. 304–14; and *'The Private Shareholder and the Corporate Report'*, The Institute of Chartered Accountants in England and Wales, 1976 (forthcoming).
23. See F. J. Soper and R. Dolphin, 'Readability and Corporate Annual Reports', *The Accounting Review*, April 1964, pp. 358–62; J. E. Smith and N. P. Smith, 'Readability: A Measure of the Performance of the Communication Function of Financial Reporting', *The Accounting Review*, July 1971, pp. 552–61; and M. D. Still, 'The Readability of Chairmen's Statements', *Accounting and Business Research*, Winter 1972, pp. 36–9.

most thoroughly read part. Financial press reports were the best used of other sources of financial information. But the most alarming finding was that the thorough reader of the annual report tended also to be the thorough reader of other information sources – many shareholders appearing to make little or no use of *any* source of information about companies. This was even more disturbing in light of two other results – thorough readers of financial information tended to have a substantially better understanding of accounting matters than less interested readers, and tended also to have a relevant accounting background or experience. In fact, there is clear evidence to suggest that many private shareholders must be unable to use existing financial information due to its complexity. It appears, therefore, that accountants have produced a reporting system which is capable of being read thoroughly and reasonably understood only by accountants or equivalent professionals. This is particularly significant when it is realised, at least from our findings, that the vast majority of the private shareholders concerned were making their own investment decisions without any expert help or advice. Many therefore must be making their decisions blindly, and a considerable number who do make use of financial reports must be in obvious danger of misunderstanding their content.

Armed with this knowledge, and coupled with suggestions from responding shareholders, two alternative and possibly complementary recommendations were made – first, to devise means of simplifying the present accrual-based annual report (both in relation to its complexity and terminology); and, secondly, to devise alternative systems to that of accruals which are likely to meet the needs of report users (and this could include cash flow reporting). Similar research is being conducted into the needs of institutional users but, meantime, the following conclusion warrants attention:

Financial reports must not be conceived solely in terms of the so-called sophisticated user. To do so would be to ignore the needs of the majority of shareholders in most companies. It could also result in the ignoring of the particular needs of other financially unsophisticated groups which, undoubtedly, are likely to be major recipients of company financial reports – for example, company employees.

Otherwise, to adapt the familiar Orwellian statement:

'All shareholders are equal. But some shareholders are more equal than others.'

Such appears to be the unintentional reality in financial reporting. It needs to be remedied. The remedy lies in the hands of members of the accountancy profession.[24]

My own firm belief in this respect, conceived from an earlier conceptual

---

24. Lee and Tweedie, ('The Private Shareholder'), *op. cit.*, pp. 234–5.

standpoint, and confirmed from empirical evidence briefly discussed above, is that cash flow reporting must be examined with a view to supplementing or replacing the existing accrual system. It could simplify financial statements (because less disclosure of accounting methodology would be required); it would avoid the complexities of accruals and remove much of the language of accruals (such as income, depreciation, reserves, assets, debtors, inventory, and accrued charges); and it would appear to be more directly compatible with the needs *and* abilities of its potential users (particularly those lacking in accounting qualification and experience).

7. The future

It would be wrong of me to suggest that the case for cash flow reporting rests or falls entirely on the basis of the above briefly-described arguments. This position can only be reached when the system has been empirically tested in relation to both the needs of sophisticated and unsophisticated report users, and its feasibility in practice. Work therefore has to be conducted in the construction of cash flow reports, using both historic and forecast data. Once this stage has been completed, and only when this is so, the resultant reports can be tested on shareholders and other users to find out whether these can be used meaningfully (both in relation to decision making and control), and whether they are able to understand cash flow data significantly better than the present accrual-based data.

I have no intention of condemning conventional accounting absolutely. It is a system which, despite its acknowledged faults, has received general acceptance in the accountancy profession and business world. It is also a system which is likely to be used for some time to come even if cash flow reporting received immediate support. There may even be a case for reporting on both bases, or the arguments for cash flow reporting may ultimately be found to be unacceptable. Indeed, cash flow reporting may not be the only conceivable alternative to accrual accounting. Therefore, whatever the future holds for financial reporting, I only ask that the case for cash flow reporting be examined fully, debated adequately, and implemented if it is found to be useful.

Appendix: specimen cash flow and exit-value financial statements

This appendix has been prepared using invented data, and on the basis of a cash flow reporting format described originally in T. A. Lee. 'A Case for Cash Flow Reporting', *Journal of Business Finance*, Summer 1972, particularly pp. 32–5. It is not a complete reproduction of such a system, and is intended only to give the reader an impression of what it might be like in practice. Much work has yet to be undertaken on the precise contents of cash flow statements, and the undernoted should be regarded as for discussion only.

Exit-value balance sheets have been appended to the cash flow report because there are convincing arguments to suggest that they complement it rather well, and prevent the loss to report users of statements of financial position. Both the cash flow report and the exit-value report have been derived from data which are described first in the traditional historic cost format. For purposes of simplicity, the latter has not been prepared in accordance with any U.K. or E.E.C. regulations.

Traditional historic cost financial statements

1. *Income Statements – calendar years 1975 and 1976*

	1975		1976	
	£	£	£	£
Sales		677,000		759,000
Less: raw materials	420,000		498,000	
direct labour	101,000		117,000	
direct overheads	37,000	558,000	41,000	656,000
		119,000		103,000
Less: indirect labour and overheads	5,000		6,000	
irrecoverable debts	2,000		12,000	
loan interest	3,000		2,000	
depreciation	55,000	65,000	61,000	81,000
		54,000		22,000
Less: loss (gain) on sale of:				
plant	—		6,000	
motor vehicles	—		(3,000)	
investments	—	—	(10,000)	(7,000)
		54,000		29,000
Less: taxation		35,000		13,000
		19,000		16,000
Less: dividends		15,000		15,000
		4,000		1,000
Add: retained income brought forward		26,000		30,000
Retained income		30,000		31,000

2. Balance Sheets – year-ends 1975 and 1976

	1975		1976	
	£	£	£	£
Fixed Assets				
Land and buildings (cost)		100,000		100,000
Plant and machinery (cost)	250,000		265,000	
Less: accumulated depreciation	100,000	150,000	139,000	126,000
Motor vehicles (cost)	25,000		40,000	
Less: accumulated depreciation	20,000	5,000	8,000	32,000
Research and development (cost)		—		28,000
		255,000		286,000
Current Assets				
Stock and work in progress	180,000		206,000	
Debtors	75,000		83,000	
Investments	30,000		15,000	
Bank	10,000	295,000	—	304,000
		550,000		590,000
Less: Current Liabilities				
Creditors	190,000		196,000	
Bank	—		65,000	
Taxation	35,000		13,000	
Dividends	15,000	240,000	15,000	289,000
		310,000		301,000
Less: loan		30,000		20,000
		280,000		281,000
Share capital		200,000		200,000
Reserves		50,000		50,000
Retained income		30,000		31,000
		280,000		281,000

3. Funds Statement – calendar year 1976

	£	£
Sources of funds		
Income before taxation		29,000
Add: transactions not involving movements in funds:		
depreciation	61,000	
net gains on sale of assets	(7,000)	54,000
		83,000
Proceeds from sale of assets:		
plant	15,000	
motor vehicles	8,000	
investments	25,000	48,000
		131,000

Less: Application of funds			
Purchase of assets:			
plant	50,000		
motor vehicles	40,000		
Research and development costs	28,000		
Repayment of loan	10,000		
Taxation paid	35,000		
Dividends paid	15,000	178,000	
		(47,000)	
Decrease in working capital			
Increase in stocks and work in progress		26,000	
Increase in debtors		8,000	
Increase in creditors		(6,000)	
Decrease in bank		(75,000)	
		(47,000)	

Outline cash flow statements

1. *Statement of total cash flow*

	Calendar Year			
	1976			1977
	Forecast	Actual	Variance	Forecast
	£	£	£	£
Bank balance brought forward	10,000	10,000	–	(65,000)
Operational transactions flow	120,000	64,000	56,000	130,000
Financial transactions flow	(10,000)	(10,000)	–	(10,000)
Capital transactions flow	(104,000)	(77,000)	(27,000)	(12,000)
Taxation transactions flow	(35,000)	(35,000)	–	(13,000)
Net distributable flow	(19,000)	(48,000)	29,000	30,000
Interest and dividends	(17,000)	(17,000)	–	(21,000)
Undistributed bank balance	(36,000)	(65,000)	29,000	9,000

2. *Statement of operational transactions flow*

	Calendar Year			
	1976			1977
	Forecast	Actual	Variance	Forecast
	£	£	£	£
Cash received from customers	765,000	739,000	26,000	800,000
Cash paid for:				
raw materials	(502,000)	(513,000)	11,000	(499,000)
labour	(100,000)	(116,000)	16,000	(121,000)
overheads	(43,000)	(46,000)	3,000	(50,000)
Net operational flow	120,000	64,000	56,000	130,000

THE CASH FLOW ACCOUNTING ALTERNATIVE

3. *Statement of financial transactions flow*

	Calendar Year			
	1976			1977
	Forecast	Actual	Variance	Forecast
	£	£	£	£
Repayment of loan	(10,000)	(10,000)	—	(10,000)

4. *Statement of capital transactions flow*

	Calendar Year			
	1976			1977
	Forecast	Actual	Variance	Forecast
	£	£	£	£
Cash paid for:				
plant	(66,000)	(61,000)	(5,000)	—
motor vehicles	(40,000)	(36,000)	(4,000)	—
research and development	(25,000)	(28,000)	3,000	(12,000)
	(131,000)	(125,000)	(6,000)	(12,000)
Cash received for sale of:				
plant	18,000	15,000	3,000	—
motor vehicles	9,000	8,000	1,000	—
investments	—	25,000	(25,000)	—
Net capital flow	(104,000)	(77,000)	(27,000)	(12,000)

5. *Statement of taxation transactions flow*

	Calendar Year			
	1976			1977
	Forecast	Actual	Variance	Forecast
	£	£	£	£
Tax paid	(35,000)	(35,000)	—	(13,000)

6. *Statement of interest and dividend payments*

	Calendar Year			
	1976			1977
	Forecast	Actual	Variance	Forecast
	£	£	£	£
Loan interest paid	(2,000)	(2,000)	—	(1,000)
Dividends paid	(15,000)	(15,000)	—	(20,000)
Total distribution flow	(17,000)	(17,000)	—	(21,000)

Note: The above statements contain a 'stewardship' accounting of the cash flows for the immediate past period, compared and contrasted with the forecasts made for the same period and originally reported in the previous financial report. I would also recommend a disclosure of explanations by management of the variances resulting from the comparison of actual and previously forecast data. The possibility of an audit of these explanations would have to be considered.

Forecast data relating to the next period are provided for purposes of decision making. I believe it to be important to ensure that these are supported by adequate managerial statements of the assumptions on which they are based. Again, the question of audit would require to be considered. (Ideally, forecasts for more than one future period should be contemplated. However, given the inherent subjectiveness of these data, it may not be feasible or credible to go beyond a one year forecast in the first instance.)

Finally, I would recommend that a ten year summary of historic cash flow should be reported in a separate statement similar to that described above as Statement of Total Cash Flow. This would provide report users with a relatively simple trend of cash flow data.

Outline exit value balance sheets

Year-ends 1975 and 1976

	1975		1976	
	£	£	£	£
Fixed Assets				
Land and buildings		360,000		396,000
Plant and machinery		80,000		67,000
Motor vehicles		9,000		31,000
Research and development		—		175,000
		449,000		669,000
Current Assets				
Stock and work in progress	115,000		136,000	
Debtors	75,000		83,000	
Investments	40,000		18,000	
Bank	10,000	240,000	—	237,000
		689,000		906,000
Less: Current Liabilities				
Creditors	190,000		196,000	
Bank	—		65,000	
Taxation	35,000		13,000	
Dividends	15,000	240,000	15,000	289,000
		449,000		617,000
Less: loan		30,000		20,000
Realisable Capital		419,000		597,000
Less: opening realisable capital				419,000
Increase in Capacity to Adapt				178,000

2 THE SIMPLICITY AND THE COMPLEXITY OF ACCOUNTING

T. A. Lee

'What's twice two?' he roared at the tortoise who could scarcely be seen through the smoke.
'Seventeen,' answered the tortoise.
'Five,' said a newt.
'Three and a bit,' said Simple Simon.
'One penny,' said the pie-man surlily.
All the students were yelling different numbers but not one of them said 'Four.'
'Very, very good!' said Ethelred. 'All the answers are quite correct.'
'Rubbish!' said Alice. 'The correct answer is four!'
[Wilson, 1959, p. 113]

THIS IS MY THIRD ATTEMPT at this paper. The first and second were lengthy efforts which, no matter how hard I tried, retained the very complexity which Bob Sterling was hoping I would avoid. Following discussions and correspondence with colleagues, I came to the conclusion that the problem might be my prior knowledge and experience of accounting, which had conditioned me to react in particular ways in specific situations, rather like a Pavlovian dog. I, therefore, resolved to start again, examine the situation afresh, and try not to be influenced by my accounting upbringing. Whether I have succeeded is open to debate. Whether I or any other accountant can be successful in this quest is equally questionable. But I firmly believe that the attempt has to be made if the problems of accounting are to be resolved. The

I wish to thank my colleagues at the Universities of Bristol, Edinburgh, and Kent, as well as the paper's referee, for their extremely helpful suggestions on earlier drafts.

following sections represent my contribution; the rest I leave to you, the reader.

Before proceeding to the analysis I have made of the situation outlined by Bob Sterling, I think it is only fair to state certain limitations to my paper. I have deliberately introduced them as part of the process of attempting to examine the problem with a fresh mind. Therefore, I have avoided direct reference to previous writings, and I have not sought empirical evidence to support my value judgments. I do not believe such matters should be considered at this stage. I would instead suggest that, should some points of agreement emerge from the a priori reasoning in this and other papers in the text, the next stage should involve literature reviews and empirical testing. To attempt everything at one time would appear likely to repeat the problems which have given rise to Sterling's plea for simplicity.

THE STATE OF ACCOUNTING

Accounting used to be a reasonably simple matter, at least until accountants became responsible for it. Cash transactions were the principal feature of financial statements because the objective of measuring venture surpluses avoided the complication of allocating and valuing data. Bygones were treated as bygones, and all expenditures were regarded as "sunk" costs to be written off immediately against revenues. There could be no argument about methods of accounting for inventory, depreciation, and similar matters. They simply did not exist in the early accounting methodologies.

Industrialization, investment opportunities, and business continuity created the foundation for a more complex form of accounting information based on periodic allocations. The accounting function, as a result, has become extremely complex, demanding the use of highly qualified experts capable of producing and using such information but creating extended arguments and debates about points of detail in the system. There is little agreement regarding appropriate definitions of such apparently crucial matters as capital, capital maintenance, and income, and it has taken a considerable amount of time for accountants to accept the fact that a program of standardization is necessary to combat the inherent flexibility of their practices.

It has also become clear that little or no attention has been paid to the information needs of financial report users in terms of their various decision models. Financial statements of a general purpose nature, based on relatively unchanging principles, have been produced for decades irrespective of the various circumstances and needs of those persons relying on them for knowledge of business activity. Only recently has the report user become the subject of serious attention in accounting circles.

The present state of affairs obviously leaves much to be desired. Financial reporting should be a system which attempts to provide information of immediate use in decision making. But, as it is presently constituted, it is based on a mixture of past transactions and future expectations. Fact and forecast are inevitably entwined in the income and capital measurements required for present-day financial statements, and it is little wonder that disagreements and debates over appropriate practices are numerous. Generally speaking, more solutions are offered than there are problems, and the result is confusion, lack of progress, and loss of credibility in accountants and their reports. A number of suggestions have been put forward over the years which have attempted to return accounting to its simpler roots. However, accountants appear to be addicted to the complexities of the allocations system, and attempts at simplification usually have been ignored.

THE SIMPLICITY OF ACCOUNTING

As the earliest accountants discovered, accounting matters need not be too complex and the ritual of complexity need not be followed. Indeed, as with any other type of written message, accounting can be obscured completely by the "mumbo-jumbo" that surrounds it. I firmly believe there is a need to take a more simplistic approach to the problems of accounting, and this, I would suggest, includes the specification of the objectives of the function and the making of judgments as to which accounting information may be said to satisfy these objectives. Further, I believe that specifying such matters depends on two familiar but elusive characteristics—common sense and experience. Too much attention has been paid in the past to searching for a formula which, as if by magic, will ensure the attainment of accounting goals.

In my opinion, the main objective of accounting should be to provide information which aids the making and monitoring of the decisions of those persons to whom it is directed. This point is relatively self-evident and has been expressed in various ways and by different writers over the years. It is a statement to the effect that accounting information should be related to the various matters which impinge on particular decisions. It provides accountants with a reasonable sense of purpose and the necessary freedom to achieve it as best they can in the specific circumstances of a given situation. In particular, it points to a knowledge of two matters:

38   Chapter 2   (Cash Flows)

1. the nature of the decisions to which the reporting of accounting information is directed (in other words, the uses to which it can be put); and

2. the type of accounting information which most adequately meets these uses.

It is to these matters that this paper is directed. The analysis, however, will evolve within the framework of a "real-life" situation. It is, therefore, a case study, and the comments and conclusions must be read in that context only.

THE GIVEN SITUATION

A taxicab company has been specified as the object of analysis by Sterling in his Introduction. I have followed his specification with one or two minor amendments and have obtained factual data to add a dimension of realism to the commentary. The following are the main features of the situation (only the name of the company and the quotation of its shares are fictitious). The period being considered is the year to 31 January 1977.

1. The Edinburgh Taxicab Co. Ltd. is a quoted company which has been in existence for many years. It owns ninety British Leyland taxicabs, all with a useful life of three years. When this expires, the cabs are traded-in and replaced with up-to-date models. There have been few significant technological changes in recent years.

2. The number of cabs owned by the company has been fixed for some years by the number of taxi hire licenses issued to it by the governing authority. Thirty cabs are replaced exactly half-way through the company's financial year to 31 January.

3. The company employs cab drivers on a commission basis of 40 per cent of fare revenue and is responsible for the upkeep and maintenance of each cab it owns.

4. All transactions of the company are on a cash basis, and all expenditures can be treated as variable.

A fictitious corporate entity has been used for purposes of this paper, but the figures used in the analysis actually relate to the operations of a fleet of ninety taxicabs in the Edinburgh region during the year to 31 January 1977. Collecting such data presented few problems; they were obtained from the main distributor of taxicabs in the area, various taxicab owners, Lothian and Borders Police Transport Department, and the files of a taxicab company kept in the Registrar of Companies.

The situation is a relatively simple one and, at least within the U.K.

context, it contains a great deal of certainty. This, I believe, has the advantage of clarifying many of the issues to be discussed. For example, I am dealing with

    a. a single fixed asset type, subject to little technological change;
    b. easily obtained new or second-hand replacement costs and a well-established pattern of net realizable values;
    c. nil growth in the taxicab fleet of the company due to the infrequent reviewing of the number of taxi hire licenses issued to it; and
    d. a well-established mileage and life for each cab.

Much of the above may make accounting somewhat easier than is the case in other situations, although there must always remain uncertainty regarding future fare structures, fuel costs, repair and maintenance charges, replacement costs of cabs, and so on. Despite its apparent simplicity, it is a real-life situation deserving of analysis.

THE USERS OF ACCOUNTING INFORMATION

The most important matter to be considered at the outset of this analysis is a specification of the potential users of the reported information for, without them, there would be no need for it. The conditions pertaining to the Edinburgh Taxicab Co. Ltd. restrict the number of users normally found in a quoted public company because of the lack of creditors and lenders in Sterling's specification. However, there are a number of familiar groups whose members can be said to have a reasonable interest in the company. Despite recent studies into such matters, there is clearly a lack of detailed knowledge of user needs and, for this reason, my comments can only be of a general nature. However, I would suggest they are sufficient to identify key factors for later analysis.

Investors. Because the company's shares are quoted, investors can buy and sell through the local stock exchange relatively easily and quickly. These shareholdings will be of both a private and institutional nature and relate to varying degrees of financial and accounting expertise and knowledge. Nevertheless, all existing and potential investors have a well-known decision model based on an evaluation of the present worth of the future cash flows which they believe will result from an investment in the company. Of particular concern to these investors are the anticipated dividend receipts over the life of such an investment and the eventual realization proceeds should it be terminated. Investors would therefore appear to need data of assistance in forecasting future dividends and share realizations. Equally, they will require information concerning past dividend flows with which to monitor the degree of success attributable to any decisions they may have made previously.

Employees. The company employs taxicab drivers whose interest in its financial activities would appear to concern employment prospects (including job security) and its ability to meet any wage claims they may make. These needs would seem to require data relating to the future activity of the company, although information concerning its performance in the past in relation to jobs, wage claims, and employee facilities would also appear pertinent.

Managers. The management of the company requires a considerable quantity of regular information to assist in the administration of its operations. This particularly relates to the collection and control of cash receipts from cab drivers and cash payments covering cab operating costs. It will also require data of use in revenue and capital budgeting exercises.

Licensing authority. The company holds ninety taxi hire licenses issued by the relevant local authority. These are conditional on the company's maintaining a specific number of taxicabs on the road at any time and keeping them at a high standard. The authority is therefore concerned that the company is financially sound enough to maintain a fleet of ninety cabs at the required specification and has the ability to continue to do so. It would require information relating to these matters.

Inland Revenue. The government, in the form of its Inland Revenue Service, is concerned with collecting tax revenue according to existing legislation. At the present time in the U.K., tax is determined in terms of the company's historic cost income, and the Inland Revenue will thus need such information.

The preceding appear to be the main user groups connected with the Edinburgh Taxicab Co. Ltd. Others could be added to the list for one reason or another—for example, if the company were borrowing money long-term, then the lenders would need to be considered. However, their needs are generally felt to be approximate to those of investors, and their omission from this analysis therefore appears to present few problems. Likewise, professional advisers and related persons such as financial analysts could be examined. But their needs should be identical to those of the groups they are advising or serving—for example, analysts providing information to investors and trade unions representing employees. Finally, other user groups (such as suppliers, trade associations, and customers) could be considered, but,

COMMON FACTORS

The previous section merely provides a list of user groups and a brief introduction to their areas of interest. It does not readily identify any of the common factors which can be deduced from the latter and which could be helpful for analysis purposes. The following are offered as the main features which I believe the stated groups have in common:

1. With the exception of the Inland Revenue, which has a very narrowly defined interest in reported information, each group has an interest in the past and anticipated performance of the company. They, therefore, require information relating to past activity and data which may help them anticipate future activity. All are concerned with how well the company has survived in the past and how well it is likely to survive in the future.

2. Again with the possible exception of the Inland Revenue, each group mentioned is concerned with making and monitoring decisions. Each of these decisions has financial consequences, and suitable information is needed to aid the decision makers.

3. The specific interests of each group in relation to their respective decisions appear superficially to be widely different—investors are concerned with dividends and stock market values, employees with job prospects and wage levels and rates, management with all aspects of day-to-day operational activity, the licensing authority with the continuity and quality of taxi service provided, and the Inland Revenue with taxable capacity. However, there are common features to be found, the main one being that all such matters depend on the existence of that most basic of contemporary economic resources in business—cash.

Dividends cannot be distributed unless there is an adequate cash flow to justify them and adequate cash resources from which payment can be made. Likewise, wage increases and payments can be justified only in terms of adequate cash flows and resources. Managerial decision making and control within this type of business also demand a close attention to cash and cash flow. The licensing authority, too, must be concerned about cash flow as this is so central to the continuity of the company's service to the public. Lastly, even the Inland Revenue cannot ignore cash flow because this provides the means by which the company's taxation liabilities can be paid and is the basis for the defined taxable income figure. Cash and cash flows, therefore, are

42   Chapter 2   (Cash Flows)

common to most persons interested in the company. It is not, of course, the only input to these various decision models but, I would submit, it is the most fundamental. I would, therefore, suggest that the most basic information needs of these user groups could be specified as follows:

   a. a statement of the company's operational activity of the immediate past period which adequately reflects its cash flow;
   b. a statement of the company's present financial situation which has resulted from the immediate past cash flow and which is the basis for the cash flow anticipated in the next period; and
   c. a statement of the company's anticipated operational activity during the next period which adequately reflects the anticipated cash flow of that period.

The problem is finding the most suitable type of information which describes the above features and thereby adequately meets the needs of the various interested user groups being considered in this paper. To do this would provide at least an information set of a general purpose nature to which additional information could be added to further satisfy the particular needs of specific users. I believe the purpose of this paper should be to establish the foundation upon which such an information structure could be built. This is obviously a point of debate, but it is my opinion that, at least in this situation, there is such a foundation. The next sections will consider it in detail.

THE BASIC FEATURES OF THE SITUATION

The conclusions of the previous section suggest, in the first instance, a specification of an opening position, a closing position, and matters which have altered these positions. This will enable statements a and b to be prepared and will provide a basis for the predictions necessary for statement c. I would argue that outlining the main features of such a situation for the company in question will provide a basis for producing relevant financial statements. These features are given in Table 2-1.

The overall statement in Table 2-1 may reasonably represent the company's activities during the year to 31 January 1977, but the problem is how best to describe it in accounting terms which are the most useful to the various user groups mentioned previously. Obviously, it would be exceedingly difficult to prepare aggregate financial statements of the above data which had any real meaning in their present form—for example, how does one add cab numbers to cash balances and compare these with share numbers?

Table 2-1

The Edinburgh Taxicab Co. Ltd.
Basic Features of the Year to 31 January 1977

	Opening Position at 1 February 1976	Closing Position at 31 January 1977	Changes During Year
Number of cabs owned and in use (1)	90	90	—
Cash resources on hand (2)	£17,500	£45,600	+£28,100
Number of ordinary shares issued	100,000	100,000	—

Notes:

(1) These data can be described in greater detail:

	6-month-old Cabs	18-month-old Cabs	30-month-old Cabs	Total Cabs
Opening position at 1 February 1976	30	30	30	90
Less: Sold on 1 August 1976	—	—	30	30
	30	30	—	60
Aging during year to 31 January 1977	(30)	30	—	—
		(30)	30	—
	—	30	30	60
Add: Purchased on 1 August 1976	30	—	—	30
Closing position at 31 January 1977	30	30	30	90

(2) These data can also be described in some detail:

Opening balance at 1 February 1976		£ 17,500
Add: Fare revenue received	£810,000	
Sale proceeds of 30 cabs	17,100	827,100
		£844,600
Less: Payments for running cabs	336,600	
Drivers' commission	324,000	
Purchase of 30 new cabs	108,000	
Payment of tax on current year's profits*	30,400	799,000
Closing balance at 31 January 1977		£ 45,600

*This assumption has been made for the sake of simplicity.

44 Chapter 2 (Cash Flows)

The problem is that there is no common measurement unit being employed in the figures in the main statement, and there is not the additivity which can be obtained when the totals are analyzed separately [as is the case with the specific data in either substatements (1) or (2)]. Some uniformity of measurement must be applied to the basic data in order to provide decision makers with meaningful information. Therefore, the first step is to employ an acceptable measurement unit. I would argue that the money unit appears to be suitable and has been used consistently for this purpose for many years. It is the usual means of exchange in developed economies and is generally understood.

STATEMENT OF PAST OPERATIONAL ACTIVITY

100 According to the figures given in the previous section, the operating activity of the Edinburgh Taxicab Co. Ltd. for the year to 31 January 1977 resulted in a trading cash flow as follows:

	£
Fare revenue	810,000
Less: Cost of running cabs	660,600
Trading cash flow	149,400

In addition, thirty three-year-old cabs were sold for £17,100 and thirty new cabs were purchased for £108,000. Taxation payments amounted to £30,400. In my opinion, these are the most fundamental financial data concerning the company's operations during the period. They are all expressed in terms of cash—the basic economic resource of the company. Therefore, I would argue that, by putting them in the form of a suitable financial statement, such as Table 2-2, the various decision makers in this case are being provided with relevant information which adequately describes the company's past operational activity in the year to 31 January 1977.

My reasons for coming to this conclusion are reasonably straightforward but obviously open to debate. They are as follows:

1. *A complete and neutral statement.* The statement describes completely the operational cash flow of the company for the period under review, each datum being expressed in cash terms. It is, therefore, as factual a report of past operational activity as any financial statement can be. It reflects what has happened in relation to cab hiring during the year and, as such, can be used as a measure of managerial achievement. It is free of all managerial influences which result from accounting

Table 2-2

The Edinburgh Taxicab Co. Ltd.
Operational Cash Flow Statement— Year to 31 January 1977

	£
Fare revenue	810,000
Less: Costs of running cabs*	660,600
Trading cash flow	149,400
Less: Net cost of replacing cabs*	90,900
Operating cash flow before taxation	58,500
Less: Taxation paid	30,400
Operating cash flow after taxation	28,100

*Details of the composition of these figures could be given where appropriate.

valuations and allocations designed to produce smoothed income flows. It has the significant advantage of being extremely objective and verifiable. Its credibility in the minds of its users should be reasonably high as a consequence.

I would further argue that the cash-flow statement is sufficiently neutral to satisfy all needs in this situation reasonably well. It does not appear to preempt any particular decision by supplying information of restricted or limited relevance but instead provides data of common concern to the various user groups interested in the company. It describes the past operational activity of the company free of any deliberate "distortions" by management due to the application of a depreciation policy for the taxicabs. It is thus not dependent on subjective judgment in the measurement process and can be used consistently over time and even between companies. In other words, assuming an agreed definition of cash flow such as that outlined in the preceding figures, similar situations should result in similar measures of cash flow. This should considerably aid comparisons and trends for decision purposes.

Finally, the cash-flow model for reporting past operational activity describes completely the company's past without reference or inference to the future. It can be measured entirely on the basis of facts. There are no forecasts to be made about the useful lives and eventual realizable values of the taxicabs (which would be necessary if the data were to be allocated) nor is there any need to measure on the basis of values which contain implications as to possible future action concerning the cabs (as is the case with new or second-hand replacement costs and net realizable values). The cash-flow alternative looks entirely back in time and is therefore faithful to its reporting of past activity.

2. *Data for decisions.* My second main reason for selecting the cash-flow format as the most appropriate means of describing the past operational activity of the Edinburgh Taxicab Co. Ltd. is its relevance to the various needs of the user groups considered in this paper. As previously indicated, each group appears to have a considerable interest in the past cash flow of the company, and it seems sensible to report precisely in these terms. I would suggest that, at least in the case of this company, most of the various user groups would be best served by the receipt of pure cash-flow data. The only possible exception is the Inland Revenue which requires a historic cost income figure as the basis for assessing the taxation due by the company for the year to 31 January 1977. Each of the other stated groups, however, is concerned with the making and monitoring of decisions of which past cash flow is an essential input. The following paragraphs amplify this point.

a. Investors. Investors are primarily concerned with assessing dividends—that is, the past dividend record of the company and its possible future dividend payments. In particular, they need to know (1) whether dividends have or can be justified in terms of available "earnings" (a sort of capital maintenance decision) and (2) whether the company has paid or will be able to pay dividends in terms of cash (a financial decision). I would argue that the cash-flow statement prepared above gives answers to both (1) and (2) and, in that sense and in this case, is a complete report for investors. They can obtain from it the "earnings" and cash apparently available to pay dividends during the year to 31 January 1977 (that is, £28,100).

b. Employees. The cash-flow statement supplies the company's employees with clues as to job security and employment prospects, as it describes not only its operating surplus but also the deployment of part of the latter to replace its taxicab fleet as it wears out over time. It also reflects the seeming availability of surplus cash from hiring operations to pay for tax and dividends, expand the fleet should this be possible in the future (thus providing more jobs), and provide a basis for future wage claims.

c. Managers. The company's management will be concerned with monitoring and controlling the cash flow which results from its hiring activities—that is, the revenues received from customers and the various payments for petrol, oil, repairs, and maintenance. Such data will be useful for comparison with trading budgets already made for the year to 31 January 1977. Management will also require data to monitor its prior investment decisions concerning the disposal and replacement of the company's taxicabs. These capital budgeting exercises should be conducted on the basis of anticipated cash flows which can be capitalized and compared with relevant replacement costs and net realizable values. The comparison of budgeted and actual results in this situation (whether of trading or capital investment) appears to demand cash-flow data.

d. Licensing authority. Periodically, the licensing authority will review the company's taxi hire licenses, and I would suggest that a statement of past cash flow provides useful information regarding the company's ability to maintain its operations at their present level. This should be significant in the authority's decisions as whether or not to renew the license and expand the number of cabs covered by it.

3. *Comprehensibility of information.* I believe the meaning of reported accounting information to be a crucial matter when discussing its overall utility in relation to financial report users. Very few of the latter will have the knowledge and expertise of qualified accountants and, yet, financial statements tend to be couched largely in the terminology of the accountant. It may be argued that, so far as financial report usage is concerned, only the highly qualified financial expert matters, but I would suggest that *all* potential users of financial reports deserve to receive information which they can reasonably understand and use.

Thus, on the basis of its fundamental comprehensibility, I would defend the use of a cash-flow statement to describe the Edinburgh Taxicab Co. Ltd.'s past operational activity. It avoids allocations, valuations, and capital maintenance decisions, all of which are likely to add to the complexities of accounting statements. Instead, it can describe operational activity in a language which avoids such terms as depreciation, holding gains, unrealized income, and so on. It is a system which is compatible with what individuals meet in everyday matters, and I would argue it is descriptive of how an investor or employee would regard changes in his financial position. It is understandable to the nonaccountant in a way which the cost allocation process (either historic or current) is not, and it states clearly and unambiguously what is actually happening to the company and its taxicabs. As such, its potential to mislead and confuse nonaccountants who form the majority of its readership is effectively minimized.

THE PRESENT SITUATION

The next stage of the analysis is to find an appropriate statement to reflect the financial situation of the Edinburgh Taxicab Co. Ltd. at 31 January 1977, the cash-flow statement analyzed previously not being capable of doing this adequately as it ignores the taxicabs held

48   Chapter 2   (Cash Flows)

by the company at this date. As a starting point, I would suggest that the fundamental features of its financial position at 31 January 1977 are as follows:

Number of cabs owned and in use	90
Cash resources on hand	£45,600
Net assets	90 cabs + £45,600 cash
Equivalent to: Number of shares in issue	100,000

Again, I would hope to take a simple, common sense approach to this analysis—the basic question being which monetary measurements adequately reflect the above data for the benefit of the defined user groups requiring some statement of the company's present position.

As with the statement of past operating cash flow, I have looked for a description of the company's financial position at 31 January 1977 which is factual, relevant to the needs of the defined user groups, and free of unnecessary subjective judgment due to managerial interference in the measurement process. This means avoiding allocation-based systems and, instead, concentrating on allocation-free models. I narrowed the search down to two alternative balance sheets—one based on second-hand replacement costs and the other on net realizable values. The former I discarded as it is not the policy of this company to replace its cabs with equivalent second-hand vehicles. Such a policy contains little sense if the quality of service to customers demanded by the licensing authority is to be maintained. I was left, therefore, with the possibility of using the net realizable value-based balance sheet. Table 2-3 represents the position expressed in these terms at 31 January 1976 and 1977. The following comments are given in support of the figures in Table 2-3.

1. *The net realizable value balance sheet.* The net realizable value balance sheet of the company describes an aggregation of the current trade-in values of its taxicabs and its cash resources. As such, it appears to be a statement reflecting what would be realized should the cabs be traded-in at 31 January 1977. It contains implications and assumptions which are not wholly in accordance with fact—particularly the assumed trading-in situation at 31 January 1977 for all cabs when, in fact, they will be realized in an orderly fashion as and when they need to be replaced in the future (thirty of the cabs will be traded in on 1 August

Table 2-3

The Edinburgh Taxicab Co. Ltd.
Net Realizable Value Balance Sheets at 31 January

	1976	1977
	£	£
Taxicabs	93,300	113,400
Cash	17,500	45,600
Capital employed	110,800	159,000

1977, the next thirty on 1 August 1978, and the remaining thirty on 1 August 1979).

In addition, the values used assume the continuity of the company in the business of taxicab hire—they are trade-in values (that is, those arising in the normal course of trade) and, as such, imply a replacement of the cabs concerned. The alternative sale value which could be used would reflect an immediate liquidation of the cabs and, in this case, would be much less than the values actually applied. Liquidation values reflect what the company could realize if it decided to cease trading as a taxicab hirer in order to conduct some other type of activity. But it is extremely difficult to establish what these immediate liquidation values might be at 31 January 1977. The taxicab market is limited, and much depends on the condition of each vehicle put up for sale. In any case, the use of trade-in values would seem to me to reflect the deliberate intention of the company to continue in the taxicab hire business, and this is useful information in itself for decision makers.

In other words, the net realizable value balance sheet would appear to contain implications and assumptions which are open to question. However, I feel it is a useful information source which deserves to be examined further in terms of meeting the information needs of the specified user groups in this case.

2. *Relevance to users.* As previously indicated in this paper, I believe the interests of the various user groups connected with the Edinburgh Taxicab Co. Ltd., with the possible exception of the Inland Revenue, are concerned with its future prospects and survival, generally, and its future cash flow and liquidity position, particularly. I have stated that a report of past cash flows could be of assistance to them when assessing these matters, but I would suggest also that a statement of current financial position would be relevant. Such a statement should describe the financial base from which future cash flows will stem and thereby provide its users with an indication of the minimum cash flow

which will be forthcoming in the future.

This would suggest a statement indicating potential cash inflows to the company, and the net realizable value-based balance sheet would appear to be suitable for this purpose being measured in potential cash inflow terms. Investors, employees, suppliers, and so forth, want to know what the net cash inflow to the company will be over the next period and beyond; and net realizable values of the taxicabs, when aggregated to existing cash balances, will provide a useful starting point for such an inquiry.

3. *A neutral and complete statement.* The measurement unit used in the net realizable balance sheet is the money unit. The money valuations being aggregated are those existing at 31 January 1977, the relevant date of reporting. Further, they are all market-based and involve no subjective judgments. They are allocation-free and require no subjective judgments to be made by management as the pattern of trade-in values in the Edinburgh region is well-established and easily evidenced.

As was the case with the operating cash-flow statements, it should be possible to maintain internal consistency over time in the accounting procedures applied to the net realizable value balance sheet. I would argue that this is certainly the case with regard to lack of accounting allocation procedures when depreciating the company's cabs. This, and the previous point regarding the objectivity of the net realizable value balance sheet, makes it, in my opinion, a neutral and complete statement for its users in this case.

4. *Comprehensibility of the balance sheet.* One of the questions to be asked of the net realizable value balance sheet is whether or not it is likely to be understood by its potential users. Intuitively, I believe people regard balance sheets as statements of current value and that the current value with which they identify is likely to be net realizable value. In fact, I would suspect that few report users would be misled or confused by the use of net realizable values. I, therefore, believe that the net realizable value aggregate gives a meaningful total with which report users can readily identify.

ANTICIPATED OPERATIONAL ACTIVITY

The third and final information set which I suggest report users in this case should receive refers to a statement of future operational activity, describing the anticipated cash flow from operations during the next financial period. In the case of the Edinburgh Taxicab Co. Ltd., this would be the year to 31 January 1978.

To date, the publication of forecast accounting data by companies is a relatively rare occurrence. Indeed, over the years there has been a fairly consistent opposition to the reporting of such data. It has been argued that they are far too subjective and lack the credibility which is necessary if they are to be used extensively. Another argument is that they would tend to reveal too many secrets of corporate activity. The latter argument is a dubious one, given the general nature and lack of detail in any accounting report, and the former one is somewhat surprising because of the amount of forecasting which necessarily takes place in the models of past income and capital which are not allocation-free. In particular, the forecasting problems associated with accounting allocations appear to me to be little different from those inherent in producing budgeted statements.

What an accounting forecast is attempting to do is indicate to the decision maker what is likely to happen during the near-future as a result of intended operational activity. It is no more than a guideline to aid him in making his decisions and to allow him to compare actual performance once it takes place. As such, I would suggest that the forecast statement of operational activity for the Edinburgh Taxicab Co. Ltd. should provide a reasonable indication of the expected cash flow for the year to 31 January 1978. It should be prepared in accordance with the expert judgments of its management, which should be producing such forecasts in any case for its internal decision-making activities. Although such data cannot be verified in the same way as actual accounting information, I would strongly urge that it at least be vetted by an independent expert, particularly so far as the underlying commercial assumptions are concerned. In this respect, I would argue for the publication of these assumptions to support the forecast statement.

If a statement of forecast data of the type described above is to make much sense, the apparently logical conclusion is that it should be described in cash-flow terms. The production of an operational cash-flow forecast provides not only a guideline for decision making but also a standard with which actual performance (in the form of an operational cash flow) can be compared and evaluated. A forecast for the Edinburgh Taxicab Co. Ltd. might be made, as in Table 2-4. The figures are obviously estimates but are based on known changes in the taxi fare structure at the time of writing, together with predicted increases in fuel, maintenance, and taxicab replacement costs. The production of the figures did not cause me undue problems, and I would expect them to be reflected fairly accurately in the actual figures produced for the year to 31 January 1978. Admittedly, the degree of certainty associated with this type of business makes forecasting a much easier task than it would be, for example, in a more complex

Table 2-4

The Edinburgh Taxicab Co. Ltd.
Forecast Operational Cash Flow Statement—Year to 31 January 1978

	£
Fare revenue (1)	891,000
Less: Costs of running cabs (2)	743,500
Trading cash flow	147,500
Less: Net cost of replacing cabs (3)	111,600
Operating cash flow before taxation	35,900
Less: Taxation paid (4)	18,700
Operating cash flow after taxation	17,200

(1) Allowing for an expected 10 per cent increase in fare rates and a taxicab fleet of 90 cabs.

(2)
Cost of running cabs	£387,100
Drivers' commission	356,400
	£743,500

(3)
Cost of replacing 30 cabs	£135,000
Less: Sale proceeds of 30 cabs	23,400
	£111,600

(4) Based on the forecast historic cost income for the period and allowing for tax depreciation allowances.

manufacturing organization. Nevertheless, there are sufficient encouraging signs in the processing of such data to confirm my view that forecast figures are required and can be produced. Obviously, such a statement should be presented with sufficient supporting disclosures to give meaning to it. I would particularly wish to see a statement of the underlying assumptions, together with full details of the main sections of the cash-flow statement. I would also wish to include an audited statement of the main differences between forecast and actual performance and a statement by the directors of the company on the reasonableness of such differences.

A forecast cash-flow statement should reflect the company management's intentions in relation to its future operational activity. It should provide data of use in assessing matters such as the earnings and cash available for future distributions, wage claims, taxation payments, replacement and supplementation of existing fixed assets, and payments to suppliers—that is, it should be relevant to the main needs of its potential users. In the case of the Edinburgh Taxicab Co. Ltd., I believe such assessments can be made on the basis of the above forecast statement. I also believe that, despite its subjectivity, it provides decision makers with useful and relevant data. The latter can be measured; the system of measurement is consistent over time and between entities and relates well to past cash-flow statements and net realizable value balance sheets; and, as with past cash-flow statements, it has meaning for its various users because they can identify with and recognize cash flows relatively easily.

OVERALL CONCLUSIONS

I have used a very simple and straightforward situation provided by Bob Sterling to explore the essential features of accounting and financial reporting. As I suspected, it is an enormously complex task, and not even this lengthy paper can do full justice to all the problems and points for debate. However, I have tried to isolate the essential features of the company's activities and to suggest the type of information which appears to me to be best suited. What I have stated may cause argument and debate. If it does, I will regard this as at least a partial success rather than a complete failure. In order to help the discussion, I offer what I believe to be the most important aspects of my analysis. They must be taken, however, only within the limited context of the Edinburgh Taxicab Co. Ltd.

1. There is an identifiable *entity* (the Edinburgh Taxicab Co. Ltd.) with an *activity* (taxicab hiring) which is worthy of being accounted for and reported. This is the starting point for all subsequent points of analysis.

2. Identifying the company and its activity helped to identify the *persons* who require reports of its operations, as well as the type of *information* or data they need. There proved to be little difficulty in identifying these groups in a general fashion in this case.

3. The identification of potential users of the Edinburgh Taxicab Co. Ltd.'s reports revealed that they all have a need for information or data which aids them in making *decisions* and monitoring previous decisions.

4. These decisions appear to relate to information about the *past operational activity* of the company, its *present position*, and its management's views on its *future operational activity*.

5. The most fundamental feature of such information, which is

relevant to the needs of all potential report users, is the company's *cash flow*. Without such a cash flow, it could not exist in the long-term.

6. The most *reasonable mix* of information and data for all user groups is a statement of cash flow reflecting operational activity of the immediate past period (together with an equivalent forecast made for the same period and a statement of the variances between actual and forecast

Table 2-5

The Edinburgh Taxicab Co. Ltd.
Suggested Financial Statements—Year to 31 January 1977

Operational Cash Flow Statements:

	Year to 31 January			
	1977			1978
	Forecast	Actual	Variances	Forecast
	£	£	£	£
Fare revenue		810,000		891,000
Less: Costs of running cabs		660,600		743,500
Trading cash flow		149,400		147,500
Less: Net cost of replacing cabs		90,900		111,600
Operating cash flow before taxation		58,500		35,900
Less: Taxation paid		30,400		18,700
Operating cash flow after taxation		28,100		17,200

Balance Sheets:

	As at 31 January	
	1976	1977
	£	£
Taxicabs at net realizable value	93,300	113,400
Cash	17,500	45,600
Capital	110,800	159,000

Notes:

Forecast figures for the year to 31 January 1977 have not been prepared for purposes of this paper. Therefore, variances for 1977 are not available. However, in practice they would be, and explanations would be required in a supporting statement. Likewise, a statement of the assumptions underlying the 1978 forecast would need to be disclosed. It would also be of advantage to have a summary of several years' actual results in order to allow adequate comparisons to be made by report users.

figures); a financial position statement in net realizable value terms at the period-end; and a forecast statement of cash flow reflecting anticipated operational activity (together with a statement of the underlying assumptions). These are given in summary in Table 2-5.

As I have stated before, this paper cannot do full justice to all the points which need to be made. However, the key features have been noted (the need for reports for decision-making purposes, the problems of accounting allocations, the simplicity of cash flow, and the relevance of net realizable values). I hope that you, the reader, have found them of use when discussing the case of the Edinburgh Taxicab Co. Ltd.

THE CONTRIBUTION OF FISHER TO CASH FLOW ACCOUNTING

T.A. LEE*

In terms of his contribution to economic thought, Irving Fisher must undoubtedly rank as one of the outstanding economic theorists of this or any other century. As some of his contemporaries at Harvard University were moved to write in 1947 (the year of his death):[1]

> "No American has contributed more to the advancement of his chosen subject than Fisher. His use of the mathematical techniques in the analysis of economic data was among the first of such applications in this country and it has remained among the best. His *Mathematical Investigations into the Theory of Prices* must, in fact, be recognised as among the best works of its time in any country.
> Fisher's *The Nature of Capital and Income* added to his international reputation, to the reputation of Yale University, and to the study of economics in this country. Together with his masterpiece, *The Rate of Interest*, it established Fisher's position by the side of J.B. Clark and F.W. Taussig as a founder of modern economic study in the United States. That he continued in his *Making of Index Numbers* and in later works the vein of originality so characteristic of his earlier productions is a tribute to his vitality and to the environment in which he worked."

However, Fisher's influence has not been limited to the study of economics. He was also an expert on health and fitness matters[2], and an inventor of some note[3]. More important to this paper is his considerable yet relatively unknown place in the evolution of contemporary accounting thought. Indeed, in his famous work on the nature of capital and income, he made considerable use of accounting techniques, explaining his approach as follows:[4]

> "Our present object, however, is to show, not the methods of practical bookkeeping, but merely the application of economic principles to such bookkeeping. The chief object is to find the philosophical basis of accounting. Careful examination shows that accounting is at bottom not a mere makeshift but a complete, consistent, and logical system. When thus conceived and understood it will be seen to be of importance, not alone to the accountant but also to the economist."

His interest in accounting was therefore very genuine and, as a result, much of his work is of use to accounting theorists, particularly in relation to the areas

*The author is Professor of Accountancy and Finance at the University of Edinburgh. (Paper received December 1978, revised February 1979).

of income measurement and capital valuation. Evidence of this can be seen in
the writings of generations of accountants from Canning[5] to Sterling[6]. Indeed,
the extent of his influence has been sufficient to arouse warnings of the dangers
of attempting to relate his essentially economic ideas to the problems of
contemporary accounting[7]. It has also given rise to particular doubts about the
relevance of his ideas to the measurement of enterprise income[8].

One area of accounting thought, however, remains relatively neglected with respect
to the pioneering work of Fisher. This concerns the fairly recent advocacy of
cash flow accounting as an alternative solution to the problems of accounting
allocations generally, and periodic income measures particularly[9]. The purpose of
this paper, therefore, is to explore the connection between Fisher and cash flow
accounting and, in so doing, to reveal that Fisher had much to teach accountants
regarding the resolution of the accounting entity concept problem[10]. As such it
is a paper reflecting a matter of historical interest as well as of contemporary
relevance to financial reporting improvements.

The Accounting Entity Concept Problem

One of the most vexed and ill-resolved of accounting problems concerns the
interpretation of the accounting entity concept when reporting in financial terms—
that is, not only what is to be accounted and reported, but also for whom the
resultant financial reports are to be produced[11]. Sadly, these matters have not
been given the attention they deserve by the professional accountancy bodies, as
has been revealed in a recent survey of accounting standards[12]. In the latter study,
it was found that the concept had been consistently ignored, with a consequent
lack of consistency in its implied treatment in recent recommended accounting
practices. This puzzling gap in professional accounting thought has done little to
aid the resolution of contemporary financial reporting problems.

There are two main ways in which the accounting concept can be interpreted in
practice—first, the proprietary viewpoint which, as the term suggests, emphasises
one or more of the proprietorial interests reflected in the financial statements of
the reporting entity (that is, either narrowly in terms of ownership groups or more
widely in terms of owners, lenders, creditors, and employees); and secondly, the
enterprise approach which concentrates on the financial results of the reporting
entity without any commitment to any proprietary group. Thus, a study of the
accounting entity concept reveals its essentially behavioural nature, and reflects
the extremes of attitude which can influence the financial reporting function—
different interpretations of the concept resulting in essentially different portrayals
of the same economic activity—particularly in relation to the measurement of
enterprise income and financial position, and the ratio data which can be derived
from such measures (for example, return on capital employed).

The accounting entity concept also reflects the conflict which can occur between different accounting objectives and concepts. For example, the entity concept can be said to support the objective of information relevance in the sense that the proprietary version (in either its narrow or broad form) tends to emphasise the need to satisfy the specific needs of potential report users—that is, ensuring that reported information is likely to bear upon the decisions of defined user groups[13]. One the other hand, it can also be argued that the neutrality concept in accounting relies on the enterprise approach to the entity concept—that is, reported accounting information should be objectively measured in order to portray adequately the activity of the enterprise for the benefit of all interested user groups (no particular group being advantaged or prejudiced in the reporting emphasis)[14].

In this way, two distinct and separable versions of the accounting entity concept, each capable of providing different accounting interpretations of the same economic reality, are each supporting basic parts of accounting thought which, in turn, are separable and relatively incompatible (at least in terms of the definitions ascribed in this paper to relevance and neutrality). In financial accounting practice at the present time, the relevance objective appears to be primary to the neutrality concept in the quest to ensure that specific financial report user needs are adequately satisfied in practice (such as shareholders and employees). This means that the proprietary approach, when extended to include various non-ownership "proprietorial" interests (including employees), is the one which is to be evidenced most widely in existing accounting practice. It is of both historical and contemporary interest, therefore, to see that Fisher advocated an accounting entity approach which implied a greater recognition of the enterprise as the central feature of reporting practice.

Fisher and the Accounting Entity Concept Problem

As is the case with a considerable amount of contemporary accounting thought (for example, when relating information to decision activity), Fisher's economic thrust was distinctly behavioural in nature. His analyses of economic problems concentrated on the individual human being as the final economic consumer, and many of his writings were obviously influenced as much by psychological ideas as those of economics. His concept of psychic income (his ultimate interpretation of income) is an example of this particular approach:[15]

> "For each individual only those events which come within the purview of his experience are of direct concern. It is these events – the psychic experiences of the individual mind – which constitute ultimate income for that individual. The outside events have significance for that individual only in so far as they are the means to these inner events of the mind. The human nervous system is, like a radio, a great receiving instrument. Our brains serve to transform into the stream of our psychic life those outside events, which happen to us and stimulate our nervous system."

Fisher thereby recognised the business enterprise only as an intermediate receptacle for the income of individual consumers. Using double-entry bookkeeping techniques, he demonstrated how the various intermediate income services cancel out, leaving what he described as the psychic items of enjoyment and labour pain[16]. In this respect, he was exceedingly adamant in his distinction between what he termed real persons (individual human beings capable of enjoying the act of comsumption) and fictitious persons (such as partnerships and companies). He stated his feelings in this respect as follows:[17]

> "Directors and managers providing income for thousands of people sometimes think of their corporation merely as a giant moneymaking machine. In their eyes, its one purpose is to earn money dividends for the stockholders, money interest for the bondholders, money wages and money salaries for the employees. What happens after these payments are made seems too private a matter to concern them. Yet that is the nub of the whole arrangement. It is only what we carry out of the market place into our homes and private lives which really counts. Money is of no use to us until it is spent. The ultimate wages are not paid in terms of money but in the enjoyment it buys. The dividend check becomes income in the ultimate sense only when we eat the food, wear the clothes, or ride in the automobile which are bought with the check."

Fisher thus recognised the impossibility of quantifying enjoyment income and, instead, recommended a surrogate measure — real income based on the measurement of an individual's cost of living. He went on to state:[18]

> "It is interesting to observe that a corporation as such can have no net income. Since a corporation is a fictitious, not a real, person, each of its items without exception is doubly entered. Its stockholders may get income from it, but the corporation itself, considered as a separate person apart from these stockholders, receives none."

At first glance, it seems that Fisher would have found it hard not to adopt some version of the proprietary approach to the accounting entity concept had he been asked to examine it in relation to business financial statements. His approach to economic matters, so eloquently and so often described in accounting terms in his books, constitutes what can only be described as the ultimate proprietary viewpoint—shareholders, lenders, suppliers and employees being the persons consuming the monetary benefits to be derived from the existence of the business enterprise. To Fisher, accounting revealed that what was important in economic terms was not the benefits realised by the enterprise from its trading activities (and distributed to its shareholders, lenders, suppliers and employees) but the ways in which these individuals consumed the benefits in their private lives[19].

"Neither these intermediate processes of creation and alteration nor the money transactions following them are of significance except as they are the necessary or helpful preliminaries to psychic income—human enjoyment. We must be careful lest, in fixing our eyes on such preliminaries, especially money transactions, we overlook the much more important enjoyment which it is their business to yield."

Despite this intensely proprietorial outlook, the Fisherian system of accounting did admit to the existence of business entities and the need to account for their activities. For example, in several of his chapters dealing with capital and income, Fisher illustrated his arguments with examples of business balance sheets and income statements[20]. In doing so, his work appears to refute the proprietary approach so evident in his economic concentration on the ultimate consumers of services. Because he regarded the business entity as a form of "clearing house" for the distribution of the monetary benefits from which enjoyment could be derived, his financial statements took on a distinctly enterprise-orientated look. For example, he portrayed the balance sheet of a railway company as follows:[21]

RAILROAD COMPANY

Assets		Liabilities	
Railway	$50,000	Bonds (held by Z)	$20,000
		Capital stock	
		(held by X) $20,000	
		(held by Y) 10,000	30,000
	$50,000		$50,000

In other words, the railway company had assets of $50,000 and obligations of $50,000. It had, according to Fisher, no capital of its own. He then went on to describe the capital of the individuals in his example as:[22]

X's capital balance	$ 70,000
Y's capital balance	40,000
Z's capital balance	80,000
R. R. Co.'s capital balance	000
	$190,000

And the personal assets represented thereby as:

Residence	$ 70,000
Personal effects	20,000
Farm	50,000
Railway	50,000
	$190,000

He therefore regarded the business entity, both in economic and accounting terms, as an inanimate enterprise rather than as a collection of individuals. Only at the level of the individual consumer was he prepared to substitute a proprietary approach in his accounting. He justified this distinction as follows:[23]

> "It is well to note here the distinction between the accounting of real persons and of fictitious persons. For a real person, the assets may be and usually are in excess of the liabilities, and the difference is the capital-balance of that person. This capital is not to be regarded as a liability, but as a balance or difference between the liabilities and the assets. For a fictitious person, on the other hand, as for instance a corporation or partnership, the liabilities are always exactly equal to the assets; for the balancing item called capital is as truly an obligation from the fictitious person to the real stockholder, as any of the other liabilities. A fictitious person, in fact, is a mere bookkeeping dummy, holding certain assets and owing all of them out again to real persons."

The lesson to be drawn from this is reasonably clear. Fisher regarded business entities as devices by which human beings could obtain enjoyment from consumption. Although in accounting terms these entities could be recognised from the point of view of measuring the economic resources underlying individual capital, and the outgo representing monetary benefits for individuals, Fisher regarded them in a completely non-proprietary way. His accounting for their activities can only be regarded as an enterprise interpretation of the accounting entity concept.

Fisher and Cash Flow Accounting

Fisher re-emphasised his enterprise approach when he continued his analysis of capital into the related area of income. As previously mentioned, he believed business entities could have no net income; any surplus achieved from trading activity being exactly balanced by the distribution made by it to its owners, lenders, suppliers and employees. In this respect, he made the following statements, again distinguishing between what he regarded as real and fictitious persons:[24]

> "When we turn from real to fictitious persons, we find, for income accounts, as for capital accounts, that the two sides necessarily balance exactly. A corporation, as an entity distinct from its stockholders, cannot enjoy income or suffer outgo. All the income not devoted to other expenses is absorbed in paying dividends."

He then produced an income statement of a railway company by way of illustration:[25]

INCOME STATEMENT OF RAILROAD CORPORATION FOR YEAR

Income		Outgo	
By passenger and freight service	$1,246,147	To operating expenses	$800,000
		To interest to bondholders	100,000
		To dividends to stockholders	200,000
		To surplus applied to (1) purchase of land	140,000
		(2) cash in treasury	6,147
	$1,246,147		$1,246,147

In this statement, a number of points of interest can be seen. First, it lacks any proprietary influence all payments being regarded as outgo to individuals for potential consumption. In this respect, Fisher felt that even the cash balance (taken from the cash register to the bank) was an outgo from the business[26]. In other words, Fisher's income statement did not produce income measurements attributable to any particular proprietary group. In this respect, he was perfectly clear as to the nature of the income statement — in his view it was designed to reflect enterprise activity:[27]

> "We see, then, that the guiding principle for the construction of the income account, either of real or fictitious persons, is simply to make a complete list of the services and disservices which flow from each and every item of the assets and liabilities."

The second point of interest in the Fisherian financial statement is that its measurement basis is allocation-free; that is, it contains no accounting allocations such as depreciation of fixed assets. Indeed, the inclusion of the purchase of land, and the year-end cash balance from trading activity, give clear indications that this is a cash flow statement, and that the accounting is cash flow-based. This tends to support the contention of Whittington that Fisher was the father of cash flow accounting[28].

Thus, in this one particular financial statement, Fisher demonstrated that it is possible to reflect the trading activities of a business entity in a way which truly reflects an enterprise approach to the accounting entity concept — that is, by utilising a cash flow statement.

Conclusions

Cash flow accounting proposals have been made on many occasions over recent years[29]. In some instances, the arguments for such a system of accounting have attempted to justify the need for it as a system in its own right[30]. At other times, the arguments for it have been equally arguments against the faults of accounting systems which utilise arbitrary allocations of data. On this occasion, the work of Fisher provides a further, and arguably more persuasive, argument for its use in practice—an argument based on economic analysis as well as accounting theory.

In terms of economic analysis, Fisher's work suggests that the business entity is only an economic vehicle for the individual consumer and that, because it lacks human qualities, the proprietary approach to accounting for its activities is somewhat inappropriate. Indeed, Fisher would appear to support the use of an enterprise approach based on what can only be described as an enterprise-orientated measurement basis—cash flow accounting (at least so far as trading activity is concerned). Such a system of accounting avoids the arbitrary periodic allocations of accounting data which are so necessary to the smoothing of income streams for dividend and other "proprietorial" purposes. Instead, it concentrates on reporting of the activity of the enterprise over a defined period of time.

From the accounting point of view, it would therefore appear that cash flow accounting is a suitable means (although not the only one) of reflecting an enterprise interpretation of the accounting entity concept. It also appears to reflect the enterprise version of economic reality propounded by Fisher. In doing so, it would also seem to provide reasonable compatability between the accounting objective of relevance and the accounting concept of neutrality. Cash flow-based "income" statements can be said to be relevant to user needs in the sense that they reflect the total revenue of the enterprise and the various ways in which it has been distributed to all interested parties (in the form of payments to suppliers, employees, government, lenders and owners). It can also be said to be neutral in the sense that its measurement basis is neutral (avoiding arbitrary allocations), and it does not attempt to emphasise in its disclosures any particular proprietary groups. To adopt a more proprietorial approach to reporting (for example, by using allocations to produce smoothed income streams for dividend purposes) may improve the relevance of the reported data vis-à-vis the needs of a particular user group (in this example, shareholders) but diminishes its neutrality in the sense adopted for purposes of this paper.

Obviously the work of Fisher in this respect should not be taken too much out of context—he was, after all, primarily concerned with economic issues. Nevertheless, his views on economic consumption and saving did result in his advocation of a form of enterprise accounting for firms, and the adoption of a form of cash flow accounting to do so. Such an early recognition of such an accounting system by a non-accountant should, at the very least, provide a pause for thought at a time when cash flow accounting is hardly in the forefront of the minds of most members of the accountancy profession as a means of improving the quality of financial reporting. The question, therefore, is not whether Fisher's particular system of cash flow accounting is of relevance to the issues of today. Rather it is that his economic arguments support the use of cash flow accounting as a means of implementing an enterprise approach to the accounting entity concept.

NOTES AND REFERENCES

1. Quoted in I.N. Fisher, *My Father, Irving Fisher*, Comet Press Books, 1956, p.338.
2. For example I. Fisher, *The Effect of Diet on Endurance*, Yale University Press, 1907; and I. Fisher and E.L. Fisk, *How to Live*, Funk and Wagnalls, 1915.
3. His Index Invisible Company was a forerunner of the Sperry Rand Corporation.
4. I. Fisher, *The Nature of Capital and Income*, Macmillan, 1912, p.140.
5. J.B. Canning, *The Economics of Accountancy*, The Ronald Press, 1929.
6. R.R. Sterling, *Theory of the Measurement of Enterprise Income*, University of Kansas Press, 1970, particularly pp.211-45.
7. R.J. Chambers, "Income and Capital : Fisher's Legacy", *Journal of Accounting Research*, Spring 1971, pp 137-49.
8. T.A. Lee, "A Note on the Nature and Determination of Income", *Journal of Business Finance and Accounting*, Spring 1974, pp 145-7; and T.A. Lee, "The Contribution of Fisher to Enterprise Income Theory : A Comment", *Journal of Business Finance and Accounting*, Autumn 1975, pp.373-6.
9. For example, T.A. Lee, "The Cash Flow Accounting Alternative for Corporate Financial Reporting," *Trends in Managerial and Financial Accounting : Volume 1*, C. van Dam (ed)., Martinus Nijhoff, 1978, pp.63-84.
10. He did not, however, comment specifically on this concept of accounting.
11. For a general coverage of this problem area, see P.E. Meyer, "The Accounting Entity", *Abacus*, December 1973, pp.116-26.
12. T.A. Lee, "The Accounting Entity Concept, Accounting Standards, and Inflation Accounting", *Accounting and Business Research*, forthcoming.
13. As defined in *A Statement of Basic Accounting Theory*, American Accounting Association, 1966, pp.9-10.
14. As defined, ibid, p.11.
15. I. Fisher, *The Theory of Interest*, Macmillan, 1930, p.4.
16. Ibid, p.20.
17. Ibid, p.5
18. Ibid, p.23
19. Ibid, p.5.
20. Fisher (Nature of Capital and Income), op cit, pp.66-98 and 119-64.
21. Ibid, p.23.
22. Ibid, p.94.
23. Ibid, p.92
24. Ibid, p.138

[25] Ibid, p.138.

[26] Ibid, p.139.

[27] Ibid, 139.

[28] G. Whittington, "Accounting and Economics", *Current Issues in Accounting*, B. Carsberg and T. Hope (eds.), Philip Allan, 1977, p.202.

[29] For example, Lee (The Cash Flow Accounting Alternative), op cit.

[30] Ibid.

[31] For example, A.L. Thomas, "The Allocation Problem : Part Two", *Studies in Accounting Research 9*, American Accounting Association, 1974, pp.119-21.

A Major Extension

Jaarverslag
Informatieverstrekking
Herkomst en besteding der middelen

REPORTING CASH FLOWS AND NET REALIZABLE VALUES*

by: Professor T. A. Lee

Introduction

The outstanding feature of corporate reporting in recent times has been the attempt by the major professional accountancy bodies to improve the relevance and quality of published reports by accounting for the various effects of inflation. This has taken place in most countries within the context of persistent price changes, and has revealed remarkably similar approaches to the problem - all recent suggestions of the professional accountancy bodies being rooted firmly in the use of entry prices[1] as an extension of the existing historic cost system.[2] In other words, inflation accounting has been the most significant reporting development of recent times, and has usually been conceived as an extension of a long-standing system - i.e. based on historic costs which have been adapted to current costs, and retaining the familiar accounting process of allocation in the measurement of such past data.[3]

The above brief commentary is intended only as a background to this paper, and no doubt it has and will continue to be commented on at length by the proponents and critics of inflation accounting.[4] However, what is intriguing and worthy of more comment is the existence during the same period of time of sustained arguments by a very few accountants for two systems of financial reporting which do not depend upon the familiar basis of allocated historic costs, being advocated as either alternatives or additions rather than extensions to it. These systems are usually described as cash flow accounting (CFA) and net realizable value accounting (NRVA). Their presence as serious contenders for improving the relevance and quality of financial reporting is made even more significant in the sense that, despite a lack of wide-spread explicit support from professional accountants, there appear to have been no major arguments constructed against them which could cast doubt on their

---

* A modified version of this paper will be published in Accountancy and Business Research. It has benefited greatly from the comments of my colleagues at Edinburgh. In particular, I must thank Rolland Munro for presenting a seminar on financial reporting and the theory of money which forced me to commit my previously unstructured and lazy thoughts on this topic to paper, and Rod Ferrier who helped to formalize my ideas on the realizability of assets.

[1] For example, historic costs are entry prices, and alternative suggestions of an entry nature include current purchasing power accounting (historic costs in current purchasing power terms) - see "Accounting for Changes in the Purchasing Power of Money", *Provisional Statement of Standard Accounting Practice 7*, 1974; and current cost accounting (usually based on current replacement costs) - see "Current Cost Accounting", *Exposure Draft 24*, 1979.

[2] Current cost accounting is a good example of this with its adjustments of historic cost income for the current cost of monetary working capital - see *Exposure Draft 24, op cit.*

[3] The term "allocation" is used consistently throughout this paper to mean the familiar accounting process of attributing financial data to particular accounting events, entities and periods. It does not cover the manipulation of accounting reports by management by means of altering the timing of transactions (a matter which is exceedingly difficult to detect and verify).

[4] There have also been suggestions for additional financial statements to supplement the existing system of corporate financial reporting, but this paper is largely concerned with the major and primary aspects of such a system. For examples of these additional statements, see Accounting Standards Committee, *The Corporate Report*, 1975, pp. 47-60.

validity and feasibility.⁵ By way of contrast, the various recent suggestions for allocation-based entry price systems have attracted a considerable amount of adverse criticism and, on occasion, such criticism has caused rejection and withdrawal of the proposal concerned.⁶

The suggestions for CFA and NRVA typically have been made separately by their advocates, who have usually related them to specific report user needs and/or the faults of other reporting systems.⁷ Rarely has any attempt been made to link the arguments for each system in such a way as to produce a convincing case for an overall system of financial reporting which contains, inter alia, both statements of cash flows and net realizable values.⁸ The purpose of this paper is therefore to attempt to demonstrate that CFA and NRVA are compatible, and can be connected in a unified system of financial reporting which has considerable advantages for its potential users - i.e. a cash-orientated, allocation-free system capable of describing both the operational activity and financial position of the reporting enterprise.

Defining CFA and NRVA

Before proceeding to the argument for combining CFA and NRVA, it would appear sensible to outline briefly the aims and structure of each system. This provides a necessary background to an understanding of later sections of the paper.

CFA is a system of reporting on the past and future activity of a business enterprise in pure cash terms - i.e. only accounting for transactions for which there has or is expected to be a cash inflow or outflow. All reported transactions therefore reconcile to a periodic change in cash resources (these including bank balances and deposits). Thus, CFA avoids arbitrary allocations of accounting data, as well as accounting accruals due to credit transactions.

---

5 The reader is invited to seek in the literature for substantial arguments against CFA and NRVA. Indeed, Chambers has pointed out the lack of such arguments in relation to NRVA (see R. J. Chambers, "Second Thoughts on Continuously Contemporary Accounting", *Abacus*, September 1970, pp. 39-55), and there appears to be a reluctance to accept CFA and NRVA despite their admitted good points (see "Inflation Accounting", *Report of the Inflation Accounting Committee*, HMSO, 1975, pp. 156-8, for evidence of this in relation to CFA, and E. O. Edwards and P. W. Bell, *The Theory and Measurement of Business Income*, University of California Press, 1961, pp. 70-109, in relation to NRVA).

6 For example, the rejection of current purchasing power accounting (as in the setting aside of *Provisional Statement 7, op cit*), and of two versions of current cost accounting (as in Accounting Standards Committee, „Current Cost Accounting", *Exposure Draft 18*, 1976 and Accounting Standards Committee, *Inflation Accounting - an Interim Recommendation*, 1977).

7 See, for example, in relation to CFA, G. H. Lawson, "Cash-flow Accounting", *The Accountant*, 28.10.71, pp. 586-9 and T. A. Lee, "A Case for Cash Flow Reporting", *Journal of Business Finance*, Summer 1972, pp. 27-36, and in relation to NRVA, R. J. Chambers, *Accounting, Evaluation and Economic Behaviour*, Prentice Hall, 1966, esp. pp. 78-102 and R. R. Sterling, *Theory of the Measurement of Enterprise Income*, University of Kansas Press, 1970, esp. pp. 319-31.

8 Only in a casual way has it been attempted before - see H. C. Edey, "Accounting Principles and Business Reality", *Accountancy*, December 1963, p. 1087; T. A. Climo, "Cash Flow Statement for Investors", *Journal of Business Finance and Accounting*, Autumn 1976, pp. 11 and 13; T. A. Lee, "The Cash Flow Accounting Alternative for Corporate Financial Reporting", in C. Van Dam (ed.), *Trends in Managerial and Financial Accounting*, Martinus Nijhoff, 1978, p. 84; and "The Simplicity and Complexity of Accounting", in R. R. Sterling and A. Thomas (eds.), *Accounting for a Simplified Firm*, Scholars Book Co., 1979, pp. 47-50.

Equally, the idea of continuing CFA and NRVA ought not to be confused with the suggestion by Ronen and Sorter of combining a market rate-determined economic value of the reporting entity with the exit values of its conventionally classified assets and liabilities - see J. Ronen and G. H. Sorter, "Relevant Accounting", *Journal of Business*, April 1972, pp. 258-82; see also J. Ronen, "Discounted Cash Flow Accounting", in J. J. Cramer, Jr. and G. H. Sorter (eds.), *Objectives of Financial Statements*, American Institute of Certified Public Accountants, 1974, pp. 143-60. The Ronen and Sorter proposal was intended to provide investors with (a) means of comparing market values with economic values of the reporting entity and its equity; (b) managerial reporting of cash flows (but only in the form of reporting one discounted measure of value); and (c) measurement of the conversion of entity asset economic values into exit values, and vice versa. Nowhere in their system was there a recommendation to specifically disclose past or forecast CFA data.

The fundamental importance of cash management is consequently emphasised and, in particular, the reader of CFA statements is made aware not only of the uses to which cash has been put but also of the internal and external sources from which it has been obtained.

As mentioned above, CFA can be envisaged in both ex ante and ex post forms, and in each there should be adequate disclosure to support and sustain the outline cash data contained in the published statements. The aim of these statements is to provide all identifiable users of financial reports with a suitable explanation of past and future cash management within the enterprise - this aspect of its activity being vital to its long-term survival, and to the protection and development of the various interests in it of these user groups. In this sense, apart from the potential for management to manipulate the timing of cash inflows and outflows in the short-term in order to distort the reported data, CFA can be regarded as a reasonably objective, verifiable, and neutral[9] reporting system. It can also be seen to be relevant to the needs of all those persons interested in the adequacy of the financial management of the reporting enterprise.

By way of contrast, NRVA is a system of reporting which concentrates on both cash and non-cash resources of the business enterprise. Using sale values which assume an orderly rather than a forced liquidation of assets, its financial position is accounted for as an aggregation of the potential money it has at its command in order to pay its way, and to develop and change over time - sale values representing potential cash available for these purposes should management believe this to be necessary. Thus, NRVA reflects the ability of the enterprise to survive in the long-term - survival being dependent on the existence of money with which to acquire resources and pay obligations.

NRVA also demonstrates the ability of the entity to adapt from its existing activities to other activities (either on a small or large scale). Net realizable values are, in the sense used throughout this paper, expressions of opportunity cost - the sacrifice the enterprise is making by holding its resources in their existing form rather than in some alternative one. Sale values are therefore either the first stage in the possible conversion of resources from one form into another or the means of paying obligations. The "surplus" figure which can be derived from comparisons of net realizable value-based financial positions describes the increase (or decrease) in the enterprise's command over money. These data provide report users of various types with essential information about its financial position, and of periodic changes in that position - particularly its capacity to grow and to change, and to survive by being able to pay its obligations at due dates.

Points of similarity

The separate arguments for cash flows and net realizable values in accounting have been made extensively elsewhere.[10] It is therefore not intended to repeat

---

[9] The term "neutral" is intended to indicate that no specific user has been contemplated in the measurement and disclosure of accounting data.

[10] See, for example, references in footnote 7.

them in this paper, except to the extent that they represent points of similarity for consideration in the case for linking the two systems. These points are given below, not so much as specific arguments for combining the systems, but more as reminders that they may be parts of the same reporting system.

1. CFA and NRVA are both allocation-free systems; neither containing subjective allocations of data by their producers. Both systems are therefore based on data which are free of the influence of accounting manipulations by managements which regard them as such a necessary part of traditional systems of accounting. This lack of accounting "interference" would appear to improve their potential objectivity, verifiability, and credibility, thereby presumably adding to its quality so far as financial report users are concerned. For example, the latter can be left in no doubt about the quality of financial reports containing only data which have arisen from either enterprise or market activity; which have not been subjected to arbitrary allocations by management and accountants; and which have been adequately evidenced by an independent auditor. Problems of flexibility in accounting measurement practice, and the attendant need for relevant standardization of such practice, are therefore not to be seen in either CFA or NRVA.[11] The problems of auditing in an environment of such flexibility are also avoided by these systems. This is not to say, however, that the use of net realizable values in NRVA will not involve problems of subjectivity (due to value estimating) for accountants and auditors alike.

2. CFA and NRVA each emphasise the condition of survival required of an enterprise. It is vital that those persons interested in it are provided with relevant information as to how its management has ensured its survival in the past, and how it plans to cope in the future. This will in part determine the "life-time" and extent of their various interests in it. CFA, for example, emphasises survival in terms of the availability of cash to pay for purchases, wages, overheads, taxation, interest, dividends, investment, and so on. The quality of cash management will determine the success of the enterprise at paying its way, and all interested user groups are represented in the above list of cash outflows.

   NRVA, too, describes the survival attribute in business - the sale values of the enterprise's assets reflecting the "cover" available for its commitments, as well as the base from which growth, development and change occur in its activities. Although an admittedly incomplete description of the resources of the entity, the realizable value aggregate for its assets is both the "security" for owners, lenders and suppliers, and the "platform" for future enterprise activity. Any increase in such a position (as measured in terms of a periodic surplus) is a description of an improvement in both the "security" and the "platform". Survival prospects are thus enhanced.

3. Both CFA and NRVA are systems of reporting which are concerned primarily with the reporting *of* enterprise activity and market effects related to it, rather than *for* the specific needs of particular user groups.

---

[11] The term "flexibility" is used throughout this paper to indicate the condition of accounting variability which results from the arbitrary allocations of data defined in footnote 3 above.

Both sets of data can be said to conform more with the "entity" view of reporting than with any of its socalled "equity" variants.[12] They therefore appear to have the considerable reporting attribute of neutrality - no particular user group or set of user decisions being contemplated in the preparation of the information concerned.

CFA, for example, describes the various cash inflows and outflows arising from the operations and other activities of the reporting enterprise. It is a system which attempts to describe such activity in factual terms which do not require to be fashioned to meet the information needs of a specific user group.[13] In particular, because it does not directly involve income and capital measurement concepts and procedures (which inevitably are orientated toward categories of specific ownership and related interests), CFA retains a user neutrality and, indeed, may be described reasonably as a "general purpose" reporting system capable of satisfying several user group needs. As previously indicated, its main aim is to describe, in summary form, the cash management of the enterprise which should be a matter of direct concern to all interested groups.

NRVA also has this "entity" characteristic - it is a system which is intended to describe the reporting enterprise's command over money which reflects its ability to fulfil its obligations, and its capacity to adapt its existing activities to alternative operations should this be required (either wholly or partly). Net realizable value balance sheets describe enterprise resources in monetary terms which inform all users of its ability to pay its way, and to evolve from one form to another, and the related periodic "surplus" measurement describe improvements or deterioration in this. All businesses have to meet their various obligations at due dates, and all businesses replace and augment their existing resources. Sale values represent the intermediate resource form (cash) which is required by the enterprise to complete these functions.

4. One of the most vital aspects of corporate activity is the reliance of the enterprise on cash resources for its survival - without cash no enterprise can survive in the long-term; no matter how good its products, and no matter how effective its management.[14] CFA and NRVA are systems of accounting which emphasise the importance of cash and cash flow to the enterprise. CFA obviously does this as it describes in detail the cash flow in and out of the enterprise over defined periods. NRVA, on the other hand, ought to be regarded also as a system which highlights the importance of cash - in this case describing the activity and financial position of the reporting enterprise in what is often termed "current cash equivalents".[15] In other words, cash can be regarded in NRVA as the

---

[12] The importance of the entity concept has long been ignored in the practice of financial reporting, as evidenced in T. A. Lee, "The Accounting Entity Concept, Accounting Standards, and Inflation Accounting", *Accounting and Business Research*, Spring 1980, pp. 1-11.

[13] A recent example of such bias in practice is seen in the latest version of current cost accounting in the UK (*Exposure Draft 24, op cit*), and a recent paper has directed accountants' attention to the bias of reporting on distributable income and the dividend decision (see D. A. Eggington, "Distributable Profit and the Persuit of Prudence", *Accounting and Business Research*, forthcoming).

[14] Cash in this sense includes cash equivalents (for example, bank transactions). It is used in this paper to denote a vital means of exchange for business enterprises, as well as its role as a unit of accounting measurement. For example, an examination of corporate failures inevitably leads to the lack of adequate cash resources and cash flow as a major contribution to such failure.

[15] A term coined by Chambers - see, Chambers (*Accounting, Evaluation and Economic Behaviour*), *op cit*, p. 92.

intermediary between existing and alternative resource forms, and net realizable values are intended to reflect the potential of the enterprise to translate its existing resources into cash available to acquire alternative or replacement resources, or to pay obligations and make distributions.

5. One of the most often-quoted arguments made for NRVA is its lack of attention to the continuity assumption used in traditional allocation-based accounting practice - i.e. the general proposition which assumes for accounting purposes that the reporting enterprise will continue in business indefinitely. Continuity is therefore used in traditional practice to at least partly justify accounting allocations (for example, in the carrying forward of fixed asset and inventory costs). NRVA, however, challenges the absolute validity of such an assumption given that enterprises tend to change over time, either taking on other forms or disappearing altogether. Thus, because NRVA does not presume any specific action on the part of the enterprise and its management with regard to the nature of its business activity and resource form, it can be said to contravene the continuity assumption. However, this is too narrow an outlook on continuity - sale values are reported in NRVA systems to indicate their availability for a variety of investment, financing and distribution functions in the future. NRVA does not therefore assume liquidation of the enterprise. In fact, the opposite is the case - continuity of the entity is assumed but not the continuity of its existing business activity and resource form. The latter can be changed in the future, and the sale values reported are intended to reflect this without prejudging the issue.

    CFA also appears to challenge the idea of continuity because of its use of cash flows without any process of accounting allocation - i.e. treating payments as committed costs, and receipts as recoveries of these costs. However, as with NRVA, CFA treats the future with a neutral approach, preferring to describe the past in purely factual terms, and to leave the future as a matter of subjective judgment (in the form of reported forecasts). CFA and NRVA therefore do not depend on the debatable assumption of an indefinite life for the reporting enterprise in order to determine the method of accounting. Instead, the method of accounting in each case reflects an expectation of a future for the entity, but not necessarily for existing resources and activities.

6. Corporate financial reporting has two main objectives - the provision of relevant information for a variety of decision functions of external interests, and as an exercise in accountability to the owners (and, possibly, also lenders, creditors and employees) of the enterprise.[16] It can be argued that CFA and NRVA both provide data for these purposes. The systems of CFA which have been advocated over the years have all included not only past data but also forecasts, thus aiding both the decision and accountability functions - i.e. forecasts (together with trends established from past data series) aiding decisions, and comparisons of forecast and actual data providing the basis for an accountability exercise whereby

---

[16] Explicitly recognised in *The Corporate Report*, op cit, and in Accounting Objectives Study Group, *Objectives of Financial Statements*, American Institute of Certified Public Accountants, 1973. This assumes accountability to be a function sufficiently important to be separated from the various other decision-orientated functions.

previously stated expectations can be used to evaluate results achieved. In addition, due to the lack of accounting allocation, past cash flows can be argued for as the most objective information base for formulating investment and other decisions, and for accountability purposes when comparing relevant forecast and actual data.

NRVA is equally a system which attempts to satisfy decision making and accountability functions. It provides data representing descriptions of the assets which are available for use and sale by the enterprise at particular points of time, as well as descriptions of the financial consequences during defined periods of such use and sale. The end-of-period position highlights the financial platform from which the enterprise can move forward into the next period in terms of its command over money, thus reflecting its potential to adapt in the future and to meet its financial obligations.

7. Following on from the previous point, one of the main features of financial information usage is the idea of data comparability - i.e. the user of information ought to be able to compare data when assessing it; between different enterprises and between different periods. For example, when company A is compared with company B; period 1 is compared with period 2; and forecast results are compared with actual results. Such comparisons demand that the data be in measurement terms which have legitimate comparability. This is reasonably the case with CFA and NRVA for both are in cash or cash equivalent terms which, when aggregated and matched, provide meaningful totals and meaningful movements in these totals.[17] Both are devoid of accounting rules which, despite standards prescribed by professional accountancy bodies, give room for potential variability of results due to different measurement procedures and, thus, for lack of comparability. Also it should be noted that, in the case of CFA, comparability of the data is achieved without the distortion of accounting adjustments when actual results are reviewed with previously forecast results.[18]

8. A major problem in financial reporting concerns the communication of accounting data. The ability of the report user to comprehend properly the meaning of accounting messages is very much in doubt because of their complexity - the complexity of the allocation procedures, together with the technical language used in financial reports, causing non-accounting users severe difficulty in terms of comprehension.[19] CFA and NRVA obviously contain as yet unresolved terminology problems but, because they avoid data allocations, could be better understood by their users (i.e. compared with their understanding of allocated data). They are also based on measurement systems which, intuitively, users of financial reports may be

---

[17] The importance of aggregation in accounting generally, and of additivity of data, particularly, has been well argued by Chambers - for example, Chambers (*Accounting, Evaluation and Economic Behaviour*), *op cit.*, pp. 93-4. The absolute additivity of even CFA and NRVA data must always be doubtful - particularly as it relates to data of *periods* as distinct from *periodic* data (the latter are additive; the former are not unless some further adjustment of the measurement unit is made to ensure additivity).

[18] This is not intended to convey the impression that forecasting, and the subsequent comparison of forecast and actual results, are unique to CFA. Merely to suggest that such forecasts and comparisons are made easier by the lack of possible distortion and variance due to accounting allocations.

[19] For evidence of this, see T. A. Lee and D. P. Tweedie, „Accounting Information: An Investigation of Shareholder Understanding", *Accounting and Business Research*, Winter 1975, pp. 3-17 and *The Private Shareholder and the Corporate Report*, Institute of Chartered Accountants in England and Wales, 1977.

expecting when they receive allocation-based statements.[20] Thus, report users may not be misled in their use of such CFA and NRVA data - they could be receiving what they expect to receive; but this requires empirical testing to be anything other than a subjective comment.

9. CFA and NRVA are systems of financial reporting which have considerable individual merit from the point of view of providing useful information regarding the financial management of the reporting entity for a variety of report users. In particular, they emphasise the ability of the enterprise to survive and adapt. In addition, the following points of similarity in the systems have been identified: both systems are allocation-free; reflect the activity of the reporting enterprise without reference to the specific needs of individual user groups; describe and highlight the key factor of cash in business activity; assume enterprise continuity but do not assume activity continuity; relate to both user decision and accountability objectives in reporting; provide reasonably comparable data; and appear to improve user comprehension. Thus, although they can be argued for as separate reporting systems, CFA and NRVA seem to be mutually reinforcing because they both reflect the importance in business of cash resources and cash management in reasonably straightforward and comprehensive terms. There therefore appear to be sufficient common features in these systems to warrant consideration of the deliberate linking of cash flows and realizable values within a complete reporting structure.[21]

Combining cash flows and net realizable values

The combining of CFA and NRVA in a unified system of corporate financial reporting can be described in a diagramatic form as follows. This hopefully aids the reader's comprehension of the main features of such a system. Its main aims and advantages will be discussed following this initial introduction. The undernoted comments are intended only as preliminary descriptions of the system.

CFA proposals normally include the publication of historic and forecast cash flows, and this has been accommodated in the above scheme - forecasts are prepared on a cash basis, thus attempting to aid user decisions regarding the future cash flow of the enterprise (step 1); these forecasts reflect managerial intentions and expectations which, given time, hopefully should be translated into the cash flow data contained in statements of historic cash flows of use for stewardship purposes (step 2); relevant forecast and historic cash flows can be compared providing, together with explanations of the resultant variances, a description and basis for evaluation of the cash management of the enterprise (step 3); the historic cash flows can be linked with measures of unrealized cash flows represented by periodic changes in (a) the net realizable values of the underlying assets and (b) liabilities, to produce a measure of total

---

[20] See D. P. Tweedie, "Cash Flows and Realizable Values: The Intuitive Accounting Concepts? An Empirical Test", *Accounting and Business Research*, Winter 1977, pp. 2-13.

[21] This is not to say that CFA and NRVA financial statements would be the only statements to include in a financial report. The cases for inclusion of further statements must, however, be made elsewhere.

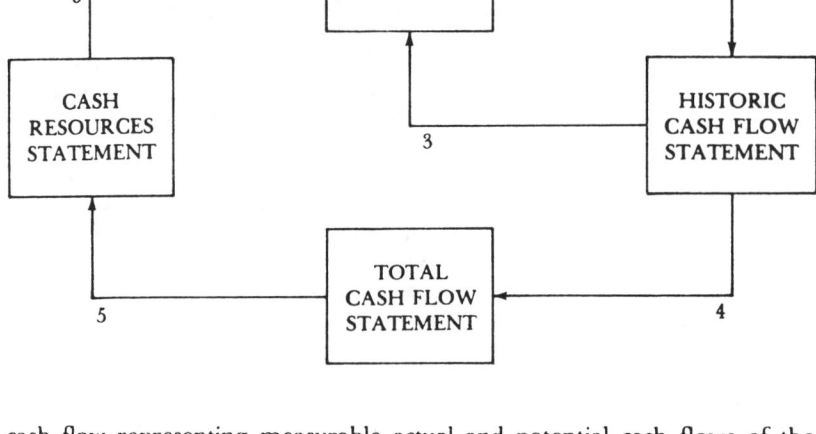

cash flow representing measurable actual and potential cash flows of the enterprise (step 4); the measurement of total cash flows results in an end-of-period cash resources statement which attempts to describe the enterprise's total command over money available for a variety of as yet unspecified purposes (step 5); and, finally, the latter statement can be used as a basis for producing the next forecast for decision making purposes - i.e. the specification of future cash uses (step 6).

The essential feature of the above system is the way in which realized cash flows can be linked to unrealized changes in net values of non-cash resources in order to produce a measure of total cash flow which represents the total money available for future investment and distribution.[22] The exact formulation can be described as follows:

$$\Delta C + \Delta N = \Delta 0$$

Where ΔC represents the net realized change in the total cash resources of the reporting enterprise for a defined period - i.e. sales revenue received minus total operational payments, minus total payments for new and replacement investment, minus interest, taxation, and dividend payments, plus or minus cash transactions relating to long-term financing (such as loans and share capital).[23]

ΔN is the total unrealized net cash flow representing the periodic change in the net realizable value of the non-cash assets of the reporting enterprise (including those assets which are readily realizable and those which are not so readily realizable).

---

[22] It must be emphasised that due to the omission of important assets (such as goodwill), and the incompleteness of valuing non-vendible assets, this total sum is itself incomplete.

[23] A great deal of work, as mentioned later in this paper, will require to be done in order to establish the most reasonable and acceptable sequence of ordering this data.

Δ O is the total change in the various obligations (or liabilities) of the reporting enterprise (including its short, medium and long-term debts, and its owner's capital measured in net realizable value terms).

This aggregation of realized cash flows and potential cash flows from the use and holding of assets provides the report user with a total cash flow figure which is equivalent to the total taxed and undistributed, actual and potential, cash funds in the enterprise. This expression of its total measured command over money reveals a potential basis for repaying its financial obligations, maintaining and changing its operations and activities, and for making distributions.

Thus, using assumed figures, the overall reporting system described above could be summarised as below:

Opening Cash Resources Statement	£	Total Cash Flow Statement	£	Closing Cash Resources Statement	£
Realized cash	5	Realized cash flow	39	Realized cash	44
Readily realizable assets	43	Increase in potential cash flow	17	Readily realizable assets	60
Not readily realizable assets	18	Increase in potential cash flow	12	Not readily realizable assets	30
	66		68		134
Short-term obligations	27	Additional credit received	23	Short-term obligations	50
Long-term obligations	10	Additional borrowings received	8	Long-term obligations	18
Indefinite obligations	29	Additional funds accruing	37	Indefinite obligations	66
	66		68		134

The above outline contains several relatively unique features which ought to be described at this stage before proceeding further:
1. The opening and closing position statements are described as cash resources statements rather than as conventional balance sheets. They treat all measurable assets of the enterprise as cash or potential cash - through the use of net realizable values. Thus, its command over money is emphasised by measuring its assets in current cash equivalent terms.
2. The assets are ordered for purposes of the position statements in order of realizability - from the already realized to the least realizable. This provides the user with some idea of the degree of certainty associated with the

enterprise's command over money (such command being more absolute with certain assets than with others). It also means a rethinking of asset classification from either the traditional fixed and current or monetary and non-monetary categories. Indeed, a further non-realizable category could be added for non-vendible durables.

3. The liabilities of the enterprise (including its ownership interests) are also ordered - in this case in terms of order of potential repayment (from the most to the least immediate obligation). Again, this will require some further thinking as to classification, but should provide report users with some impression of the timing of repayments of obligations for which cash resources will be required (and are available as described in the earlier part of the cash resources statement).

4. The total cash flow statement reflects all actual and potential cash flow changes affecting the measured assets and obligations of the enterprise over a defined period - i.e. the total increase or decrease in its command over money. The separate parts of this total cash flow are attributable to the various actual and potential cash and cash equivalent resources and obligations in the cash resources statement. Thus, the entire emphasis in all statements in the system is on cash flow and cash resources (actual and potential). The system is essentially one concerned with the cash management function within the enterprise.

5. The cash-orientated system described in outline above describes the activities of the reporting enterprise in as neutral a fashion as possible. It does not attempt to identify particular report users and, for this reason, is hopefully a genuinely multi-purpose reporting system.

Outline financial statements

The above outline is obviously insufficient for reporting purposes. It requires to be expanded and presented in such a way as to be comprehensible and meaningful to its readers. Thus, as a first step in this difficult process, the undernoted statements have been prepared. They are given in outline only, and contain many matters of terminology and presentation sequence which would require to be resolved before such statements become part of a formal system of reporting by the enterprise to its various external interests.[24] In addition, the following statements at this stage concern only the reporting of the events and activities of the enterprise during the immediate past period. The statements concerned are a summary statement of realized cash flow; a total statement of cash flow (realized and potential); and a statement of cash resources (again, realized and potential).

---

[24] See the conclusions to this paper.

CF LTD.

SUMMARY STATEMENT OF CASH FLOWS

Period $t_1 - t_2$

	£
Cash receipts from customers	187
Less: cash payments for materials, wages and overheads	124
CASH OPERATING MARGIN	63
Less: loan interest paid	2
PRE-TAX CASH FLOW	61
Less: taxation paid	13
DISTRIBUTABLE CASH FLOW	48
Less: dividends paid	10
OPERATING CASH FLOW AVAILABLE FOR INVESTMENT	38
Add: long-term loans received	8
TOTAL CASH FLOW AVAILABLE FOR INVESTMENT	46
Less: cash payments for new buildings	7
TOTAL INCREASE IN CASH RESOURCES	39

The above statement provides its reader with a portrayal of the actual cash inflow and outflow for the defined period. The next statement looks beyond the point of realization, and describes increases in potential cash flows which are being held by the enterprise in various non-cash forms but which, with varying degrees of certainty, could be converted into cash.

m a b blz 93

CF LTD.
SUMMARY STATEMENT OF TOTAL INCREMENTAL CASH FLOWS
Period $t_1 - t_2$

	£	£
REALIZED CASH FLOW INCREMENTS		
Net realized cash flow for the period		39
READILY REALIZABLE CASH FLOW INCREMENTS		
Potentially realizable cash flows represented by an increase (decrease) in the net realizable values of:		
Amounts due by customers	7	
Stocks of finished goods	8	
Motor vehicles	(6)	
Land and buildings	8	17
		56
NOT READILY REALIZABLE CASH FLOW INCREMENTS		
Not readily realizable cash flows represented by an increase (decrease) in the net realizable values of:		
Work in progress	15	
Plant and machinery	(3)	12
Total Potential Increase in Cash Resources		68
INCREMENTAL CHANGE IN SHORT-TERM OBLIGATIONS		
Potential cash outflows in the near future because of increases in:		
Amounts due to suppliers	9	
Taxation due to Inland Revenue	12	
Distributions due to owners	2	23
INCREMENTAL CHANGE IN LONG-TERM OBLIGATIONS		
Potential cash outflows in the long-term because of increases in:		
Borrowings from merchant bank		8
INCREMENTAL CHANGE IN INDEFINITE OBLIGATIONS		
Indeterminate future cash outflows because of increases in:		
Funds pertaining to owners		37
Total Potential Increase in Obligations		68

m a b blz 94

If reported, the above data would provide an explanation of the total increase in the enterprise's command over money during the period. It is a general statement of the cash management exercised within the enterprise, resulting in a realization of cash flow and an increase in potential cash flow. In particular, it reveals the incremental changes in cash and cash equivalent resources available to cover the incremental changes in financial obligations - in the case of resources, highlighting the range of potential realizability; and in the case of obligations, highlighting the range of possible repayment timing.

The final statement supporting these descriptions of cash flow is the end-of-period cash resources statement. Together with corresponding figures relating to the beginning of the period, it contains descriptions of the total resources of the enterprise in cash equivalent terms. As such, it provides a total reporting of the actual and potential cash resources available to cover the enterprise's total financial obligations. Thus, it not only describes the assets and liabilities of the enterprise in current value terms which are understandable and not subject to the arbitrariness of data allocations; it also reveals (in an admittedly limited way) the financial resources available to management to meet existing financial obligations and future commitments.

CF LTD.
STATEMENT OF TOTAL CASH AND EQUIVALENT RESOURCES
as at t_1 and t_2

RESOURCES

	t_1 £	t_2 £
REALIZED CASH RESOURCES		
Bank, cash and deposit balances	5	44
READILY REALIZABLE NON-CASH RESOURCES		
Amounts due by customers	11	18
Stocks of finished goods	10	18
Motor vehicles	10	4
Land and buildings	12	20
	43	60
NOT READILY REALIZABLE NON-CASH RESOURCES		
Work in progress	9	24
Plant and Machinery	9	6
	18	30
	66	134

m a b blz 95

OBLIGATIONS

SHORT-TERM OBLIGATIONS

Amounts due to suppliers	9	18
Taxation due to Inland Revenue	8	20
Distributions due to owners	10	12
	27	50

LONG-TERM OBLIGATIONS

Borrowings from merchant bank	10	18

INDEFINITE OBLIGATIONS

Funds pertaining to owners	29	66
	66	134

The above outline statements contain the following advantageous features which appear to strengthen the case for reporting in such a way:
1. The cash flow statements clearly separate the objectively measured realized cash flow data from the far more subjective potential data described in large part by the unrealized value changes in the enterprise's assets. This is not entirely a new suggestion,[25] and the idea of distinguishing factual from judgmental data in accounting statements should be capable of aiding their users in assessing the varying degrees of credibility inherent in such information. In addition, the "ranking" of actual and potential cash flows in order of realizability provides users with indications of what cash is or will be available for future activities of the enterprise.
2. Although it can be argued that there is no need to ensure the articulation of the "surplus" and "position" statements,[26] the above scheme of reporting ensures a proper reconciliation of cash flows with cash resource changes. It is thus intended as a complete cash system with all reported data being capable of being matched, compared and justified. In this way, the cash-based statements are available for an assessment of the extent and quality of the reporting enterprise's cash management. If the managing of cash flow is regarded as a vital ingredient in the survival of the enterprise in both the short-term and long-term, it appears to be sensible to report on such matters.

Therefore, it could be anticipated that these statements would be useful primarily for (a) bankers, lenders and suppliers concerned with evaluating the liquidity of the enterprise in connection with the amount and risk

---

[25] For example, see R. A. Rayman, "Is Conventional Accounting Obsolete?", *Accountancy*, June 1970, pp. 422-9.
[26] An interesting argument for this has been made by G. Macdonald in relation to income and capital - see "Deprival Value: Its Use and Abuse', *Accounting and Business Research*, Autumn 1974, pp. 263-9.

associated with their existing and potential cash claims on it; (b) investors anxious to predict the amount and risk associated with the future cash distributions by the enterprise which are such a vital ingredient in their investment decisions; (c) employees desiring to assess the financial position of the enterprise in connection with future job and pay prospects; and (d) government monitoring the effects of its taxation policies and procedures on the cash flow of business enterprises. In addition, it does not appear unreasonable to presume that enterprise management may find such statements useful when involved in the process of managing cash flow and resources - for example, when determining distribution levels, and when deciding on borrowing requirements.

3. The accounting practices used in the above statements are simple and straightforward - no complex data allocation procedures have been undertaken, and no extensive explanation of such procedures are necessary to the report user.[27]

There are, however, several problems which have yet to be discussed and resolved. For example, the ordering of the presentation of the realized cash flow data can produce differing interpretations of particular cash uses (should new investment expenditure be deducted from the operating margin before the deduction of tax and dividends; and where should loan and share capital changes be introduced?). Also there is the question of how much explanation and disclosure to provide in support of each of the figures contained in the above statements (for example, in relation to cash payments for operational activity, new and replacement investment, and so on).

In addition, it would be wrong to believe that cash flow could not involve any allocation procedure. Allocations may be made by management without adequate disclosure (by delaying or accelerating payments), and may also be required (for example, should expenditure on investment be split between replacement and new investment in order to give the report user some idea of growth and development in the enterprise; and, if so, what can be classed as new investment, and what can be classed as replacement expenditure?). Finally, and perhaps surprisingly, the feasibility in practice of using cash flows and net realizable values is not exactly proven. Because reporting enterprises are so dependent on accounting allocations and accruals, it may not be too easy to determine cash inflows and outflows with the amount of detailed analysis required for the above system of financial reporting.[28] Equally, although several studies have examined and established proof of the feasibility of using net realizable values in practice,[29] there are areas where obtaining such valuations would be extremely hazardous and subjective (for example, in the case of not readily realizable assets).

---

27 As, for example, required in historic cost accounting in the UK by "Disclosure of Accounting Policies", *Statement of Standard Accounting Practice 2*, 1971.
28 In other words, companies may not be able to adequately label their cash inflows and outflows, as such details are normally related to the original credit transactions in the bookkeeping system.
29 For example, in J. C. McKeown, "An Empirical Test of a Model Proposed by Chambers", *The Accounting Review*, January 1971, pp. 12-29.

Completing the system
One final matter requires to be described in order to complete the linking of CFA and NRVA within one system of financial reporting, and that is the need to disclose forecast data. In this respect, it would appear to be sensible to limit the suggestion to the forecasting of realized cash flows rather than also including predictions of future net realizable values. This is not to say that the latter cannot be contemplated - it is simply an admission that the process of forecasting enterprise activity is subjective enough without extending it into the arguably more subjective area of anticipating market behaviour in the form of sale prices.[30]

Forecasting of cash flows is a large and controversial area,[31] and cannot really be covered properly in this paper - for example, the question of the period of time to which the forecast relates is open to question; should it be for one period or several, and how long should these periods be? For purposes of this paper, the illustration provides for a one period forecast, but this should not be taken as a firm suggestion (much has yet to be considered for any definite proposal to be made). The following illustration uses the assumed figures already described above. It shows the need to disclose, first the previous period's forecast to compare with the actual results of the current period; and, secondly, the forecast for the next period. In addition, variances between actual and previously forecast results could be shown, together with suitable explanations of the differences (distinguishing between operational factors and forecasting errors, and between controllable and uncontrollable factors).[32] An explanation of the assumptions underlying the forecast for the next period would also appear to be worthy of consideration for reporting purposes, although there are considerable problems to be faced in this area regarding the commercial secrecy and such disclosure (yet again, another matter requiring much more thought and space than this paper can allow).

---

[30] A search of Literature reveals no argument made for forecasting in net realizable value terms. In fact, Chambers is very doubtful about making predictions in financial reporting - see Chambers (*Accounting, Evaluation and Economic Behaviour*), *op cit*, pp. 83-4.
[31] See, for example, S. Dev and M. Webb, "The Accuracy of Company Profit Forecasts", *Journal of Business Finance*, Autumn 1972, pp. 26-39.
[32] As in conventional standard costing analyses for internal management accounting purposes.

CF LTD.
SUMMARY STATEMENT CONTAINING FORECAST AND ACTUAL REALISED CASH FLOWS

	Forecast $t_1 \cdot t_2$	Actual $t_1 \cdot t_2$	Variance $t_1 \cdot t_2$	Forecast $t_2 \cdot t_3$
	£	£	£	£
Cash receipts from customers	173	187	14	195
Less: cash payments for materials, wages and overheads	116	124	8	121
CASH OPERATING MARGIN	57	63	6	74
Less: loan interest paid	2	2	–	2
PRE-TAX CASH FLOW	55	61	6	72
Less: taxation paid	9	13	4	20
DISTRIBUTABLE CASH FLOW	46	48	2	52
Less: dividends paid	10	10	–	11
OPERATING CASH FLOW AVAILABLE FOR INVESTMENT	36	38	2	41
Add: long-term loans received	8	8	–	–
TOTAL CASH FLOW AVAILABLE INVESTMENT	44	46	2	41
Less: cash payment for new and replacement investment	11	7	(4)	23
TOTAL INCREASE IN CASH RESOURCES	33	39	6	18

The above description cannot do full justice to the presentation and explanation of such information, but it is hoped that it will provide some flavour of the place of forecasts in the suggested reporting system. Suffice to say that it is believed that such predicted data will provide the various user groups mentioned previously with information which ought to further aid their respective decision activities.

Conclusions and unresolved issues

What this paper has attempted to do us to bring its readers' attention to the possibility of linking CFA and NRVA to provide information relating to past and future enterprise cash flows and cash resources. Points of similarity between CFA and NRVA provide the impetus for this suggestion, and outline financial statements have been described as a starting point for any discussion on the merit of these proposals. These statements were supported by brief explanations of their aims and advantages.

What has been described in this paper is only a small step along the road to providing a system containing CFA and NRVA which is acceptable enough in practice. There appear, however, to be considerable arguments for pursuing this theme. In particular, the emphasis on allocation-free cash data in CFA and NRVA for purposes of evaluating cash management ought to provide the basis for this. There are also arguments for separating realized and unrealized cash flows, thereby deriving measures of realized and potential cash resources available to the reporting enterprise and its management. The production of both forecast and actual results on the same basis, together with supporting explanations and disclosures, are a further matter requiring discussion and debate.

Inevitably, the above comments lead to more questions than answers. This is as it should be. Accounting is a process which should be allowed to evolve gradually in response to the needs and requirements of the times. The present times, with their emphasis on business liquidity and cash flow, appear ripe for systems such as CFA and NRVA but these matters should always be of importance. They certainly must be considered more seriously than hitherto. But they also require a consideration of a number of significant issues on which this paper has only managed to touch. For example:

1. The extent of detailed disclosure to back up the aggregate data presented in the CFA and NRVA statements; and the possibility of other statements to include in the overall reporting package.
2. The sequence of presentation of data in the cash flow and resource statements in order to provide the most meaningful and least biased disclosure of such information.
3. The way in which non-cash transactions (such as assets acquired by the issue of shares and loan stock) can be coped with in the suggested system (this is an issue which has not been covered in this paper)[33].
4. The terminology to be adopted in CFA and NRVA statements. Particularly of concern is the way in which the unrealized cash flows might be presented in the total statement.
5. The way in which the suggested CFA and NRVA statements might be tested for use and feasibility.[34]
6. The number of periods to be covered by the disclosed CFA and NRVA data - both actual and forecast - and the extent to which the nature of the reporting enterprise and its normal operating cycle ought to determine this issue.[35]

These issues, of course, only become live ones once the general principle of reporting in CFA and NRVA terms has been accepted by the reader. Hopefully, by this stage in the paper, the latter person has not felt obliged to treat them as unacceptable. If this is the case then the discussion can commence on the various assertions, arguments and proposals contained in this paper.

---

[33] It has been touched on briefly in Lee (A Case for Cash Flow Reporting), *op cit*, pp. 31-2.
[34] Work on this has already commenced - see T. A. Lee, "A Test of the Use of Cash Flow Reporting", and "A Survey of Accountants' Opinions on Cash Flow Reporting", both discussion papers at the University of Edinburgh, 1979.
[35] This is an issue which has rarely, if ever, been discussed by accountants. In fact, company law and accounting regulations imply that a requirement to report at least every twelve months is suitable for all companies - irrespective of the nature of their trade and operations.

Reporting Cash Flows and Net Realisable Values *

T. A. Lee

Several arguments have been advanced for financial reporting to be based on cash flow accounting (CFA).[1] The literature also contains many items explaining the case for net realisable value accounting (NRVA).[2] Typically, however, these systems of reporting have been examined and presented separately, and rarely has any detailed attempt been made to link them.[3] The purpose of this paper is to make such a connection, in the hope of revealing to the interested reader that CFA and NRVA are parts of a single system of reporting which concentrates on the importance and accessibility of cash in business enterprise activity. As such, it is concerned particularly with describing how CFA and NRVA data can be brought together in a series of articulating financial statements which provide more relevant information for the report user about cash and cash management than can be given in either a CFA or NRVA system on its own.

It is not concerned with advancing individual arguments for the reporting of either CFA or NRVA data. These have already been well rehearsed in the accountancy literature, and should be familiar to the interested reader. Equally, it is not concerned with demonstrating that CFA is a particular sub-set of NRVA, or vice versa. Such artificial distinctions are futile if, as is suggested in this paper, both are parts of a single cash-orientated system of financial reporting. In other words, the writer is concerned that advocates of CFA and NRVA have been working separately, and may well have ignored the possibility that their arguments and recommendations are similar but incomplete without each other, and could be strengthened through unification.

Points of similarity

Before proceeding to the main part of the paper, it would appear to be relevant to describe briefly the main points of similarity in CFA and NRVA as they are presently and separately constituted. These are made in order to demonstrate that linking the two systems within one reporting framework is not a casual *ad hoc* exercise, and that they are compatible.

1. CFA and NRVA are both based firmly on the importance of cash as a business resource. CFA describes in detail cash flows to and from various sources, and NRVA describes the adaptability of the reporting enterprise in terms of its command over money (resources being valued using net realisable values, or 'current cash equivalents').

---

*This paper is based on an earlier one presented to the annual conference of the European Accounting Association, Amsterdam, March 1980. It has benefited considerably from comments on the earlier paper by Professors R. J. Chambers and M. C. Wells and an anonymous referee.

[1] For a summary of CFA arguments, and a full bibliography on the subject, see T. A. Lee, 'Cash Flow Accounting and Corporate Financial Reporting,' *Discussion Paper 6*, University of Edinburgh, 1980.

[2] For a full bibliography on the case for NRVA, particularly as expounded by R. J. Chambers and R. R. Sterling, see T. A. Lee, *Income and Value Measurement*, Nelson, 2nd. ed. 1980, pp. 185–7.

[3] Only in a casual way has it been attempted before: see R. Edwards, 'The Nature and Measurement of Income,' in *Studies in Accounting*, W. T. Baxter and S. Davidson (eds.), Institute of Chartered Accountants in England and Wales, 3rd. ed. 1977, pp. 126–38; H. C. Edey, 'Accounting Principles and Business Reality,' *Accountancy*, December 1963, p. 1087; T. A. Climo, 'Cash Flow Statements for Investors,' *Journal of Business Finance and Accounting*, Autumn 1976, pp. 11 and 13; T. A. Lee, 'The Cash Flow Accounting Alternative for Corporate Financial Reporting,' in *Trends in Managerial and Financial Accounting*, C. van Dam (ed.), Martinus Nijhoff, 1978, p. 84; and T. A. Lee, 'The Simplicity and Complexity of Accounting,' *Accounting for a Simplified Firm*, in R. R. Sterling and A. Thomas (eds.), Scholars Book Co., 1979, pp. 47–50. Edwards' contribution was originally published in 1938 and appears to have been the first, although it must be noted that his recommendations relating to cash flow and net realisable value were effectively limited to what he described as merchanting businesses (that is, retail concerns). In fact, he specifically excluded total valuations for industrial businesses, with a recommendation that only individual assets ought to be valued where this would produce relevant information. Additionally, his cash flow recommendations were vague, being based on cash receipts and expenditures with certain unspecified adjustments, and lacking any illustration or numerical example. The cash flow accounting recommended appears to have been based for industrial businesses on the nineteenth century double-account system of accounting and reporting.

2. CFA and NRVA are both allocation-free systems. Neither contains arbitrary allocations due to short-term periodic reporting, and thus both are free of such accounting interference.

3. The condition of enterprise survival is greatly emphasised in CFA and NRVA the former being concerned with the way in which cash has been generated to meet its obligations and requirements, and the latter with the availability and accessibility of cash for future activity and needs.

4. Both systems concentrate on reporting on the activity of the enterprise and its management. Neither assumes continuity of this activity, and both appear capable of providing essential information on the financial management of the reporting entity (particularly that pertaining to its liquidity).

5. Cash, current cash equivalents, and cash flows are matters which appear to underlie most of the decision models to which financial reporting is directed—for example, shareholders concerned about dividends; lenders, bankers and creditors concerned about interest and capital repayments; employees concerned about wages and security of employment; and so on. Both CFA and NRVA would therefore appear to be of relevance to these potential report users.[4]

Linking CFA and NRVA

In its historic form, CFA describes the realisation and utilisation of cash—that is, the conversion of non-cash resources into cash, and the use of cash funds generated from various sources to acquire resources and meet obligations. NRVA, on the other hand, describes, within aggregate totals, a mixture of both the realisation and utilisation of cash (as in CFA), and the pre-realisation changes in the net realisable values of non-cash resources and the amounts due on various obligations. The 'linking' of the two systems can be achieved relatively easily by the segregation of NRVA data into realised cash flows and unrealised cash flows—the former described in detail in CFA terms, and the latter represented by the aforementioned changes in the net realisable values of reported assets, and changes in the amounts of reported obligations. In this way, it can be argued that CFA-based financial statements would thereby cease to be incomplete because of their present failure to deal with unrealised cash flows (and thus with statements of financial position); and NRVA-based statements would provide much greater information on the realised cash flows which presently are contained, but not separately identified, in its measures of realisable income. The exact formulation required for the 'linking' can be described as follows:

$$\Delta C + \Delta N = \Delta O$$

where ΔC represents the net realised change in the total cash resources of the reporting enterprise for a defined period—that is, sales revenues received minus total operational payments, minus total payments for new and replacement investment, minus loan interest, taxation, and dividend payments, plus or minus cash transactions relating to long-term financing (such as loans and share capital).

ΔN is the total unrealised net cash flow representing the periodic change in the net realisable value of the non-cash assets of the reporting enterprise (including those assets which are readily-realisable, those which are not-so-readily realisable, and those which are non-realisable). ΔO is the total change in the various obligations or liabilities of the reporting enterprise (including its short, medium and long-term debts, and its owner's capital measured in net realisable value terms). This aggregation of periodic realised and potential cash flows from the use and holding of assets provides the report user with a total cash flow figure which is equivalent to the net increase (or decrease) during the period in taxed and undistributed, actual and potential, cash funds in the enterprise. It is an expression of the change in its total measured command over money, and reveals the increment (or decrement) in the enterprise's potential for repaying its financial obligations, maintaining and changing its operations and activities, meeting wage claims and making distributions. In other words, it represents financial information which ought to be of interest to most report users.

Because of the flow nature of this data, they should be contained within a statement which reconciles with position statements at the beginning and end of the period concerned. Thus, using assumed figures for purposes of demonstration, the overall reporting system described above could be summarised as in Figure 1.

This outline contains several features which ought to be described at this stage before proceeding further:

1. The opening and closing position statements

---
[4] This has been recognised in at least one major study of financial reporting: Accounting Objectives Study Group, *Objectives of Financial Statements*, American Institute of Certified Public Accountants, 1973, pp. 17–20.

Figure 1

Opening Cash Resources Statement		Total Cash Flow Statement		Closing Cash Resources Statement	
	£000		£000		£000
Realised cash	5	Realised cash flow	39	Realised cash	44
Readily-realisable assets	43	Increase in potential cash flow	17	Readily-realisable assets	60
Not-readily-realisable assets	18	Increase in potential cash flow	12	Not-readily-realisable assets	30
Non-realisable assets		Increase in potential cash flow		Non-realisable assets	
	66		68		134
Short-term obligations	32	Additional credit received	18	Short-term obligations	50
Long-term obligations	10	Additional borrowings received	8	Long-term obligations	18
Indefinite obligations	24	Additional funds accruing	42	Indefinite obligations	66
	66		68		134

are described as 'cash resources' statements rather than as conventional balance sheets. They treat all measurable assets of the enterprise as cash or potential cash—through the use of net realisable values. Thus, its command over money is emphasised by measuring its assets in current cash equivalent terms.

2. The assets are ordered for purposes of the position statements in order of realisability—from the already-realised to the non-realisable. This provides the user with some idea of the degree of certainty associated with the enterprise's command over money (such command being more absolute with certain assets than with others). It also means a rethinking of asset classification from either the traditional fixed and current or monetary and non-monetary categories.[5] If a system of reporting is being advocated which emphasises the realisation or potential realisation of the reporting enterprise's resources, it appears only sensible to ensure that the latter are described in a way which accords with the notion of realisability. The above formulation does this; the traditional classification, although intended originally to do so in terms of fixed and current assets, does not.

3. The liabilities of the enterprise (including its ownership interests) are also ordered—in this case in terms of order of potential repayment (from the most to the least immediate obligation). Again, this will require rethinking as to classification, but should provide report users with some impression of the timing of repayments of obligations for which cash resources will be required (and are available as described in the earlier part of the cash resources statement).

4. The total cash flow statement reflects all actual and potential cash flow changes affecting the assets and obligations of the enterprise over a defined period—that is, the total net increase or decrease in its command over money. The separate parts of this total cash flow are attributable to the various actual and potential cash and cash equivalent resources and obligations in the cash resources statement. Thus, the entire emphasis in the system is on cash flow and cash resources (actual and potential). It is essentially one concerned with the cash management function within the enterprise although, as will be seen later, it can also be used for purposes of income assessment as a means of evaluating the success or failure of enterprise management in terms of returns on capital employed, etc.

5. It is possible to derive a measure of income from the reported data, this being based on net realisable values. The datum describing additional funds accruing to indefinite obligations forms the basis for this, as it represents (assuming no new

---

[5]This is not entirely a new idea—a somewhat different variation of it can be seen in M. C. Wells, 'Costing for Activities,' *Management Accounting* (USA), May 1976, pp. 35–6; and in S. G. Gray and M. C. Wells, 'Corporate Liquidity and Disclosure of Financial Position: A Comment on European Developments and a Counter Proposal,' *Journal UEC*, 3/1977, pp. 156–8.

capital issued or capital repayments) the income retained for the period after taxation and distribution. Thus realisable income (Y_r) could be formulated as follows:

$$Y_r = \Delta R + t + d \pm l$$

where ΔR represents the additional funds accruing to capital in net realisable value terms; t represents taxation provided for the period; d represents dividends provided for the period; and I represents capital repayments (+) or new capital (−).

6. The non-realisability of certain specialised assets, and therefore their lack of potential in providing cash from sale as distinct from use, is recognised in this scheme with nil values and value changes being attributed to these items.

Outline financial statements

The above outline is obviously insufficient for financial reporting purposes. It requires to be expanded and presented in such a way as to be comprehensible and meaningful to its readers. Thus, as a first step, the undernoted outline statements have been prepared—that is, a Statement of Realised Cash Flow; a Statement of Total Cash Flow Movements (realised and potential); a Statement of Net Cash and Cash Equivalent Resources (again, realised and potential); and a Statement of Realisable Income (see Figures 2, 3, 4 and 5).

Figure 2 provides its reader with a portrayal of the actual cash inflow and outflow for the defined period. It could be supported by detailed schedules analysing the composition of individual figures given in it. As such, it describes the cash flow underlying the retained income measure based on net realisable values, and represents the factual and incontrovertible part of the latter datum (although the ordering and presentation of data are open to debate). The next statement looks beyond the point of realisation, and describes potential increases and decreases in cash resources which, with varying degrees of certainty, could be converted into actual cash movements.

If reported, Figure 3 would provide an explanation of the total potential increase in the reporting enterprise's command over money during the period. It is a general statement of the cash management exercised within the enterprise, resulting in a net realisation of cash flow and a net increase in potential cash flow. In particular, it reveals the incremental changes in cash and cash-equivalent resources available to cover the incremental changes in financial obligations—in the case of resources, highlighting the range of potential realisability; and, in the case of obligations, the range of possible repayment timing.

As such, it provides more information concerning the realisability of assets, and repayment of obligations, than does the equivalent NRVA-based income statement. The latter does not

---

Figure 2
CF Ltd.
Statement of Realised Cash Flows
Period $t_1 - t_2$

	£000
Cash receipts from customers	187
Less: cash payments for materials, wages and overheads	124
Cash Operating Margin	63
Less: loan interest paid	2
Pre-tax Cash Flow	61
Less: taxation paid	13
Distributable Cash Flow	48
Less: dividends paid	10
Operating Cash Flow Available for Investment	38
Add: long-term loans received	8
Total Cash Flow Available for Investment	46
Less: cash payments for new buildings	7
Total Increase in Cash Resources	39

Figure 3
CF Ltd.
Statement of Total Cash Flow Movements
Period $t_1 - t_2$

	£000	£000
Realised Cash Flows		
Net realised cash flow for the period (as per Statement of Realised Cash Flows)		39
Readily-Realisable Cash Flows		
Potential cash flows represented by an increase (decrease) in the net realisable values of readily-realisable assets:		
Amounts due by customers	7	
Stocks of finished goods	8	
Motor vehicles	(6)	
Land and buildings	8	17
		56
Not-Readily-Realisable Cash Flows		
Potential cash flows represented by an increase (decrease) in the net realisable values of not-readily-realisable assets:		
Work-in-progress	15	
Plant and machinery	(3)	12
Total Potential Increase in Cash Resources		68
Change in Short-Term Obligations		
Potential cash outflows in the near future resulting from increases in:		
Amounts due to suppliers	9	
Taxation due to Inland Revenue	7	
Distributions due to owners	2	18
Change in Long-Term Obligations		
Potential cash outflows in the long-term resulting from increases in:		
Borrowings from merchant bank		8
Change in Indefinite Obligations		
Indeterminate future cash outflows resulting from increases in:		
Funds pertaining to owners (see Statement of Realisable Income)		42
Total Potential Increase in Obligations		68

reveal specific details of cash or cash equivalent movements in individual asset categories, and it also fails to report changes in many of the obligations of the reporting enterprise. In other words, the Statement of Total Cash Flow Movement is effectively a funds statement based on net realisable values; its data are rearranged to be compatible with the position statement—the Statement of Total Net Cash and Cash Equivalent Resources—which is based on a reasoned ordering of the enterprise's assets and liabilities.

The next statement supporting these descriptions of cash flow is the end-of-period 'cash resources' report—the Statement of Net Cash and Cash Equivalent Resources (Figure 4). Together with corresponding figures relating to the beginning of the period, it contains descriptions of the total resources of the enterprise in cash or cash equivalent terms. As such, it provides a total reporting of the actual and potential cash resources and obligations of the reporting enterprise. Thus, it not only describes the assets and liabilities of the enterprise in current value terms which are understandable and not subject to the arbitrariness of periodic data allocations; it also reveals the financial resources currently available to management to meet existing financial obligations and future commitments. The uniqueness of this 'balance sheet' is that it is a statement of financial position which attempts to reflect the liquidity of the reporting enterprise in reasonably clear and understandable terms which do not

Figure 4
CF Ltd.
Statement of Net Cash and Cash Equivalent Resources
as at t_1 and t_2

Resources

	t_1 £000	t_2 £000
Realised Cash Resources		
Bank, cash and deposit balances	5	44
Readily-Realisable Non-Cash Resources		
Amounts due to customers	11	18
Stocks of finished goods	10	18
Motor vehicles	10	4
Land and buildings	12	20
	43	60
Not-Readily-Realisable Non-Cash Resources		
Work-in-progress	9	24
Non-specialist plant and machinery	9	6
	18	30
Non-Realisable Non-Cash Resources		
Specialist plant and machinery	–	–
	66	134

Obligations

	t_1	t_2
Short-Term Obligations		
Amounts due to suppliers	9	18
Taxation due to Inland Revenue	13	20
Distributions due to owners	10	12
	32	50
Long-Term Obligations		
Borrowings from merchant bank	10	18
Indefinite Obligations		
Funds pertaining to owners (see Statement of Retained Income)	24	66
	66	134

Figure 5
CF Ltd.
Statement of Retained Income
Period t_1 to t_2

	£000
Realised income	74
Less: taxation provided	20
Distributable Income	54
Less: dividends provided	12
Retained Income for Period	42
Add: retained income of previous periods	24
Total Retained Income (as per Statement of Net Cash and Cash Equivalent Resources)	66

adhere to the rather misleading fixed and current asset categories of traditional accounting, and are compatible with the cash flow analysis contained in the previous cash-based funds statement. It is therefore a rearranged NRVA-balance sheet, and provides a position statement which has for so long been missing from CFA systems of reporting.

The final Statement of Retained Income (Figure 5) also provides a means of filling a gap in CFA—in this case, the lack of a measure of income in the latter.

This statement thus completes the combined CFA and NRVA system by providing the NRVA-based measure of income which reconciles with the equivalent position statement. Thus the complete system comprises a realised cash flow statement, a cash-based funds statement, a realisable income statement, and a net realisable value position statement.

Advantages of the combined system

The above outline statements contain the following advantageous features which appear to strengthen the case for reporting in such a way:

1. The two cash flow statements clearly separate and identify the objectively measured realised cash flow data from the far more subjective potential cash flow data described by the unrealised movements in the enterprise's assets and liabilities. The idea of distinguishing factual from judgmental data in accounting statements in this way should be capable of aiding their users in assessing the varying degrees of credibility inherent in such information. In addition, the 'ranking' of actual and potential cash flows in order of realisability and repayment provides them with indications of what cash is or will be available for future activities and commitments of the enterprise.

2. Although it can be argued that there is no need to ensure the articulation of the 'surplus' and 'position' statements, the above scheme of reporting ensures a proper reconciliation of actual with potential cash flows. It is thus intended as a complete cash-orientated system with all reported data being capable of being matched, compared and justified. In this way, these cash-based statements are available for an assessment of the extent and quality of the reporting enterprise's cash management. If the managing of cash flow is regarded as a vital ingredient in the survival of the enterprise in both the short-term and long-term, it appears to be sensible to report on such matters.

Thus, it can be anticipated that these statements would be useful primarily for, for example, (a) bankers, lenders and suppliers concerned with evaluating the liquidity of the enterprise in connection with the amount and risk associated with their existing and potential cash claims on it; (b) investors anxious to predict the amount and risk associated with the future cash distributions by the enterprise which are such a vital ingredient in their investment decisions; (c) employees desiring to assess the financial position of the enterprise in connection with future job and pay prospects; and (d) government monitoring the effects of its taxation policies and procedures on the cash flow of business enterprises. Each of the decision models inherent in the above descriptions of users relies to a considerable extent on the short or long-term availability of cash within the reporting enterprise. The recommended system provides information likely to meet these requirements. Income is there as well, but this system destroys the notion of the all-embracing importance of income in relation to such matters as interest and capital repayments, credit settlements, dividend distributions and wage claims.[6] With respect to each of these matters, cash appears to be just as, if not more, important.

In addition, it does not appear unreasonable to presume that enterprise management would find such statements useful when involved in the process of managing cash flow and resources—for example, when comparing with previously forecast activity, determining distribution levels, and deciding on borrowing requirements. Indeed, as has been recently suggested, the aims of enterprise management should be compatible with those persons interested in its financial reports, and thus the information needs of management and external interests should be just as compatible.[7]

3. The accounting practices used in the above statements are simple and straightforward—no complex data allocation procedures have been undertaken, and no extensive explanation of such procedures is necessary to the report user.

4. The combined system ought to satisfy the advocates of both CFA and NRVA. It contains all the data normally required in each of these systems, but in such a way as to highlight the crucial feature of both—cash and its accessibility.

---

[6]This was originally suggested by Edwards, *op. cit*, p. 135, and more recently implied in H. C. Edey, 'The Logic of Financial Accounting,' *The Deloitte, Haskins and Sells Lecture*, Cardiff University College Press, 1980, pp. 8–11.

[7]This idea has been most elegantly explored in Edey, *op cit*, pp. 6–7.

Conclusion

The above points have been put forward as matters for debate by those who regard improvements to the financial reporting function to be essential. In particular, they are presented as a means of extending CFA and NRVA to the point at which it can be said that the reported data are complete so far as liquidity management assessment at least is concerned. It is not a case of adding CFA and NRVA data together; it is an admission that each is incomplete without the other, and that financial reports are irrelevant without both. Finally, it might be suggested that this cash-orientated system may only have a limited application to certain types of enterprise whose asset structure is mainly composed of readily-realisable assets (such as banks, property and insurance companies).[8] To limit the system in this way is to deny that liquidity matters, generally, and cash flow and cash accessibility, particularly, are of no concern to industrial organisations. The non-realisability of assets in the latter due to their specialised nature is recognised in the system outlined in this paper—they have no sale value, and therefore do not add to the reporting entity's command over money until such time as they generate cash flows from use.

---

[8] As suggested in Edwards, *op cit*, pp. 132-3.

Obtaining the Data

7
Cash Flow Accounting and Reporting

THOMAS A LEE

*Professor of Accountancy and Finance,
University of Edinburgh*

Introduction

This essay is concerned with accounting for and reporting on cash flow information by enterprises to various external report user groups. As such, cash flow accounting is a relatively recent addition to the numerous proposals which have been made to improve the relevance and utility of the external financial reporting function. However, it must be remembered that cash flow accounting is not a new concept — not only was it the main form of reporting before inter-period data allocation became part of generally accepted accounting practice, but it has also developed as an essential element in internal management decision-making and control (for example, in capital budgeting and working capital management). In addition, it ought not to be forgotten that cash flow data underlie all the main systems of external financial reporting which depend on data allocations for production of financial information. Thus, the advocation of external cash flow reporting which is made in this essay is but a natural extension of accounting practices which have developed over many years. It is making the implicit explicit in financial reporting terms.

CASH FLOW ACCOUNTING AND REPORTING

Cash flow accounting is concerned with describing the financial activities and performance of the reporting enterprise in purely cash terms — that is, it is a system of accounting which is devoid of arbitrary accounting allocations of data between activities and periods. It also ought to be free of credit transactions (although some advocates would define cash in terms of cash plus credit). It therefore attempts to match relevant cash inflows and outflows for defined entities over defined periods of time. It avoids the subjectivity of data allocations such as depreciation of fixed assets, and accounting for unsold stock and incomplete work-in-progress. Its major measurement problem is one of adequate identification of cash flows — that is, ensuring that cash inflows and outflows are identified properly with the entities, activities and time periods to which they relate. But this latter problem of potential manipulation of cash flows is one which is inherent in any system of accounting and reporting which involves their use.

The system of cash flow reporting which is typically advocated is one which involves the production of a number of related financial statements which attempt to focus their readers' attention on the reporting enterprise's liquidity and financial management — that is, how the liquid resources of the enterprise have changed over a defined period, and what specific inflows and outflows of cash have caused this change. As such, therefore, it is only fair to state that cash flow accounting and reporting does not purport to be an all-embracing, all-inclusive system (it does not report measures of profit, nor does it look beyond liquid resources to other resources which comprise the enterprise's overall financial position[1]).

The main cash flow statement is essentially a 'surplus' statement — that is, a 'master' statement describing the total inflows and outflows which reconcile with the periodic change in cash resources. It can be described in the following simple identity:

$$O - I - T - D \pm L \pm C = \Delta R$$

---

[1] These particular issues will be explored later in the essay when the relationship between cash flows and realisable values is examined.

where O = the net cash inflow or outflow from operational activity (that is, cash received from customers minus cash payments for trading expenditure); I = the cash cost of new and replacement investment on long-lived assets, net of cash receipts for asset disposals and government grants); T = cash payments for taxation; D = cash payments for dividends to the owners of the enterprise; L = cash receipts from or payments to long-term lenders to the enterprise; C = cash receipts from and payments to the owners of the enterprise; and ΔR = the resultant change in the defined cash resources of the enterprise (usually cash and bank balances and deposits, but capable of including near-cash items such as trade debtors if credit transactions are included with cash transactions in any of the previous items in the identity).[2]

Although the above identity captures all the various cash inflows and outflows, it would be inappropriate to leave it as the basis for a single cash flow statement. In fact, each major item in the main statement should be supported by a detailed subsidiary statement. For example, item O could be expanded as follows.

$$s - m - w - o - i = O$$

where s = sales receipts; m = cash payments for goods for resale; w = wage repayments; o = overhead payments; and i = loan interest payments.[3] It could be extended to separate new from replacement investment, as well as purchases from disposals. Also, T could distinguish foreign from non-foreign taxation.

In addition to the above-mentioned expanded disclosure of cash flow information, a number of other extensions to the system can be recommended. In some instances, they are compatible with existing disclosure practice; in others, they

---

2 It should also be noted that the various cash inflows and outflows can result in a decrease in cash resources or, indeed, in an increase in 'cash' liabilities — that is, bank overdraft and similar borrowings.

3 The extent of disclosure on each of these items would depend on the circumstances of the enterprise and the judgment of its management as to what was relevant and useful to report users.

CASH FLOW ACCOUNTING AND REPORTING 151

extend the latter (in a way compatible with other recommendations covered in this book).

First, cash flow accounting lends itself to segmental reporting, with particular regard to the disclosure of operational cash flows (O).[4] Secondly, the cash flow data which are reported can be forecast, as well as historical, in order to provide report users with guidelines to the future as well as statements of the past.[4] Thirdly, if forecast cash flow statements are provided, they could be supported by relevant statements of the various commercial and financial assumptions on which they are based (together with explanations of the variances which have occurred between actual and previously-forecast results; and a suitable audit review of the forecasts, assumptions and variances). Fourthly, because not all transactions of the reporting enterprise will involve cash inflows and outflows, it would appear appropriate to produce also a statement describing these transactions, thereby avoiding an incompleteness in the system (examples might include the purchase of other enterprises, satisfied by the issuing of share capital or loan stock). Finally, cash flow reporting suggestions have, until recently, ignored the question of providing relevant and compatible information on the reporting enterprise's overall financial position. With this in mind, it is conceivable for it to report on the latter in terms of realisable values (a topic which will be dealt with in greater depth later in this chapter).

The importance of the previously-mentioned additions to the basic cash flow reporting system is that each enhances its relevance and utility to the report user — segmentation identifies individual parts of the enterprise which are strengths or weaknesses in its overall liquidity position; forecasting adds a further dimension to the reporting data bank on which various decisions may be based; supporting forecasts by assumptions and explained variances puts the actual and forecast results within a suitable context and improves the accountability of enterprise management to the various report user groups; non-cash transactions (which will almost certainly influence

---

[4] Both these suggestions are made on the basis of the arguments for the respective systems given in the relevant chapters in this book.

future cash movements) must be reported to ensure report users are not deprived of data relevant to their decisions; and an overall statement of financial position which relates to cash flows would appear also to avoid gaps in the reporting system.

The above comments are intended as no more than brief introductions to the remaining sections in this chapter. They hopefully provide the reader with a flavour of the structure, purpose and problems associated with cash flow accounting and reporting. Of particular relevance in this context is the fact that, even at this introductory stage, the most crucial element of the reporting system has been touched upon on several occasions — that is, the provision of relevant and useful information to a variety of persons concerned with and interested in the reporting enterprise. It is to this issue that we now turn.

Uses and Users

No financial reporting system can ignore the vital topic of report users — particularly, the specific uses to which the reported information can be put. In this respect, cash flow reporting is no different from any other system. Following numerous recommendations by individual writers, the importance of report users was formally recognised in the early 1970s on both sides of the Atlantic (AICPA 1973; and ASC 1975). However, the US *Trueblood Report* rejected cash flow reporting in favour of periodic earnings (despite acknowledging the importance of cash flow information to various external report users); and in the UK, *The Corporate Report* ignored the topic completely (despite its analysis of the needs of various user groups). Nevertheless, the Sandilands report on inflation accounting in 1975 (HMSO 1975) provided the first institutional recognition of the potential utility of cash flow reporting. Surprisingly, despite such recognition, it did not regard the system as being a feasible addition to financial reports (pp. 156–8). It has therefore to be seen whether or

CASH FLOW ACCOUNTING AND REPORTING   153

not the present study on liquidity reporting by the US Financial Accounting Standards Board will reverse this relative lack of attention to and recognition of the topic of cash flow reporting by professional accountancy and other bodies.

In other words, despite an increasing attention to the needs of financial report users, and despite limited 'official' support for cash flow reporting in relation to these users, it has been left to individual writers to argue the merits and utility of cash flow accounting reports. The evidence of these arguments (see, for example, Lee 1972 and 1978) reveal that the system is conceived as a multi-purpose one, being capable of meeting the specific needs of a variety of report users. In general terms, this broad utility refers to the provision of cash flow data as part of the exercise of managerial accountability, and for a variety of decisions. To be more specific, however, at least some description of these accountability and decision functions is required.

As previously mentioned, cash flow reports describe the liquidity flows and position of the reporting enterprise and, as such, inform their users of the actual and/or potential achievements of its financial management. It is therefore this aspect of accountability with which cash flow reporting is designed to cope — forecast cash flows providing a statement of what management is hoping or expecting to achieve in cash terms during the period(s) to come; and actual cash flows describing the results which have been achieved in the same terms. These statements, together with supporting explanations of variances, undoubtedly aid the process of accountability by making the reporting management commit to paper the results of their financial stewardship both *ex ante* and *ex post*. All report users concerned with the well-being of the reporting enterprise (particularly its potential to survive long-term) should be aided by the provision of this information.

In this sense, therefore, the general utility of cash flow reporting is in line with the ever-widening accountability of enterprise management to the outside world — that is, liquidity and financial management appear to be suitable topics for which enterprise managers can be held accountable; and accountability is increasingly being conceived in terms of a multiplicity of user groups (investors, lenders, bankers, creditors, employees, customers and government, each being concerned to a greater or lesser extent with the quality of the reporting enterprise's financial management which is so crucial to its long-term survival).

The relevance of cash flow reports to the decisions of various report users can also be commented on. Investors' decision models are mainly based on cash dividend flows from the enterprise; lenders and bankers are concerned with the cash receipt of interest and capital sums when due by the enterprise; creditors, too, are mainly concerned with the enterprise's ability to meet its obligations in cash to them on due dates; the availability of cash within the enterprise is crucial to the well-being of employees concerned with payment of wages, wage claims, future jobs, and the provision of facilities from which they can benefit; customers buying goods and services from the enterprise are interested in whether it will be able and available to meet its potential 'sale of goods' commitments; and government relies on the enterprise having sufficient cash to pay its taxation liabilities when due. In other words, despite the brevity of the above comments, it is clear from them that all potential report user groups are interested in some way or another in matters to which cash is strongly related — that is, the enterprise's ability to pay dividends to investors, interest and capital to lenders and bankers, amounts due to suppliers, wages and other benefits to employees, rectification and maintenance services for customers, and taxation to government. Cash is therefore a universal resource of the reporting enterprise, and it ought to be no surprise that reported information about cash flows and resources should have a universal appeal to a variety of report users.

Computing Cash Flow Data

Writings advocating the implementation of cash flow reporting have rarely commented on the computation of cash flow data

CASH FLOW ACCOUNTING AND REPORTING 155

for reporting purposes. Instead, they have given the impression that the latter are readily available. Whether this is so is debatable and yet to be proven one way or another but, meantime, it is clear that external report users do not have access to cash flow data as they are not presently reported. Thus, some means of obtaining surrogate data has to be found in order to provide interested users with information about the reporting enterprise's cash position.[5] The way to do this is to recognise the principles of double-entry bookkeeping, and reverse the effect of these principles in allocation and credit-based accounting information (that is, to cancel the effects of depreciation, stock, debtors, creditors, etc., and reveal the underlying cash base to it). The approach in this respect is a relatively simple one — if three separate items of data relating to a piece of accounting information are known, then the fourth datum can be derived if the basic accounting identity is to remain in balance. For example, assume the following sales information:

Credit sales, as reported in the income statement for period t_0 to t_1, were:	£100,000
Debtors, as reported in the accompanying balance sheet, were:	
at t_0	£ 10,000
at t_1	£ 15,000

Thus, given that opening debtors plus credit sales minus closing debtors equal cash received from customers, then:

$$£10,000 + 100,000 - 15,000 = £95,000$$

In other words, the cash-equivalent figure for sales for period t_0 to t_1 was £95,000.

---

5 The existence of predominantly credit transaction-based accounting systems may make the provision of allocation-free, credit-free data a difficult task. In addition, even the surrogate approach can only give very limited information on cash flows (for example, it is not possible to produce forecast data by this means).

Similar computations, following equivalent principles, can be made for trading costs (by adjusting for opening and closing creditors and stock and work-in-progress), as can those for taxation[6] and dividends. But they may be made more easily if the reporting enterprise includes within its financial statements a statement of source and application of funds. In the latter report, it is usual within the UK and elsewhere to contain data which are either in cash terms (such as taxation and dividend payments) or can be easily converted into cash terms. (Trading profits are usually stated after adjusting for the accounting effects of allocations such as depreciation, losses on sale of fixed assets, and other bookkeeping write-offs; and the periodic change in working capital — stock, debtors and creditors — is normally also given.) Thus, the major adjustments to be made to funds data to convert them to their cash equivalents are as follows:

Trading profits before taxation
Add: depreciation and other accounting allocations[7]
Less: increase in working capital[8]
Giving: cash operating income before taxation.

In other words, the above adjustments cancel out the effects of accounting allocations and credit transactions in traditional financial statements. They make some heroic assumptions about the linking of debtors and creditors entirely to trading costs (and not in part to the costs of expenditure on long-lived assets). Thus, they must always be regarded as approximations only to actual cash flows.

The next stage is to prepare figures for the net cash cost of expenditure on new and replacement investment in long-lived

---

6 Opening and closing taxation provisions require figures for deferred tax and advance corporation tax to be included (where relevant).

7 If a funds statement is not available, these will require to be searched for in the relevant income statement and supporting notes. Accounting 'gains' of this nature would require to be deducted.

8 A decrease in working capital would be added to trading profits. If such changes were not available because of the lack of a funds statement, they could be computed from the relevant income statement and balance sheets.

assets (such as land, buildings, plant and vehicles). As mentioned above, because of lack of data, it is impossible to adjust the figures in the funds statement (or the balance sheet notes to accounts if no funds statement is available) for relevant debtors and/or creditors. Thus, the reported figures must be taken, separating out the cost of new assets from the disposal proceeds for assets realised.[9]

As previously mentioned, the funds statement usually gives taxation and dividend payments in cash terms. If this is not the case, or a funds statement is not disclosed, the relevant cash data can be derived by taking the income statement deductions, adding the opening balance sheet figures and deducting the closing balance sheet figures. Once this has been done, most of the data for the main cash flow statement should be available, and can be reconciled to the relevant cash changes in capital, loans and the defined cash resources (which are either in the funds statement or can be derived from a comparison of relevant balance sheet information). The following simple examples, based on the published funds statement of a small UK public company, illustrate these various stages of adjustment and the eventual main cash flow statement (Table 7.1).

Table 7.1 is not the only way in which the cash flow data could be reported (for example, it could be in a form which closely follows the notation in the identity given earlier in this chapter). However, the stated format provides a neutrality of disclosure which allows its user to make his or her judgment as to the key relationships and the significance of the latter (for example, the proportion of total cash available to each of the various 'commitments' of the enterprise). However, it also omits certain potentially-relevant information, and this ought to be noted.

First, as stated earlier, the data shown are only approximations to the actual cash flow if they are based upon allocated accounting information provided in the traditional set of financial statements. Therefore, not all the information needed

---

9 If not disclosed, sale proceeds can be calculated by relating the net book value of the assets sold (as per balance sheet) to the gain or loss on realisation (as per the income statement, if material).

Table 7.1 Producing a Main Cash Flow Statement

Assume the following summarised funds statement for the company:

	1980 £	1979 £
Profits before taxation	842,000	779,000
Adjustments for items not involving movements of funds:		
depreciation	104,000	85,000
profit retained by company	19,000	37,000
	965,000	901,000
Funds from other sources:		
proceeds of rights issue	–	610,000
regional development grants	–	32,000
disposal of fixed assets	78,000	52,000
	1,043,000	1,595,000
Application of funds:		
dividends paid	(184,000)	(115,000)
taxation paid	(320,000)	(240,000)
additions to fixed assets	(823,000)	(382,000)
	(1,327,000)	(737,000)
	(284,000)	858,000
Increase (decrease) in working capital:		
stocks	(81,000)	140,000
debtors	70,000	214,000
creditors	(51,000)	(86,000)
	(62,000)	268,000
Increase (decrease) in cash resources	(222,000)	590,000
	(284,000)	858,000

Adopting the adjustments described above, the following cash flow computations can be made from this funds statement:

	1980 £	1979 £
Profits after adding back accounting allocations	965,000	901,000
Add decrease; *less*: increase in working capital	(62,000)	268,000
Operating cash flow	1,027,000	633,000
Less: additions to fixed assets	823,000	382,000
less:		
disposals of fixed assets	(78,000)	(52,000)
regional development grants	–	(32,000)

	745,000	298,000
	282,000	335,000
Less: taxation paid	320,000	240,000
	38,000	95,000
Less: dividends paid	184,000	115,000
	(222,000)	(20,000)
Add: rights issue receipts	—	610,000
Increase (decrease) in cash resources	(222,000)	590,000

The above working schedule can next be put into the form of a reportable financial statement:

Statement of Total Cash Flow Year to 31 December

	1980 £	1979 £
Internally-generated cash		
Cash receipts from customers for sale of goods	6,900,000	6,100,000
Less: cash payments for goods, wages and overheads	5,873,000	5,467,000
*Cash operating margin**	1,027,000	633,000
Externally-generated cash		
Proceeds of rights issue	—	610,000
Total cash available for commitments	1,027,000	1,243,000
Less: cash commitments met during year:		
net cash cost of new and replacement investment in long-lived assets	745,000	298,000
taxation to government	320,000	240,000
dividends to shareholders	184,000	115,000
	1,249,000	653,000
Increase (decrease) in cash resources	(222,000)	590,000

Note:* The detailed receipts and payments have been derived from the relevant income statements and balance sheets.

to make the necessary adjustments is given, and the direct production of actual cash flow statements by enterprises ought to be encouraged. Secondly, only two years of data have been given in the above statement and, in order to avoid the problem of interpreting the meaning of isolated peaks and troughs in a trend of cash flow, the report user should be provided with five to ten years of data, depending on the circumstances of the reporting enterprise.[10] Thirdly, the use of existing published data to produce cash flow statements (as above) means that they will be limited to descriptions of past events and activities only, and will not reflect cash flow prospects. Thus, the issue of forecast statements remains. Fourthly, a related problem to the previous one arises from the use of surrogate data to derive cash flow statements, for very little detail of the individual figures can be disclosed (for example, segmental data; the composition of trading cost data; and the split between new and replacement investment data). In other words, each of these points reveals that, although it is possible to produce a summary and total cash flow statement for each past period (through the use of funds statements and/or adjustments to published allocated data), it is no substitute for a full system of cash flow reporting as outlined earlier in this chapter.

---

10 For example, the cash flow of a retail concern is so quick that a five-year report should be more than adequate to identify cash flow trends and avoid the distortions in cash flows of individual periods. However, with a civil engineering contractor involved in building roads or bridges, the long-term nature of individual contracts ensures that ten-year reports would be more suited to this type of business if the report user is not to be confused by receiving the data of individual years. In fact, there is an argument that cumulative cash flow statements ought to be produced to allow the user to become conversant with aggregate cash flow trends.

Cash Flow Statements

Having explained briefly how cash flow data may be derived from published financial reports (as a stepping stone to a full system of cash flow reporting), it may be useful to the reader to examine the financial results of four well-known public companies in the retail stores business when cash flow adjustments have been made to their published funds statements. These data are given for the last five years for each company, and have been subjected to the types of adjustment made in the previous section (they are therefore subject to the various assumptions and simplifications on which these adjustments are founded). The four companies are Great Universal Stores, Marks and Spencer, United Draper Stores and Woolworths. They are all operating in a business which is as near as one can get to being cash flow-based, and yet reveal substantial differences between cash flow changes and their equivalent historic cost profits (table 7.2).

For each company, the relevant cash flow data reflect actual transactions taking place during the periods concerned, mainly because they are unaffected by subjective accounting allocations. Despite the basically cash flow nature of the businesses concerned, it is interesting to note that the use of cash flow accounting retains the 'lumpiness' of particular and total periodic cash flows. In the case of the two largest companies (Great Universal Stores and Marks and Spencer), despite the relative constancy in the growth of their operating, investment, taxation and dividend cash flows, the combination of these data resulted in fluctuating net cash performances. On the other hand, the two smaller companies (United Drapery Stores and Woolworths) (with the exception of one year each) had a constancy in the trend of their net flows after investment, taxation and dividends, yet, again in each case, the operating, investment, taxation and dividend cash flows reveal a distinct 'lumpiness'.

The latter quality is the hallmark of cash flow accounting — it allows the peaks and troughs which pertain to cash flow trends to be retained in financial statement form — something which the inclusion of credit transactions and accounting

Table 7.2 Cash Flows for Four Retail Stores Groups

	1976 £m	1977 £m	1978 £m	1979 £m	1980 £m	Total £m
Great Universal Stores Ltd						
Operating cash flow	70.2	76.8	95.0	148.2	147.2	537.4
Less: investment net of disposals	11.9	21.0	30.8	58.0	50.9	172.6
	58.3	55.8	64.2	90.2	96.3	364.8
Less: taxation paid	36.2	52.0	47.9	46.8	49.2	232.1
	22.1	3.8	16.3	43.4	47.1	132.7
Less: dividends paid	15.8	17.4	19.4	21.6	27.3	101.5
	6.3	(13.6)	(3.1)	21.8	19.8	31.2
Add: net loans received (repaid)	1.9	1.4	2.5	(1.4)	(1.4)	3.0
Increase (decrease) in cash resources	8.2	(12.2)	(0.6)	20.4	18.4	34.2
	1976 £m	1977 £m	1978 £m	1979 £m	1980 £m	Total £m
Marks and Spencer Ltd						
Operating cash flow	78.5	93.5	136.2	178.5	167.6	654.3
Less: investment net of disposals	39.9	36.4	47.1	58.0	73.2	254.6
	38.6	57.1	89.1	120.5	94.4	399.7
Less: taxation paid	36.1	41.3	49.8	53.5	76.7	257.4
	2.5	15.8	39.3	67.0	17.7	142.3
Less: dividends paid	21.6	23.3	27.4	31.5	38.6	142.4
	(19.1)	(7.5)	11.9	35.5	(20.9)	(0.1)
Add: net loans received (repaid)	14.0	4.7	(3.5)	(8.5)	(3.4)	3.3
Increase (decrease) in cash resources	(5.1)	(2.8)	8.4	27.0	(24.3)	3.2
	1976 £m	1977 £m	1978 £m	1979 £m	1980 £m	Total £m
United Drapery Stores Ltd						
Operating cash flow	17.8	11.7	8.7	16.0	11.4	65.6
Less: investment net of disposals	3.9	2.9	1.1	(14.4)	9.8	3.3

	1976 £m	1977 £m	1978 £m	1979 £m	1980 £m	Total £m
Less: taxation paid	13.9	8.8	7.6	30.4	1.6	62.3
	8.0	7.5	7.4	5.7	6.8	35.4
Less: dividends paid	5.9	1.3	0.2	24.7	(5.2)	26.9
	6.8	7.3	7.3	7.8	8.6	37.8
Add: rights issue proceeds	(0.9)	(6.0)	(7.1)	—	(13.8)	(10.9)
	—	—	—	16.9	34.4	34.4
Add: net loans received (repaid)	(0.9)	(6.0)	(7.1)	16.9	20.6	23.5
	0.9	6.2	2.9	(10.1)	(9.1)	(9.2)
Increase (decrease) in cash resources	—	0.2	(4.2)	6.8	11.5	14.3

Woolworths Ltd

	1976 £m	1977 £m	1978 £m	1979 £m	1980 £m	Total £m
Operating cash flow	34.0	30.7	40.8	28.0	42.0	175.5
Less: investment net of disposals	13.9	12.7	8.0	12.6	21.4	68.6
	20.1	18.0	32.8	15.4	20.6	106.9
Less: taxation paid	12.3	9.5	12.2	11.5	15.2	60.7
	7.8	8.5	20.6	3.9	5.4	46.2
Less: dividends paid	14.9	14.9	14.9	15.8	17.4	77.9
Net (increase) decrease in loans	(7.1)	(6.4)	5.7	(11.9)	(12.0)	(31.7)

Equivalent Historic Cost Income for Four Retail Stores Groups*

	1976 £m	1977 £m	1978 £m	1979 £m	1980 £m	Total £m
Great Universal Stores Ltd	40.3	45.4	50.7	67.3	68.1	271.8
Marks and Spencer Ltd	20.7	29.7	36.9	51.5	49.5	188.3
United Drapery Stores Ltd	3.0	4.9	5.4	12.1	6.7	32.1
Woolworths Ltd	0.4	3.0	8.5	22.5	22.2	56.6

Note: * Income defined as reported trading profits after deduction of depreciation of fixed assets, and taxation and dividend provisions, and including extra-ordinary items.

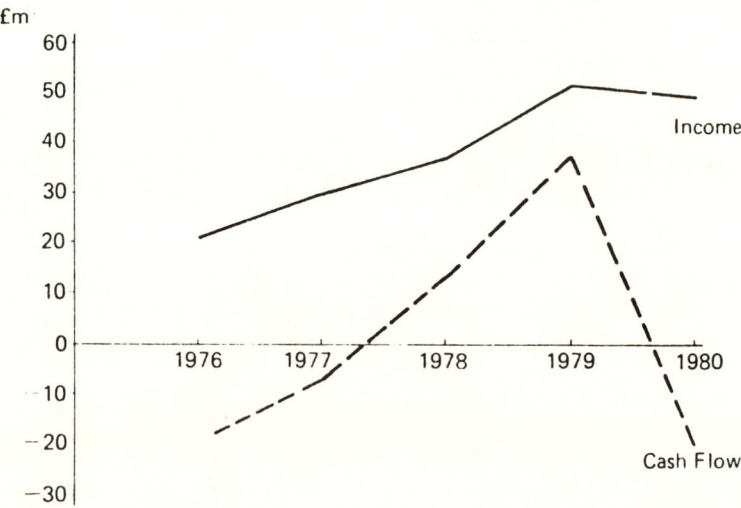

Figure 7.1 *Cash Flow and Income Data — Marks and Spencer Ltd*

allocations does not allow. This can be seen when the traditional historic cost-based income figures (after depreciation, taxation and dividends) of the four companies are examined. They reveal a constancy of trend over the five-year period in each case (with a levelling or falling off in figures in 1980 due to the effects of the economic recession), but they are distinctly different from their equivalent cash flow data. This can be best demonstrated graphically by taking the post-dividend cash flow and income figures for a large company (Marks and Spencer) (figure 7.1) and for a smaller one (Woolworths) (figure 7.2).

In both figures 7.1 and 7.2, it is clear that cash flows do underlie income measurements (by very substantial amounts), and that income is a very much smoothed version of cash flow. This is not to argue against the reporting of income — merely to demonstrate that, should income measurements be reported, it is misleading not also to disclose the underlying cash flow. Accounting allocations such as stock valuations and fixed asset depreciation have the effect of removing the peaks and troughs in enterprise liquidity with which financial management is concerned. For example, in the case of

CASH FLOW ACCOUNTING AND REPORTING

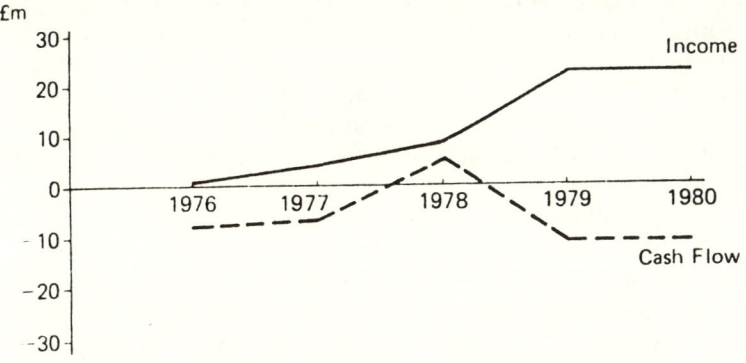

Figure 7.2 *Cash Flow and Income Data — Woolworths Ltd*

Woolworths, it is reasonably clear from an inspection of figure 7.2 that, despite its recent growth in profits, there is an underlying liquidity problem which is necessitating continuous borrowing to cover the cash flow deficits. From the figures given in table 7.2, it is also apparent that this has much to do with a distinct unevenness in operational activity when expressed in cash terms (operating cash flows of the company moving from £34m to £31m to £41m to £28m to £42m over the five-year period from 1976 to 1980). It is doubtful whether these matters would have been apparent from a reading of the year-by-year traditional income statement, balance sheet and funds statement.

A Statement of Financial Position

As previously mentioned, suggestions for cash flow accounting and reporting have rarely contained provision for the disclosure of a statement of financial position which relates to and is compatible with the reporting of periodic cash flows. This gap has recently been bridged in some detail with the recommendation that statements of financial position based on net realisable values appear to be linked with cash flows by means of an overall statement of realised and potentially-realisable cash flows (Lee 1981). In other words, realisable values reflect future cash flows and, when applied to statements of financial position, provide a report of enterprise assets and liabilities which is compatible with its statement of realised cash flows (which has been the main object of attention in this chapter).

The similarity between cash flow accounting and net realisable value accounting appears to be reasonably strong, and for a number of reasons: each system is allocation-free in its use of accounting data, the condition of enterprise survival and its relation to cash is strongly emphasised in both; neither assumes the rather improbable situation of the reporting enterprise having an indefinite life; and each appears to be relevant to the decision needs of a variety of report users. But the most important reason appears to be that they are effectively part of the same system of financial accounting and that, by expanding one or other out to include realisable as well as realised cash flows, a more relevant information source is available to report users. This can be demonstrated in table 7.3 which provides (in outline only) the main parts of the total cash flow system.

The figures in table 7.3 would require a great deal of additional disclosure to provide a set of meaningful financial statements for report users. However, it should be sufficient to give the reader a flavour of the total information being reported, and of how a statement of realised cash flow is only a small part of the overall picture. The use of realisable values allows the reporting accountant to give much more information about, first, the realisability of assets and the payability of obligations (classifications of assets, particularly, requiring amendment from the traditional fixed and current categories); and, secondly, the *potential* changes in cash inflows and outflows which result from changes in the realisable values of assets and the recorded amounts of liabilities.

CASH FLOW ACCOUNTING AND REPORTING

Table 7.3 Cash Flows and Realisable Values

Balance Sheet as at t_0	£	Total Cash Flow Statement t_0 to t_1	£	Balance Sheet as at t_1	£
Realised cash assets	15,000	Realised cash flow*	29,000	Realised cash assets	44,000
Readily-realisable assets	92,000	Increase in potential cash flow	13,000	Readily-realisable assets	105,000
Not-readily-realisable assets	47,000	Increase in potential cash flow	6,000	Not-readily-realisable assets	53,000
Non-realisable assets	—	Increase in potential cash flow	—	Non-realisable assets	—
	154,000		48,000		202,000
Short-term obligations	54,000	Additional credit received	9,000	Short-term obligations	63,000
Long-term obligations	30,000	Additional borrowings received	20,000	Long-term obligations	50,000
Indefinite obligations	70,000	Additional funds accruing**	19,000	Indefinite obligations	89,000
	154,000		48,000		202,000

Notes: * The net change in realised cash assets which is detailed in the cash flow statements of an historic nature explained in previous sections of this chapter.
** Assuming no capital introduced or repaid during the year, this figure would represent the realisable income for the period (after taxation and dividend provisions have been deducted).

Benefits of Cash Flow Accounting

This chapter can give only a flavour of the nature of cash flow reports and the utility of cash flow accounting. The latter is at a relatively primitive stage of its development, despite the longevity of cash accounting in business, and despite the apparent simplicity of the methods of accounting applied to it. Much has yet to be done regarding such matters as disclosure and presentation of cash flow data; the production of forecast cash flow statements; and the various ways in which cash flow data can be used and interpreted. Meantime, however, the reader's attention is drawn to a number of significant benefits which can be derived from cash flow accounting and reporting.

First, cash flow accounting avoids arbitrary accounting allocations, and thus there is little need for concern over the question of accounting flexibility and the need for accounting standards. Nor does there appear to be need for concern over matters of price and price-level changes (except, insofar as the use of net realisable values are contemplated). In other words, the issues of current cost accounting and/or current purchasing power accounting do not concern cash flow accounting — past cash flows adequately reflect actual price movements, forecast cash flows capture future price movements, and realisable values state current prices.

Secondly, because cash flow accounting avoids allocations, it can be argued that it allows the 'bare facts' of the reporting enterprise's finances to be reported. Thus, essential differences can be seen in financial terms between similar types of business (where such differences should not exist) and different types of business (where differences are to be expected). It is unfortunate that the process of accounting allocation can distort or remove these differences to such an extent that it is impossible, when comparing the financial results of two enterprises, to say whether differences in the results are due to operational activity or accounting measurement procedures. Cash flow accounting avoids this dilemma.

Thirdly, two of the most vital features of enterprise management are highlighted by cash flow accounting — that is, its financial management generally, and its liquidity management particularly. These would appear to be something in which all report user groups ought to be interested, because they are so crucial to the decision functions of these groups. Thus, cash flow accounting has a general utility which should commend itself to a profession which has emphasised the general-purpose nature of financial reports over many decades.

Finally, of all the available systems of financial reporting, cash flow accounting is one of the most objective and understandable. It attempts to state facts in financial accounting terms without the accountant having to become involved in making subjective judgments as to which period the data relates. And it is expressed in terms which should be familiar to all non-accountants — cash resources and flows are things which anyone in a developed economy has to administer from day to day. Thus, cash flow reports are potentially comprehensible, a matter which is of increasing concern to accountants as the number of report users and groups increases year by year.

Cash flow accounting and reporting has a long and honourable history in the development of business enterprises. It was superseded by the sophisticated statements of allocated data which are now such a familiar part of financial reporting practice. Perhaps, with liquidity such a vital issue in business today, the wheel will turn full circle, and cash flow accounting will again be restored to its rightful place as a useful and relevant source of financial information about business enterprises for a variety of report users.

References

Coughlan, J.W. (1964), Funds and income, *NAA Bulletin*, September, pp. 23–34.

Heath, L.C. (1978), Financial reporting and the evaluation of solvency, *Accounting Research Monograph 3*, American Institute of Certified Public Accountants (AICPA).

Ijiri, Y. (1978), Cash flow accounting and its structure, *Journal of Accounting, Auditing and Finance*, May, pp. 331–48.

Lawson, G.H. (1971), Cash-flow accounting, *The Accountant*, 28 October, pp. 586-9 and 4 November, pp. 620-22.

Lawson, G.H. (1978), The rationale of cash flow accounting, in C. van Dam (ed.), *Trends in Managerial and Financial Accounting*, Martinus Nijhoff, pp. 85-104.

Lee, T.A. (1972), A case for cash flow reporting, *Journal of Business Finance*, Summer, pp. 27-36.

Lee, T.A. (1978), The cash flow accounting alternative for corporate financial reporting, in C. van Dam (*op. cit.*), pp. 63-84.

Lee, T.A. (1981), Reporting cash flows and net realisable values, *Accounting and Business Research*, Spring, pp. 98-105.

Accounting Objectives Study Group (1973), *Objectives of Financial Statements*, American Institute of Certified Public Accountants (AICPA).

Accounting Standards Committee (1975), *The Corporate Report*, ASC.

Inflation Accounting Committee (1975), Inflation accounting, *Report of the Inflation Accounting Committee*, HMSO Cmnd. 6225, pp. 156-8.

Funds Statements and Cash Flow Analysis

T. A. Lee, Professor of Accountancy and Finance University of Edinburgh

Companies fail because of lack of cash flow and cash resources. Although there be many reasons for this point being reached, the life of a company ends when its cash flow ceases, and its sources of cash disappear.

It is doubtful if many investment analysts would disagree with this conclusion, and presumably few would not be interested in receiving and using financial information relating to cash flow and cash resources. But recent research evidence suggests otherwise.

The Lee and Tweedie Studies

In a series of studies, Lee and Tweedie have sought to demonstrate that investors generally have a relatively small interest in reported information which would be helpful in assessing and predicting corporate liquidity. In 1975, for example, in a study of both private and institutional investors,[1] they found that only 16% of respondents indicated liquidity data to be the most significant part of annual financial statements. A later study in 1977 of private shareholders[2] revealed that only 7% of respondents classified liquidity data as particularly relevant to their investment needs. Indeed, 43% did not read the funds statement (which is arguably the single most valuable information source on liquidity matters). 18% read its content thoroughly, and it was typically classified as of slight importance.

Institutional investors were reported on similarly in 1981,[3] and the results were somewhat more encouraging. 67% of respondents read the funds statement thoroughly (although 7% failed to read it at all). It was generally considered to be of moderate to considerable importance in investment matters. But only 27% of respondents believed liquidity data to be particularly important; 7% predicted liquidity data; and an alarming 64% appeared to have no understanding of the content of funds statements.

Profit and Cash Flow

In all three studies, profitability and profit statements were the focal point for most investors. Thus, this general pattern of behaviour appears to ignore a vital and elementary financial lesson concerning the relationship between profits and cash flows.

Realised profit before depreciation (defined in terms of historic costs) is a product of two separable measurements – first, the operating cash flow (defined as operating cash receipts minus operating cash payments); and, second, the associated periodic change in working capital (defined restrictively in terms of stocks and work-in-progress plus debtors and minus creditors – each such item relating to operational receipts and payments, and debtors and creditors including prepayments and accruals, respectively). Thus, the conventionally reported profit can be described as operating cash flow $\pm$ the periodic change in working capital (+ if it is a decrease, and – if it is an increase). Alternatively, operating cash flow can be derived by netting the realised profit and working capital data.

Put more basically, operating cash flow can be seen to be an expression of the realised profit of a company after maintenance of its working capital at levels determined by its financial management. It is therefore a description of the cash flow which is available from its trading operations for purposes of such matters as capital expenditure (possibly including research and development), taxation, distribution, and borrowing repayments.

Investment analysts ought to be concerned to receive information not just about realised profits but also about the underlying operating cash flows – the former to inform him of corporate profitability and the latter to "fine tune" profits data in liquidity terms. A company, for example, will consume cash from realised profits whenever it increases its stocks or debtors, or decreases its creditors. Likewise, realised profits can be augmented by financial management which results in decreased stocks or debtors, or increased creditors.

Thus, operating cash flow is the product of the actions of financial management as well as profitable activity, and it is information about this which aids the investment analyst in assessing whether or not a company is viable in terms of *both* profitability and liquidity. The latter, particularly, is the key to corporate survival, although each interacts with the other. The problem with conventional corporate accounting and reporting is that related data are so articulated as to hide the liquidity information within the reported data on profitability.

For example, suppose realised profit before depreciation for a defined period is £560,000. When received, this figure can be related for analysis purposes to others such as capital employed, total assets, turnover, etc. in order to assess its quality and meaning by means of familiar ratios. But suppose also that, over the same period, stock has increased by £305,000, debtors by £211,000, and creditors by £100,000 (a net increase in these working capital items of £416,000). By definition, this means that the underlying operating cash flow is £560,000 − 416,000 or £144,000, a decidedly less inspiring figure in terms of the cash flow available to fund capital expenditure, taxation, dividends and borrowing repayments. Equally, if the change in the stated working capital items had been a net decrease of £416,000, the operating cash flow equivalent would have been nearly double the profit as £560,000 + 416,000 or £976,000. Both operating cash flow figures reflect the results of profitable operations coupled with financial management.

It is therefore being argued in this paper that the combination of profitability and liquidity data in this way provides the investment analyst with a view of both sides of the same coin when assessing corporate viability over time − business survival depending on both profits from operations and sound financial management. In addition, this approach to investment analysis has the considerable advantage of avoiding many of the subjective judgments involved in profit measurements which tend to cast doubt on the latter's reliability. The netting of profit and the working capital change negates all such judgements concerning the accounting for stocks and work-in-progress, debtors and prepayments, and creditors and accruals. If they exist in working capital, they must also exist in realised profit. Netting therefore cancels them, and leaves the investment analyst with objective cash flows.

The remainder of this paper is concerned to develop the above-mentioned points by introducing a method of cash flow analysis which is based on profit and related data, minimises the accounting problem of subjective judgment, provides needed information on the liquidity situation underlying profitability, and makes specific use of the funds statement. In fact, the latter document is the key to such analysis given the lack of reporting of actual cash flow information by companies.

Using the Funds Statement

Since 1975 in the UK,[4] the funds statement has become a familiar part of corporate financial reporting − the relevant provision being applicable to all companies with an annual turnover of £25,000 or more. The usual presentation format is the reconciliation of various sources of funds (such as profit before depreciation, share capital issues, and fixed asset disposal proceeds) with various uses of these funds (including capital expenditure, increases in working capital, and tax and dividend payments), and often balancing with movements in defined monetary resources or borrowings. Thus, a typical funds statement might appear in an annual report as follows:

Source of Funds	£	£
Trading profits after interest and depreciation		383,000
Add: adjustments for depreciation and other non-fund items		177,000
Funds from operations		560,000
Rights issue proceeds		100,000
Long-term loan		110,000
Investment grants		15,000
Disposal of fixed assets		16,000
		801,000
Application of Funds		
Capital expenditure		156,000
Increase in working capital:		
Stock and work-in-progress	305,000	
Debtors	211,000	
(Creditors)	(100,000)	
		416,000
Taxation paid		209,000
Dividends paid		168,000
Repayment of loan		30,000
		979,000
Increase in bank overdraft		178,000

The above financial statement contains much useful data for the investment analyst but arguably it is not in a form which easily aids his understanding of the liquidity position of the company as it has progressed over the period concerned. Much of the reported funds data are already in a cash form, and a modest rearrangement provides the analyst with information which is on a relatively pure cash basis. The steps involved in this rearrangement are as follows:

1. Net the funds from operations with the increase in working capital to obtain an operating cash flow for the period of £144,000 (£560,000 − 416,000). The profit and the working capital change would be added if the latter represented a decrease.

2. Net the flows for capital expenditure, asset disposals and investment grants to get the total net cash flow on new investment. For liquidity purposes, the analyst is concerned to know how much cash was spent by the company on the latter, and in this case the figure is £125,000 (£156,000 − 16,000 − 15,000).

3. Net the borrowing flows to obtain the aggregate change in total borrowing for the period as this will reflect the additional cash received or repaid by the company. The above funds statement reveals an aggregate additional borrowing of £258,000 (£178,000 + 110,000 − 30,000).

4. The remaining figures require no further adjustment usually, and are now available with those in 1, 2 and 3 above to produce a cash flow statement for the period which can be the basis for further analysis. It would take the following format:

Cash Inflows	£
Operating cash flow	144,000
Share capital	100,000
Additional borrowing	258,000
	502,000
Cash Outflows	£
Capital expenditure	125,000
Taxation paid	209,000
Dividends paid	168,000
	502,000

In this way, the detail of the funds statement has been reduced to a relatively few key datum, each expressed in cash terms, and devoid of subjective accounting practices. It reflects the contribution to the cash needs of the company from operations, shareholders, and lenders and bankers. In particular, it provides a cash flow-based portrayal of changes in the gearing of the company − by comparing operational cash flow and share capital issues with additional borrowing (in this case, £144,00 + £100,000 or £244,00 related to £258,000). In addition, the cash uses can be typically split between "plough back" expenditure in the form of new net investment (in this case, £125,000) and "distributional" payments such as tax and dividends (in this case, £209,000 + 168,000 or £377,000). In other words, the inflow section describes the company's reliance on internal and external generation of cash, and the outflow section also makes a similar distinction in terms of expenditure. In the above example, the company has required more external cash funding than could be generated internally. It has used a minority of the available cash on new investment.

Further Adjustments and Aggregations

It would be wrong for any analyst to judge the profitability and financial position of a company solely on the basis of an isolated year's results. To do so would be meaningless because it would not allow for comparability generally, and the assessment of trends particularly. The issue of liquidity analysis is no different. In fact, due to the inevitable lumpiness of cash flows (which conventional accounting sets out to defeat by smoothing practices), it is essential that the analyst examines cash flow data in the form of a multi-period trend analysis.

The length of these period aggregates will depend on what the analyst regards as a normal operational cycle for the company concerned. With retail concerns such as stores, a trend using single-year results may be perfectly adequate to detect long-term changes and movements. On the other hand, for a civil engineering contracting company, the use of four or five-year aggregates may be more appropriate if significant trends are to be spotted, and if the distortions of the cash results of individual years are to be avoided.

The first step in this process of meaningful aggregation prior to interpretation is to obtain the requisite number of years' cash flow results laid out as described in the previous section (that is, equating cash inflows with outflows). For example, assuming that the normal operating cycle of the company is judged to be three years (which would be a usual manufacturing situation), the following cash flow data have been prepared from available funds statements. In order to obtain a minimum of three multi-period aggregates, at least five years of individual results are required for example, 1978, 1979, 1980, 1981 and 1982 provide aggregates of 1978–9–80, 1979–80–1, and 1980–1–2. Four multi-period aggregates require six years of results.

Five aggregates need seven years; and so on. In this case, four three-year aggregates have been prepared from six sets of individual cash flow data (in addition to a six-year summary):

	1977	1978	1979	1980	1981	1982	Total
Cash Inflows	£000	£000	£000	£000	£000	£000	£000
Operating cash flow	532	501	144	80	90	178	1,525
Share capital	—	—	100	—	—	—	100
Additional borrowing	50	113	258	306	365	49	1,141
	582	614	502	386	455	227	2,766
Cash Outflows							
Capital expenditure	222	214	125	138	267	105	1,071
Taxation paid	240	260	209	101	54	62	926
Dividends paid	120	140	168	147	134	60	769
	582	614	502	386	455	227	2,766

The above single period results are reduced in the first instance to three-year "rolling" totals:

	1977–9	1978–80	1979–81	1980–2	1977–82
Cash Inflows	£000	£000	£000	£000	£000
Operating cash flow	1,177	725	314	348	1,525
Share capital	100	100	100	—	100
Additional borrowing	421	677	929	720	1,141
	1,698	1,502	1,343	1,068	2,766
Cash Outflows					
Capital expenditure	561	477	530	510	1,071
Taxation paid	709	570	364	217	926
Dividends paid	428	455	449	341	769
	1,698	1,502	1,343	1,068	2,766

And these data can be further reduced to a simpler form by conversion to percentages of the total flow for each multi-period aggregate:

	1977–9	1978–80	1979–81	1980–2	1977–82
Cash Inflows	%	%	%	%	%
Operating cash flow	69	48	24	33	55
Share capital	6	7	7	—	4
Additional borrowing	25	45	69	67	41
	100	100	100	100	100
Cash Outflows					
Capital expenditure	33	32	39	48	39
Taxation paid	42	38	27	20	33
Dividends paid	25	30	34	32	28
	100	100	100	100	100

The analyst has thus reduced the relevant data to manageable proportions which can be updated as each new year's results are received – that is, when the results for 1983 are available, those for 1977 could be left out of the analysis.

Interpreting Cash Flow Data

Producing cash flow data from funds statement, and aggregating them into multi-period totals, are only first steps in the direction of assessing corporate liquidity. The next stage is to take the data and interpret them within the context of the particular company and the other available sources of information about it. Interpretation in this context is not a matter where specific rules or guidelines can be laid down. Much depends on the expert judgment of the analyst but general principles can be stated:

1. Companies with liquidity problems will tend to be those with a diminishing operating cash flow contribution, and increasing reliance on external funding such as additional borrowing. In other words, a failing company is one which is not generating sufficient cash flow from its realised profits in the long-term. This may be due to inadequate profitability, and this can be best judged through conventional profit-based analyses using profit margins and returns on capital employed. However, another reason may be the quality of financial management which is allowing working capital to exceed minimum required levels. Increased working capital must be converted into cash flow eventually otherwise it remains as, for example, costly and unsaleable stock and uncollected debts. Equally, decreased working capital results in cash flows additional to those represented by the realised profits of the period.

Successful companies in cash flow terms are therefore those which over a considerable period, convert their reported profits into cash flows, and thereby minimise their need for external funding. Unsuccessful companies fail to maximise on operating cash flow, and inevitably increase their dependence on borrowings to compensate. A comparison of operating cash flows to additional borrowings provides the analyst with a useful measure of this additional gearing in cash terms – that is, devoid of the subjective judgments affecting conventional gearing calculations which are based on equity data containing retained profits. An increasing and continuous cash-based gearing is a sure indicator of liquidity problems due to poor profitability and/or poor financial management.

This general principle can be reasonably seen in the admittedly exaggerated example used earlier in this section. Using three-year rolling totals, the trend has been quite clear – the contribution from operating cash flow has dropped steadily from a 1977–9 figure of 69% to a 1980–2 equivalent of 33%; and this has been compensated for by an equal and opposite rise in the additional cash funding from borrowing – from 25% in 1977–9 to 67% in 1980–2.

2. The total cash flow pool available to a company from such sources as operations and borrowings mentioned above is usually required in the first instance to provide for the cost of capital expenditure representing either a maintenance or a change in the physical structure of the company. It is this new investment which is the key to the generation of operating cash flows in the future. Without an adequate investment in the past, operating cash flows are bound to decline as such things as plant and equipment deteriorate and the company loses its competitiveness in a rapidly-changing technological age.

What is therefore of crucial importance in cash flow analysis in this respect is the degree to which available cash is being invested in needed capital expenditure. In particular, the analyst ought to be concerned to learn of the balance over time between capital expenditure and distributions. The less cash which is being spent on the former and the more on the latter may be a clue to predictions of operating cash flows (and, thus, borrowings) in the future.

Of course, much will depend on the individual circumstances of the company and the nature of its activities and operations. For example, manufacturing companies may have a considerably greater use of available cash for replacement and new fixed assets than, say, retail concerns such as stores and supermarkets. Also, companies may reinvest by selling off assets such as land and buildings and use the proceeds to acquire needed alternative assets. In these cases, the net cash investment may appear relatively small, and the analyst ought to take care in his interpretation of the detailed figures. Likewise, the analyst will require to exercise caution in this respect with companies funding capital expenditure by leasing.

This topic will be dealt with later as will the entire question of assets acquired by non-cash funding. Meantime, the CFA figures provided in the example in this section reveal a growing use of cash for investment – from 33% in 1977–9 to 48% in 1980–2 – although much of the latter contribution was due to the surge of expenditure in 1981 to £267,000 (a level similar to those of 1977 and 1978 and roughly twice as much as in 1979, 1980 and 1982). By contrast, the level of cash spending on taxation was falling – from 42% in 1977–9 to 20% in 1980–2. Distributions, on the other hand, were at a relatively high level throughout the six years concerned – averaging 28% of the available cash.

3. One further interpretative principle also concerns the use of available cash and that is the level of taxation paid by the company being analysed on a cash basis. Apart from the considerable advantage for the analyst of using a tax figure which is devoid of the largely uninterpretable adjustments of accountants using deferred tax practices, the overall tax payment as a percentage of the total cash "pool" available in particular periods provides him with an indication of the effective cash rate of taxation which can be expected for the company concerned. Corporate taxation is not neutral in the sense that all companies are treated by tax provisions in the same way – for example, with regard to such matters as capital allowances. Thus, by taking operating cash flow minus capital expenditure, and relating this with tax payments, it is possible to obtain a tax rate on a cash basis which can be compared with similar companies. In the previous example, the tax rate for each of the years is as follows:

	1977	1978	1979	1980	1981	1982	Total
	%	%	%	%	%	%	%
Cash tax rate	77	91	1100	(174)	(31)	98	204

Thus, it can be seen that tax rates can become very high and, in cases when capital expenditure exceeds available operating cash flow, they become negative. In order to avoid these distorting single-period results, the use of three-year totals reveals the following data:

	1977–9	1978–80	1979–81	1980–2
	%	%	%	%
Cash tax rate	115	230	(169)	(83)

The company in this case would appear to be suffering confiscatory levels of taxation, and this (not unusual) situation would be revealing to an analyst concerned to identify problem areas affecting the company.

Cash Flow Analysis Problems

The above explanations of the use of cash flow data derived from funds statements to analyse corporate liquidity would be incomplete unless some mention was made of the problems of judgement which exist in such analyses.

1. The natural "lumpiness" of cash flows is difficult to deal with unless some attempt is made to "smooth" them by trend analysis techniques as explained above. This requires judgments to be made concerning the appropriate operating cycle to apply but this will probably be detectable from other sources of information available to the analyst – for example, reviews of operations. However, it must be remembered that, despite such available information, cash flow analyses depend on judgments by the analyst (rather than by the information producer).

2. The setting off of realised profits against working capital changes makes an assumption that all working capital items relate to profit and operating cash flow. The analyst must therefore be vigilant in detecting items within the working capital context which may relate to other matters (for example, creditors applicable to capital expenditure). Not to make these corrections can distort the operating cash flow and other data. However, company report disclosures may not be sufficient to make these distinctions – in which case the analyst must cope with the data as best he can, remembering that multi-period rolling totals may well minimise the effects of such errors.

3. In a similar vein the analyst may require to deal with non-cash transactions – for example, assets purchased and financed by the issue of share capital or loan stock. On these occasions, there are two schools of thought – either to leave these simultaneous but quasi-cash transactions in the CFA analysis as if they were cash inflows and outflows (because they would have been such if negotiated at different times); or to exclude them but note their existence (because they did not result in a cash movement, and because much depends on the valuation judgments made in relation to the assets and the funding). Because of the latter problems, it may be thought to be prudent to exclude rather than include such non-cash items unless the valuation issue is one about which there is little doubt. One of the biggest examples of this problem area concerns the matter of long-term

leasing of assets. The individual analyst will require to interpret such data in a cash flow analysis context as he see fit.

4. A crucial classification problem affects cash flow-based analysis, and that is the question of what should be regarded as capital expenditure. If funds statements are used to derive cash flow data, the analyst is dependent on the company's classification of capital expenditure. It may well be that items which could be defined as the latter have been written off to profit (for example, as on research and development). In these instances, if sufficient disclosure of the relevant items has been made by the company in its annual financial statements, then some adjustment can be made to the capital expenditure item and the operating cash flow (appropriately increasing both items by the same amount). If no disclosure is made, the analyst has to rely on the company's classification of capital expenditure.

5. In relation to cash flow-based analysis, the crucial matter of investment in capital expenditure can be described in net terms – that is after deduction of the proceeds of the sale of fixed assets and the receipt of investment grants. The net cash outflow is the significant feature. However, this may mean that such an aggregation may hide information, particularly in circumstances where disposal proceeds are large in relation to acquisitions. In these cases, the analyst must take care to note the simultaneous investment and disinvestment which is taking place in the company concerned.

6. One of the most vexed accounting problems is that concerning the translation of foreign currencies when the company concerned has business operations and net assets overseas. In these circumstances, translation normally takes place in order to render the overseas data compatible with its home-based equivalent. In particular, however, there is a difficulty with funds statements in that movements in funds (whether sources or uses) may be shown which are nothing more than currency restatements – that is, they do not represent actual sources or uses of funds.

In these circumstances, the funds statement ought to eliminate such restatements and thereby reflect funds movements at the time of the appropriate transactions. Some companies do this; others do not. If the latter is the case, the analyst who makes use for cash flow purposes of a funds statement which contains restatement surpluses and/or deficits may find his computation of such matters as operating cash flow, borrowings and capital expenditure to be seriously distorted. On the basis of whatever is disclosed about foreign exchange translation in the financial statements, the analyst must make some adjustment to avoid these distortions. If he does not, an increase in borrowing in a cash flow statement or an increase in operating cash flow may appear to be cash inflows when, in part, they represent translation "surpluses". If there is inadequate disclosure of these matters then cash flow analysis must be regarded as subject to unquantifiable distortions. That this should be possible reflects badly on the present state of funds statement practice which makes no mention of the translation problem.

An Example of Cash Flow Analysis

The above sections have attempted to outline the structure and form of cash flow-based financial

	1975	1976	1977	1978	1979	1980	1981	1982
	£m	£m	£m	£m	£m	£m	£m	£m
Cash Inflows								
Operating cash flow	43.6	52.8	45.0	50.4	85.6	92.7	94.2	123.9
Additional borrowing	—	—	—	4.3	—	—	—	10.6
Decrease in cash assets	7.8	—	—	—	—	—	—	—
	51.4	52.8	45.0	54.7	85.6	92.7	94.2	134.5
Cash Outflows								
Extra-ordinary items	—	—	—	—	—	2.0	6.6	5.3
Capital expenditure	19.2	22.8	17.5	11.6	25.6	43.7	3.2	62.6
Taxation paid	20.0	17.4	14.4	18.9	20.2	21.7	30.6	28.4
Dividends paid	8.5	9.2	10.2	11.2	16.9	15.5	18.8	21.4
Borrowing repayments	3.7	2.1	0.1	—	4.2	7.0	5.9	—
Increase in cash assets	—	1.3	2.8	13.0	18.7	2.8	29.1	16.8
	51.4	52.8	45.0	54.7	85.6	92.7	94.2	134.5

analysis. They have also provided explanations of the main reasons for and problems associated with the latter activity. In order to complete this exposition, the reader may find it useful to examine the cash flow results of a large U.K. public company and its subsidiaries – Sears Holdings PLC. The undernoted data have been taken from the available funds statements of the group for the last eight years. The data are free of foreign exchange distortions, and the trend analysis uses three-year rolling aggregates to avoid the peaks and troughs of Sears' very diverse operations. The results are first given as those of individual years, then these are aggregated and shown as percentage contributions to total cash inflow or outflow.

Although, in this case, a review of the above figures may be reasonably straightforward because of the relatively steady increase in most of the inflows and outflows, it has been argued in this paper that the analyst ought to use simple trend analysis techniques to aid the interpretation of cash flows. In this case, the use of three-year totals has been judged to be sufficient to smooth the lumpiness of individual years' results, and to reflect the diverse retail and manufacturing activities of Sears Holdings.

	1975–7	1976–8	1977–9	1978–80	1979–81	1980–82	1975–82
Cash Inflows	£m	£m	£m	£m	£m	£m	£m
Operating cash flow	141.4	148.2	181.0	228.7	272.5	310.8	588.2
Additional borrowing	—	2.1	—	—	—	—	—
Decrease in cash assets	3.7	—	—	—	—	—	—
	145.1	150.3	181.0	228.7	272.5	310.8	588.2
Cash Outflows							
Extra-ordinary items	—	—	—	2.0	8.6	13.9	13.9
Capital expenditure	59.5	51.9	54.7	80.9	72.5	109.5	206.2
Taxation paid	51.8	50.7	53.5	60.8	72.5	80.7	171.6
Dividends paid	27.9	30.6	38.3	43.6	51.2	55.7	111.7
Borrowing repayments	5.9	—	—	6.9	17.1	2.3	8.1
Increase in cash assets	—	17.1	34.5	34.5	50.6	48.7	76.7
	145.1	150.3	181.0	228.7	272.5	310.8	588.2

The above figures now enable the analyst to discern more clearly the trends underlying the single-period figures. In this case, the group is clearly funding itself from its operations – available cash being used increasingly on capital expenditure, tax, dividends and cash assets. Borrowing has also been decreased over the eight-year period. However, the relativity of the various inflows and outflows cannot be easily examined until the above data are further converted into percentage form to provide a picture of ratio-based contributions.

	1975–7	1976–8	1977–9	1978–80	1979–81	1980–82	1975–82
Cash Inflows	%	%	%	%	%	%	%
Operating cash flow	97	99	100	100	100	100	100
Additional borrowing	—	1	—	—	—	—	—
Decrease in cash assets	3	—	—	—	—	—	—
	100	100	100	100	100	100	100
Cash Outflows							
Extra-ordinary items	—	—	—	1	3	4	2
Capital expenditure	41	35	30	35	27	35	35
Taxation paid	36	34	30	27	27	26	29
Dividends paid	19	20	21	19	19	18	19
Borrowing repayments	4	—	—	3	6	1	2
Increase in cash assets	—	11	19	15	18	16	13
	100	100	100	100	100	100	100

The cash flow analysis is now a matter of interpretation of relatively unambiguous data presented in a simple format. In the case of Sears, the stability of inflows and outflows throughout the eight-year period is obvious. The almost single inflow has been operating cash flow (the three-year aggregate increasing by 120% from 1975–7 to 1980–82's figure of £310.8m.

Capital expenditure has accounted for 35% of cash outflow (relatively consistently throughout the period), but has varied considerably through the eight years. It has averaged £25.8m per annum – that is, 35% of the equivalent figure for operating cash flow. Although this figure may appear to be relatively low, the level of new investment has been considerably higher at £330m for the eight years – sale disposals for the period totalling £123.8m.

Taxation payments have amounted to approximately 30% of outflow between 1975 and 1982, and 20% approximately of the outflow has met dividend payments (in both cases consistently throughout). Thus, about 50% of total outflow has accounted for cash outgoings for which little direct benefit is received in return. Despite this, the company has increased its cash assets considerably – by £76.7m in total (13% of outflow), and reduced its borrowings by a net £8.1m.

A Final Comment

The above admittedly brief analysis of the cash flow of Sears Holdings is given solely for illustrative purposes. In cash terms, it has been a successful group of companies during the last decade. In some sense, it is relatively cash rich and a major criticism may be made that not enough has been done with the cash flow which has been available. This having been said, however, analysts will find it a much easier case for cash flow analysis than many other companies, particularly where there is a lack of operating cash flow over the long-term.

The latter is the key to a company's business survival. Unless, over a number of years, it is capable of generating cash flow from its operations to meet its needed capital expenditure, tax and dividends, it will require to seek external funding which, in turn, will tend to diminish future operating cash flows – a trend which can develop into an uncontrollable spiral despite the existence of reported realised profits. The latter are only an intermediate accounting step to the cash flows needed to survive.

References

(1) T. A. Lee and D. P. Tweedie, "Accounting Information: An Investigation of Shareholder Usage," *Accounting and Business Research*, Autumn 1975, pp. 280–91.
(2) T. A. Lee and D. P. Tweedie, *The Private Shareholder and the Corporate Report*, Institute of Chartered Accountants in England and Wales, 1977.
(3) T. A. Lee and D. P. Tweedie, *The Institutional Investor and Financial Information*, Institute of Chartered Accountants in England and Wales, 1982.
(4) "The Funds Statement," *Statement of Standard Accounting Practice 10*, 1975.

SSAP 10 and cash flow analysis

T A Lee, MSC, CA, ATII, FRSA

The report user is not well served by SSAP 10, argues Professor Tom Lee. Using the accounts of housebuilders, Barratt, he shows how a reconstructed, multi-period funds statement produced on a cash flow basis can supply vital information about a company's liquidity.

There is a clear need for CCAB's Accounting Standards Committee (ASC) to amend SSAP 10 in order to improve financial reporting for the benefit of a wide range of potential users.[1] The approach of SSAP 10 is to report on funds flow with respect to entity liquidity,[2] but there is little formal prescription concerning the structure and content of a funds statement which reports on liquidity matters (other than the disclosure of certain cash inflows and outflows[3]). The result is that, despite the existence of SSAP 10, there is a considerable flexibility in funds statement reporting practices.[4] A mixture of cash and non-cash data are reported, often in no apparent order, and usually not easily reconcilable with related profit statement and balance sheet data.[5]

The report user is therefore not particularly well served by the present standard. Despite the explicit objective of ASC to narrow differences in financial reporting practice, SSAP 10 does little to achieve such an aim. In addition it is conspicuously silent on the purpose of funds flow reporting—preparers and users of funds statements being ill-informed as to the uses to which they may be put. The relevant literature is equally poor, concentrating on detailed explanations of funds statement preparation rather than on usage. The purpose of this article, therefore, is to redress this imbalance by concentrating on funds statement analysis, generally, and on the need to adjust SSAP 10 statements in order to derive analysable data, particularly.[6]

A major principle underlying present-day funds statement practice is the need to match various sources of funds (for example, profits after adjustments for non-cash items, capital or borrowing receipts, and asset disposals) with various applications (such as capital expenditure, tax and dividend payments, and changes in working capital items). The difference between the two flows when aggregated is reconciled usually to the periodic movement in net liquid funds. This matching principle can be seen in the 1981 funds statement of a well-known building group, Barratt Developments plc.

SOURCES	£m	£m
Profit before tax		30·5
Less: items not involving funds movements		0·6
		29·9
Rights issue		21·8
Loans received		8·9
Disposal of assets		3·6
		64·2
APPLICATION		
Investment properties and fixed assets		5·8
Taxation		1·9
Dividends		5·0
Increase in working capital:		
Stock	46·7	
Debtors	10·0	
Creditors	(14·8)	
		41·9
Movement in net liquid funds:		
Increase in cash	—	
Decrease in borrowing	9·6	
		9·6
		64·2

Thus, in terms of the main data, a combination of realised profits and new share capital has been used by Barratt largely to fund a substantial increase in working capital. However, as suggested in the provisions of SSAP 10, what is required by financial report users is a full understanding of changes in Barratt's liquidity position. It is doubtful if the above form of funds statement provides this directly.

A business will survive only if it is profitable and liquid—that is, profitability must always be accompanied by a cash flow which meets the liquidity needs of the reporting entity. It is possible to earn profits without necessarily generating an equivalent amount of cash flow. Equally, the reverse is true. What enables the entity to survive is the tangible resource of cash—not profit, which is merely a man-made indicator of entity performance. Reporting profits is important to financial report users, but so too is the disclosure of the resultant cash flows.[7]

In order to provide report users with information about liquidity and cash flow, the funds statement ought to be produced on a cash basis.[8] This would disclose details of cash inflows and outflows. In particular, financial report users would be informed on how the various cash outflows for capital expenditure, taxation and dividends had been funded by cash inflows from trading operations, new capital and additional borrowings. However, funds statements are produced in accordance with the general principles of SSAP 10, and in a variant of the Barratt format shown here. What is therefore required is a series of simple adjustments and rearrangements in order to derive cash flow data from that reported in the conventional funds statement.[9]

The main adjustment is to utilise the basic principles of double-entry bookkeeping in order to remove the influence of working capital items from realised profits, and thereby derive the net cash flow from trading operations. This is done by netting the adjusted profits figure in the funds statement with the reported change in working capital (deducting an increase, and adding a decrease). This can be illustrated by using the Barratt data above.

	£m
Profit after adjustment	29·9
Less: increase in working capital	41·9
Operating cash flow	(12·0)

This simple exercise reveals to the financial report user that, despite its realisation of nearly £30m of profits, Barratt has incurred a £12m cash deficit on operations due to a working capital investment of approximately £42m. In other words, trading operations in 1981 did not contribute a net cash inflow to meet the cash outflow needs of the group. This is something which a conventional funds statement such as Barratt's did not make obvious.

In order to provide a complete cash picture of the reporting entity it is necessary to rearrange the remaining data in the funds statement (including a netting of capital expenditure and asset disposals) to derive a net investment figure, and borrowings received and repaid). The relevant 1981 figures for Barratt would be as follows.

	£m
CASH INFLOW	
Share capital	21·8
CASH OUTFLOWS	
Operating cash flow (as above)	12·0
Net investment*	2·2
Tax paid	1·9
Dividends paid	5·0
Net borrowing repaid†	0·7
	21·8

*£m 5·8 3·6
†£m 9·6–8·9

By means of this simple rearrangement of funds flow data the liquidity picture becomes clearer and, in this case, appears far less attractive in its cash flow form. The sole cash inflow came from the rights issue and this has funded the outflows due to the operating deficit, capital expenditure, tax and dividend payments, and a small net borrowing repayment. This gives the financial report user the opportunity of questioning the appropriateness of capital receipts being used to finance revenue payments such as dividends. Such liquidity issues are rarely revealed in the conventional funds statement. The rearranged cash flow statement is intended to make such disclosures obvious.

However, the analysis of cash flow data must be multi-period. The variations which can occur in cash flows from period to period can be significant, making the analysis of a single period exceedingly hazardous. For example, the 1981 cash flow figures for Barratt may give concern to the financial report user if viewed in isolation. But, by placing the 1981 data within a multi-period format it is possible to examine the cash flow performance over a reasonable length of time. Despite the distortions of individual periods, what the financial report user is attempting to detect are indications of cash flow problems which could seriously affect the entity's cash generation potential generally and its survival prospects particularly. Such problems do not usually occur at one point in time (although that is possible); they are more likely to develop over time, and cash flow analysis is aimed at monitoring this progression.

Using the adjustments and rearrangements described above, a multi-period statement of cash flows for Barratt has been prepared from its published funds statements, see Table 1. This has been produced over a five-year period, a reasonable length of time for a group concerned with long-term property development and building. The format for the purposes of this article has been kept reasonably simple, although it could be made more complex with the use of trend analysis techniques.[10]

The figures provide the financial report user with a detailed overview of Barratt's cash flow performance. Despite its realisation of £171m of profits before depreciation during the five-year period, the group has generated only £24m of operating cash flow following additional working capital investment of £147m. The cash contribution from operations has been augmented by £59m of additional borrowing and £70m of net capital. In other words, only 15% of the total cash inflow for the five-year period has been generated from Barratt's trading activities. The additional borrowing contributes 39% and the remaining 46% comes in the form of net capital. Thus, during the period, Barratt has been reliant mainly on external funding due to the low contribution from operations. Obviously the group cannot continue indefinitely to fund its cash needs in this way. Such dependence on external funding, with its attendant costs and repayment requirements, needs a substantial cash contribution from operations during the next few years. Hopefully, the surpluses of 1982 and 1983 will be improved on, and the lack of contribution from operations in 1979, 1980 and 1981 will not be repeated.

The rights issue in 1983, largely still in the form of cash balances at the end of that year, tends to distort the cash outflow picture for the five-year period. Nevertheless, it is reasonably clear that the largest outflow has been capital expenditure (£58m), with tax payments (£17m) and dividend payments (£30m) representing significant items. One of the most important features of this aspect of the analysis is that only £24m of operating cash flow has been available to fund £47m of tax and dividend payments. Assuming a priority of tax payments of £17m, this suggests that only £7m of operating cash flow was available to fund £30m of dividend—further suggesting that £23m of the latter was financed by borrowings. The additional borrowing for the five-year period was 2·5 times the operating cash flow, and dividends were 1·3 times operating cash flow.

It is open to debate how much concern these cash flow findings should give financial report users. Certainly, the relatively poor operating cash flow contribution has taken place during a period when profits before depreciation have improved by 195%, with an average annual increase of 30%; the quick ratio has improved from 0·11 to 0·54; and the gearing ratio has also improved from 0·3 in 1980 to 0·2 in 1983. Equally certainly, it is doubtful if conventional funds statements would have revealed the cash flow data outlined above from which important liquidity questions can be asked. Thus, if SSAP 10 continues in force, it is inevitable that financial report users will require to make adjustments and rearrangements to derive the required cash flow data.

References
[1] "Statements of Source and Application of Funds", *Statement of Standard Accounting Practice 10*, 1975.
[2] Ibid, paragraphs 1, 3, 8 and 11.
[3] For example, dividends paid, changes in fixed and other non-current assets, changes in medium and long-term borrowing, and movements in working capital items (ibid, paragraph 11).
[4] Evidence of this can be found in L C L Skerratt, *Survey of Published Accounts 1981–82*, ICAEW, 1981, pp 228–52.
[5] See S Hamilton, "Among the Company Accounts", *The Accountant's Magazine*, July 1976, pp 267–70.
[6] These adjustments have been described in greater detail in T A Lee, "Funds Statements and Cash Flow Analysis", *The Investment Analyst*, July 1983, pp 13–21.
[7] This is the theme of a forthcoming text, T A Lee, *Cash Flow Accounting*, Van Nostrand, 1984.
[8] This has been argued for on many occasions. See, for example, T A Lee, "A Case for Cash Flow Reporting", *Journal of Business Finance*, Summer 1972, pp 27–36.
[9] For further details, see Lee (1983), *op cit*.
[10] See, for example, Lee (1983), *op cit* and Lee (1984), *op cit*.

Table 1	1979	1980	1981	1982	1983	Total
CASH INFLOWS	£m	£m	£m	£m	£m	£m
Operating cash flow	—	0·1	—	16·4	28·8	23·6*
Additional borrowing	14·8	19·5	—	18·2	7·3	59·1*
Share capital	2·6	—	21·8	—	45·9	70·3
	17·4	19·6	21·8	34·6	82·0	153·0
CASH OUTFLOWS						
Operating cash flow	9·7	—	12·0	—	—	—*
Net investment	2·5	13·5	2·2	22·8	17·4	58·4
Tax paid	2·2	2·0	1·9	4·1	7·2	17·4
Dividends paid	3·0	4·1	5·0	7·7	10·4	30·2
Borrowing repaid	—	—	0·7	—	—	—*
Cash balance increase	—	—	—	—	47·0	47·0
	17·4	19·6	21·8	34·6	82·0	153·0

* Cash inflows and outflows netted

Further news on Barratt

Professor Tom Lee updates the cash flow position of Barratt Developments.

In the June 1984 issue of TAM (p 232) I used the published funds statements of Barratt Developments plc to illustrate the utility of a cash flow-based financial analysis. Since then, the 1984 annual financial report of the group has been issued and has revealed a further deterioration in its cash flow situation. In order to complete the analysis by bringing it up to date, this brief note integrates the 1984 results with those already presented in the June 1984 TAM. This will provide interested readers with a more contemporary picture of Barratt's liquidity performance.

The cash flow results for the group, including those for 1984, can be shown as follows:

	1979-83 £m	1984 £m	1979-84 £m
CASH INFLOWS			
Operating cash flow	23·6	—	—
Additional borrowing	59·1	54·4	113·5
Share capital	70·3	—	70·3
Cash balance decrease	—	46·2	—
	153·0	100·6	183·8
CASH OUTFLOWS			
Operating cash flow	—	65·8	42·2
Net investment	58·4	9·7	68·1
Tax paid	17·4	11·6	29·0
Dividends paid	30·2	13·5	43·7
Cash balance increase	47·0	—	0·8
	153·0	100·6	183·8

The cash flows for 1979-83 were explained in detail in the earlier TAM article. The addition of the 1984 figures reveals that the cumulative operating cash flow deficit (cash received from customers minus cash paid to suppliers, employers, etc) is £42m. Indeed, during the last six years the group has generated operating cash flow surpluses of any significance only in 1982 and 1983. As it is, the tangible resource of cash rather than reported profit which funds dividend payments and borrowing repayments, it is pertinent to question what cash has funded £44m of dividends during the last six years. The analysis indicates that no cash flow was available from operations and that the remaining sources were £113m of additional borrowing and £70m of new capital.

A further question is posed by the analysis. What is the prospect of cash flow surpluses from operations to reduce the level of borrowing, which amounted to £138·8m at 30 June 1984? The service cost of this debt will require a considerable cash flow funding from operations in 1985 onwards.

Cash flow analysis of this type should not be regarded as the only form of analysis, and ought to be considered together with older, more traditional methods. However, although it does not necessarily provide completely clear answers for the analyst, it does allow pertinent points to be considered. ☐

Tom Lee

Analysis of Entities

What cash flow analysis says about BL's finances

BY TOM LEE

THE BL saga appears never-ending. Its continuing commercial, financial and human problems would provide the basis for a record-breaking TV soap opera. But, behind the music hall jokes and the constant lemming-like rushes to the cliff edge, lurks the grim financial reality of government or government-secured money being pumped in at an enormous rate.

Surprisingly, therefore, although individual loans, share issues and government promises to BL have been adequately highlighted in the press and elsewhere, very little detailed analysis has been made of its cumulative financial position. The purpose of this article is to present such an analysis on the basis of available published results, and to make one or two comments about the implications of it. The basis of investigation will be the cashflow data of BL, for cash availability and flow must be the name of the game in this particular case.

Cash flow analysis is receiving increasing professional attention and acknowledgment as a useful means of highlighting the financial strengths and weaknesses of companies. By taking the published funds statements of companies, adjusting for working capital and rearranging certain other data, it is possible to produce their financial results on a pure cash basis (free of credit transactions, accruals, and most arbitrary allocations such as depreciation—in other words, merely showing cash flowing in and out of the organisation concerned). The perfectly

TABLE 1 — BL LTD. CASH FLOW RESULTS

	1974 £m	1975 £m	1976 £m	1977 £m	1978 £m	1979 £m	1980 £m	Total £m
Sales receipts	1,603	1,805	2,835	2,557	3,031	2,940	2,991	17,762
Less: operating payments	1,560	1,890	2,848	2,594	3,029	2,960	3,034	17,915
	43	(85)	(13)	(37)	2	(20)	(43)	(153)
Less: capital payments	99	84	118	144	226	238	250	1,159
	(56)	(169)	(131)	(181)	(224)	(258)	(293)	(1,312)
Less: interest payments	17	38	47	54	56	66	94	372
	(73)	(207)	(178)	(235)	(280)	(324)	(387)	(1,684)
Less: tax payments	7	7	13	13	11	10	5	66
	(80)	(214)	(191)	(248)	(291)	(334)	(392)	(1,750)
Less: dividend payments	9	3	—	—	—	—	—	12
TOTAL CASH DEFICIT	(89)	(217)	(191)	(248)	(291)	(334)	(392)	(1,762)
Financed by:								
Share issues	—	—	198	—	444	148	295	1,085
Bank borrowings	89	217	(7)	248	(153)	186	97	677
	(89)	(217)	(191)	(248)	(291)	(334)	(392)	(1,762)
Historic cost loss after tax and dividends	(24)	(124)	(44)	(52)	(38)	(145)	(536)	(963)

TABLE—2

	1974 £m	1975 £m	1976 £m	1977 £m	1978 £m	1979 £m	1980 £m	Total £m
Cash flow deficits expressed in 1980 prices ...	(217)	(420)	(327)	(361)	(394)	(391)	(392)	(2,502)

legitimate and defensible work of the accountant in "smoothing" data to produce profit figures is thus ignored, and the underlying cash reality is revealed.

This approach has been undertaken with BL's financial results for 1974 to 1980 inclusive. The funds statements for the last seven years have been suitably adjusted and rearranged, and Table 1 summarises the cash flow situation. (Although not all the necessary figures are available, the table gives a broad but reasonably accurate approximation of BL's cashflow.)

The upshot of these results is fairly apparent.

(1) Only in two years out of seven has BL produced an operating cash flow surplus to finance capital expenditure, interest payments, etc. (1974 and 1978). In fact, over the seven years it has accumulated a deficit of £153m. Which business would normally have managed to raise capital and borrow when not covering its day-to-day cash expenditure with sales receipts over a period of seven years? Cash flow analysis highlights the harshness of this reality.

(2) BL has contributed no cash to its £1.16bn capital expenditure programme of the past seven years.

(3) The result of point (2) is that BL has an increasingly crippling interest burden—rising from £17m in 1974 to £94m in 1980, and likely to go much higher.

(4) Paradoxically, BL has paid tax of £66m over the past seven years, and the tax planning of its management must be brought into question regarding the siting of its profitable plants.

(5) The overall deficit of £1.76bn over the past seven years has been financed by share issues subscribed by government or borrowings guaranteed by government. This compares with the equivalent accounting-based loss of £963m in total. In other words, cash flow analysis of data is much more critical of BL's financial condition than that which uses conventional accounting figures. When this is coupled with the cash flow of at least £1.14bn which it has projected it will need for 1981 to 1984 inclusive, the total cash deficit over 11 years will have been in the order of £3bn—and this only getting to a break-even point, it hopes, by 1984.

The cash flow position can also be put in better perspective if the above data are described in the same price-level terms—in this case in terms of the prices used in the 1980 financial statements. The undernoted figures represent a rough translation of the total annual cash flow deficits in these price terms.

The results reveal a remarkable consistency in the "real" cash flow deficits—at a staggeringly high level which ought to concern anyone interested in the wisdom or otherwise of allowing BL to survive in its present form.

Of course there are issues just as, if not more, serious than the financial ones in this particular case. And, of course, arguments can be made for supporting BL in this way. However, cash flow analysis provides information with which to aid the proper judgment of these arguments.

For example, do BL's operating cash flow deficits indicate that in the future surpluses from operations will be produced at a sufficiently high level to finance capital expenditure, pay for interest, and repay borrowings? What is meant by "recovery" in terms of BL when the pit it has fallen into is akin to a financial black hole? And would cash flow analysis of other companies and other industries raise the same questions concerning financial common sense?

The niggling doubt is that cash flow analysis is not even being applied in an obvious case such as BL.

Tom Lee is professor of Accountancy and Finance at the University of Edinburgh.

Financial reporting

by Professor Tom Lee

Laker Airways – the cash flow truth

Could cash flow analysis have prevented the tragedy or lessened its consequences?

In February 1982, Laker Airways ceased operations. Its bankers withdrew their continuing support, and a receiver was appointed. Since then, much has been said and written about the changes in fortune of the company and its chairman; and a certain amount of comment has been made about its accounting and disclosure practices.

However, little or no attention has been given to the major issue of how Laker Airways was permitted by its bankers to continue into large-scale bankruptcy at a considerable cost to customers, suppliers and employees, as well as lenders.

The answer lies in an analysis of Laker Airways' published financial statements for the last few years. This reveals not so much bad or dubious accounting, as apparent lack of attention by the bankers to warning signs of an impending crash. It is therefore the purpose of this article to outline this analysis briefly, and to indicate the signs to which an alert banker ought to respond with a business customer who is growing rapidly, or is having to cope with difficult trading situations.

Laker Airways' published statements for the years to 31 March 1976, 1977, 1978, 1979 and 1980 have been examined in detail (those for 1981 are not available, as they are in the hands of the receiver). The statements have been analysed, particularly with a view to providing a summary of the company's profitability and cash flow. The emphasis in this article is much more on the latter than the former, as it was cash flow (or the lack of it) which caused the downfall of Laker Airways. Also, as the company's bankers ought to have been primarily concerned with cash flow and liquidity matters, a cash flow analysis appears appropriate.

The use of cash flow accounting techniques to examine the financial performance of companies is not new, and has been applied by the writer to a number of such organisations. However, it is little used by bankers and investors, and it can be reasonably argued that, by ignoring it, potential financial crises are not identified until it is too late.

Specifically, the technique used the data contained in the published statements and, by means of the principles of double-entry bookkeeping, reduced them to their cash equivalent – that is, the financial results are described in pure cash terms (cash inflows from trading operations, new capital and additional borrowing; and cash outflows on new investment, taxation, dividends, and repaid borrowing). In the case of Laker Airways, the main objective is to establish over a number of years how much cash was made available from operations and borrowings, and how much was spent on investment and repaying borrowings.

The analysed data for this article are

Figure 1
Laker Airways (International) Ltd: reported profits climbed from 1976 to 1980

	1976 £m	1977 £m	1978 £m	1979 £m	1980 £m	Total £m
Trading profits	0.7	2.0	6.9	2.4	—	12.0
Less: foreign exchange losses:						
realised	0.2	1.2	1.1	—	(0.3)	2.2
unrealised	—	—	4.3	—	—	4.3
	0.2	1.2	5.4	—	(0.3)	6.5
Reported group profits	0.5	0.8	1.5	2.4	0.3	5.5
Add: extraordinary gains:						
realised[1]	—	—	—	2.3	—	2.3
unrealised[2]	0.4	—	—	—	(0.5)	(0.1)
	0.9	0.8	1.5	4.7	(0.2)	7.7
Add: exceptional gains:						
unrealised[3]	—	—	—	3.3	1.9	5.2
	0.9	0.8	1.5	8.0	1.7	12.9
Add: prior-year gains:						
realised[4]	—	—	—	—	7.6	7.6
unrealised[5]	—	—	—	0.1	0.1	0.2
	0.9	0.8	1.5	8.1	9.4	20.7
Less: transfers to foreign exchange reserve	—	—	—	3.3	1.3	4.6
Total reported profits	0.9	0.8	1.5	4.8	8.1	16.1

[1] Profit on sale of aircraft etc
[2] Revaluation of aircraft and write off of goodwill
[3] Foreign exchange surpluses
[4] Recovery of operating expenses and revenue
[5] Associated company profits

Figure 2
Laker Airways (International) Ltd: analysing the cash flow from 1976 to 1980

	1976 £m	1976 %	1977 £m	1977 %	1978 £m	1978 %	1979 £m	1979 %	1980 £m	1980 %	Total £m	Total %
Operating cash flow	4.5	100	4.5	65	12.1	52	10.7	27	17.6	25	49.4	34
Additional borrowing	—	—	—	—	11.2	48	27.3	68	52.0	74	90.5	62
Decrease in cash assets	—	—	2.4	35	—	—	2.0	5	0.8	1	5.2	4
	4.5	100	6.9	100	23.3	100	40.0	100	70.4	100	145.1	100
Additional investment	0.5	11	3.5	51	19.1	82	40.0	100	70.4	100	133.5	92
Repayment of borrowing	2.1	47	3.4	49	—	—	—	—	—	—	5.5	4
Increase in cash assets	1.9	42	—	—	4.2	18	—	—	—	—	6.1	4
	4.5	100	6.9	100	23.3	100	40.0	100	70.4	100	145.1	100

contained in Figures 1 and 2. In Figure 1, the aim has been to simplify the reported figures to reveal the basic composition of profits. As with all measurements of profit, Laker Airways' profit statements contain a great deal of complex data. In particular, it can be seen that the trading profits after depreciation (there was little or no taxation in any of the five years) totalled £12m (annual average of £2.4m). But these were augmented or depleted by a variety of non-trading, extraordinary, exceptional and prior-period gains and losses of both a realised and unrealised nature.

The upshot of this was that, in total, the £12m of trading profits were increased to £16.1m of total net gains in the profit statement. What then was the profitability of Laker Airways during the five years to 31 March 1980?

Some might argue that it should be defined only as trading profits. But what should be done with the prior-period item of £7.6m in 1980, representing the recovery of previous operating costs and revenues, but not further explained in the published statements? To treat it as trading profit would increase the total to £19.6m (annual average of £3.9m). But should profit be determined inclusive of all trading items, but less all foreign exchange losses (giving a five-year total of £13.1m and an annual average of £2.6m)?

Whichever way it is (or was) done, the return on an average shareholders' equity of £8.9m for the period could vary from 12% up to 46% (the full trading return being an average of 44%). These figures are sufficiently large (given no tax) possibly to have convinced an examining banker that the company was not only profitable but, in most years examined, very profitable. And it should also be noted that these profit figures are after deduction of substantial amounts of interest on borrowings.

But relying on the traditional financial analysis of profitability would have been disastrous in the case of Laker Airways. The full and stark picture of impending bankruptcy can only be seen in the cash flow analysis in Figure 2. From a 100% contribution of cash inflow from operations in 1976, the figure falls steadily to 25% by 1980, and averages 34% over the five years. Borrowing, on the other hand, increased in an opposite direction with equivalent speed – 47% of cash outflow was committed to borrowing repayment in 1976, deteriorating rapidly to a position where 74% of cash inflow was received from net borrowings in 1980.

Over the five years, 62% of the total inflow came from borrowings – roughly speaking, for every 34p that the company contributed, the lenders contributed over 62p. And most of it went on new aircraft (92% overall), leaving little available to repay borrowings in the future, and a prospect of operational cash flows in future periods having to meet an ever-increasing interest burden.

If cash flow analysis techniques had been used by the bankers responsible for the Laker Airways account, they ought to have become worried in 1978, and taken action after the 1979 reporting – at least to the extent of providing no further long-term funding. Instead, they continued through 1980, 1981 and 1982, despite the appalling cash flow results of 1980.

Conclusion

It is a fact of financial life that no business, over a number of years, can afford not to contribute the majority of cash inflow needed to pay for new investment, tax, dividends and borrowing repayments. The signs with Laker Airways were glaringly obvious in 1979, and ignored. A lot of innocent individuals may well have been hurt by the lack of attention to basic fundamentals of financial analysis and, presumably, of banking.

These points appear self-evident and, of course, are made with the benefit of hindsight. But, whenever Laker Airways reported during the last few years, a very few minutes of adjustment of the reported figures would have provided the cash flow data which have been described above. They should have confirmed the need to restrain or terminate Laker Airways' fight for survival by geometric growth.

That this came too late is a matter of regret. But cash flow analysis can be applied by bankers and others before the event with every chance, at worst, of minimising the agony and, at best, preserving needed resources. ■

The Lonrho phenomenon

Harrods problems have brought Lonrho back into the news; indeed the group is rarely far from the front page. Its growth record has been staggering, but is it the commercial rock it may appear? PROFESSOR T. A. LEE, head of accounting and business method at Edinburgh University takes a close look at the group.

THE growth and development of the Lonrho Group over the last decade has been considerable. At the end of 1973, it reported total equity of £144 million. By 1982, this had expanded to £651 million; a 4.5 times increase despite poor results in 1982. Trading profits (before depreciation, tax, etc) rose by three times during the same decade to £104 million in 1982.

Other features of the group's financial structure have not been so favourable. Total borrowing of £42 million (including the permanent feature of net short-term borrowing) amounted to 22.5 per cent of total funding at the end of 1973. Ten years later, the equivalent statistics were £589 million and 47.5 per cent. Gearing had therefore doubled in a decade. And this in a group exceedingly sensitive to economic factors outwith management control such as commodity prices, foreign exchange rates, interest rates and general inflation.

RISK

The economic risk the group has had to face is perhaps best revealed in the statistics of 24 per cent of its 1982 turnover coming from African operations and providing 50 per cent of total profits before interest.

Much of the above should not be new to the financial community if the efficient market hypothesis is to be believed. But, given the minimal comment concerning Lonrho's recent 1982 results, it is surely useful to take stock of the group's financial performance and position in recent years. The approach used is that of cash flow analysis which examines Lonrho's cash inflows and outflows over a ten year period. This avoids the subjectivity of conventional accounting measurements (to which Lonrho is much prone), and reflects both profitability and liquidity in a convenient format at the same time.

The figures have been taken from the published funds statements of Lonrho for 1973 to 1982, inclusive, and are free of the distortions of foreign exchange translation. The technique has been used by the writer in recent times in relation to BL (*Financial Times*, October 23, 1981) and Laker Airways (*Accountancy*, June 1982). Its application to Lonrho concerns a large and (apparently) viable going concern.

These figures provide a view of Lonrho's financial performance during the last decade. In seven out of ten years, borrowing has been heavy in relation to internal funding; £575 million of operating cash flow has been matched by £530 million of additional borrowing. The majority has been spent on capital expenditure (net of disposal proceeds), and increasing tax and distribution payments. During the same period, the group generated £852 million of realised profits before depreciation and tax; £277 million was invested in additional stocks and debtors (minus creditors) leaving £575 million of operating cash flow.

The inevitable lumpiness of operating cash flow reveals a five-year trading cycle. In order to avoid these fluctuations, a five-year trend analysis has been produced with the figures reduced to percentage contributions (thus avoiding the problem of aggregating different money totals during a period of price inflation).

BORROWING

It is now clear that, only in the period 1977 to 1981 has Lonrho generated a majority of its required cash from operations, the overall trend being remarkably consistent at 47 per cent. The most worrying feature has been the increasing contribution from borrowing, rising from 37 per cent in the first five-year period to 46 per cent in

> '**The economic risk the group has had to face is perhaps best revealed in the statistics of 24 per cent of its 1982 turnover coming from African operations and providing 50 per cent of total profits before interest**'

Table 1: Lonrho – the last 10 years

	1973 £m	1974 £m	1975 £m	1976 £m	1977 £m	1978 £m	1979 £m	1980 £m	1981 £m	1982 £m
CASH INFLOW										
Operating cash flow	20	46	(30)	35	107	73	81	27	151	65
New share capital	—	—	35	14	16	1	17	39	8	—
Additional borrowing	(1)	(16)	58	30	69	52	9	116	55	158
	19	30	63	79	192	126	107	182	214	223
CASH OUTFLOW										
Capital expenditure	15	14	44	51	135	70	55	114	142	149
Taxation paid	2	13	16	18	46	39	31	43	46	45
Dividends paid	2	3	3	10	11	17	21	25	26	29
	19	30	63	79	192	126	107	182	214	223

LONRHO

> *'This cash flow picture is not a happy one and reflects disquiet concerning Lonrho's borrowing levels'*

the last period (averaging 43 per cent over the decade).

In other words, between 1973 and 1982, Lonrho has contributed 47p in the pound to its capital, tax and dividend expenditure, with 43p in the pound coming from borrowing and the remainder from share issues. In addition, capital expenditure (net of disposals) reduced proportionally over the period from 68 per cent of available cash to 62 per cent. With taxation payments amounting to a relatively constant one quarter of available cash, there was a proportional doubling of dividends from 7 per cent to 14 per cent.

The above cash flow picture is not a happy one, and reflects disquiet about Lonrho's borrowing levels.

> *'It is alarming how large the burden of debt has become to the group and its cash flow'*

Vast amounts have had to be borrowed in one form or another because the group consistently has contributed a minority of needed cash flow.

INTEREST

Much of the reason for this low contribution has been due to the size and cost of the group's total debt. In 1973, the interest cost was £4 million. By 1982, it was £75 million. Over the ten-year period examined, 36 per cent of available operating cash flow was consumed by interest charges. During the last three years, the equivalent statistic was up to 46 per cent.

The increasing use of cash flow to cover interest payments has inevitably increased borrowing. Given the risk associated with profits, it is alarming to see how large the burden of debt has become to the group and its cash flow. It is also not difficult to speculate what would happen if overseas profits and operating cash flows were substantially reduced in the future. Is this one reason why the banking risk is spread between ten principal banks? □

Table 2. Lonrho — Trends	1973-7	1974-8	1975-9	1976-80	1977-81	1978-82	1973-82
CASH INFLOW	%	%	%	%	%	%	%
Operating cash flow	46	47	47	47	53	47	47
New share capital	17	14	15	13	10	7	10
Additional borrowing	37	39	38	40	37	46	43
	100	100	100	100	100	100	100
CASH OUTFLOW							
Capital expenditure	68	64	63	62	63	62	64
Taxation paid	25	27	26	26	25	24	24
Dividends paid	7	9	11	12	12	14	12
	100	100	100	100	100	100	100

A CASH FLOW DISCLOSURE OF GOVERNMENT-SUPPORTED ENTERPRISES' RESULTS

T.A. LEE AND A.W. STARK*

INTRODUCTION

Government-supported industries and companies receive financial aid because they are believed to be vital to the economic and social well-being of the nation. They provide goods, services and employment which cannot be financed and protected adequately through the normal functioning of the private enterprise system. At the present time, these entities in the UK would include manufacturing organisations such as BL, Rolls Royce and the British Steel Corporation; energy producers such as the National Coal Board, the Electricity Council and the British Gas Corporation; and transportation concerns such as British Rail and British Airways.

The financial results of each of these organisations are required legally to be reported in the traditional terms of profitability, financial position and funds flow. However, it is open to debate whether the traditional accounting and reporting practices of private enterprise ought to be the only ones applied to entities where the key financial factor appears to be survival in cash terms through government support, rather than survival and progress in profit terms by means of the normal mechanisms of the market place. If it is accepted that cash flow is at least as critical as profitability to these concerns, then the provision of cash flow-based financial results provides a means whereby the interpretation of financial results can be undertaken in a way more compatible with the economic objectives and structures of the entities concerned.

It is the intention of this short paper to provide the cash flow-based annual results of certain government-supported organisations. In this way, it is hoped that persons interested in or involved with these entities will find the data useful when making judgments about them. In particular, the aim is to disclose the extent to which each such entity contributes cash from its trading operations, and how each receives cash flow contributions from the public purse. The uses to which cash inflows are put will also be evident. The note is therefore concerned primarily with the provision of factual data.

---

* T.A. Lee is Professor of Accountancy and Finance at the University of Edinburgh and Director of Accounting and Auditing Research at the Institute of Chartered Accountants of Scotland. A.W. Stark is Lecturer in Accounting at the University of Manchester. (Paper received January 1983, revised March 1983)

The organisations selected for this purpose are those mentioned earlier—that is, BL, Rolls Royce, British Steel, the National Coal Board, the Electricity Council, British Gas, British Rail and British Airways. They all cover essentially different industries (motor vehicles, engines, steel, energy and transport); are all under government control and supervision; and receive (or have received) substantial government support in various financial forms (by subsidy, borrowing or share capital).

THE FINANCIAL RESULTS

The financial results used in this paper have been taken from the published annual reports of the organisations involved. Cash flow accounting (CFA) techniques have been applied where necessary to convert accounting allocations to their cash flow equivalents (Lee, 1981a, 1981b, 1982a and 1982b). The results refer to the seven-year period beginning with a financial year ending in 1975 and completing with a year ending in 1981.

The CFA techniques involved have been applied to the published funds statements, particularly with regard to reorganising the data contained in the latter, and setting off working capital changes against profits to derive operating cash flows. They follow a general 'funds' format of matching cash inflows with outflows. Where relevant, government and related subsidies have been isolated from operating cash flows; interest payments have been treated as outflows, with government interest separated from external interest (the former being regarded more as a return on investment than a cost); government borrowings have been separated from other borrowings to indicate the extent of government support; and the cost of reconstruction and closures has been shown as an outflow separate from operating cash flow.

The presentation of the results of the eight organisations will be conducted in groupings; the first dealing with the manufacturing concerns of BL, Rolls Royce and British Steel; the second with the energy entities of the Coal Board, British Gas and the Electricity Council; and the third with the transport organisations of British Rail and British Airways.

THE MANUFACTURERS

The three manufacturing concerns in public ownership were all formerly substantial parts of private enterprise. BL is government protected because of its size as an employer and exporter, and the need to maintain a UK-based vehicle manufacturer; Rolls Royce has a technological expertise vital to UK defence; and British Steel covers a basic industry for so many UK manufacturers. This section will deal with each in turn (Tables 1, 2 and 3).

(a) *BL* BL contributed little cash flow from its operations between 1975 and

Table 1
BL: Detailed Cash Flow Results—1975 to 1981

	1975 £m	1976 £m	1977 £m	1978 £m	1979 £m	1980 £m	1981 £m	Total £m
CASH INFLOW								
Operating cash flow	—	—	—	29	26	33	—	88
Government capital	—	197	—	444	148	295	515	1599
Government borrowing	—	—	150	—	—	—	—	150
Other borrowing	218	—	98	—	194	104	—	614
	218	197	248	473	368	432	515	2451
CASH OUTFLOW								
Operating cash flow	39	1	38	—	—	—	24	102
Reconstruction costs	42	12	3	26	54	83	111	331
Investment	89	118	139	226	238	250	153	1213
Taxation	7	13	14	11	10	5	3	63
Government interest	—	—	14	25	22	6	—	67
Other interest	41	47	40	31	44	88	88	379
Other borrowing	—	6	—	154	—	—	136	296
	218	197	248	473	368	432	515	2451

1981. Only in three of the seven years was there a small operating surplus and, in aggregate, there was a monetary deficit of £14m. Cash has therefore been raised to cover operating deficits before other essential outflows could be funded. Because of the latter factor, BL relied increasingly on government support which was received largely in the form of share capital issues (nearly £1,600m in total, and comprising 77% of total inflow for the seven-year period). The remainder of the cash required came from external borrowing from banks (usually government guaranteed).

The uses to which BL put its available cash were varied. The most substantial proportion of the seven-year total (59%) was spent on replacement and new investment (for example, plant for new product ranges). But an increasing amount was spent on the costs of plant closures and redundancies. This comprised 16% of the total cash outflow between 1975 and 1981 inclusive. A small cash flow was committed to taxation despite the heavy loss-making nature of the business, and the remainder was used to meet interest costs (mainly to the banks). The latter, although doubling in the seven-year period to £88m by 1981, remained as a relatively small proportion of total cash outflow at between 17% and 24%.

(b) *Rolls Royce* The operating cash flow performance of Rolls Royce was consistently poor between 1975 and 1981—only in 1977 and 1978 was there a surplus. In absolute money terms, the deficit on operations aggregated £315m. Admittedly, this was after substantial research and development costs had been met (£331m was disclosed between 1975 and 1980).

Table 2

Rolls Royce: Detailed Cash Flow Results—1975 to 1981

	1975	1976	1977	1978	1979	1980	1981	Total
CASH INFLOW	£m	£m	£m	£m	£m	£m	£m	£m
Operating cash flow	—	—	41	71	—	—	—	112
Government capital	77	38	21	7	31	94	130	398
Government borrowing	33	17	9	—	—	96	19	174
Other borrowing	—	21	—	23	75	22	50	191
Taxation refund	—	7	—	—	—	—	—	7
Decrease in cash assets	—	—	—	—	45	10	—	55
	110	83	71	101	151	222	199	937
CASH OUTFLOW								
Operating cash flow	63	51	—	—	89	145	79	427
Reconstruction costs	—	—	—	—	—	—	17	17
Investment	33	23	18	30	50	44	28	226
Taxation	2	—	2	—	—	—	—	4
Interest	6	9	11	11	12	33	41	123
Government borrowing	—	—	—	22	—	—	—	22
Other borrowing	6	—	22	—	—	—	—	28
Increase in cash assets	—	—	18	38	—	—	34	90
	110	83	71	101	151	222	199	937

The aforementioned lack of liquidity from Rolls Royce's operations meant a substantial funding in almost every year from government (mainly by share capital issues totalling £398m and providing a seven-year contribution to inflow of 56%; but also increasingly from borrowing—particularly in 1980 and 1981). The company also regularly borrowed externally from banks, etc. — this too tending to rise in recent years.

The cash inflow situation has considerably influenced the way in which available cash was used over the seven years 1975 to 1981. In absolute terms, investment barely increased, being £33m in 1975 and only £28m in 1981. As the operating cash deficits increased, so investment as a proportion of total outflow consistently fell and averaged 32% for the seven-year period. In addition, the company commenced a major and costly reconstruction in 1981. The rising cost of borrowing from £6m in 1975 to £41m in 1981 constituted a sizeable outflow.

(c) *British Steel* Between 1975 and 1981, the financial results of British Steel reveal its lack of operating viability and need for government support. It has had continuous operating cash flow deficits which have amounted to 21% of total cash outflow between 1975 to 1981 inclusive. In money terms, the change was from a surplus of £36m in 1975 to a deficit of £563m in 1981. This has been accompanied by a reconstruction and closure programme costing £636m between 1975 and 1981, and representing 12% of the seven-year outflow.

GOVERNMENT-SUPPORTED ENTERPRISES' RESULTS

Table 3

British Steel: Detailed Cash Flow Results—1975 to 1981

	1975	1976	1977	1978	1979	1980	1981	Total
CASH INFLOW	£m	£m	£m	£m	£m	£m	£m	£m
Operating cash flow	36	—	—	—	—	—	—	36
Government capital	45	345	490	445	850	905	1233	4313
Government borrowing	—	130	161	216	—	—	—	507
Other borrowing	338	184	280	140	27	—	—	969
	419	659	931	801	877	905	1233	5825
CASH OUTFLOW								
Operating cash flow	—	1	202	168	147	58	563	1139
Reconstruction costs	5	28	48	35	76	106	338	636
Investment	262	524	524	412	296	228	84	2330
Government interest	51	56	72	95	102	80	63	519
Other interest	23	50	85	91	94	95	108	546
Government borrowing	78	—	—	—	162	209	50	499
Other borrowing	—	—	—	—	—	129	27	156
	419	659	931	801	877	905	1233	5825

These operating results were largely and increasingly financed by government share capital—£45m in 1975 rising to £1,233m in 1981. Government support between 1975 and 1981 was 84% of inflow, the remainder coming from external borrowing. The cash spent on new investment diminished from £262m in 1975 to £84m in 1981. The remainder of the available cash was spent on interest costs (£74m in 1975 and £171m in 1981, but remaining constant in proportional terms at about 21% of outflow over the seven years).

THE ENERGY PRODUCERS

The next three entities to be examined constitute a very substantial part of the total UK energy industry. The organisations are the National Coal Board, the British Gas Corporation and the Electricity Council (Tables 4, 5 and 6).

(a) *National Coal Board* The operating cash flows of the Coal Board changed from a deficit of £8m in 1975 to a surplus of £176m in 1981. Over the seven-year period, the aggregate surplus was £449m and comprised 13% of the total cash inflow. However, the Coal Board received total subsidies over the seven years from government and elsewhere of £1,035m (2.3 times the total operating surplus), and this comprised 29% of the total inflow. In addition, government borrowing increased consistently throughout the period—from a £21m repayment in 1975 to a £479m receipt in 1981, and comprised 31% of the seven-year inflow. The remainder of the cash funding came from external borrowing (27%

Table 4

National Coal Board: Detailed Cash Flow Results—1975 to 1981

	1975	1976	1977	1978	1979	1980	1981	Total
CASH INFLOW	£m	£m	£m	£m	£m	£m	£m	£m
Operating cash flow	—	—	53	108	89	92	176	518
Government subsidies	196	32	55	75	92	331	254	1035
Government borrowing	—	102	8	64	223	263	479	1139
Other borrowing	6	127	236	176	192	130	106	973
	202	261	352	423	596	816	1015	3665
CASH OUTFLOW								
Operating cash flow	8	61	—	—	—	—	—	69
Investment	137	148	272	336	458	631	759	2741
Government interest	9	29	45	41	64	101	166	455
Other interest	27	23	35	46	74	84	90	379
Government borrowing	21	—	—	—	—	—	—	21
	202	261	352	423	596	816	1015	3665

of inflow). In total, 60% of cash inflow for 1975 to 1981 inclusive, came either from subsidy or government borrowing, and the seven-year cost of borrowing of £834m was 186% of the equivalent operating cash flow total.

The Coal Board's cash outflow position remained stable in proportional terms throughout the period 1975 to 1981—77% being used for investment and 23% on interest. In money terms, investment increased from £137m in 1975 to £759m in 1981; the equivalent interest figures are £36m and £256m, respectively.

(b) *British Gas Corporation* The total inflow of British Gas between 1975 and 1981, inclusive, came almost exclusively from operations; increasing from £344m in 1975 to £1,144m in 1981. A small subsidy in 1975, and occasional borrowing in 1975, 1976 and 1979, formed the only other contributions to cash inflow.

The operating cash flow contribution of British Gas is further emphasised by its ability to generate sufficient cash to meet its investment needs (£2,862m in total and 52% of the total seven-year inflow) and to repay borrowings. In fact, during the seven-year period, government borrowing decreased by £1,365m through repayment, and the equivalent external borrowing reduction was £43m.

The effect of these changes was most evident when the cost of borrowing is examined. In 1975, the cost was £163m (mainly to government). By 1981, the net interest was £5m (solely to external lenders). Indeed, in 1980 and 1981, British Gas increased its cash or near-cash assets by a total of £448m (20% of outflow) and received £35m in interest from investments in government securities, etc.

GOVERNMENT-SUPPORTED ENTERPRISES' RESULTS

Table 5
British Gas: Detailed Cash Flow Results—1975 to 1981

	1975	1976	1977	1978	1979	1980	1981	Total
CASH INFLOW	£m	£m	£m	£m	£m	£m	£m	£m
Operating cash flow	344	424	724	967	870	1014	1144	5487
Government subsidies	42	—	—	—	—	—	—	42
Government borrowing	68	—	—	—	—	—	—	68
Other borrowing	13	236	—	—	150	—	—	399
Government interest	—	—	—	—	—	7	28	35
Decrease in cash assets	—	—	—	10	30	—	—	40
	467	660	724	977	1050	1021	1172	6071
CASH OUTFLOW								
Investment	304	406	317	288	353	470	724	2862
Government interest	126	133	124	93	46	—	—	522
Other interest	37	44	62	48	45	57	33	326
Government borrowing	—	77	131	510	606	109	—	1433
Other borrowing	—	—	52	38	—	163	189	442
Increase in cash assets	—	—	38	—	—	222	226	486
	467	660	724	977	1050	1021	1172	6071

(c) *Electricity Council* The cash flow results of the Electricity Council reveal increasing cash flows from operations, from £183m in 1975 to £1,360m in 1981. The remainder of the inflow came from subsidies (£477m in 1975 and 1976), additional government borrowing (£999 in total, mainly received in 1980 and

Table 6
Electricity Council: Detailed Cash Flow Results—1975 to 1981

	1975	1976	1977	1978	1979	1980	1981	Total
CASH INFLOW	£m	£m	£m	£m	£m	£m	£m	£m
Operating cash flow	183	640	995	1054	1192	1012	1360	6436
Government subsidies	176	301	—	—	—	—	—	477
Government borrowing	—	303	—	—	—	837	296	1436
Other borrowing	415	—	360	81	—	—	—	856
Decrease in cash assets	—	—	8	—	—	17	—	25
	774	1244	1363	1135	1192	1866	1656	9230
CASH OUTFLOW								
Investment	478	596	639	559	622	770	880	4544
Government interest	261	308	302	284	290	326	452	2223
Other interest	29	94	102	168	147	106	82	728
Government borrowing	1	—	320	110	6	—	—	437
Other borrowing	—	231	—	—	123	664	208	1226
Increase in cash assets	5	15	—	14	4	—	34	72
	774	1244	1363	1135	1192	1866	1656	9230

1981). In fact, most of the government borrowing appears to have been used to reduce external borrowing (the latter being repaid over the seven years to the extent of £370m).

A seven-year total of £4,544m was spent on investment, and this comprised a relatively constant 57% of total cash outflow. Apart from the aforementioned repayment of external borrowing, the remainder of the cash spending was on interest (a total of £2,951m), and mainly to government. This expenditure amounted to 37% of the seven-year outflow.

TRANSPORTATION

British Rail and British Airways are the two transport entities examined in this paper, and Tables 7 and 8 provide the required data.

(a) *British Railways Board* British Rail has received substantial and consistently increasing subsidies from government in the years 1975 to 1981 inclusive. Stretching from £324m in 1975 to £810m in 1981, and totalling £3,408m, this has been augmented by a further £218m of government lending. In fact, over the seven-year period, government provided 96% of the total cash inflow. The remainder came from external borrowing of £171m.

The government finance received by British Rail has met its increasing operating cash deficits. The latter have extended consistently from £260m in 1975 to £630m in 1981. Proportionally, these have amounted to 63% of available cash during the seven-year period. Interest payments were approximately 10% of total cash outflow during the same period, and totalled £378m (64% of which were to government). The remaining 27% of total outflow comprised new investment—rising from £92m in 1975 to £147m in 1981.

Table 7

British Rail: Detailed Cash Flow Results—1975 to 1981

	1975	1976	1977	1978	1979	1980	1981	Total
	£m	£m	£m	£m	£m	£m	£m	£m
CASH INFLOW								
Government subsidies	324	319	364	434	523	634	810	3408
Government borrowing	63	26	—	11	41	47	30	218
Other borrowing	—	26	35	69	33	—	15	178
	387	371	399	514	597	681	855	3804
CASH OUTFLOW								
Operating cash flow	260	214	222	315	348	423	630	2412
Investment	92	114	134	150	187	183	147	1007
Government interest	20	31	31	33	37	40	50	242
Other interest	13	12	12	16	25	30	28	136
Other borrowing	2	—	—	—	—	5	—	7
	387	371	399	514	597	681	855	3804

GOVERNMENT-SUPPORTED ENTERPRISES' RESULTS

(b) *British Airways* British Airways has consistently produced operating cash flow surpluses—£722m in monetary total for the years 1975 to 1981, inclusive, but in 1981 being little different at £14m from the £12m figure of 1975. Over the seven-year period, the contribution was 45% of total cash inflow. The remainder of the cash funding required came from government—share capital (£194m) and external borrowing (42% of total inflow, and totalling £683m). Inevitably, this has meant an increased cost of borrowing (£16m in 1975 and £72m in 1981) and this totalled 13% of total cash outflow for 1975 to 1981 inclusive. Most of the cash outflow, however, was used for new investment—£1,273 in total, and 79% of total cash outflow for the seven-year period.

Table 8
British Airways: Detailed Cash Flow Results—1975 to 1981

	1975	1976	1977	1978	1979	1980	1981	Total
	£m	£m	£m	£m	£m	£m	£m	£m
CASH INFLOW								
Operating cash flow	12	71	134	151	213	127	14	722
Government capital	80	64	10	10	10	10	10	194
Government borrowing	—	28	—	—	—	—	—	28
Other borrowing	51	—	16	100	71	167	300	705
Decrease in cash assets	20	—	—	—	—	41	—	61
	163	163	160	261	294	345	324	1710
CASH OUTFLOW								
Investment	102	117	117	201	223	280	233	1273
Taxation	9	1	1	9	4	19	8	51
Government interest	15	8	11	19	22	20	11	106
Other interest	1	2	—	8	8	20	61	100
Government borrowing	36	—	24	23	14	6	6	109
Other borrowing	—	22	—	—	—	—	—	22
Increase in cash assets	—	13	7	1	23	—	5	49
	163	163	160	261	294	345	324	1710

OVERALL VIEW

There are several points to be drawn from the previous brief analyses. These are as follows:

1. All eight entities required government support at some time or another during the seven-year period 1975 to 1981. Only in the case of British Gas was this small. In most instances, the support was of a considerable amount. In terms of proportions of total cash inflow, 85% for BL; 77% for Rolls Royce; 84% for British Steel; 60% for the Coal Board; and 96% for British Rail. British Airways required a total of 14% inflow

from government (but borrowed 42% from banks); and the Electricity Council had a 19% inflow from the public purse.

2. Looking at the seven-year period as a whole, and again judging the data in terms of cash inflow contributions, only British Gas and the Electricity Council produced a majority of cash funds from operations (100% and 81%, respectively). British Airways (45%) and the Coal Board (13%) were the only other organisations to report overall cash surpluses from operations. The remainder produced deficits—Rolls Royce, 44% of total cash outflow; British Steel, 21%; and British Rail, 63%.

3. The operating cash flows of all the energy producers increased during the seven-year period; that of BL was relatively static; and the remainder revealed diminishing situations.

4. Government support usually came in the form of either share capital or a mixture of capital and borrowing. British Rail was financed solely by subsidy, and the Coal Board received regular subsidies supplemented by borrowing.

5. All three manufacturing organisations (BL, Rolls Royce and British Steel) were involved in reconstruction programmes resulting, in the cases of the first and last, in considerable outflows of cash.

6. All eight organisations had a major outflow of cash in the form of replacement and new investment. In the cases of BL, the Coal Board, British Gas, the Electricity Council, and British Airways, this outflow constituted more than 50% of the total outflow for the seven-year period 1975 to 1981. The highest proportions were the Coal Board (77%) and British Airways (79%). The lowest proportions were Rolls Royce (32%) and British Rail (27%).

7. Few entities paid any taxation in any of the years 1975 to 1981, inclusive. Only BL, Rolls Royce and British Airways did so and, in each such case, the amounts involved were small.

8. Interest payments constituted a substantial cash outflow for most of the organisations examined. The highest proportional outflow for the seven-year period was that of the Electricity Council with 37% and the lowest was British Rail at 10% (presumably because of its subsidy financing).

9. Only British Gas made net borrowing repayments during the seven

years; the remainder of the entities analysed were net additional borrowers.

10. The government support received by each of the eight organizations during the seven-year period was aggregated (that is, capital borrowings, subsidies, tax recovered and interest received). These totals were netted off against equivalent aggregations of cash outflows to government (that is, tax and interest payments, and borrowing repayments). Ideally, the matching should have been made following suitable price-level adjustments. However, lack of disclosure by each of the eight organisations prevented this being done with sufficient accuracy. The effect of the monetary aggregations and matchings was as follows (figures represent net receipts unless bracketed to indicate net payments to government): British Steel, £3,802m; British Rail, £3,384m; BL, £1,619m; Coal Board, £1,698m; Rolls Royce, £494m; British Airways £(44)m; Electricity Council, £(747)m; and British Gas, £(1,810)m. In other words, whereas the first five organisations have been recipients of considerable government support during the seven-year period, the last three have been significant contributors of cash to government.

CONCLUSIONS

The above CFA-based data of government-owned and supported organisations has provided an insight into the nature and degree of dependence by them on government for cash during the years 1975 to 1981, inclusive. In particular, it has revealed the operational cash contributions of these enterprises, and the substantial use of available cash to meet interest costs. It therefore adds to existing knowledge of the financial position and development of such entities.

REFERENCES

Lee, T.A. (1981a), "Cash Flow Accounting and Corporate Financial Reporting", in M. Bromwich and A. Hopwood (eds.), *Essays in British Accounting Research* (Pitman, 1981), pp.63–78.
____ (1981b), "What Cash Flow Analysis Says About BL's Finances", *The Financial Times* (23 October 1981), p.15.
____ (1982a), "Laker Airways—the Cash Flow Truth", *Accountancy* (June 1982), pp.115–6.
____ (1982b), "Towards a Practice of Cash Flow Analysis", *Discussion Paper 13* (University of Edinburgh, 1981).

5. THE FINANCIAL STATEMENTS OF THE HONGKONG AND SHANGHAI BANKING CORPORATION, 1865-1980

by T A Lee*

An Application of Cash Flow Accounting

This study is unique for two reasons. First, no previous study has examined the financial statements of a bank through its entire history. Secondly, no such analysis has employed the techniques of cash flow accounting to highlight financial developments over such a considerable period of time. The study is therefore a pioneering venture which focuses attention on accounting and financial matters, but is not concerned directly with the wider business, economic and social issues dealt with in other papers contained in this volume.

The history of the Hongkong and Shanghai Banking Corporation (HSBC) is presented in this paper through its published financial statements from its inception on 1 January 1865 to 31 December 1980. These statements summarise its activities, events and transactions over these one hundred and sixteen years, and serve as a useful bird's eye view of the changes which have occurred to the Bank during such a long period.

This particular approach to business history has been rarely used, and only by accounting historians. The first such study was by Claire (1945) of United States Steel. Hill (1955) investigated the statements of the Continental Gas Association, and Hodgkins (1975) the first twenty-one years of Unilever. In addition, Edwards (1981) has examined a limited run of financial statements of various UK steel companies. But Lee (1977) was the first study of a major public company's financial statements throughout its then entire history.

The technique of long-term, multi-period analysis of company financial statements has been rarely used by historians because of a number of factors--first, the lack of published financial statements for the complete period (not a problem in the case of HSBC); secondly, the difficulty of a changing corporate and trading structure for the reporting entity due to takeover and merger, and the need to diversify and adapt to changing circumstances and tastes (again, not a problem with HSBC as it has remained a bank throughout the one hundred and sixteen years of analysis); and, thirdly, limited accounting and disclosure of information in company financial statements, particularly prior to the 1950s and 1960s (and especially with banks such as HSBC due to generally accepted but restricted legal provisions which exist to this day in certain countries including Hong Kong).

Thus, the non-accounting historian may not have been sufficiently tempted to use financial statements to describe business histories even

---

*I am grateful for the considerable help given to me by officials of the Hongkong and Shanghai Banking Corporation when interpreting figures, and to my colleague, Rod Ferrier, for his careful comments on earlier drafts.

when these sources of information were available. However, Lee (1977) has sought to demonstrate that it is possible for the qualified accounting historian to do so, and to employ the technique of funds flow accounting over long periods of time to avoid certain of the problems of subjective accounting practices in early financial statements. Funds flow also has the considerable merit of measuring financial change and development over periods of time--a matter of some importance to the business historian.

The funds flow accounting technique involves taking successive balance sheets and related profit statements and, by comparing them, preparing funds statements reflecting the major sources of finance (for example, capital, loans and profit retained) and the major sources to which the total funding has been put (for example, the purchase of fixed assets, increases in working capital, payment of tax and dividends, and repayment of loans). These statements, when covering extensive periods of time, allow the business historian to assess the overall progress of the reporting entity. However, because they contain data relating to inventories, debtors and creditors (that is, working capital) they remain influenced by any subjective accounting practices which have been applied to these items. For this reason, the conversion of funds flow to cash flow statements has been used in this paper, and avoids much of the problems affecting these or equivalent data in the financial statements of HSBC. This will be explained further in a later section.

HSBC financial statements

Banks are no strangers to subjective accounting practices and limited disclosure, and it should be no surprise to associate HSBC with such a situation. In fact, it has usually been the case in most developed free-enterprise societies that banks have been allowed legally to 'smooth' their financial results by use of techniques such as 'inner' or 'hidden' reserves and to disclose far less information than is expected or required for other trading concerns. The reason for this approach to reporting requirements is the need to reflect financial stability in banks for the benefit of depositors.

But smoothing profits, and over- or undervaluing assets and liabilities in the balance sheet as a consequence, no matter how necessary and acceptable, make financial analysis a difficult process for the business historian. This in no way is meant to cast doubt on bank managements; it is merely a factual statement of banking practice. However, it can to a considerable extent be avoided by the use of an accounting technique which minimises the effects of movements to and from hidden reserves--particularly those which relate to the assets and liabilities of a bank which can reasonably be classified as working capital--that is, most items with the exception of properties and related assets, and investments. As the latter typically constitute a minority of a bank's total net assets, the effect of the technique on smoothing procedures is significant.

The technique is entitled cash flow accounting, and has usually been described and used in relation to retail or manufacturing concerns. It aims to describe their operational financial results in pure cash terms,

FINANCIAL STATEMENTS

devoid of any arbitrary allocations and valuations. In effect, it takes the funds statement and, by netting the working capital change against the periodic profit (with depreciation and other arbitrary allocations eliminated) it produces a measure of operational cash flow without the influence of stocks, debtors and creditors. By rearranging the other funds items, which are usually in the form of cash anyway (for example, fixed asset purchases and sales, taxation, dividends and borrowings), it is possible to produce a cash flow statement free from any accounting smoothing. The technique is explained in Lee (1981) and, should a funds statement not be available (as in the case of HSBC) it is possible to derive one from the available balance sheets and linking profit statement.

Given that HSBC is essentially a cash business, and has been so throughout its one hundred and sixteen year history, it appears to be suitable to apply cash flow accounting to its available financial statements and produce cash-based data which avoid subjective accounting practices (in the main but not entirely) and do not depend on the availability of detailed disclosures and explanations of published figures. In essence, it reveals the underlying cash flow elements of HSBC.

Applying cash flow accounting

Due to the lack of full disclosure in all of the one hundred and sixteen years of reported information, the compilation of HSBC cash data has not been easy, but it has been possible to undertake in a reasonably approximate way. The following sections are therefore not intended to be anything other than limited analyses which are near enough the truth of the underlying cash flow to warrant comment and explanation. As stated previously, it has not been possible to eliminate all the hidden reserve movements affecting properties, furnishings and investments (including those in subsidiary companies).

The overall framework in cash flow terms is to describe the periodic changes in financial position as operational cash flow minus acquisitions of properties and investments (net of disposals) plus note issues and capital issues--reconciling these movements to the change in cash and near cash assets. This concentrates attention on the main sources of funding for the latter items which are required to meet the immediate needs of depositors. It highlights in a defined period how much additional cash has been generated from depositors, after allowing for increased lending to customers and interest flows; and how much has come from the subscription of new capital by shareholders (new note issues have usually required deposits to be made with the Hong Kong government, and thus should be related directly with investments in any cash flow analysis). It avoids the notion of profit which is difficult to interpret in banking terms because of accounting allocations and valuations. And it describes, in relatively simple terms, how much of the available cash from banking and related operations has been used to invest in new property, furnishings, deposits and securities, and subsidiary and associated companies, and how much has been made available for dividend distributions.

Producing the above cash flow data is not easy, and does not avoid all the problems brought about by generally accepted bank accounting. For example, HSBC has never disclosed its tax figures and therefore the following cash flow analyses will contain no mention of tax payments--the operational cash flow being stated as 'after-tax'. In addition, although careful scrutiny of every scrap of information in the published financial statements can reveal to the experienced accountant considerable data on hidden reserve movements, not all of them can be detected. Those affecting properties and investments which fall into this category are considered to be small in relation to the adjusted figures which have been used.

When applying cash flow accounting to a company such as HSBC, the main problem is identifying a bank's working capital and cash resources. This is not easy as no such classification is usually made--throughout its history, HSBC has followed generally accepted practice and listed its assets and liabilities without the major asset and liability headings which would appear in the financial statements of non-banking organisations. The problem is establishing what is the banking equivalent of stocks, work-in-progress, debtors and creditors. In a bank, all such items are monetary but are no less stocks, debtors and creditors for that. It was eventually decided for purposes of this paper that HSBC's working capital constitutes advances and loans to customers, trade bills and time deposits, minus current, deposit and other accounts, and drafts and other sums in transit. This left cash and short-term funds to be defined as period-end cash resources, and properties, investments and certificates of indebtedness as equivalent to fixed assets. These definitions were applied as consistently as possible to similar or equivalent items in the financial statements of HSBC over one hundred and sixteen years.

Basic data

The primary purpose of this paper is to examine the financial progress of HSBC in terms of its basic business--the flow of cash within the economic community. Thus the financial reports of the company from 1865 to 1980 have been converted into cash flow terms, and the resultant data are contained in Table 1. As suggested previously, this avoids the measurement of profit in traditional accounting terms, and makes it easier for the historian to interpret the financial progress of HSBC.

The calculated data have been divided for convenience into five main periods of time. This reduces the complexity and enormity of the data to manageable proportions. It also deals with significant periods in the bank's history--the first (1865 to 1875) representing the initial decade of activity in which the bank sought to survive in financial terms; the second (1876 to 1900) covers the crucial and difficult period leading up to the First World War, and in which economic conditions in the Far East were consistently difficult; the third (1901 to 1925) is mainly concerned with the influence of the First World War; the fourth (1926 to 1950) related to the bank's development during world-wide depression, and its management of the crippling effects of the Second World War; and the last (1951 to 1980) explains the post Second World War expansion in HSBC activities.

The splitting of the financial history of the bank into these periods

FINANCIAL STATEMENTS

TABLE 1

THE HONGKONG AND SHANGHAI BANKING CORPORATION

Summary of Cash Flow Results from 1865 to 1980
(in millions of Hong Kong Dollars)

Period of Activity	1865-1875	1876-1900	1901-1925	1926-1950	1951-1980	Total
Operating cash flow	3.7	76.0	204.4	1,442.5	65,757.9	67,484.5
Less: investment in securities	2.5	14.5	76.2	1,147.2	17,418.9	18,659.3
properties	0.2	1.5	33.3	26.3	2,717.5	2,778.8
subsidiaries and associates	–	–	–	2.1	2,799.4	2,801.5
	2.7	16.0	109.5	1,175.6	22,935.8	24,239.6
	1.0	60.0	94.9	266.9	42,822.1	43,244.9
Less: dividends paid	3.5	33.1	139.5	264.6	3,039.5	3,480.2
	(2.5)	26.9	(44.6)	2.3	39,782.6	39,764.7
Add: new capital received	5.0	9.3	35.9	–	409.5	459.7
new notes issues	1.9	10.6	32.8	710.4	6,618.3	7,374.0
Increase in cash assets	4.4	46.8	24.1	712.7	46,810.4	47,598.4

of activity is obviously open to question, but they do contain the most significant financial events affecting its progress. In any case, the major emphasis is on <u>periodic</u> analysis; the results of individual years are of little significance as an annual period is too short to judge a bank's financial performance. The point of the following analyses is to concentrate on major periods of activity; varying the length of the chosen periods by several years has been found to make little difference to the overall picture in each period.

Table 2 outlines the main financial ratios of the bank as indicators of its progress over time and deals with its growth in terms of profits, cash flow, dividends, assets, and liquidity. These appear to be matters with which the historian ought to be concerned when assessing HSBC's progress. It should be noted that, in order to provide proper comparisons of data over time, two corrections should be made where relevant--the data ought to be described in constant general price-level terms in order to avoid the distorting effects of inflation and deflation (this has not been

EASTERN BANKING

possible in this case due to the lack of a suitable price index to make the necessary adjustments from 1865 to 1980); and data must be put in comparative terms when events have rendered them non-comparative (in this case, the number of shares in issue has changed over time due to disaggregation and bonus issues and, as in normal accounting practice in such situations, all share numbers are expressed in terms of 1980 equivalents).

Tables 1 and 2 will form the basis of the remaining analyses in this paper. However, attention will also be paid to any significant changes in reporting practice which have occurred during the one hundred and sixteen years of activity being examined, as these are of specific interest to the accounting historian.

TABLE 2

THE HONGKONG AND SHANGHAI BANKING CORPORATION
Key Financial Indicators 1865 to 1980

Period of Activity	1865-1875	1876-1900	1901-1925	1926-1950	1951-1980	1865-1980
	(in millions of Hong Kong Dollars)					
Average annual operating cash flow	0.34	3.04	8.18	57.70	2,191.93	581.76
Average annual profit before dividend	0.35	1.78	6.92	11.98	212.90	59.55
Average annual dividend paid	0.32	1.32	5.58	10.58	101.32	30.00
Point of time: 31 Dec	1865	1875	1900	1925	1950	1980
Earnings per share ($)	0.0021	0.0010	0.0131	0.0169	0.0212	1.2846
Dividends per share ($)	0.0016	0.0009	0.0081	0.0162	0.0192	0.6499
Assets per share ($)	0.1591	0.2057	0.6280	1.0450	5.1326	218.0447
Cash assets/current, deposit and other accounts (%)	14	16	30	14	31	22

FINANCIAL STATEMENTS

The foundation: 1865 to 1975

The first eleven years of HSBC's life were exceedingly difficult due to the then world depression, and with the bank taking over banking arrangements previously undertaken by the merchant companies of Hong Kong.
 The bank's published financial statements during this period were simple summaries of figures, produced on a half-yearly basis. The balance sheet was typically a simple listing of assets in order of realisability and liabilities in order of priority of repayment. No classifications were made, and no corresponding period figures were given. The profit statement was merely a report of recommended appropriations of figures, the balance sheet having been prepared excluding these appropriations. There were no detailed notes to the accounts although the reserve fund was disclosed as a separate statement from 1867 onwards. Transfers to reserve appeared to be the method of accounting for the potential replacement of fixed assets rather than by means of formal depreciation policies. The auditor's report, signed by two individuals, was a simple statement that the financial statements had been examined and found correct. It was therefore likely to have been a very limited audit, mainly concerned with checking the accuracy of the bookkeeping procedures and the arithmetic of the financial statements.
 The accounting, reporting and auditing can be summarised during this period as being typical of the times. The figures provide little direct insight into the financial progress and position of HSBC by 1875. Its profits before dividend for the year 1865 were $0.2 million and had fallen by 7% to $0.19 million in 1875, and earnings per share had decreased by 52% over the same period. Dividends per share, on the other hand, fell by 44% between 1865 and 1875 (despite an increase in dividend levels of 13%) and this reflects the difficult trading situation of the times. Total reported assets increased from $13.4 million in 1865 to $34.6 million in 1875 (158%). In terms of data per share, the equivalent assets increase for the period was 29%.
 Thus, the levels of profits, dividends and assets appeared to have grown substantially in the first decade of activity, but, when expressed in 1980 equivalent per share terms, the increases were substantially less in the cases of profits and assets, and a decrease in the case of dividends. The cash flow situation more accurately reflects the problems of the bank during these times (as shown in Table 3).
 An operating cash flow of $3.7 million was generated over the eleven years (an annual average of $0.34 million) something less than the total reported profits before dividend of $3.8 million. It represented 35% of the total inflow of $10.6 million--the remainder comprising capital issues (47%) and note issues (18%). Remembering the need to invest to cover new note issues, investment (mainly of securities) constituted a low 25% of the total funds available; dividends represented a higher 33% (at $3.5 million, just less than the ten year operating cash flow); and cash assets were increased by the remaining 42%. However, by the end of 1875, the latter amounted to only 14% of the liability to depositors. All of these figures reflect the financial difficulties of the times which HSBC had to face--it depended on new capital for its long-term survival, and dividend levels had

213

TABLE 3

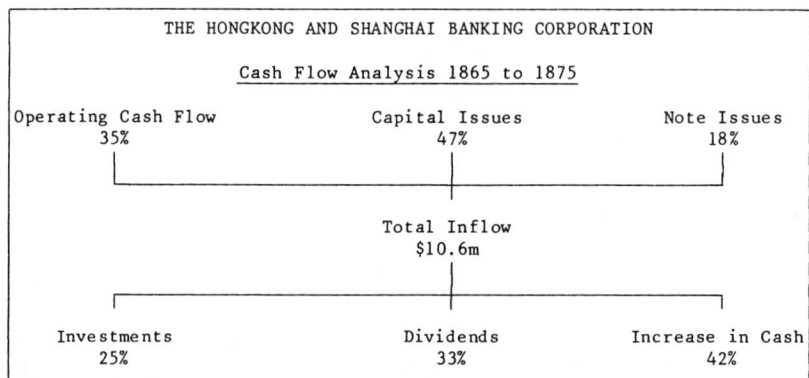

Data source: Table 1; all percentages are of total inflow.

to be sufficient to attract such capital. Much of the available cash was put in the form of realisable assets to provide cover for the increasing liability to depositors.

The next twenty-five years: 1876 to 1900

The period from 1 January 1876 to 31 December 1900 represents the first major trading era of HSBC. Despite a continuing world depression and a slump in silver prices, the bank was aiding Chinese governmental finance and expanding its activities across the Pacific as well as into India and Europe. It therefore expanded its operations considerably although the resultant financial data continued to be reported in the very limited way of the previous decade. In fact, there were no major changes in reporting format or accounting procedures between 1876 and 1900.

Operating cash flow totalled $76 million for the period--an annual average of $3.04 million and an annual increase of 794% over the previous period's average. This total flow constituted 79% of the total inflow of HSBC, the remainder coming from capital (10%) and notes (11%). 17% of the total inflow was spent on securities and properties (presumably covering new notes), with 34% being used for dividends (a similar proportion to the previous period). The remaining 49% increased cash or near cash assets. In other words, there was a considerable improvement on the cash flow situation of the previous period. Much more cash had been generated from depositors and other account holders, and the net result was an improvement of $46.8 million in cash assets (the latter being 30% of the liabilities to depositors, etc at 31 December 1900). (These data are summarised in Table 4).

FINANCIAL STATEMENTS

TABLE 4

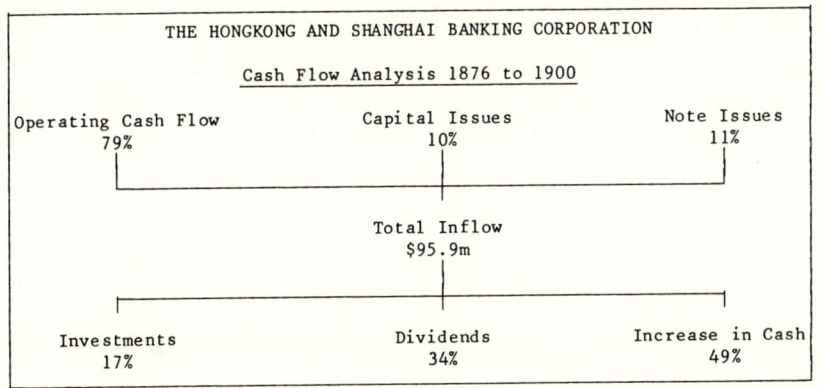

Data source: Table 1; all percentages are of total inflow

The profitability of the bank had also improved during the period. The average annual profit before dividend was $1.78 million, a 409% increase over the equivalent 1865 to 1975 figure. The adjusted earnings per share figure by 1900 had moved to $0.0131 from $0.0010 in 1875 (an increase of 1210%). Dividends per share had improved also over the period --by 800% to $0.0081 in 1900. The average annual dividend of the period was $1.32 million, having increased by 313% from the equivalent average of 1865 to 1875. The assets per share had expanded from $0.2057 in 1865 to $0.6280 (a 205% increase). In other words, during the twenty-five years covered in this analysis, cash flow, profits, dividends and assets had expanded in a considerable way (usually by several hundreds per cent and surely in excess of general price-level movements) and the relative frailties of the first ten years from 1865 to 1875 were nullified. By far the greatest improvement was in cash flow which in net terms resulted in a 1064% increase in cash assets. In the sense that profits had overstated the underlying cash flow situation between 1865 and 1875, it can be reasonably said that profits between 1876 and 1900 understated it.

Consolidating years: 1901 to 1925

The next period in the history of HSBC was one in which the efforts of the earlier periods were consolidated, particularly in China, despite trading uncertainty caused by the War Lord problem, the Japanese Russian War and the First World War. During the same period, several accounting and reporting changes took place.

In 1911, acceptances and other contra liabilities appeared in the balance sheet for the first time, and in 1915 the statements were produced

- 85 -

EASTERN BANKING

on an annual basis (to 31 December) with all provisions and appropriations accounted for in the balance sheet. Figures were presented in both Pounds and Dollars in 1919 onwards and in 1922 the authorised share capital was disclosed. A year earlier in 1921, the auditor's report had a long-form content, stating that the balance sheet had been audited with head office records and branch returns; all necessary information and explanations had been received by the auditors, and that the balance sheet was full and fair, and gave a true and correct view of the bank's state of affairs. Thus, the audit was limited to the balance sheet, and the latter was described in undefined terms of fullness, fairness, truth and correctness. The published financial statements remained very sparse indeed in terms of disclosure, despite these assurances from the auditors (a situation not unusual at that time).

A study of the available financial results for HSBC between the years 1901 and 1925 reveals considerable growth over the period as well as compared with the previous twenty-five year period. The average annual profit before dividend was $6.92 million, an increase of 289% over the equivalent datum for the previous period. Earnings per share had, by 1925, increased by only 29% when compared with a similar ratio for the year 1900. Thus, profitability, when adjusted by a 1980 share equivalent, did not rise as materially as the absolute profit figures indicate.

Dividend data describe similar growth--the average annual dividend paid was $5.58 million, thus well covered by the average profit (1.24 times), and an increase of 323% compared with the previous period. But the dividend per share for 1925 had increased by only 100% from the 1900 equivalent figure. Total assets of the bank grew, too, by 233% from $211.5 million in 1900 to $703.8 million by the end of 1925. The assets per share data for the same points of time were $0.6280 and $1.045--an increase of 66%.

Therefore, the profit, dividend and asset increases of the period 1901 to 1925 inclusive reflect considerably less advance than was the case in the period 1876 to 1900 inclusive. In fact, when measured in 1980 share equivalent terms, the increases are small considering the twenty-five year length of period. This relative slowness in progress was presumably due to the war-influenced economic conditions of the time and is more accurately reflected in the cash flow results of HSBC for the period.

The total operating cash flow for the twenty-five years was $204.4 million, representing 75% of the total inflow (13% came from new capital and the remaining 12% from notes issues). The average annual cash flow for the period was $8.18 million, an increase of 169% over the prior period equivalent. However, when outflows are examined, the picture changes. 40% of the total inflow of $273.1 million acquired necessary securities (for example, to cover the new notes), and premises and fittings. A very high 51% of inflow (68% of operating cash flow) was used to make dividend payments of $139.5 million. This left funds available to produce an increase in total cash assets of $24.1 million--47% of such assets reported at the end of 1900. The cash assets available to cover depositors and other accounts dropped to 14% of the latter at the end of 1925 compared with 30% at the end of 1900. In other words, the cash generated from banking operations did not appear sufficient to meet the need to pay for securities

FINANCIAL STATEMENTS

(other than to cover note issues), premises and dividends, and the receipt of new capital was inadequate to prevent the cash asset cover of immediate liabilities dropping drastically between 1900 and 1925. The main problem appeared to be the high level of dividend payments in relation to the total operational cash flow. (Table 5 summarises the foregoing situation.)

TABLE 5

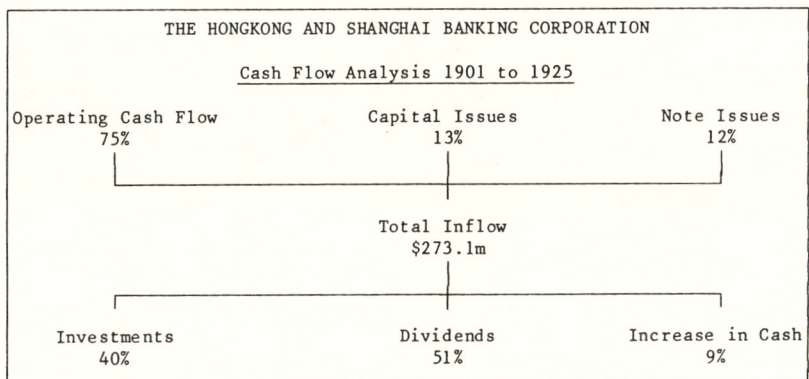

THE HONGKONG AND SHANGHAI BANKING CORPORATION

Cash Flow Analysis 1901 to 1925

Operating Cash Flow	Capital Issues	Note Issues
75%	13%	12%

Total Inflow
$273.1m

Investments	Dividends	Increase in Cash
40%	51%	9%

Data source: Table 1; all percentages are of total inflow.

The troubled years: 1926 to 1950

The years 1926 to 1950 presented further difficulties for HSBC. This was particularly the case between 1939 and 1946 due to the effects of the Second World War and the Japanese invasion and confiscation of Hong Kong. The published financial statements of the period reflect this. With most of the bank's assets in enemy hands in the early 1940s, it is not surprising to see the disclosed profit statements, balance sheets and auditor's reports making full mention of the problem. For example, in the year of 1942, notes to the financial statements were produced for the first time, largely because of the war, and continued as an accounting practice thereafter. In 1941, no financial statements were produced for a year in which the large majority of the bank's assets (and liabilities) fell into enemy hands. In 1942, a balance sheet only was produced from London, revealing that (at book value) 49% of HSBC assets suffered such a fate, and 58% of its liabilities were being similarly treated. The auditor's report (for the first time issued by a firm of professional accountants rather than by individuals) made a clear statement of the inevitable lack of verification of assets and liabilities and qualified the audit opinion on the financial statements accordingly. It was not until the financial statements of 1946 were produced that some semblance of accounting normality returned.

Other significant accounting changes during the period were limited. The financial statements continued throughout to be of a brief and simple kind. Summarised profit statements and balance sheets lacked detailed classification and explanation and had no comparative figures. In addition, although investments in subsidiary companies were introduced to the 1942 statements, it was not felt necessary to produce consolidated statements.

The total operating cash flow of the period of $1,442.5 million constituted an increase of 606% over that of the previous twenty-five years. It also represented 67% of the total inflow, the remaining 33% coming in the form of notes issues (no new capital was issued). 55% of funds was utilised to acquire securities (much of which were to act as cover for the notes issues), premises and subsidiary investments. The security purchases formed 92% of all security investments made since 1865. Only 12% of the total inflow was used to meet dividend payments for the period of $264.6 million. In fact, dividends amounted to only 18% of operating cash flow; the high security purchases having diminished considerably the cash availability for distribution.

The average annual cash flow of the period was $57.7 million, an increase of 605% over the previous period's statistic, and this would have been sufficient to meet the average annual dividend payment of $10.58 million (an increase of only 90% from the previous period) but for the securities which were required to be purchased. Equally, the average annual profit figure of $11.98 million (73% increase) appears to have been sufficient to provide dividend cover. Generally speaking, however, the financial performance of HSBC was understandably static--earnings per share increased by only 25% between 1925 and 1950 (to $0.0212); dividends per share only increased by 19% during the same period (to $0.0192); although assets per share increased by 391% (largely in the form of securities and cash assets, and with the latter providing a 31% cover for immediate liabilities at the end of 1950, compared with 14% at the end of 1925). In other words, the financial position of the bank had improved considerably by 1950 although improvements in its profitability, distribution and cash flow during the previous twenty-five years had been at a lesser level. (Table 6 outlines the cash flow position.)

The years of expansion: 1951 to 1980

Whereas each of the previous periods of analysis have indicated difficult economic and trading conditions for HSBC, the last period to the present date reflects the post Second World War boom which the bank has enjoyed by using the platform of financial position it had built by 1950. Indeed, it is only in the last thirty years that the bank has expanded to its present condition of size and importance.

During the period a great many accounting and reporting changes took place in the published financial statements of HSBC, and the main ones are worthy of note. In 1951, comparative figures for the previous year were produced for the first time, and from 1955 onwards separate financial statements were disclosed for the main subsidiary companies. Only in 1959,

FINANCIAL STATEMENTS

TABLE 6

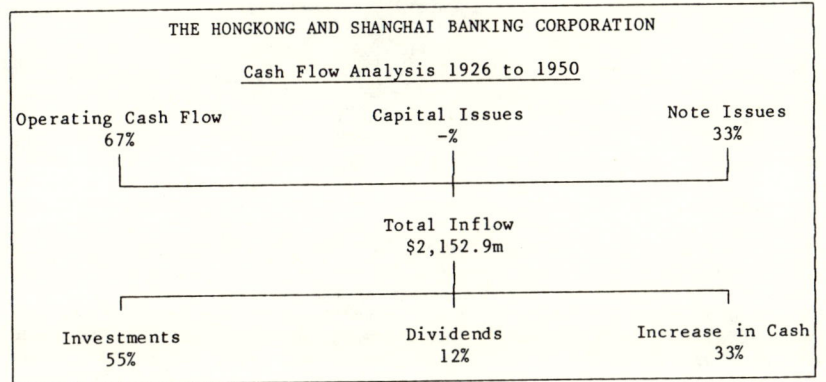

Data Source: Table 1; all percentages are of total inflow.

long after a similar change in other countries, was the practice of producing consolidated financial statements introduced. In the same year, a vertical profit statement appeared, as did the curious (and unexplained) practice of providing two audit opinions--a 'true and correct' one for the holding company statements, and a 'true and fair' one for the consolidated statements (the subtle difference between 'correctness' and 'fairness' could have been confusing for the shareholder recipient). This practice continued until 1967 when a 'true and fair' opinion was given on the holding company statements, and the consolidated statements were said to comply with the provisions of the Companies Acts. In 1975, the 'true and fair' opinion was given to cover all published financial statements. Finally, in relation to subsidiary companies, their reserves were included with holding company reserves (instead of being placed in undisclosed inner reserves) for the first time in 1966; and in 1971 onwards, subsidiary company investments were revalued on the basis of their net asset values, thus continuously updating their consolidated reserves for reporting purposes. (Inner reserves were not and are not disclosed separately. Instead, they form part of the general liability heading including deposit and current accounts, and provisions.)

Despite these changes, however, the published financial statements of HSBC remain relatively stark listings of assets and liabilities, supported by considerably more explanation and analysis of detail (wholly in line with generally accepted banking practice). They continue to be subject to inner reserve movements of an undisclosed nature and are relatively typical of all banks' financial statements. Thus, they required as much care to be applied in analysis in 1980 as was the case in 1865.

The financial results of HSBC over the last thirty years have been spectacular by any standards. Annual profits before dividends increased from $14.2 million in 1950 to $1,431.0 million, an increase of 998% (far in excess of general price-level changes). Average annual profits for the period increased by 1,559% to $215.67 million. Earnings per share were $0.0212 in 1950 but $1.2846 in 1980 (an increase of 5,962%). Dividends, too, grew out of all proportion--the average annual payment for the period was up by 858% over the previous period at $101.32 million, and the dividends per share increased by 3,285% between 1950 and 1980. The cash situation of the bank mirrored this 'accounting' success--the total operating cash flow for the thirty years totalled $65,757.9 million (up by 4,459% on the previous period) and the annual average was $2,191.93 million (up by 3,699%). This huge influx of cash was more than adequate to cover the acquisition of securities (27%), premises and fittings (4%) and subsidiaries (4%). Total dividend payments of $3,039.5 million represented only 4% of the total inflow and only 5% of operating cash flow (in both cases, considerably below anything seen in earlier periods). 90% of the aggregate inflow of funds came from operations, 9% from notes, and the remainder from capital issues. The increase in cash assets of $46,810.4 million comprised a 5,940% increase in them, and provided at the end of 1980 a 22% cover for immediate liabilities (31% at the end of 1950). The growth of total assets over the period is reflected in the assets per share statistics--in 1950 it was $5.1326 and by 1980 it was $218.0447, an increase of 4,148%. (Cash flow developments are summarised in Table 7.)

TABLE 7

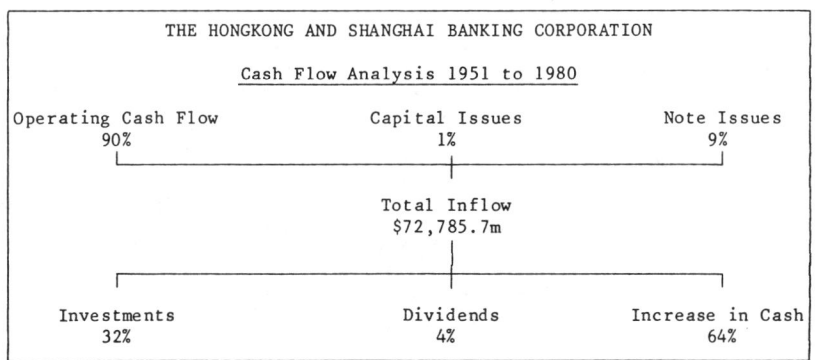

Data source: Table 1; all percentages are of total inflow.

In summary, therefore, the last thirty years of HSBC's history represent the point at which it has 'taken off' and grown at an almost geometric rate. This is reflected in all its figures for profits, dividends, cash flow and assets, and of particular interest is the generation of cash which has been more than sufficient to meet the needs of management, shareholders

FINANCIAL STATEMENTS

and depositors.

Overall summary

Before closing this analysis of the financial reports of HSBC, it is useful to examine the overall position as reflected in the total columns of Tables 1 and 2, and in the summary Table 8. In total over the one hundred and sixteen years concerned, $75,318.2 million of inflow has been generated-- 90% from banking operations, 9.8% from notes, and 0.2% from capital. 24% has been used to buy securities, 4% to purchase property and fittings, and 4% to acquire subsidiary and associated companies. 5% has met dividend payments, and 63% has increased cash assets. The average annual cash flow from operations over the entire one hundred and sixteen years has been $581.76 million, whereas the annual average profit before dividend has been $59.55 million. The average annual dividend payment was $30.0 million. Thus, overall, operating cash flow has vastly exceeded profits, and dividends have been more than adequately covered by both cash flow and profits.

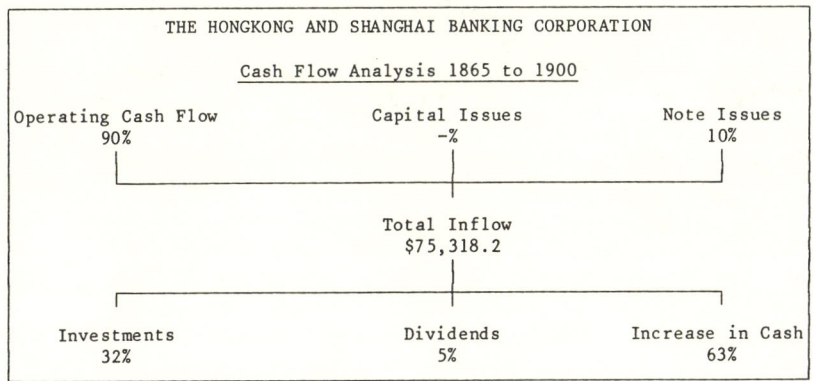

TABLE 8

THE HONGKONG AND SHANGHAI BANKING CORPORATION

Cash Flow Analysis 1865 to 1900

| Operating Cash Flow | Capital Issues | Note Issues |
| 90% | -% | 10% |

Total Inflow
$75,318.2

| Investments | Dividends | Increase in Cash |
| 32% | 5% | 63% |

Data source: Table 1; all percentages are of total inflow.

The period from 1951 to 1980 has undoubtedly distorted these data. The extraordinary growth in banking activity and related financial results is to be witnessed in the following bare statistics relating to HSBC's cash flow--in the years 1951 to 1980 inclusive, the undernoted proportions of the one hundred and sixteen years totals were achieved: 97% of operating cash flow, 93% of securities purchased, 98% of property and fittings purchased, nearly 100% of subsidiary investments, 87% of dividends paid, 89% of new capital raised, 90% of new note issues, and 98% of cash assets. The early years reflect merely the gradually evolving platform on which this financial success has been built. Interestingly, despite the lack of detail and disclosure in all the financial reports of the bank since 1865, this detailed analysis of cash flow and related results has been possible, and reflects well on past and present managers of HSBC.

References

R S Clair, 'Evolution of Corporate Reports', Journal of Accountancy (LXXIX, 1945), pp. 39-51.

J R Edwards, Company Legislation and Changing Patterns of Disclosure in British Company Accounts: 1900-1940 (ICAEW, 1975).

N K Hill, 'Accountancy Developments in a Public Utility Company in the Nineteenth Century', Accounting Research (VI, 1955), pp. 382-90.

P Hodgkins, 'Unilever--The First 21 Years', Coopers' Journal (Sept 1975), pp. 15-19.

T A Lee, 'Company Financial Statements: An Essay in Business History: 1830-1950,' in S Marriner, ed. Business and Businessmen (University of Liverpool Press, 1977), pp. 235-62.

T A Lee, 'Cash Flow Accounting and Corporate Financial Reporting', in M Bromwich and A Hopwood, eds. Essays in British Accounting Research (Pitman, 1981), pp. 63-81.

Empirical Findings

T. A. LEE

A Survey of Accountants' Opinions on Cash Flow Reporting

> The results of a survey of members of the Institute of Chartered Accountants of Scotland is reported. The survey gives evidence of the views of professionally qualified accountants concerning their support for, and the feasibility of reporting on, a cash flow basis. Considerable support was discerned for preparing company annual financial reports on a cash flow basis.
>
> **Key words:** Accounting theory, Financial Statements, Cash flow statements.

INTRODUCTION

The merits of cash flow accounting (CFA) as a basis for corporate financial reporting have been well documented (for details, see Lee [1981]). But nowhere in the literature is there a statement of whether it has support within the report producer and user communities. This paper is a report on the results of a fact-finding survey into CFA. In particular, it describes the views of certain professionally qualified accountants who are at least partly responsible for the corporate financial reporting function; views not only about whether they favour the introduction of CFA in financial reports but also concerning its form and feasibility. In addition, the opportunity was taken to evidence the opinions of these accountants on the external reporting of cash flow forecasts, and to find out whether CFA is used for internal reporting purposes within their companies.

Research Method

The survey was conducted by means of a simple mailed questionnaire which had been pretested. This was sent to 488 members of the Institute of Chartered Accountants of Scotland designated in its *1978-79 Directory* as working in companies in industry and commerce (approximately 500 was judged to be the absolute limit beyond which time and cost factors would impinge on the research). The selection of the sample of accountants was not random. As the study was intended as the first necessary step in a much larger programme of research into CFA, the respondents were limited to Scottish CAs employed by companies in Scotland. In fact, almost all Scottish-based industrial and commercial companies employing Scottish CAs were represented in the sample — one qualified accountant only being selected for each company. The result of this stratification was that the companies concerned were located throughout Scotland with the majority inevitably being within the main central industrial belt around Edinburgh

---

T. A. LEE is Professor of Accountancy and Finance, University of Edinburgh.

and Glasgow. A reasonable spread of job function and post-qualifying experience was also demanded in the selection process. In other words, although the sampling procedure was not entirely 'scientific', it did allow for stratification according to type and location of employing company, and job function and date of qualification of the surveyed accountants. This will be seen more clearly in a later analysis of the background characteristics of the responding and non-responding accountants, and, considering the nature of the questions to be asked, it was judged to be sufficient to justify proceeding with the questionnaire.

The Questionnaire

The questionnaire was sent to the potential respondents, together with a covering letter which explained the nature and reasons for the research and described precisely what was meant by CFA. As part of the latter description, a specimen cash flow statement was also provided, and this is reproduced in the Appendix to this paper. The questionnaire required answers to questions in the following general areas:

1. Whether the respondents were in favour of CFA for external reporting purposes (and the reasons why) and, if they were, for whom CFA would be useful (again with supporting reasons) — that is, to evidence whether the respondents believed CFA to have utility in the external reporting function.
2. How the respondents in favour of CFA felt it could be sustained in practice — for example, in relation to the availability of cash flow data, the form of cash flow statements, how many years of cash flow data to be reported, and whether they should be audited (in all cases with supporting reasons) — that is, to evidence whether the respondents believed CFA to be practicable.
3. Whether the respondents were in favour of producing forecast cash flow statements for external reporting purposes and, if so, how many years of data should be reported, and whether they should be audited (supporting reasons were also asked for) — that is, to evidence whether the respondents believed CFA should include forecasts for external reporting purposes.
4. Whether the respondents' companies produced cash flow statements for internal reporting purposes and, if so, in what form — that is, to evidence whether the respondents had experience of CFA for internal purposes which could aid its implementation for external purposes.

Each of these general areas will form the basis for a discussion of the relevant research results achieved by the survey.

SURVEY RESPONSE

The response achieved in the survey is given in Table 1 and indicates that approximately four out of every ten accountants surveyed responded to the main questionnaire, with a further 6 per cent providing background detail responses only. Given the notoriously difficult task of obtaining good survey responses on accounting matters in the U.K., the response rate of 39 per cent was felt to be reasonable enough to justify the analysis and further consideration of the questionnaire results.

TABLE 1
ACCOUNTANTS SURVEY RESPONSE

	n	%
Total questionnaires mailed	488	100
Less: questionnaires returned because addressees not known, left employment etc.	24	5
Maximum possible response	464	95
Questionnaires completed and analysed	182	39
Questionnaires completed and not analysed because they were returned late	2	—
Background details questionnaires returned by non-respondents	29	6
Absolute non-response	251	55
	464	100

Respondents' Background

The questionnaire contained a section dealing with the background characteristics of the respondents — that is, occupation, internal and external reporting experiences, reporting responsibilities and size of the employing companies (size being determined in terms of turnover, assets and employees). These were felt to be sufficient to create variables for further analyses of the main data if this was necessary (see Lee and Tweedie [1977, 1981]). A relevant summary is given in Table 2. The data reveal several interesting features about the respondents to the main questionnaire.

1. Typically, the respondents appeared to hold relatively senior accounting or financial positions in their companies, as was to be expected because of their professional accountancy qualification — 72 per cent were finance directors, chief accountants or financial controllers, and 43 per cent had achieved company board status.

2. However, although their job titles may indicate seniority, the reporting experience of respondents was more varied. In terms of internal experience, something below half (45 per cent) had less than five years, and only 27 per cent had more than eleven years. This record was less impressive in relation to external reporting — more than half of the respondents had less than five years' experience and only 17 per cent had more than eleven years. In other words, in reporting terms, the respondents were relatively short of reporting experience when examined at the aggregate level — a situation not inconsistent with a rapidly growing profession.

3. So far as the reporting responsibilities of the companies employing the respondents were concerned, these tended to vary, the main recipient groups being identified by the respondents as (in order of magnitude) bankers (64 per cent), shareholders (57 per cent), holding companies (49 per cent), lenders (30 per cent) and employees (26 per cent). In other words, there is evidence from this study of a multi-purpose reporting responsibility for a typical company, with the recipients of its external financial reports going well beyond the strict legal requirement of shareholders. The importance of bankers is this regard, and particularly in relation to liquidity as a feature in this study of CFA, is noteworthy. The multiplicity of the reporting function is seen in the further analysis revealing that only 28 per cent of the 'responding' companies had a single

SURVEY ON CASH FLOW REPORTING

TABLE 2
BACKGROUND VARIABLES OF ACCOUNTANTS

	Respondents		Non-Respondents		Chi Square Significance
	n	%	n	%	
Occupation					
Finance directors	77	43	13	44	
Chief accountants or financial controllers	52	29	8	28	
Other accountants	51	28	8	28	
	180	100	29	100	*
Internal Reporting Experience					
1-5 years	79	45	15	52	
6-10 years	49	28	6	21	
11+ years	48	27	8	27	
	176	100	29	100	*
External Reporting Experience					
1-5 years	78	52	9	43	
6-10 years	47	31	8	38	
11+ years	26	17	4	19	
	151	100	21	100	*
Reporting Responsibility to					
Holding company	88	49	18	62	
Shareholders	102	57	11	38	
Employees	47	26	2	7	
Banks	114	64	14	48	
Lenders	54	30	7	24	
Others	16	9	1	3	
	421	235	53	182	**
Reporting Responsibility to					
1 group	51	28	15	52	
2 groups	44	25	9	31	
3 groups	58	32	2	7	
4+ groups	26	15	3	10	
	179	100	29	100	**
Size of Turnover (£m)					
10 or less	99	56	20	69	
11-30	38	21	6	21	
31+	40	23	3	10	
	177	100	29	100	*
Size of Total Assets (£m)					
5 or less	104	60	25	86	
6-15	33	19	1	4	
16+	37	21	3	10	
	174	100	29	100	**
Number of Employees					
500 or less	97	54	22	76	
501-1,000	36	20	1	3	
1,001+	46	26	6	21	
	179	100	29	100	**

Note
Total numbers of respondents and non-respondents were 182 and 29 respectively. Differences between n and these totals are due to 'no answers'.
* Not significant at $p = 0.05$.
** Significant at $p \leq 0.05$.

reporting responsibility, but that 47 per cent had three or more groups to which they were responsible.

4. The remaining background factors in Table 2 concern the size of the 'responding' companies. The evidence is not surprising in terms of the Scottish industrial scene — relatively few very large companies being located in Scotland, and the main emphasis being on small to medium-sized concerns. For example, in terms of their latest published financial statements, more than half the companies concerned in this survey had either a turnover of £10m or less; total assets of £5m or less; or 500 or less employees. A considerable proportion of these companies had all three such characteristics (43 per cent of the 182 companies 'responding' to the survey). The remaining companies were divided relatively equally between the other size categories given — that is, approximately one out of every five in each category (but only 9 per cent of the 182 'responding' companies had all three of the largest category of these size characteristics).

Summarizing on the above, it would appear that the majority of respondents held accounting and/or finance posts of some seniority in their employing companies; their reporting experience was varied but tending in aggregate to the small rather than the large end of such a scale; their employing companies had multi-purpose external reporting responsibilities, including bankers particularly; and their companies tended typically to be small to medium-sized entitites in terms of turnover, assets and employees.

Table 2 also contains data relating to the background characteristics of non-respondents. These are provided as a means of testing for non-response bias by comparing the characteristics of non-respondents with those of respondents, and submitting the resulting matrices to the chi square test of significance. (It should be noted, however, that this test can be upset by the smallness of aggregates in some cells of a matrix and, because only 29 accountants can be classed as non-respondents, this may be the case with certain of the analyses.) Nevertheless, there appears to be sufficient strength in the remaining results to arrive at the following conclusions:

1. There were no significant differences in the occupation and experience characteristics of respondents and non-respondents. There appears to be no response bias in terms of the personal backgrounds of the accountants concerned.
2. By way of contrast, the characteristics of the 'responding' and 'non-responding' companies appeared to be different — at times, significantly so in terms of the chi square test. For example, the 'non-responding' companies appeared to be more concerned with reporting to holding companies and less so to shareholders and bankers (results significant at the .05 level). This is more clearly seen in relation to the reporting responsibilities of these companies — 52 per cent of 'non-respondents' having a single reponsibility compared with an equivalent datum of 28 per cent for 'responding' companies; and only 17 per cent of the former being responsible to three or more groups compared with 47 per cent of the latter (results significant at less than the .05 level).
3. The company differences are further evidenced in relation to size — despite insignificant differences in terms of turnover ('non-respondents' typically being somewhat smaller than 'respondents', but with the results not being significant at the .05 level), total asset and employee differences were significant at less than the .05

level. Few 'non-responding' companies (14 per cent) had total assets of more than £5m (compared with 40 per cent of 'respondents'). A less dramatic difference occurred with employee numbers (76 per cent of 'non-respondents' and 54 per cent of 'respondents' having 500 or less employees).

Summarizing, the above analysis reveals few significant differences between respondents and non-respondents in terms of the personal characteristics of the accountants concerned. However, in terms of the characteristics of their employing companies, there were significant differences between 'respondents' and 'non-respondents' — the former typically having more reporting responsibilities, total assets and employees than the latter. Why these differences existed is difficult to answer (perhaps accountants in larger companies had more time to answer questionnaires), but they have been noted, and the analysis of the survey results must be made within this context. They are not felt, however, to be serious enough to prevent such an analysis being made.

OPINIONS ON REPORTING PAST CASH FLOWS

The first major question asked of respondents was whether they were in favour of companies producing past CFA statements for external reporting purposes. Their responses are summarized in Table 3. The respondents were equally divided on this issue — 49 per cent in favour of it and 49 per cent against it. The strength of support for CFA, however, should be encouraging for its proponents, given the newness of the CFA proposal and its lack of practical application. (Indeed, seven respondents believed it should be introduced as a complete substitute for the present system of allocation-based accounting data.)

Of the 89 respondents in favour of CFA, 36 per cent gave the need to supply liquidity data in financial reports as the main reason for their support. Eighteen per cent stated that CFA data would provide a clearer insight into the quality of management, and 15 per cent believed CFA could provide lay readers with a better understanding of financial results. These are all reasons that have been given in support of CFA proposals in the literature (see Lee [1981]).

TABLE 3
ACCOUNTANTS' OPINIONS ON EXTERNAL REPORTING OF PAST CASH FLOWS

	n	%
CFA should be introduced as a complete substitute for the present system of allocation-based accounting data	7	4
CFA should be introduced as an addition to the present system of allocation-based accounting data	82	45
Total positive response	89	49
CFA should not be introduced as a complete substitute for, or addition to, the present system of allocation-based accounting data	90	49
No opinion given	3	2
	182	100

The objections to CFA by the 90 respondents concerned were equally clear: 36 per cent stated that the proposal was a waste of time as the existing system of reporting was adequate; 25 per cent believed funds statements were adequate; and a further 8 per cent felt that CFA would merely add to the present complexity of financial reporting. In other words, there appears to have been a considerable body of opinion amongst the respondents which supported the 'status quo' in external reporting. On the other hand, 11 per cent of these respondents stated that future and not past cash flows were required in external financial reports (a matter that will be examined in greater detail later in the paper).

Users of Past Cash Flows

The 89 respondents supporting the idea of CFA in historic terms were further asked to state the main user groups for which they felt such data would be useful in practice. Table 4 outlines the results of this inquiry, the user groups being listed in order of the magnitude of support given to them by the respondents concerned.

TABLE 4
ACCOUNTANTS' OPINIONS OF THE POTENTIAL UTILITY OF PAST CASH FLOW DATA TO REPORT USERS

	Useful	Not Useful	No Opinion	Total
	%	%	%	%
Bankers	88	10	2	100
Lenders	85	10	5	100
Institutional shareholders	83	12	5	100
Private shareholders	78	15	7	100
Employees	64	29	7	100
Suppliers	58	27	15	100
Government	34	40	26	100
Customers	33	49	18	100

$n = 89$ in all cases

Past cash flow data were regarded by the majority of respondents to be useful to bankers, lenders, institutional and private shareholders, employees and suppliers (the 'useful' response ranging from 88 per cent for bankers to 58 per cent for suppliers). The emphasis in this respect appeared to be on groups that traditionally have been stated to be interested in cash flow — that is, bankers, lenders and creditors (see ASC [1975] and AICPA [1973]). However, the other groups (particularly shareholders and employees) also were felt to be capable of finding CFA useful. Only in the cases of government and customers was there a minority of 'useful' responses (34 and 33 per cent, respectively, but with only 40 and 49 per cent, respectively, of the relevant respondents stating CFA would not be useful). In other words, those respondents who supported a past CFA system generally regarded it as useful to a wide variety of potential user groups, and were in substantial agreement on such utility in relation to a number of these groups.

The reasons given by respondents in support of their beliefs in the utility of CFA for particular groups usually concerned the need to provide report users with meaningful data on the quality of cash management — for example, of those indicating the potential utility of CFA, 40 per cent provided this reason in relation to bankers; 43 per cent in relation to lenders; 46 per cent in relation to institutional investors; 40 per cent in relation to private shareholders; 26 per cent in relation to employees; and 37 per cent in relation to suppliers. There was therefore considerable agreement as to the reason for supplying past cash flow data to these particular user groups. Interestingly, in relation to the two groups most likely to contain significant numbers of lay readers with no accounting expertise (private shareholders and employees), 37 and 65 per cent, respectively, of the respondents providing 'useful' responses gave their reason as the need to supply simple and comprehensible accounting data to these users.

When cross-analysing the 'utility' responses with the background characteristics of the respondents concerned, few analyses proved to be statistically significant in terms of the chi square test applied. However, a number of tests did prove significant at or below the .05 level — that is, with regard to the utility of reporting cash flows, significant differences relating to private shareholders and employees occurred (figures are given as a portion of those of the 89 'supporting' respondents providing relevant background data). For example, although approximately 9 out of every 10 (45) chief accountants and other accountants believed CFA to be useful to private shareholders, a lesser proportion of approximately 7 out of every 10 (24) finance directors had the same opinion. In relation to employees, little more than one half (19) of finance directors, 7 out of 10 (16) chief accountants, and nearly 9 out of 10 (21) of the other accountants supported the utility of CFA. In other words, those respondents at directorial level appeared to be significantly less enthusiastic than other respondents for reporting past cash flows to private shareholders and employees.

In terms of reporting experience related to opinions of the utility of CFA to private shareholders, significant differences also existed (figures are again given as a proportion of the total of 89 respondents providing background factors) — for example, two-thirds (16) of the relevant respondents with eleven or more years of internal reporting experience supported its utility in this respect compared with more than 9 out of 10 (51) respondents with less experience. In relation to external reporting experience, 94 per cent (30) of respondents with five or less years of experience stated the usefulness of CFA to private shareholders, with just less than 7 out of 10 (22) of the more experienced respondents having the same opinion. In other words, those respondents with more reporting experience appeared to believe less in the utility of CFA for private shareholders than did those with less experience (all such differences were significant at or below the .05 level).

Finally, two other variables revealed significant differences in attitude to the reporting of past cash flows to employees (each figure being a relevant portion of the 89 respondent total as before) — approximately one-half (22) of the relevant respondents in companies with turnover of £10m or less, but more than 8 out of every 10 (33) relevant respondents in companies with turnover of more than £10m, supported the idea. A similar difference was evidenced in relation to the number of employees of the 'responding' companies — respondents in companies with more than 1,000 employees were almost all (20) in favour of reporting in CFA terms to employees, compared with approximately 6 out of every 10 (35) in companies with less than 1,000 employees. In other words, respondents in the larger companies appeared to be more in favour of reporting past cash flows to employees than were those in the smaller companies (all such differences were significant at or below the .05 level).

Summarizing on the perceived utility of reporting past cash flows, therefore, it appears there was substantial support for it within a multi-purpose context, but mainly related to shareholding and lending user groups. The prevalent supporting reason for this opinion appeared to be the need to improve reporting on the quality of company cash management. There were few significant differences in attitude in this respect in terms of the various background variables of the respondents: directors were less enthusiastic about CFA than other respondents in relation to reporting to private shareholders and employees; respondents with more reporting experience tended to be less favourably disposed to reporting in CFA terms to private shareholders; and respondents in the larger companies were more in favour of CFA reporting to employees.

Thus, different background characteristics of the respondents did not appear to be significant in determining the differences in their stated views as to the utility of reporting past cash flows. However, there is also clear evidence of the distinction made by respondents between lay readers of reports (private shareholders and employees) and the more expert readers — respondents of all types being reasonably agreed (with insignificant differences at the .05 level) about the utility of reporting past cash flows to persons with the available expertise to make proper use of such data (that is, bankers, lenders, institutional investors and suppliers).

OPINIONS ON THE STRUCTURE OF CFA STATEMENTS

Table 5 outlines the respondents' opinions on the structure of reporting in past cash flow terms. Seventy-two per cent of the relevant respondents believed CFA statements could be prepared from pure cash data, with a further 10 per cent stating this could not be done. Only one-half of respondents felt that these statements could be prepared by adjusting allocated data (see Lawson [1976]). Interestingly, a further 40 per cent were puzzled enough by this possibility to have no opinion to declare. Generally speaking, however, respondents felt CFA statements could be prepared, and approximately 4 out of every 10 specifically stated that appropriate data were available for this purpose (whether in cash terms or as adjusted allocations).

Respondents were provided with a specimen cash flow statement, and 80 per cent of those in favour of reporting in CFA terms supported this as a reasonable way of reporting. Twenty per cent also felt the relevant cash flow data could be put in some other format — all such respondents stating that what was needed was a more detailed CFA statement. Whatever the viewpoint, however, respondents were generally agreed that cash flow data could be disclosed either in the form of the illustration provided (see Appendix) or in a more detailed format.

Almost two-thirds of the respondents believed three or more years of data should be reported in past cash flow terms (indeed, 44 per cent wanted to provide five or more years). Thus, the idea of extending financial reporting to provide reasonable trends of results was adequately evidenced in this study, 38 per cent of respondents making this clear in an explicit statement to this effect. The need to audit past cash flow statements was also made clear by the respondents concerned, almost 8 out of every 10 supporting the idea, and typically stating in their reasons that such an audit would lend credibility to the reported data (26 per cent), be consistent with the need to audit existing statements (25 per cent), and safeguard the interests of report users (16 per cent). In summary, therefore, those respondents supporting CFA typically believed several years of audited cash flow data should be reported.

TABLE 5
ACCOUNTANTS' OPINIONS ON THE STRUCTURE OF PAST CASH FLOW STATEMENTS FOR REPORT USERS

	Yes	No	No Opinion	Total
(a) *Feasibility of Preparation*				
	%	%	%	%
From pure cash flow data	72	10	18	100
From allocated accounting data (suitably adjusted)	52	8	40	100
(b) *Disclosure Format*	Yes	No	No Opinion	Total
	%	%	%	%
As per illustration in questionnaire (see Appendix)	80	9	11	100
Some other format	20	3	77	100
(c) *Number of Years' Data*				
1–2 years			32	
3–4 years			21	
5+ years			44	
No opinion			3	
			100	
(d) *Need for Audit*				
			%	
Yes			77	
No			16	
No opinion			7	
			100	

n = 89 in all cases.

The occupation and reporting experience variables revealed no significant differences in the attitudes of these respondents to the CFA reporting structure. The variables relating to the size of 'responding' companies, however, did produce significant differences, but only in relation to attitudes concerning the format of the illustrated cash flow statement (all such differences being significant at or below the .05 level using the chi square test). In the case of turnover size, the respondents in favour of the illustrated statement (as a percentage of those providing relevant background data) comprised 98 per cent (39) of those employed in companies with turnover of £10m or less, 86 per cent (18) of those with turnover of between £11m and £30m, and 75 per cent (12) of those with turnover of more than £30m. Thus, the illustration was less well supported by respondents from the larger companies in terms of their turnover, as compared with those from the smaller 'responding' companies.

A similar trend of results was evidenced in relation to asset size (percentages again being expressed as a proportion of the relevant respondents supporting the illustration and who also provided such background data). Ninety-three per cent (40) of respondents from companies with total assets of £5m or less, and 94 per cent (17) from the £6m to £15m category, gave a vote of confidence for the illustration, but 71 per cent (10) from the £15m plus category held a similar opinion. Employee numbers produced similar results — the 'in favour' responses in the '500 employees or less' category, the '501 to 1,000 employees' category, and the 'more than 1,000 employee' category being 98 per cent (41), 88 per cent (14) and 75 per cent (15), respectively. The size of the 'responding' company therefore appeared to be a significant variable (whether in terms of turnover, assets or employees); the larger the 'responding' company, the more likely was the respondent to reject the form of illustrated cash flow statement (all such results were significant at or below the .05 level). This, perhaps, should not be surprising, given the accounting resources available in the larger companies to produce their own distinctive style of financial statement.

OPINIONS ON REPORTING FORECAST CASH FLOWS

The subject of reporting forecast data has been a matter of considerable debate for a number of years (see, e.g., Dailey [1971] and Schattke [1962]). However, little or no

TABLE 6
ACCOUNTANTS' OPINIONS ON EXTERNAL REPORTING
OF FORECAST CASH FLOWS

		n	%
CFA forecasts should be introduced as part of a system of external financial reporting:	%	76	42
With audit	29		
Without audit	46		
No opinion	25		
	100		
	%		
With stated assumptions	84		
Without stated assumptions	6		
No opinion	10		
	100		
	%		
1–2 years' data	68		
3+ years'	25		
No opinion	7		
	100		
CFA forecasts should not be introduced as part of a system of external financial reporting		100	55
No opinion		6	3
		182	100

research has been undertaken to establish the opinions of accountants (or, indeed, any other interested group) as to the credibility of this proposal. The questionnaire used in this study contained questions relating to this matter, and the answers from respondents are summarized in Table 6.

Only 42 per cent of respondents favoured forecast reports, with the majority (55 per cent) being against the idea. Of the 76 respondents supporting it, approximately 3 out of every 10 believed an audit of the forecasts was essential; more than 8 out of every 10 advocated stated assumptions to support the reported forecast data; and a clear majority (68 per cent) felt that no more than one or two years of forecast results was desirable. In other words, the support for forecast CFA was less than for past CFA, and it was generally conceived in a limited format — without audit, with assumptions, and covering a relatively short period of time. Of those respondents who were not in favour of forecast CFA, 36 per cent stated that forecasts were too uncertain, with too much of a margin for error; 32 per cent claimed the idea was an unnecessary intrusion on management; and 17 per cent believed forecast cash flows could mislead report users (presumably because of the inherent uncertainty involved in their preparation). Despite this, there is evidence of a substantial minority supporting the production of forecast cash flows in financial reports — of the 76 respondents providing such support, 46 per cent stated a preference for future cash flow reporting only, the remaining 54 per cent desiring that financial reports contain both forecast and past cash flows. The latter respondents constituted 23 per cent of all respondents.

RESPONDENTS' COMPANIES' USE OF CASH FLOW DATA

Respondents were asked to indicate the purposes for which cash flow data were used within their employing companies. Table 7 summarizes their answers in this respect. The first part of Table 7 outlines the five main areas in which cash flow data were stated to be used. The most popular use was in the management of working capital (90 per cent of respondents), followed by the making of investment decisions (76 per cent) and long-range planning (66 per cent). A minority of 'responding' companies monitored investment decisions with cash flow data (44 per cent) and made dividend decisions with them (28 per cent). In one sense, it is surprising not to see cash flow data being used by all the companies in each of the five areas concerned — only in the case of the first three mentioned is the use extensive. In the other two, there appears to be a definite under-use so far as the 'responding' companies were concerned. In fact, of the 172 responses providing the necessary information, 10 per cent used cash flow data for a single purpose, 20 per cent for two purposes, 26 per cent for three purposes, 26 per cent for four purposes, and 18 per cent for five purposes. In other words, the evidence of this survey is that the 'responding' companies tended to use cash flow data internally for a variety of purposes. Such use, however, was not extensive in some areas.

So far as the type of cash flow data used was concerned (that is, past, future or a combination of both types of data), the second part of Table 7 describes this aspect of the survey. In the case of working capital management, approximately 3 out of every 4 of the companies concerned used a combination of past and forecast data, the remainder using forecast data only. With investment decision making, the equivalent statistics were

TABLE 7
INTERNAL USE OF CASH FLOW DATA

	Yes %	No %	No Answer %	Total %
Managing working capital	90	6	4	100
Making investment decisions	76	14	10	100
Long-range planning	66	19	15	100
Monitoring investment decisions	44	39	17	100
Dividend decisions	28	47	25	100

n = 182 in all cases

	n	Past Data Only %	Forecast Data Only %	Past and Forecast Data %	Total %
Managing working capital	164	—	24	76	100
Making investment decisions	138	—	42	58	100
Long-range planning	120	—	39	61	100
Monitoring investment decisions	80	13	15	72	100
Dividend decisions	51	6	38	56	100

approximately 6 out of every 10 respondents for the combined data, and approximately 4 out of every 10 for forecast data only. Similar results to these were found in the other three areas — that is, the majority of 'responding' companies used a combination of data, the remainder usually using forecasts only. However, in the case of monitoring investment decisions and dividend decisions, certain companies used past cash flow data only.

The overall impression of this part of the survey was that a good deal of use is being made of both past and forecast cash flow data for internal management purposes within the companies concerned, although this was not as extensive as it might have been in particular areas (for example, with the dividend decision). The other aspect of this survey, however, was to evidence that the respondents, when providing their answers concerning external CFA, were writing from a position of knowledge in the sense that they were employed within finance and accounting functions that utilized past and forecast flows for internal management purposes.

CONCLUSIONS

A number of interesting conclusions can be drawn from this admittedly limited survey of accounting opinions on CFA systems for external report users. These are as follows:

1. There was substantial support from survey respondents for the idea of reporting to external parties in cash flow terms — only 58 of 182 (32 per cent) did not desire any form of CFA. Support was greatest for past CFA but there existed substantial support also for forecast CFA.

2. Past CFA was seen by respondents to be useful to many of the main financial report user groups, particularly those most concerned with assessing corporate liquidity.

3. No particular problems in obtaining cash flow data for reporting purposes were

envisaged by the respondents, past CFA typically being conceived as containing several years of audited cash flow data.

4. Forecast CFA, on the other hand, was conceived by respondents as a more limited system — typically only one or two years of unaudited data being what should be reported.

5. Respondents were employed in companies in which substantial use was being made of both past and forecast CFA. In fact, only 7 (4 per cent) respondents came from companies not using cash flow data at all. There therefore appears to be a considerable internal experience of CFA should it ever be contemplated for external reporting purposes.

Thus, the evidence of this survey is quite clear. Amongst those responsible for producing corporate financial reports there exists considerable support for and experience of CFA systems. The extent of the support for the latter amongst the accountants surveyed on this occasion is certainly sufficient to warrant further research into the nature and structure of CFA for external reporting purposes.

REFERENCES

Accounting Standards Committee, *The Corporate Report*, 1975.
American Institute of Certified Public Accountants, *Objectives of Financial Statements*, 1973.
Dailey, R. A., 'The Feasibility of Reporting Forecast Information', *The Accounting Review*, October 1971.
Lawson, G. H., 'Initial Reactions to ED 18', *Certified Accountant*, December 1976.
Lee, T. A., 'Cash Flow Accounting and Corporate Financial Reporting' in M. Bromwich and A. J. Hopwood, *Essays in British Accounting Research*, Pitman, London 1981.
Lee, T. A. and D. P. Tweedie, *The Private Shareholder and the Corporate Report*, Institute of Chartered Accountants in England and Wales, London 1977.
———, *Institutional Use and Understanding of Corporate Financial Information*, Institute of Chartered Accountants in England and Wales, London 1981.
Schattke, R., 'Expected Income — A Reporting Challenge', *The Accounting Review*, October 1962.

APPENDIX

SUGGESTED STATEMENT OF CASH FLOW
For the Year Ended 31 December 1978

	1978	1977(1)
	£	£
Cash receipts from customers	6,873,000	6,100,000
Less: cash payments for materials, wages and overheads (2)	5,884,000	5,541,000
Cash operating margin	989,000	559,000
Less: cash payments for new and replacement investment in fixed assets (3)	707,000	298,000
Taxable cash surplus	282,000	261,000
Less: taxation paid in cash	320,000	240,000
Distributable cash (deficit) surplus	(38,000)	21,000
Less: dividends paid in cash	184,000	115,000
Total cash deficit	(222,000)	(94,000)
Add: loans received in cash (4)	—	684,000
Increase in cash resources (5)	(222,000)	590,000

Notes

Cash flow financial statements are defined as those which have been produced using only cash data, and which are therefore free of any accounting allocation or valuation judgements (such as with depreciation or stock valuation). They are not sources and application of funds statements, although they can be derived from the latter. There are two ways of producing them: either
- (a) by using actual cash data before they are subjected to the processes of accounting allocation and valuation; or
- (b) by using allocated accounting data and adjusting them for non-cash transactions and working capital movements in order to reduce them to cash equivalents.

(1) Several years' past data could be disclosed with the statement.
(2) Full details of this item could be disclosed in a note to the statement. No accounting would be made for stock and work in progress because of the cash basis used.
(3) This item could be disclosed net of disposal proceeds, and the split between new and replacement investment could be disclosed in a note to the statement.
(4) This item could involve loan repayments; proceeds of rights issues, etc.
(5) This item could be defined as including cash and near-cash resources (such as deposits and sundry investments).

A Note on Users and Uses of Cash Flow Information

T. A. Lee

In a recent review of a collection of essays on UK accountancy research [Bromwich and Hopwood, 1980], Muis commented on the case for cash flow accounting (CFA) which has been extensively but, in his opinion, unsuccessfully made in the UK [Muis, 1981]. It is difficult to interpret these remarks, but presumably he was concerned not so much with the weakness of the CFA argument, but with the fact that it had not achieved general acceptance in the UK accountancy and business communities. It is true that the CFA case has been made in great detail [Lee, 1980]. It is not so true that it has been unsuccessful—no convincing argument has been attempted against it, and the widespread production of the funds statement in annual reporting [ASC, 1975] indicates at least an official awareness in the UK of the need to disclose some form of financial information related to cash flow and liquidity. In the US, the more recent work of the Financial Accounting Standards Board is evidence of a similar recognition of need [FASB, 1980].

The importance of financial information related to cash flow and liquidity analysis has been accentuated by the recent economic recession. The need for business management to assess and control cash flow is a continuing problem, but it becomes critical in times of high inflation, low demand for goods and services, high interest rates, and so on. The particular requirement for CFA data to be disclosed in these conditions has been highlighted in relation to such matters as wage negotiations [Lawson and Stark, 1977] and government aid to ailing companies [Lee, 1981a]. A recent survey has also revealed that there is support amongst reporting accountants in the UK for the disclosure of both actual and forecast CFA data—particularly for the purpose of aiding bankers, lenders and shareholders (in that order) [Lee, 1981b].

However, despite the apparent need for CFA data in times when cash flow management is crucial, and despite indications of an apparent support for it by reporting accountants, the funds statement in the UK remains the sole source of formal information from which CFA data about corporate liquidity could be derived by report users. There also does not appear to be an obvious and general demand for CFA reports by users, and this therefore begs the question as to whether or not they are interested in liquidity matters (as is usually postulated in the accountancy literature), and whether or not they make use of data related to liquidity when they assess available financial information (as is also implied in the literature).

To date, no specific research project has been undertaken into these matters, but several studies of user needs and financial information uses have been reported. From the latter, it is possible to derive specific results which bear upon user interest in CFA and liquidity. The studies can be divided into two main groupings—the first relating to inquiries into user information needs; and the second concerned with user behaviour associated with available financial information. The purpose of this paper is to examine these studies in order to determine evidence of user interest in liquidity matters generally and CFA particularly.

Studies of information needs

One of the best known information needs studies was published in the early 1970s [Baker and Haslem, 1973]. This was limited to specific information topics to be ranked in order of importance by the responding US private investors. Thus, it revealed little to indicate an interest in cash flow or liquidity—the matters of greatest importance were economic outlooks for companies and industries, and the quality of management. The financial strength (undefined) of companies, which may have been an indirect reference to liquidity, was a topic considered of only moderate importance. The Baker and Haslem study is therefore of little help to this paper because of the specific questions asked of the respondents, none of which directly related to liquidity and CFA.

But the investor responses also indicated little obvious interest in these matters at that time in the USA.

Chenhall and Juchau [1977] conducted a similar study of mainly private investors in Australia, specifically stating that they were looking, *inter alia*, for investor interest in information relating to liquidity. However, they failed to ask questions directly in this area. The financial strength (undefined) of companies was ranked as of great importance, but Chenhall and Juchau deliberately interpreted this in terms of reported earnings rather than liquidity (because of the respondents' high placing of other earnings matters). Questions loosely connected with liquidity, such as the sale value of assets, were ranked as only of slight importance by these investors.

More experienced and professional report users in the USA were questioned in a similar way by Benjamin and Stanga [1977]. Bankers and financial analysts were asked to rank stated reporting topics in order of importance (and need). Again, little was directed specifically at cash flow and liquidity, and the main emphasis for both groups appeared to be on reported and forecast sales and earnings. Bankers, who ought to be much concerned with cash flow and liquidity, indicated little obvious interest in either topic the age of debtors and the sale value of finished stock and plant being ranked as of only moderate importance.

The overall conclusion from these studies is that there are few signs that investors (particularly) and users (generally) were, at the times concerned, seeking information related to corporate liquidity and cash flow, preferring instead data on company profitability and general 'environmental' information concerning economic outlook. But these remarks must be made within the context of the questions asked the researchers not appearing to be overly concerned with cash flow and liquidity. The studies are of little use in this context, and thus the next section on use and understanding will form the main part of this paper.

Studies of use and understanding

If studies of information needs have failed to provide evidence of interest in CFA and liquidity, then research results concerned with the use and understanding of financial information remain to be examined. They are limited to investor responses because, to date, investors form the main user group which has been examined by the various writers concerned.

The pioneers in this area have been Lee and Tweedie. Since 1975, they have conducted three major studies one on a mixture of private and institutional shareholders [Lee and Tweedie, 1975a, 1975b and 1976], one on private shareholders [Lee and Tweedie, 1977], and one on institutional investors and stockbrokers [Lee and Tweedie, 1981].

The earliest Lee and Tweedie research [1975a] contained no specific question on liquidity, and omitted reference to the funds statement (although respondents could comment on such omissions). The income statement was found to be the most important and used financial statement; 47"„ of respondents read it thoroughly with a further 40"„ reading it briefly. It was classed as of great to moderate importance (mean 2.66 on a scale of 1 to 5). Respondents revealed little interest in liquidity; 16"„ stated that liquidity data were the most significant in annual reports, and 7"„ gave a similar response in relation to other sources of financial information. These results on private shareholder reading and perceived importance of the annual report were largely replicated in a New Zealand study [Wilton and Tabb, 1978].

A more extensive private shareholder study by Lee and Tweedie [1977] remedied the earlier omissions, and specific questions on liquidity matters and funds statements were asked. The relative importance of profitability and cash flow was evident in the responses received. Income data were felt to be of particular relevance to 52"„ of respondents, whereas only 7"„ categorised liquidity data in the same way. 39"„ read the income statement thoroughly, 46"„ briefly, and 15"„ not at all. The corresponding figures for the funds statement were 18"„, 39"„ and 43"„, respectively. The income statement was ranked as of considerable to moderate importance by the respondents, with the funds statement classified by them as of slight importance. When asked to state which data were of particular relevance in the annual report, 35"„ of respondents gave income data and only 6"„ preferred liquidity data.

Although the results regarding income and funds statements reflect a sharp contrast, it should not be forgotten that liquidity data can be derived to a very limited extent from the balance sheet and notes to the accounts (both of which were used by the respondents marginally more extensively than the funds statements 29"„ read the balance sheet thoroughly and 21"„ the notes). However, as only 37"„ had a reasonable understanding of the balance sheet, it is doubtful if these statements were being used as compensation for an under-use of the funds statement.

These results must be taken in the context of the time at which the research was undertaken that is, 1975. The funds statement had only recently become a professional accountancy requirement in the UK [ASC, 1975], although in the year to 30 June 1975, 73% of the top 300 manufacturing companies produced funds statements [ICAEW, 1976]. However, respondents were given the opportunity to comment on their need for liquidity or CFA data. As the results indicate, very few did. These UK results were supported in a later Australian study by Winfield [1978]—income data being regarded as much more informative to private investors than funds data.

Lee and Tweedie [1981] continued their research into investor use and understanding of financial information by examining the behaviour and views of institutional investors and stockbrokers. In this study, despite the expertise and available resources for analysis of these experts, the evidence is similar to that of the private shareholder study profitability being regarded as much more significant as a financial indicator than liquidity. The income statement was read thoroughly by 91% of respondents, briefly by 7%, and not at all by 2%, (the balance sheet was relatively similarly used). The funds statement, by contrast was read thoroughly by 67%, briefly by 26%, and not at all by 7%. The income statement was ranked as of maximum to moderate importance by the respondents (as was the balance sheet), with the funds statement being rated of considerable to moderate importance. 67% of the responding experts attempted to predict earnings per share (particularly) and 57% predicted income (generally). Only 7%, attempted to predict liquidity. When asked what information was of particular relevance to them in the annual report, 48% of respondents indicated income and 27%, liquidity. The corresponding responses regarding other sources of financial information were 38% and 11%, respectively.

Thus, although considerably better than that of private shareholders, the interest of institutional shareholders and stockbrokers in corporate liquidity was clearly secondary to that of profitability. Perhaps not surprisingly, their understanding of income statements was found to be materially better than of funds statements 57% of respondents had a reasonable understanding of the nature of the income statement compared with 23%, for the funds statement (15% did not understand the income statement, and 64% did not understand the funds statement).

These results, at least so far as usage is concerned, were largely supported in a Dutch study of various user groups (including institutional investors and investment analysts) [Klaassen and Schreuder, 1981]. It found that 58%, of respondents read the income statement completely, with 39%, behaving similarly with the funds statement. Respondents, as in all the Lee and Tweedie studies, placed the income statement first in ranking importance. The funds statement was ranked fifth, after income statements, balance sheets, notes to accounts, and statements of accounting policies. None of the respondents specifically indicated liquidity matters as being of importance in their various decisions.

In Australia, Anderson [1981] has also conducted a similar survey of institutional investors. 79% of his respondents read the income statement thoroughly and 59%, also dealt similarly with the funds statement. The income statement was stated to be the most important financial statement (mean 2.26 on a scale of 1 to 5; and 54%, of respondents ranked it as of maximum or great importance). The funds statement was considered to be only of moderate importance (mean 3.19).

The results of each of these research studies appear to bear upon the preliminary findings of Walker [1981]. He examined accountants' and accounting students' reactions to the inclusion of funds statements in a financial information package used to form judgments about the financial performance, position and prospects of the reporting entity. His findings indicated that the funds statement did not improve the accuracy of these judgments, the confidence of the respondents, the time taken to make the judgments, and the degree of consensus amongst respondents. In other words, there were clear signs that the funds statement in its traditional allocation-based form was of limited use to its recipients. This would suggest that a cash flow-based statement might be more appropriate. But, as has already been indicated, other research studies reveal little user interest in cash flow.

Conclusions

The above comments have not attempted to describe the various research studies in full. Instead, they have concentrated on specific results which reveal a consistency of behaviour and attitude in terms of time, location and user. Without doubt, income data are a primary information source for the user, with liquidity data either being largely ignored or being regarded as secondary material when analysing corporate results. As companies usually cease trading because of lack of liquidity (accompanied, in many cases, by lack of profitability), it is worrying that both the expert and the non-expert user fail to appreciate the full importance of liquidity analysis and the need for CFA. In these circumstances, it is not surprising that even expert investors, bankers and lenders are caught out when companies fail due to illiquidity. A study of profits in these cases will not reveal the crucial warning signals. A study of CFA would, on the other hand, be of considerable benefit in this respect.

References

Accounting Standards Committee, 'Statements of Source and Application of Funds,' *Statement of Standard Accounting Practice 10* (1975).

Anderson, R., 'The Usefulness of Accounting and Other Information Disclosed in Corporate Annual Reports to Institutional Investors in Australia,' *Accounting and Business Research* (Autumn 1981), pp. 259–65.

Baker, H. K. and Haslem, J. A., 'Information Needs of Individual Investors,' *Journal of Accountancy* (November 1973), pp. 64–9.

Benjamin, J. J. and Stanga, K. G., 'Differences in Disclosure Needs of Major Users of Financial Statements,' *Accounting and Business Research* (Summer 1977), pp. 187–92.

Bromwich, M. and Hopwood, A. G. (eds), *Essays in British Accounting Research*, Pitman (1980).

Chenhall, R. H. and Juchau, R., 'Investor Information Needs—An Australian Study,' *Accounting and Business Research* (Spring 1977), pp. 111–19.

Financial Accounting Standards Board, 'Reporting Funds Flow, Liquidity, and Financial Flexibility,' *FASB Discussion Memorandum* (1980).

Institute of Chartered Accountants in England and Wales, *Survey of Published Accounts 1975* (1976).

Klaassen, J. and Schreuder, H., 'Corporate Report Readership and Usage in the Netherlands,' *Maanblad Voor Accountancy en Bedrijfshuishoudkunde*, Volume 55, 2/3 (1981), pp. 101–17.

Lawson, G. H. and Stark, A. W., 'Does Ford Cash Really Flow?', *Accountancy Age* (12 August 1977), pp. 8–9.

Lee, T. A. and Tweedie, D. P., 'Accounting Information: An Investigation of Shareholder Usage,' *Accounting and Business Research* (Autumn 1975), pp. 280–91.

Lee, T. A. and Tweedie, D. P., 'Accounting Information: An Investigation of Shareholder Understanding,' *Accounting and Business Research* (Winter 1975), pp. 3–17.

Lee, T. A. and Tweedie, D. P., 'The Private Shareholder: His Sources of Financial Information and His Understanding of Reporting Practices,' *Accounting and Business Research* (Autumn 1976), pp. 304–14.

Lee, T. A. and Tweedie, D. P., *The Private Shareholder and the Corporate Report*, Institute of Chartered Accountants in England and Wales (1977).

Lee, T. A., 'Cash Flow Accounting and Corporate Financial Reporting,' in M. Bromwich and A. Hopwood [1980].

Lee, T. A., 'What Cash Flow Analysis Says About BL's Finances,' *Financial Times* (23 October 1981), p. 15.

Lee, T. A. and Tweedie, D. P., *The Institutional Investor and Financial Information*, Institute of Chartered Accountants in England and Wales (1981).

Lee, T. A., 'A Survey of Accountants' Opinions on Cash Flow Reporting,' *Abacus* (December 1981), pp. 130–44.

Muis, J. W., 'Essays in British Accounting Research,' *The Accountant's Magazine* (December 1981), pp. 427–8.

Walker, R. G., 'Funds Statements and the Interpretation of Financial Data—An Empirical Investigation', *Working Paper Series 18*, University of New South Wales (1981).

Wilton, R. L. and Tabb, J. B., 'An Investigation into Private Shareholder Usage of Financial Statements in New Zealand,' in J. K. Courtis (ed.), *Corporate Annual Report Analysis*, University of New England (1978), pp. 169–75.

Winfield, R. R., 'Shareholder Opinion of Published Financial Statements,' in J. K. Courtis (ed.), *Corporate Annual Report Analysis*, University of New England (1978), pp. 176–94.

TOM LEE

Cash Flows and Net Realizable Values: Further Evidence of the Intuitive Concepts

> This paper reports the results of a survey of students with and without prior knowledge of accounting with a view to identifying any differences in their perception of the relevance of current prices of assets.
>
> The combination of cash flows and net realizable values appears to have an intuitive appeal to students with no prior exposure to accounting concepts or practices. In the process of learning about accounting, it seems that students learn to abandon net realizable values in favour of historical costs.
>
> Key words: Cash flows; Financial statements; Net realizable values.

INTRODUCTION

In 1977, Tweedie (1977) reported an experiment to test the intuitive characteristics of non-accountants' behaviour when faced with financial accounting problems. He concluded from his study of students with no prior experience[1] of accounting that they tended generally to think in cash flow terms when dealing with income statement problems. In contrast, they thought in net realizable value terms when confronted with balance sheet items. The evidence, therefore, was that such persons do not think automatically in the relative complexities of accrual and allocation-based accounting. Although the research dealt with students rather than report users such as shareholders and employees, students appeared to be relevant surrogates for the latter groups. The study has been quoted with approval on numerous occasions (for example, Sterling, 1979) and, to date, no adverse comment has been made regarding its methodology or results.

The Tweedie study provides valuable evidence to support the case for the use of cash flows and net realizable values in external financial reporting (see Lee, 1981). In particular, it provides an understanding of what financial report users may perceive when they read financial statements based on the principles of conventional accounting. However, the study contained several limitations. First, the student respondents dealt with a series of independent transactions rather than a complete reporting situation involving articulated financial statements. Second, the respondents

---

[1] The term 'experience' is used throughout this paper to indicate a previous involvement with accounting matters in courses taken at high school prior to entry to university.

TOM LEE is Professor of Accountancy and Finance, University of Edinburgh, and Director of Accounting and Auditing Research, The Institute of Chartered Accountants of Scotland.

did not include students with a prior knowledge of accounting. This prevented comparative analyses being made. And third, the experiment was not repeated to discover the effects of a learning process.[2]

With these points in mind, this paper reports on the results of a research project to develop the work of Tweedie, in which students with and without prior knowledge of accounting were invited to produce an income statement and a related balance sheet from a series of basic transactions. They were provided also with information of different prices at relevant dates. These students also completed the same exercise several months later, and a comparative analysis of the two sets of results was made. Although the basic transactions were identical for all students, the physical amounts and prices were varied both during and between each exercise in order to avoid collaboration and to minimize familiarity. The basic data are contained in the Appendix to this paper.

The propositions which were tested in this study were as follows:
(a) Inexperienced students tend to think about entity income in terms of cash flows, and financial position in terms of net realizable values. (This hypothesis is therefore similar to that used in the Tweedie study but relies on an integrated transactions base) (Hypothesis 1).
(b) Experienced students tend to think about both entity income and financial position in terms of the conventional principles of historic cost. (Again this is similar to the Tweedie study but uses an integrated base) (Hypothesis 2).
(c) Exposure to conventional accounting practices tends to cause inexperienced students to think about both entity income and financial position in terms of the conventional principles of historic cost rather than, respectively, cash flow and net realizable value (Hypothesis 3).

The following sections describe the evidence with which to support or reject each of these hypotheses. The data are contained in Tables 1 to 11 inclusive, and have been tested for statistical significance—in each case using the chi square test with the level of significance set at the 5 per cent level. NPE relates to respondents with no prior experience of accounting, and PE indicates those with prior experience. The number of student respondents in each case is denoted by the symbol n. All respondents were members of a first-level class in acccounting at the University of Edinburgh who had no prior warning of either of the two exercises. The first exercise took place at the beginning of the course, and the second towards its end. There was no feedback or comment to the students on the results of the first exercise. Students were not allowed to retain any papers from either exercise, and each exercise was conducted under the supervision of members of staff of the Department of Accounting and Business Method at the University of Edinburgh. The results of the first exercise are headed 'First Test' in the tables, and those of the second exercise are headed 'Second Test'.

Limitations of the Exercises

The exercises conducted as part of this research can be regarded as substitutes for the 'real-life' use of financial accounting information by shareholders, lenders,

[2] The learning process of the students in this study was limited to a course on traditional historic cost-based financial accounting.

employees etc. However, it would appear reasonable to suggest that first-level students of accounting should not be taken as surrogates for experienced report users such as investment analysts. However, they do appear to be reasonable substitutes for the inexpert with little or no accounting knowledge and experience. In particular, student respondents are believed to be suitable surrogates for report user groups such as private shareholders and employees where the level of accounting knowledge and experience is typically low (see Lee and Tweedie, 1977).

The use of two tests at different times can be construed as an approximate simulation of the learning process in accounting by less experienced report users. However, it is recognized that this is a less than perfect surrogate for 'real-life' experience. It also is of interest to assess the specific influence of a formal learning experience on the prior intuitions of respondents. This provides evidence of the possible role of the educational system in matters relating to accounting comprehension. The study thus has relevance for accounting educators as well as policy-makers.

Analysis of results

The student respondents were invited to prepare statements of income and financial position from the data provided. Most attempted the task. But it was apparent that the different levels of accounting knowledge amongst respondents resulted in statements ranging from very sophisticated to very rudimentary. However, it was possible to determine relatively easily what each student was attempting to achieve in accounting terms, and to classify specific responses as being either cash-flow based (that is, with no accruals or time-period allocations); net realizable value-based (that is, with accruals but no time-period allocations); or cost-based (that is, with both accruals and time-period allocations). Obviously, a certain amount of judgement had to be applied in individual cases to make these distinctions but in no case was it found to be impossible.

Students were asked to produce financial statements. Many did. The variety of their responses was such that the analysis of those statements was conducted in the first instance on an 'item by item' basis—that is, each main transaction was examined separately. The results are contained in Tables 1 to 5 and 7 to 9. An overall review of the cash flow-based response to income statement items is contained in Table 6, and an overall review of the use of net realizable values in the balance sheet is given in Table 10. Table 11 provides an overview of the accounting attempted in both financial statements.

Appreciating Fixed Asset in the Income Statement

One of the transactions dealt with by respondents was the purchase of shop premises which had appreciated both in replacement cost and net realizable value terms during the reporting period. The problem in the first instance was how to account for the asset in relation to the income statement. Table 1 shows there were various accounting treatments. In the first test, three-quarters of respondents with no prior experience either wrote the property off completely against income (35%) (thus adopting a cash flow basis); or accounted for the appreciation in its net realizable value by including the gain with income (40%). Few respondents accounted for the property on an allocated cost basis, and more than one-fifth did not account for it in the income statement.

TABLE 1
APPRECIATING FIXED ASSET – I

	First test		Second test	
	(1) NPE %	(2) PE %	(3) NPE %	(4) PE %
Cash flow accounting	35	11	7	4
Net realizable value accounting	40	21	–	–
Historic or replacement cost accounting	3	–	–	–
No accounting	22	68	93	96
	100	100	100	100
n*†	108	56	89	51

* Chi square statistic (significance level at <5%).
  (1) and (2) Significant.   (1) and (3) Significant.
  (3) and (4) Not significant.   (2) and (4) Significant.
† 5, 1, 14 and 2 respondents, respectively gave no answer to any of the five items, and have been omitted from the analysis.

The latter approach was the one followed by nearly seven out of ten (68%) respondents with prior experience of accounting. With the remainder of these participants utilizing either a cash flow (11%) or net realizable value (21%) basis, it is clear that prior experience was a significant reason in the first test for following the conventional accounting approach for this type of asset. Lack of prior experience appeared to cause the respondents concerned to use either the cash flow or net realizable value basis.

The effect of a learning process can be seen in the results of the second test. The almost unanimous and significant approach of respondents with and without prior experience was to account on the conventional historic cost basis (the cash flow basis almost disappearing, and the net realizable value basis being completely ignored). The learning process appears to have compensated for the previous differences in accounting experience between the two groups.

Depreciating Fixed Asset in the Income Statement

A similar analysis was conducted with respect to a depreciating fixed asset (shop fittings) – one which could be depreciated in either historic cost, replacement cost or net realizable value terms, despite an increase in its gross replacement cost (Table 2). In the first test, respondents with no prior experience tended to use either the cash flow (35%) or net realizable value (33%) basis to a greater extent than those respondents with prior experience (11% and 23% respectively). Again the picture is of the less sophisticated respondent tending to use the cash flow and net realizable value bases, although many prior experience students also used these bases. The surprise was the relatively large proportion of the latter group (30%) which did not account for the asset in the income statement.

TABLE 2
DEPRECIATING FIXED ASSET—1

	First test		Second test	
	(1) NPE %	(2) PE %	(3) NPE %	(4) PE %
Cash flow accounting	35	11	7	6
Net realizable value accounting	33	23	5	14
Historic or replacement cost accounting	15	36	82	78
No accounting	17	30	6	2
	100	100	100	100
n*†	108	56	89	51

* Chi square statistic (significance level at $< 5\%$).
(1) and (2) Significant.   (1) and (3) Significant.
(3) and (4) Not significant.   (2) and (4) Significant.
† 5, 1, 14 and 2 respondents, respectively gave no answer to any of the five items, and have been omitted from the analysis.

The second test reveals evidence of the effect of the learning process. Almost eight out of ten respondents in each group utilized a cost-based allocation practice. Again, in both groups, a minority continued to account in cash flow or net realizable value terms. Particularly significant is the 14 per cent of students with prior experience who used net realizable values. However, the various significant and insignificant results reveal that the learning process again appears to have minimized differences due to prior accounting experience.

Non-Monetary Current Asset in the Income Statement

Inventory (in this case, washing machines) was a further subject for testing (Table 3). To students with no prior experience, the method of accounting usually was cash flow-based (91%). Few (4%) used cost allocation-based cost accounting. A much bigger proportion (37%) of respondents with prior accounting experience adopted the latter basis, although a majority of 50 per cent used the cash flow basis. Thus, in the case of a non-monetary asset such as inventory, the predominant method of accounting by these respondents was cash flow-based.

The situation changed somewhat in the second test, with significant differences between the two groups of respondents. A majority of both groups utilized cost-based techniques (mainly historic cost) as might be expected following the specific learning experience which took place between the tests. Net realizable value-based accounting did not figure in the results of the second test but the cash flow system remained popular (48% of those respondents with no experience and 24% of those with prior experience). Inventory therefore appears to be an asset which continued to be associated with cash flow accounting in the minds of these students irrespective of prior experience—a situation somewhat different from the results achieved with fixed assets.

TABLE 3
NON MONETARY CURRENT ASSET—1

	First test		Second test	
	(1) NPE %	(2) PE %	(3) NPE %	(4) PE %
Cash flow accounting	91	59	48	24
Net realizable value accounting	5	4	–	–
Historic or replacement cost accounting	4	37	52	76
	100	100	100	100
n*†	108	56	89	51

* Chi square statistic (significance level at <5%).
   (1) and (2) Significant.   (1) and (3) Significant.
   (3) and (4) Significant.   (2) and (4) Significant.
† 5, 1, 14 and 2 respondents, respectively gave no answer to any of the five items, and have been omitted from the analysis.

Monetary Current Asset in the Income Statement

TABLE 4
MONETARY CURRENT ASSET

	First test		Second test	
	(1) NPE %	(2) PE %	(3) NPE %	(4) PE %
Cash flow accounting	74	32	51	18
Accrual accounting	26	68	49	82
	100	100	100	100
n*†	108	56	89	51

* Chi square statistic (significance level at <5%).
   (1) and (2) Significant.   (1) and (3) Significant.
   (3) and (4) Significant.   (2) and (4) Not Significant.
† 5, 1, 14 and 2 respondents, respectively gave no answer to any of the five items, and have been omitted from the analysis.

Respondents were introduced in each test to the practice of accounting for receivables (Table 4). In the first test, the predominant approach (74%) by those with no prior experience was to use a cash flow basis for sales with no provision being made for receivables. This result was opposite to that of respondents with prior experience (almost 7 out of 10 of that group used the accruals basis). The second test indicated that the learning experience had been insufficient to persuade the majority of participants with no prior experience to change from the cash flow basis (51% continued to utilize the latter). There remained also a persistent minority (18%) of respondents with prior experience who used the same basis. Receivables therefore was an item which was not associated with the income statement by the majority of participants with no prior experience despite an intervening learning process. For those with prior experience, the accrual basis was the typical procedure adopted.

Short-Term Liability in the Income Statement

The final separate item dealt with by the respondents in relation to the income statement was payables (Table 5). The results for the first test were similar to those for receivables — three-quarters of respondents with no prior experience used the cash flow basis, and 70 per cent of those with prior experience adopted the alternative accrual basis. The second test revealed that, for both groups, the majority (71% and 82% respectively) opted for the latter basis. Thus, the learning process was a significant reason for this change in approach and negated the effect of the previous experience levels. The learning process was not a significant reason for strengthening the accrual approach of the experienced group.

TABLE 5
SHORT-TERM LIABILITY

	First test		Second test	
	(1) NPE %	(2) PE %	(3) NPE %	(4) PE %
Cash flow accounting	75	30	29	18
Accrual accounting	25	70	71	82
	100	100	100	100
n*†	108	56	89	51

* Chi square statistic (significance level at $< 5\%$).
   (1) and (2) Significant.   (1) and (3) Significant.
   (3) and (4) Not significant.   (2) and (4) Not significant.
† 5, 1, 14 and 2 respondents, respectively gave no answer to any of the five items, and have been omitted from the analysis.

Summary on the Income Statement

Table 6 examines specifically the degree to which the cash flow basis was adopted by respondents in the income statement. For those with no prior experience in the first test, this basis was used by 80 per cent of that group on at least three out of a possible five occasions. This contrasts with only 30 per cent of the more experienced group behaving in the same way. In the second test, the influence of learning is evidenced. Only 25 per cent of respondents with no prior experience used the cash flow basis at least three times (42% made no use of it). The equivalent data for those with a prior experience were 12 and 72 per cent respectively. This comparison of significant results in the two tests within each group reveals also the influence of the learning process.

Thus, taking the results of Tables 1 to 6, it is clear that respondents with no prior experience in accounting typically used a cash flow basis in the first instance for income statement purposes but, due to a later learning process, tended towards the conventional practices of accrual and historic cost allocation. For those respondents with prior experience, the initial majority response was a conventional accounting one, and this was strengthened by the learning experience. Hypotheses 1 to 3 thus appear to be supported in the case of the income statement by the available evidence.

TABLE 6
USE OF CASH FLOW ACCOUNTING

Number of times used	First test		Second test	
	(1) NPE %	(2) PE %	(3) NPE %	(4) PE %
5	20	5	4	4
4	6	5	1	2
3	54	20	20	6
2	5	3	17	8
1	8	29	16	8
0	7	38	42	72
	100	100	100	100
n*†	108	56	89	51

* Chi square statistic (significance level at $< 5\%$).
 (1) and (2) Significant.   (1) and (3) Significant.
 (3) and (4) Significant.   (2) and (4) Significant.
† 5, 1, 14 and 2 respondents, respectively gave no answer to any of the five items, and have been omitted from the analysis.

The remaining sections concentrate on the valuation procedures attributed to non-monetary assets in the balance sheets.

Appreciating Fixed Asset in the Balance Sheet

The approach of respondents to balance sheet accounting for the appreciating shop premises has been outlined in Table 7. In the first test, the predominant approach for both groups was a net realizable value one (67% of those with no prior experience, and 53% of those with prior experience). The alternative approach for both groups was to include the item in the balance sheet at its historic cost (10% and 35% respectively).

TABLE 7
APPRECIATING FIXED ASSET—II

	First test		Second test	
	(1) NPE %	(2) PE %	(3) NPE %	(4) PE %
Historic cost accounting	10	35	80	88
Replacement cost accounting	6	2	—	—
Net realizable value accounting	67	53	19	12
No accounting	17	10	1	—
	100	100	100	100
n*†	97	51	101	51

* Chi square statistic (significance level at $< 5\%$).
 (1) and (2) Significant.   (1) and (3) Significant.
 (3) and (4) Not significant.   (2) and (4) Significant.
† 16, 6, 2 and 2 respondents, respectively, gave no answer to any of the three items, and have been omitted from the analysis.

In the second test, almost identical results were obtained for the two groups — over 8 out of 10 respondents in each group using historic cost, and a small minority in each continuing with net realizable value. The results were not significant, indicating the learning process had eliminated the experience difference between the groups in relation to this asset. The significant differences between the results of each test for each group confirm this point.

Depreciating Fixed Asset in the Balance Sheet

The treatment accorded by respondents to the problem of balance sheet accounting for a depreciating fixed asset is evidenced in Table 8. The significant results reveal a preference for net realizable values by a large minority of respondents with no prior experience (41%), and historic costs by those with prior experience (57%). The second test, as for the appreciating asset, provided almost similar results — 85 and 88 per cent respectively of the two groups utilizing historic costs. The significance tests once again reveal the influence of the learning process in causing attitudes to change and experience differences to disappear.

TABLE 8
DEPRECIATING FIXED ASSET – II

	First test		Second test	
	(1) NPE %	(2) PE %	(3) NPE %	(4) PE %
Historic cost accounting	19	57	85	88
Replacement cost accounting	12	—	1	2
Net realizable value accounting	41	29	13	10
No accounting	28	14	1	—
	100	100	100	100
n*†	97	51	101	51

* Chi square statistic (significance level at $< 5\%$).
   (1) and (2) Significant.   (1) and (3) Significant.
   (3) and (4) Not significant.   (2) and (4) Significant.
† 16, 6, 2 and 2 respondents, respectively gave no answer to any of the five items, and have been omitted from the analysis.

Non-Monetary Current Asset in the Balance Sheet

With receivables and payables accounting dealt with in relation to the income statement and not involving a valuation issue in the balance sheet, Table 9 provides data concerning respondents' attitude to accounting for a working capital item in the balance sheet (in this case, inventory). The significant results give an overall impression of a more definite response from those respondents with prior experience than those without it. In the first test, only 28 per cent of the first group made any attempt to account for inventory (22% using net realizable values), compared with 72 per cent of the second group (most of whom, 65%, utilized historic costs). The second group confirmed its use of historic costs in the second test (84%), but the first group were first group were less sure (only 47% used historic costs, and even fewer 7% continued with net realizable values).

TABLE 9
NON-MONETARY CURRENT ASSET

	First test		Second test	
	(1) NPE %	(2) PE %	(3) NPE %	(4) PE %
Historic cost accounting	6	65	47	84
Net realizable value accounting	22	7	7	—
No accounting	72	28	46	16
	100	100	100	100
n*†	97	51	101	51

* Chi square statistic (significance level at <5%).
  (1) and (2) Significant.   (1) and (3) Significant.
  (3) and (4) Significant.   (2) and (4) Significant.
† 16, 6, 2 and 2 respondents, respectively gave no answers to any of the three items, and have been omitted from the analysis.

Overall Review of Balance Sheet Accounting

With replacement cost accounting used rarely by respondents in either test, the crucial valuation issue was the choice made between historic costs and net realizable values. The general impression from Tables 7 to 9 is that respondents with no prior experience of accounting tended to use net realizable values in the first test, and then switched to historic costs in the second test. For respondents with prior experience, the tendency was for a use of historic costs in the first test, and an almost universal use of the same data in the second test.

TABLE 10
USE OF NET REALIZABLE VALUE ACCOUNTING

Number of times used	First test		Second test	
	(1) NPE %	(2) PE %	(3) NPE %	(4) PE %
3	12	2	—	—
2	31	22	2	—
1	31	41	35	22
0	26	35	63	78
	100	100	100	100
n*†	97	51	101	51

* Chi square statistic (significance level at <5%).
  (1) and (2) Not significant.   (1) and (3) Significant.
  (3) and (4) Not significant.   (2) and (4) Significant.
† 16, 6, 2 and 2 respondents, respectively gave no answer to any of the three items, and have been omitted from the analysis.

Table 10 examines specifically the use of net realizable values by respondents. In the first test, the results reveal that prior experience of accounting may not have been a significant reason for differences in approach. In fact, a large number of both groups used net realizable values — 43 per cent of the no prior experience group used it on at least two out of three occasions, and 24 per cent of the second group did the same. Little more than a quarter and a third respectively of both groups made no use whatsoever of this valuation basis.

However, in the second test, the clear majority of both groups made no use of net realizable values (63% and 78% respectively) and, when it was used, it was usually on one occasion only. The overwhelming evidence from these data, and those explained earlier, supports those parts of the three hypotheses dealing with valuation and financial position.

Conclusions

The results of the two tests in this case support the earlier results of Tweedie — that is, persons with no prior knowledge of accounting tend to use cash flows and/or net realizable values in the income statement, and net realizable values in the balance sheet; and persons with prior experience tend to use historic costs in both statements. There is little evidence of a preference for the use of replacement costs either in the income statement or the balance sheet.

One important feature of this research is that the use of cash flows and net realizable values by persons with no prior experience of accounting is evidenced within the context of complete financial statements rather than individual financial transactions. The use of cash flows was particuraly strong in this case in the income statement, and the use of net realizable values was strong in the balance sheet.

A further important aspect of the research was the effect of the learning process in accounting on persons with little or no prior experience. In the case of those with no prior experience, it is clear that learning causes cash flow and net realizable value accounting to be abandoned for allocated historic costs in most cases. In the situation of those persons with prior experience, the effect is to reinforce the use of historic costs amongst members of that group.

Articulation of Financial Statements

Table 11 attempts to provide a judgment concerning the nature of articulation in the financial statements produced by the respondents in the two tests — that is, the basis used in the income statement together with the basis used in the balance sheet. The first test revealed that a large minority (43%) of respondents with no prior experience of accounting utilized a cash flow basis in the income statement, and a net realizable basis in the balance sheet (only 11% of respondents with prior experience adopted the same combination). A further 17 per cent of the first group linked cash flows and historic costs (compared with 18% of the second group). None of the first group used a complete historic cost approach whilst nearly four out of every ten of the second group did so.

By the time of the second test, the main approach for both groups was a complete

TABLE 11
COMBINED ACCOUNTING TREATMENTS

	First test		Second test	
	(1) NPE %	(2) PE %	(3) NPE %	(4) PE %
Cash flow/net realizable value	43	11	5	—
Cash flow/historic cost	17	18	14	7
Historic cost/historic cost	—	39	44	75
Others	40	32	37	18
	100	100	100	100
n*†	109	56	113	57

* Chi square statistic (significance level at $<5\%$).
  (1) and (2) Significant. (1) and (3) Significant.
  (3) and (4) Significant. (2) and (4) Significant.
† 4 and 1 respondents, respectively gave no answer either to the income statement or the balance sheet, and have been omitted from the analysis.

historic cost system (44% and 75% respectively). Only 5 per cent of those respondents with no prior experience used the cash flow-net realizable value combination (none of the other group followed this approach). Thus, the learning process between the tests appeared to be a significant reason for the switch from cash flows and net realizable values to historic costs.

The combination of cash flows and net realizable values had intuitive appeal to those students previously uninvolved in accounting. The teaching process, perhaps not surprisingly, was sufficiently persuasive to override these intuitions and replace them with what was being taught. Thus, it will be a considerable task to persuade those accounting policy-makers, report producers and accounting report users that alternatives to historic cost accounting are relevant and acceptable, irrespective of their early intuitions. This is to be evidenced in the present U.K. debate on current cost accounting (see Lee, 1983). However, those intuitions do exist if the evidence of this and Tweedie's study is to be believed. The problem is one of seeking means of persuading those concerned with accounting policy-making to take note of them, and not to forget the effect of accounting learning processes on report users.

REFERENCES

Lee, T. A., 'Reporting Cash Flows and Net Realisable Values', *Accounting and Business Research*, Spring 1981.

———, 'The Neville Report: Simplicity and Confusion', *The Accountant's Magazine*, October 1983.

Lee, T. A. and D. P. Tweedie, *The Private Shareholder and The Corporate Report*, Institute of Chartered Accountants in England and Wales, 1977.

Sterling, R. R., *Towards a Science of Accounting*, Scholars Book Co., 1979.

Tweedie, D. P., 'Cash Flows and Realisable Values: The Intuitive Accounting Concepts? An Empirical Test', *Accounting and Business Research*, Winter 1977.

CASH FLOWS AND NET REALIZABLE VALUES

APPENDIX

John Bloom commenced business on 1 January retailing washing machines. During the following year to 31 December, he accounted for the undernoted transactions:
1. On 1 January he opened a business bank account with £50,000 from his personal savings. At the same time, he made a cash purchase of shop premises costing £30,000. By 31 December the latter's sale value was £44,000 and the cost of building similar premises was £60,000.
2. During the year to 31 December, shop fittings costing £10,000 were purchased for cash. They were estimated to have a useful life of 10 years. At 31 December, their replacement cost was £20,000 and their sale value was £2,000.
3. Also during the year to 31 December, 2000 washing machines were purchased at £80 each (at 31 December, payment for 200 machines had not been made to suppliers). Of the purchased machines, 1600 were sold during the year for £100 each (customers had not paid for 120 of these machines at 31 December). Purchase and sale prices remained constant during the year.

From the above data, you are required to prepare a statement of John Bloom's profit for the year to 31 December, and a statement of his financial position at 31 December.

Cash flow decomposition and business failure

T A Lee

This paper has been based on a researching of data provided from the files of a leading UK bank. Grateful thanks are due to the bank officials who provided such access and also to two colleagues (Falconer Mitchell and Rolland Munro) who commented on an earlier draft of the paper and contributed ideas which improved that draft. A great deal of the research was undertaken whilst the writer was on secondment to The Institute of Chartered Accountants of Scotland as its Director of Accounting and Auditing Research. The views and comments expressed in the paper are, of course, those of the writer and not necessarily those of the Institute.

INTRODUCTION

In a recent study of corporate cash flow data Casey and Bartczak (1984) generalised that operating cash flow[1] data were poor indicators of corporate operating performance. In terms of operating cash flow figures over a five-year period they were unable to distinguish surviving and failed companies. Indeed, operating cash flow appeared to be a worse predictor of failure than a combination of several conventional accounting measures.

As argued elsewhere [Egginton (1984) and Lee (1985)], cash flow data are not intended to describe corporate operating performance; they are more concerned with the important issue of liquidity. However, the Casey and Bartczak results appear counter-intuitive — the expectation being that the operating cash flow results of failed companies would be significantly different from and worse than those of surviving companies. This suggests that the Casey and Bartczak study may have been too simplistic in its cash flow approach and that a more detailed examination of the nature and composition of operating cash flow may have been appropriate.

This paper attempts to provide such an examination at an exploratory level. It is hoped that this will aid those who are interested in developing cash flow reporting and analysis to appreciate the complexities involved in an apparently straightforward measure such as operating cash flow. In particular it emphasises the inter-relationships between the latter and measures of profit, working capital and borrowing.

SAMPLE COMPANIES

Because of the exploratory nature of the study it was limited to an examination of failed companies in order to determine whether or not these entities behaved similarly in a cash flow sense prior to failure. The period chosen for this study was that containing the last three years of reported financial results; in the UK there is typically a gap between the date of ultimate reporting and that of failure which is not reported. The three-year period was felt to be sufficient to monitor changes in cash flow performance prior to failure. It was hoped that any patterns emerging from this examination of failed companies could be used as the basis for a more extensive comparison of the cash flow performance of failed and surviving companies.

A major UK bank was approached in order to provide access to the financial statements of a sample of recently failed corporate customers. The sample selected was not random but provided a reasonable spread in terms of size, location and nature of business. Thirty seven companies were selected, each with three years of financial results prior to failure.[2] There was an average gap of 15 months between the last date of reporting and the date of failure.[3]

Expressed as percentages of 37, the companies were mainly private (95%), under directorial control (89%), in manufacturing, engineering or building (59%), put into receivership prior to liquidation (65%) because of floating charge securities (86%), and audited by small to medium-sized auditors (95%). In addition, and in terms of their ultimate financial reports, the companies typically had turnover of £1m or less (70%), total assets of £1m or less (70%), positive working capital (68%)[4], positive equity (81%), gearing of 50% or more (76%), losses before tax (57%), and operating cash flow deficits (51%).

Standardisation
As described in Lee (1984), the cash flow results of the 37 companies were derived from their published funds statements, supplemented where necessary by data from the other main financial statements. The format for analysis was as shown in Illustration 1:

was adopted based on the proposals of Theil (1969) and Lev (1971 and 1974). These writers were concerned to measure changes in the relative shares of items in financial statements in order to determine the degree of stability associated with the contents of the latter. By using relative shares for assets and liabilities a natural, log-based measure of deviation from the proportional development of these items was derived to indicate their variability over time. The general principles of this approach appeared to be relevant to this study, cash flow having constituent elements which vary over time and which can be standardised in terms of proportional shares of inflow and outflow. Of special concern in this study was the degree of variability of such standardised data, the expectation being that the "natural" variability of cash flow would be accentuated by managerial actions caused by financial difficulties (for example, as in working capital management to reduce cash outflow).

Illustration 1

Inflow   *Outflow*
Share capital issues   Dividend payment
Additional borrowing   Borrowing repayments
Operating cash flow surpluses   Operating cash flow deficits
Net disinvestment[5]   Net investment[5]
Taxation refunds   Taxation payments

In order to study cash flow developments over the three year period for each company, the cash flow results were placed in the above format and expressed as percentage proportions of inflow and outflow. This prevented distortion arising from the absolute size of the monetary figures and allowed for aggregation of research data describing company results.

In addition, as the study was concerned principally with operating cash flow generally and its constituent elements particularly, a decomposition approach

The decomposition approach produced two further proportionate share formats, the first (in Illustration 2) a decomposition of that described in Illustration 1, and the second (in Illustration 3) a further decomposition of the first.

When placed in either of the formats (Illustrations 2 and 3) in percentage terms, the data describe the proportionate contributions of the various items to funds inflow and outflow. With three years of data, changes in these shares can be observed.[6]

The following sections contain analyses

> **Illustration 2**
> *Inflow*
> Share capital issues
> Additional borrowing
> Profits before depreciation
> Working capital decreases
> Net disinvestment
> Taxation refunds
>
> *Outflow*
> Dividend payments
> Borrowing repayments
> Losses before depreciation
> Working capital increases
> Net investment
> Taxation payments
>
> (Operating cash flow decomposed to realised profit (loss) before depreciation and working capital increase (decrease).)

> **Illustration 3**
> *Inflow*
> Share capital issues
> Additional borrowing
> Profits before depreciation
> Stock decreases
> Debtors decreases
> Creditors increases
> Net disinvestment
> Taxation refunds
>
> *Outflow*
> Dividend payments
> Borrowing repayments
> Losses before depreciation
> Stock increases
> Debtors increases
> Creditors decreases
> Net investment
> Taxation payments
>
> (Working capital change decomposed to stock, debtors and creditors changes.)

which are based on these decompositions of cash flow data. In each case, with data expressed as percentages of the 37 failed companies, the frequency distributions describe contributions to or consumption of cash flow in broad categories — that is, either "none" (when the data are deficits, repayments, losses, etc); "little" (when the data represent ≤33% of inflow or outflow); and "some" (when the data represent >33% of inflow or outflow). Because of the absence of a control group it has been difficult to test the data statistically. However, differences between the means for each year have been tested using z tests with the level of significance set at the 5% level; and, by comparing data in terms of "little and none" and "some", chi square tests of association have been applied to 2 × 2 tables (again, with the significance level at 5%).[7] The contingency coefficient has been used to test the degree of such associations. Where relevant, data are stated as either $ns_{0.05}$ = not significant at 5% or $s_{0.05}$ = significant at 5%.

Cash flow performance

Table 1 examines the general cash flow performance of the 37 companies in the broad format of Illustration 1 and specifically analyses operating cash flow, borrowing and investment (other flows being ad hoc and infrequent).

The data in Table 1 reveal that the operating cash flow performance of the 37 companies was relatively poor and declining over the three years. This was particularly the case in the ultimate year of reporting — 35% of companies generated a surplus greater than one third of total inflow, and the mean was a 9% outflow. In no year did a majority of companies achieve more than a one third contribution to cash inflow. The standard deviations evidence consistently large

Table 1 Overall cash flow performance

	Pre-penultimate reporting year	Penultimate reporting year	Ultimate reporting year
Operating cash flow			
Deficit	38	35	54
⩽ 33% inflow	19	19	11
	57	54	65
> 33% inflow	43	46	35
	100	100	100
Mean inflow	17	27	(9)
Standard deviation	72	67	74
z test	$ns_{0.05}$	$s_{0.05}$	
Chi square test	$ns_{0.05}$	$ns_{0.05}$	
Contingency coefficient	0.00	0.08	
Borrowing			
Repayment	24	27	22
⩽ 33% inflow	19	22	3
	43	49	25
> 33% inflow	57	51	75
	100	100	100
Mean inflow	37	31	50
Standard deviation	66	65	66
z test	$ns_{0.05}$	$ns_{0.05}$	
Chi square test	$ns_{0.05}$	$s_{0.05}$	
Contingency coefficient	0.03	0.22	
Investment			
Disinvestment	16	14	30
⩽ 33% outflow	19	19	14
	35	33	44
> 33% outflow	65	67	56
	100	100	100
Mean outflow	50	58	38
Standard deviation	51	41	53
z test	$ns_{0.05}$	$ns_{0.05}$	
Chi square test	$ns_{0.05}$	$ns_{0.05}$	
Contingency coefficient	0.00	0.08	

dispersions around the means, and thus considerable variation in individual company achievement. The z test indicates a significant difference between the means of the penultimate and ultimate years, but the chi square tests and contingency coefficients suggest little association between the operating cash flow contributions in each year. These results evidence a considerable variety of performances within each year, but a lack of association between years.

The declining operating cash flow performance of the 37 companies was matched by a consistent and substantial dependence on external funding from mainly bank borrowing. In each year a small minority of companies achieved a reduction in borrowing, but more than 70% required additional debt. The latter was particularly the case in the ultimate reporting year, with 75% of companies obtaining more than one third of cash inflow in the form of debt. The mean dependence on debt increased over the three years from 37% to 50%, with consistently large dispersions around the means. However, the z tests provide no reason to justify the rejection of the null hypothesis of no difference between the means at the 5% level of significance. On the other hand, the chi square test indicates a significant association between the borrowing activities of the companies in the penultimate and ultimate years (although the association was relatively weak in terms of the contingency coefficient).

Capital investment forms the remaining material element in this overall analysis of cash flow. A large majority of companies in each year expended more than one third of total cash outflow on investment (but reducing to 56% in the ultimate reporting year). This latter decline is reflected also in the mean outflow declining from 58% in the penultimate year to 38% in the ultimate year. The dispersion around the mean was large in each year but less than that associated with either operating cash flow or borrowing. The z and chi square tests indicate that at the 5% level of significance no rejection should be made of the null hypotheses of, respectively, no difference in means, and no association of cash flow results between years.

Overall, the above analyses provide certain distinct features in proportionate terms — a declining operating cash flow performance, an increasing dependence on debt, and a decreasing investment activity. The most pronounced and significant changes are to be found when comparing the penultimate and ultimate reporting years — the latter having the least favourable cash flow results of the three years concerned.

Profit and working capital

The poor and declining cash flow performance of the 37 failed companies is examined in more detail in terms of the two main elements comprising operating cash flow — realised profit before depreciation and other non-cash accounting adjustments, and the related periodic change in trading working capital. This analysis is presented in Table 2 and follows the proportional format given in Illustration 2 (data being expressed as percentages of 37 companies).

The profit data in Table 2 describe the declining profitability of the 37 failed companies in terms of the contribution of realised profit to operating cash flow. Fifty four per cent of companies achieved at least a one third contribution to total inflow from profits in the pre-penultimate year; but this proportion halved to 27% in the ultimate year. The decline is made clear in the mean statistics — 31%

Table 2 Profit and working capital

	Pre-penultimate reporting year	Penultimate reporting year	Ultimate reporting year
Realised profit			
Loss	30	30	57
≤33% inflow	16	24	16
	46	54	73
>33% inflow	54	46	27
	100	100	100
Mean inflow (outflow)	31	21	(13)
Standard deviation	54	46	53
z test	$ns_{0.05}$	$s_{0.05}$	
Chi square test	$ns_{0.05}$	$ns_{0.05}$	
Contingency coefficient	0.05	0.17	
Working capital			
Increase	67	43	49
≤33% inflow	16	14	8
	83	57	57
>33% inflow	17	43	43
	100	100	100
Mean (outflow) inflow	(20)	3	6
Standard deviation	49	59	69
z test	$ns_{0.05}$	$ns_{0.05}$	
Chi square test	$s_{0.05}$	$ns_{0.05}$	
Contingency coefficient	0.26	0.03	

reducing to 21% and then to (13)%. The considerable variety of profit contribution is reflected in the large standard deviations. Differences in the means are significant at the 5% level between the penultimate and ultimate years, suggesting a rejection of the null hypothesis of no difference. However, the chi square test and the contingency coefficient for these years indicate a weak association between profit performances.

A proportionally reduced use of funds to finance working capital increases is evident from the above data (67% of companies in the pre-penultimate year, reducing to 49% in the ultimate year, and the mean outflow of 20% in the former period changing to a 6% mean inflow in the latter period). However, the variety of working capital changes increased over the three years from a standard deviation of 49% to one of 69%. At the 5% level of significance the z test is not significant in either of the two differences in means. The chi square test is significant at the 5% level of significance when applied to the data of the pre-penultimate and penultimate years — indicating, with the relevant contingency coefficient, a weak association in working capital changes.

Overall, therefore, at least in proportional terms, the 37 failed companies appear to have had a declining profitability and to have been disinvesting increasingly from working capital. The most significant decline in profits took place between the penultimate and ultimate years. The most significant disinvesting of working capital occurred between the pre-penultimate and penultimate years.

Stock, debtors and creditors
The working capital changes which contributed to operating cash flow either positively or negatively can be decomposed to changes in stock, debtors and creditors. These are described in Table 3, follow the format of Illustration 3, and are expressed as percentages of 37 failed companies.

A diminishing majority of companies in each period increased stock levels. Conversely, an increasing proportion (from 11% to 46%) decreased stock in order to generate cash flow. This is reflected in the declining mean outflows (18%, through 9%, to 3%). The standard deviations reflect a large dispersion around the mean of each year, but the z test does not indicate a rejection of the null hypothesis of no difference in means. The chi square test is also insignificant at the 5% level of significance.

The data concerning debtors changes are similar to those concerning stock, with the exception of the ultimate reporting year with a mean outflow of 15%. The z tests, chi square tests and contingency coefficients do not provide evidence to suggest the rejection of the null hypotheses of, respectively, no difference between means and debtor changes between years.

The data reflecting creditor changes describe relative stability over time — a sizeable minority of companies in each year reducing creditors and a consistent but larger minority providing a greater than one third inflow from increased creditors. The mean inflow remained consistently at or just below the 25% level and the z value and chi square tests reveal no significant differences in either means or associations between years.

The above results reveal three relatively clear results — the 37 failed companies tended to be proportionally reducing stock and debtors and maintaining a considerable dependence on creditors. The various standard deviations indicate a wide variety of changes for each of these items. However, the various statistical tests indicate no significant differences in means, and weak associations between the working capital changes and time.

Specific associations
The previous analyses have revealed little or no association between the cash flow results of the three years reported prior to failure. However, by cross-tabulating the cash flow variables within each year, it is possible to test for association between variables. This provides a somewhat clearer picture of the cash flow performance of the companies concerned. The first such cross-analysis is between

Table 3 Changes in stock, debtors and creditors			
	Pre-penultimate reporting year	Penultimate reporting year	Ultimate reporting year
Stock			
Increase	89	62	54
≤33% inflow	5	27	32
	94	89	86
>33% inflow	6	11	14
	100	100	100
Mean outflow	18	9	3
Standard deviation	32	32	41
z test	ns$_{0.05}$	ns$_{0.05}$	
Chi square test	ns$_{0.05}$	ns$_{0.05}$	
Contingency coefficient	0.05	0.00	
Debtors			
Increase	81	59	65
≤33% inflow	14	22	16
	95	81	81
>33% inflow	5	19	19
	100	100	100
Mean outflow	21	9	15
Standard deviation	31	41	47
z test	ns$_{0.05}$	ns$_{0.05}$	
Chi square test	ns$_{0.05}$	ns$_{0.05}$	
Contingency coefficient	0.16	0.03	
Creditors			
Reduction	30	19	27
≤30% inflow	30	40	27
	60	59	54
>30% inflow	40	41	46
	100	100	100
Mean inflow	22	25	23
Standard deviation	39	42	42
z test	ns$_{0.05}$	ns$_{0.05}$	
Chi square test	ns$_{0.05}$	ns$_{0.05}$	
Contingency coefficient	0.03	0.03	

operating cash flow and borrowing (Table 4). Operating cash flow data are split between those companies generating "little or none" (deficits and ≤33% inflows) and "some" (>33% inflows). Borrowing data are split similarly — "little or none" (repayments and ≤33% inflows) and "some" (>33% inflows).[8] The statistical test applied for association in this and later analyses is the Fisher exact probability test (set at the 5% level of significance), which avoids the problem of small expected frequencies in 2 × 2 tables.

The data below describe the relative

Table 4 Operating cash flow and borrowing									
	Pre-penultimate reporting year			Penultimate reporting year			Ultimate reporting year		
Operating cash flow	Borrowing			Borrowing			Borrowing		
		Little or none	Some		Little or none	Some		Little or none	Some
	n	%	%	n	%	%	n	%	%
Little or none	21	5	95	20	5	95	24	4	96
Some	16	94	6	17	100	—	13	62	38
Fisher exact test	s$_{0.05}$			s$_{0.05}$			s$_{0.05}$		

dependence on additional borrowing of those companies generating little or no operating cash flow and the relative reduction in dependence on borrowing of those companies generating some operating cash flow. The Fisher test in each year indicates a highly significant association between operating cash flow performance and borrowing behaviour, and the null hypothesis of no such association can be rejected in each case.

Operating cash flow and investment can be compared similarly (Table 5). Operating cash flow is split as in Table 4, and investment data are categorised as "little or none" (disinvestments and ≤33% outflows) and "some" (>33% outflows).[8]

majority of companies with the poorer operating cash flow performance made little or no investment, whereas a large majority of companies generating "some" operating cash flow made "some" investment. With the Fisher test giving a significant result at the 5% level, there is sufficient evidence to reject the null hypothesis and accept the alternative one of an association between operating cash flow performance and investment in the ultimate period.

The above cross analyses are concerned mainly with associations with operating cash flow. Using the available decomposed data it is possible to cross-tabulate realised profit with working capital change (Table 6). The data are split

Table 5 Operating cash flow and investment

Operating cash flow	Pre-penultimate reporting year Investment			Penultimate reporting year Investment			Ultimate reporting year Investment		
	Little or none		Some	Little or none		Some	Little or none		Some
	n	%	%	n	%	%	n	%	%
Little or none	21	38	62	20	35	65	24	54	46
Some	16	31	69	17	29	71	13	23	77
Fisher exact test	ns$_{0.05}$			ns$_{0.05}$			s$_{0.05}$		

Irrespective of generating "little or none" or "some" operating cash flow, the majority of companies in each of the pre-penultimate and penultimate years made "some" investment. The Fisher test in each case supports this conclusion, the probability data suggesting the acceptance of the null hypothesis of no association between operating cash flow performance and investment. However, in the ultimate year, the cross-analysis reveals that the

in a similar fashion to those in Tables 4 and 5 — "little or none" (losses and ≤33% inflows for realised profit; and increases and ≤33% inflows for working capital change); and "some" (>33% inflows for both realised profit and working capital change).[9] Table 6 therefore describes the degree to which profitable and less profitable companies augmented cash flow by working capital management.

Table 6 Profit and working capital

Realised profit	Pre-penultimate reporting year Contribution from working capital			Penultimate reporting year Contribution from working capital			Ultimate reporting year Contribution from working capital		
	Little or none		Some	Little or none		Some	Little or none		Some
	n	%	%	n	%	%	n	%	%
Little or none	17	71	29	20	55	45	27	44	56
Some	20	95	5	17	59	41	10	90	10
Fisher exact test	s$_{0.05}$			ns$_{0.05}$			s$_{0.05}$		

Companies generating little or no funding from realised profit tended, with the exception of the penultimate year, to utilise proportionally less funding for working capital investment than did companies generating "some" profit funding. The most significant difference occurred in the ultimate year — a majority of the relatively less profitable companies making "some" contribution to cash flow from working capital reduction compared with a very small minority of the more profitable companies. Only in the penultimate year can there be said to be no significant difference between the companies (the null hypothesis therefore not being rejected in that case).

Finally, Table 7 examines the relationship between borrowing and the creditor position of the companies by comparing borrowing behaviour (split as in Table 4) with changes in creditors (split as follows — "little or none" = reductions and ≤33% inflows; and "some" = >33% inflows).[10] The cross-tabulation therefore describes the degree to which companies switched from borrowing to credit and vice versa as a means of generating cash flow.

substituting a credit dependency for a borrowing dependency.

A number of conclusions can be drawn from the above cross-analyses. First, failed companies with the poorer operating cash flow results tended to compensate by additional borrowing; companies with a better operating cash flow achievement tended to reduce their debt dependence. Second, the poorer the operating cash flow performance, the less the investment made by the failed companies. Third, the less profitable failed companies tended to contain or reduce their working capital to a greater extent than did the more profitable failed companies. Fourth, the most debt dependent failed companies tended to be the least credit dependent. Finally, from each of the cross-analyses it is clear that the above differences or associations are least strong in the penultimate reporting year and most strong in the ultimate year (the order in terms of decreasing significance being ultimate, pre-penultimate and penultimate).

CONCLUSIONS

This study has been an initial response to

Table 7 Borrowing and credit

Additional borrowing	Pre-penultimate reporting year			Penultimate reporting year			Ultimate reporting year		
	Additional credit			Additional credit			Additional credit		
	n	Little or none %	Some %	n	Little or none %	Some %	n	Little or none %	Some %
Little or none	24	46	54	25	52	48	22	36	64
Some	13	85	15	12	75	25	15	80	20
Fisher exact test	$S_{0.05}$			$ns_{0.05}$			$S_{0.05}$		

With the Fisher test indicating significant results in the pre-penultimate and ultimate periods, the above data suggest that companies which were less dependent proportionally on borrowing were more dependent on credit from suppliers. The strength of the results warrants the rejection of the null hypothesis of no association in the pre-penultimate and ultimate years, and invites support for the alternative hypothesis that companies were

the generalised conclusion of Casey and Bartczak that operating cash flow data are poor performance indicators. It has been exploratory in nature and has been constrained by the lack of a random selection of companies and a control group with which to compare the results of the failed companies. Nevertheless, it appears to have produced findings which warrant further exploration without these constraints. Specifically, it has attempted to avoid the bias of previous failure studies which have concentrated on very large companies and has developed a cash flow framework for analysis beyond the one-line measure of Casey and Bartczak.

The general findings are of declining operating cash flow performance and realised profitability compensated for by increased borrowing and/or credit. The most significant changes in these matters tended to take place in the ultimate reporting year, and the most significant associations between them occurred, respectively, in the ultimate and pre-penultimate reporting years.

Judgments were required to be made in this study regarding the categorisation of companies by frequency distribution splits. This was aided by the use of a proportionate share basis for analysis derived from decomposition analysis. It is believed that this approach is worthy of further development. It removes the problem of size distortion and allows for inter-entity and inter-period comparisons. It provides also a possible basis for establishing pre-determined cash flow guidelines for auditors and bankers concerned to detect early signals of company failure. It is hoped that the latter persons therefore may find sufficient evidence in this study to warrant further investigation and development.

Endnotes

(1) Defined as cash receipts from customers minus cash payments to suppliers and other providers of trading resources (including interest payments).
(2) Failure was defined as receivership or liquidation.
(3) Considerably greater than that reported by Lawrence (1983).
(4) Defined as stock and work in progress plus trading debtors and prepayments minus trading creditors and accruals.
(5) Disposals exceeding expenditure.
(6) Informational decomposition measures, as described by Lev (1971 and 1974), have not been computed as the formulae concerned cannot cope with negative numbers which cash and funds flow analyses tend to generate. Indeed, it is doubtful if such measures can be used for anything other than relatively stable financial statements such as balance sheets.
(7) Adjusted, where necessary, with the Yates's correction for expected frequencies of less than 5.
(8) Proportions used are as in Illustration 1 and Table 1.
(9) Proportions used are as in Illustration 2 and Table 2.
(10) Proportions used are as in Illustration 3 and Table 3.

References

C J Casey and N J Bartczak, "Cash Flow — It's Not the Bottom Line", *Harvard Business Review*, July-August 1984, pp 61-6.
D A Egginton, "In Defence of Profit Measurement: Some Limitations of Cash Flow and Value Added as Performance Measures for External Reporting", *Accounting and Business Research*, Spring 1984, pp 99-111.
E C Lawrence, "Reporting Delays for Failed Firms", *Journal of Accounting Research*, Autumn 1983, pp 606-10.
T A Lee, *Cash Flow Accounting*, Van Nostrand Reinhold, 1984, pp 94-107.
T A Lee, "Cash Flow Accounting, Profit, and Performance Measurement — a Response to a Challenge", *Accounting and Business Research*, Spring 1985, pp 93-7.
B Lev, "Financial Failure and Informational Decomposition Measures", in R R Sterling and W F Bentz (eds), *Accounting in Perspective*, South-Western Publishing, 1971, pp 102-11.
B Lev, *Financial Statement Analysis: A New Approach*, Prentice-Hall, 1974, pp 47-60.
H Theil, "On the Use of Information Theory Concepts in the analysis of Financial Statements", *Management Science*, May 1969, pp 459-80.

Criticisms

CASH FLOW ACCOUNTING AND THE ALLOCATION PROBLEM
T.A. Lee*

In a recent paper, Rutherford (1981) has argued that cash flow accounting (CFA) is not allocation-free, and therefore contains many judgmental problems similar in nature and impact to those inherent in the traditional allocation-based systems of accounting. Such criticism is not new to CFA, and tends to mirror consistent, unwritten comments made about it over the years. For this reason, it would be wrong to ignore such fault-finding as if it were no more than a straw man. Instead, it should be regarded as a serious misconception of CFA proposals, and the necessary introduction to an attempt to tighten up the argument underlying such advocations. This paper is therefore concerned to do this — that is, to discuss a possible misconception, and to strengthen an argument. The subject concerns the nature and existence of arbitrary allocations in CFA.

Defining an Allocation

Thomas is the leading critic of arbitrary allocations, and he has consistently defined them in *increasingly* broad terms. For example:

'An accounting allocation divides a monetary magnitude among recipients (inputs to the firm, accounting periods, and so forth)'. (1971, p.472)

'An allocation is a partitioning of a set (and the assignment of the resulting subsets to different groups, periods of time, or other loci)'. (1974, p.1)

'An allocation is any partitioning of a whole into parts, any division of a subject among objects'. (1980, p.1)

(It should be noted that Thomas's definitions appear to have been kept deliberately broad in order to cover most types of allocation which might appear in the accounting measurement process.)

If the above definitions are accepted (and there is no evidence in the accounting literature to suggest their rejection), their general nature would make it most surprising to find *any* system of accounting which avoided all allocations — because of the indirect nature of certain revenues and costs, and also because of the need to classify other revenues and costs (classification in this sense coming within the above definitions of allocation provided by Thomas). It would therefore be equally surprising to evidence any CFA advocate making a statement that CFA data were absolutely allocation-free. In fact, as a search of the relevant literature reveals, they do not often qualify their arguments accordingly. But they are guilty of making ambiguous statements, particularly if read carelessly. For example:

'The measurement of financial performance (or financial reporting) on a cash-flow basis thus allows management to escape from most if not all the

---

The author is Professor of Accountancy and Finance at the University of Edinburgh. (Paper received September, 1981)

controversial problem areas which have bedevilled traditional accountancy for the bigger part of this century'. (Lawson, 1971b, p.40)

'Financial accountants could substitute at least three potentially allocation-free reporting systems for our contemporary, allocated ones: current-entry-value reporting, current-exit-value reporting and cash-flow (or net-quick-asset-flow) reporting'. (Thomas, 1980, p.220)

'CFA avoids dubious accounting allocations and thus, unlike periodic income measurements, cash flows provide relatively unambiguous measures of entity financial performance'. (Lee, 1981a, p.72)

Each of these statements contains a hint that the writer concerned might have believed that CFA is allocation-free. But care must be exercised in judging them. Each statement can only be interpreted as no more than a qualified one — Lawson stated that CFA escapes from *most* of the controversial problems of traditional accounting: Thomas only described CFA as *potentially* allocation-free; and Lee stipulated that CFA avoids allocations but did not say it avoids *all* allocations.

CFA advocates have also been at pains to make specific and explicit qualifications regarding the existence of allocations in CFA. Lawson (1971a, p.150), for example, when suggesting that a cash flow-based analysis could be applied to divisional performance measurement, warned that this could only be accomplished adequately if the division concerned was truly independent of the remainder of the reporting entity. Thus, he appeared to recognise the problems associated with an accounting for revenues and costs of segments which may well lead to arbitrary allocations. Thomas (1980, p.220) has also recognised the segmentation process as a possible means of introducing arbitrary allocations to CFA-based data — that is, particularly in relation to the problem of deciding 'how much global cash receipts from sales of transfer goods to outsiders should be attributed to each division'.

Despite these qualifications, the criticism of CFA persists in this respect, or the CFA proposals are being misinterpreted. For example, Glautier and Underdown (1976, p.664) state:

'The problems associated with distinctions between capital, revenue, income and expenditure, or of allocations of costs between a series of arbitrary time periods, do not arise under cash-flow accounting'.

Thus, Rutherford (1982, p.17) — would appear to be correct to conclude:

'We must be careful, though, not to bring a system of cash flow accounting rapidly and wastefully into disrepute by imposing on its measurements interpretations which they cannot bear'.

Allocations appears to be much too broad a function to be avoided completely in any system of accounting; and, fortunately, the literature does not contain many statements of the Glautier and Underdown type. But the fact that they can be made by respected writers should be cause for concern for CFA advocates. They reflect a potential ambiguity and looseness in the latters' writings. For example, Lee (1971, p.326) has stated when explaining CFA techniques:

> 'The somewhat artificial distinction between capital and revenue transactions, and the development of criteria to classify business assets, would be equally unnecessary'.

As will be argued later in this paper, this is true in relation to CFA, but only to the extent that it does not contain notions of income and capital which require such distinctions and criteria to exist. It does not mean that they are unnecessary in *any* system of accounting. If, for example, as suggested by Lee (1981b), CFA is combined with net realisable value-based income and capital accounting, they will be required to be made and used.

The remainder of this paper will therefore attempt to at least minimise the ambiguity in the CFA proposals in relation to their comments on allocation. Hopefully, this will reveal that arbitrary allocations can affect CFA; but can also be avoided. The major contribution in this respect will be to recognise that there are different types of allocation — some of which can be inadvertently contained in CFA systems if not guarded against.

Different Types of Allocation

Defined broadly as above, allocation is the act of apportioning or distributing. In the case of accounting, this relates to data for reporting purposes, and judgmental problems occur because such data require to be matched to defined time periods or entities. The time-period type of allocations is the most familiar one to financial accountants because it underlies the debate and thinking concerning accounting standards and the measurement of income and capital. Because of the long-lived accounting requirement to report on discrete periods of business activity, the reporting accountant apparently accepts the need to divide arbitrarily the continuous stream of recorded accounting data and 'match' it to particular periods to which he regards the divided parts to be appropriate. Thus, he accounts for such allocated data as fixed asset depreciation, stock and work-in-progress valuations, and deferred taxation.

Rutherford (1981, p.1) has coined these allocations as *metrical*. They are labelled in this paper instead as *time-period* allocations. They are derived in most instances from the long-held belief in accountancy that measures of financial progress and position should be related for reporting purposes to periods of twelve or less months. They are also justified on the basis that these measures are best achieved by matching revenues and costs which can be attributed to a defined period, irrespective of when the revenues were received and when the costs were paid.

Time-period allocations contrast with another form of allocation involving what Rutherford (1981, p.1) describes as 'decisions about the disposition of resources between alternative applications' — that is, *distributional* allocations caused by management decisions to use business resources in separate locations and/or for different purposes. He provides several examples of these in his paper (1981, pp.5-15) — including segmented reports, capital and revenue data, recurrent transactions, operating and financing flows, cash flow cut-offs, and non-cash transactions.

In each of these areas, the accountant would appear to have subjective judgments to make in order to determine the accounting allocations concerned. Segmented reports provide a good example of allocating to specific entities (hereafter labelled *entity* allocations); capital/revenue, recurrent/non-recurrent, and operating/financing distinctions are forms of accounting classification (hereafter described as *classificatory* allocations); cash flow cut-offs appear to be examples of time-period rather than distributional allocations; and non-cash transactions can be coped with by reducing them to problems of classificatory allocations.

Each type of allocation (time-period, entity and classificatory) is somewhat different in its intention, although all involve some arbitrary judgment by the reporting accountant. Each should therefore be examined separately in relation to CFA to ensure that its potential impact on the latter system is properly evaluated and put into context.

CFA and Time-Period Allocations

As all CFA proposals reveal, it is unnecessary to introduce time-period allocations to accounting for external reporting purposes. Measurement of financial *progress* can be made in cash terms by ignoring or reversing the effects of time-period allocations such as inventory and depreciation, (for details, see Lee (1981a pp.63-78)). Equally, statements of financial *position* can be presented devoid of time-period allocations — for example, Stamp (1979, p.173) suggested the use of second-hand replacement costs and net realisable values; and Chambers (1967, 1970 and 1974) advocated net realisable values. Indeed, Lee (1981b) has suggested a combined cash flow and net realisable value system to provide measures of financial progress *and* position which not only articulate but lack dependence on time-period allocations.

According to the arguments of the proponents of time-period allocation-free systems of accounting such as CFA, the absence of such allocations does not appear to reduce or impair their relevance to potential users. In fact, each system has been argued for as having considerable relevance for its users (in relation to the CFA arguments, see the summary in Lee (1981a, p.68)).

The fundamental reason for requiring time-period allocations in traditional accounting would appear to be the fixed and arbitrary nature of the financial reporting period — usually a twelve month one for external purposes, but diminished on occasion by interim reports. It must be presumed, in light of little or no specific evidence to the contrary, that the potential short-term variability of cash flow is generally felt by reporting accountants to be sufficient reason for introducing allocations which 'smooth' the figures for purposes of providing information for decisions concerning such matters as distributing and borrowing. But, as it can be argued that these decisions have as much to do with cash flow and liquidity as with profitability, the question has to be asked as to why 'smoothing' of cash flows is necessary. To preserve the variability of cash flow would appear to provide useful information for owners, lenders, managers and others concerned with assessing such matters as business and investment risk. Cash flows 'smoothed' by time-period allocations appear to hide the periodic peaks and troughs about which these various user groups should be concerned to have information when making their various predictions (the latter being based invariably on some aspect of cash flow).

As previously mentioned, a further time-period allocation problem has been highlighted within the context of CFA — that is, the potential 'window-dressing' of CFA reports caused by entity management responsible for cash flow 'cut-off' accelerating or delaying cash receipts or payments (Rutherford, 1981, pp.13-14). This type of 'smoothing' (which must also exist within all other systems of accounting in which cash transactions are involved) presumably would also arise for the same reason as other time-period allocations occur — that is, the fixed and short-term nature of the financial reporting period creating cash flow variability which requires to be 'smoothed' in an attempt to 'improve' either the financial reports of a particular period or the trend of financial results over a number of periods.

However, such 'window-dressing' procedures can only have a short-term effect in most instances — one period benefiting at the expense of the next, or vice versa. But, if CFA reports are structured as *multi-period,* and if the data are reported periodically and *cumulatively,* the influence of managerial manipulation could be neutralised. Adequate systems of internal control, and the existence of the external audit function, would also act at least as preventative measures in this respect.

The 'smoothing' influence of time-period allocation serves to remind accountants of the reporting problems which can be created by the use of a fixed and arbitrary reporting period. The usual one is of twelve months and has been determined for many decades as appropriate for accounting, fiscal and legal uses; apparently without attention to the nature of the reporting entity to which it is related. It is surprising that, for external reporting purposes, accountants have been content to ignore differences in business activity which could necessitate the use of reporting periods of significantly different lengths. Of particular concern in this respect is the normal completion time for transactions in an individual business — presumably extending from a matter of a few days or weeks in a retail concern to several years for some civil engineering contractors. These material differences in operational and trading activity are well recognised in management accounting systems; they are ignored in external financial reporting.

The reporting period was not a problem for early accountants reporting on single trading ventures — the length of the latter determined the period for reporting; they were identical. And then the continuous nature of business activity, and the apparently consequential accounting assumption of the going concern, led to the legal convenience of the calendar year for reporting purposes. However, the complexity and range of business activity demands a more thinking approach akin perhaps to the plant classifications which have failed to daunt botanists and biologists over the centuries (Robertson, 1981). Meantime, CFA is a constant reminder of the reporting period problem — the fixed and arbitrary reporting period being less suited to CFA data then their time-period allocation-smoothed equivalents. In turn, the reporting period is a reminder of a fundamental concept which underlies all accounting, and which is also usually ignored by accounting standard-setters — the entity concept (Lee, 1980). The following section examines this concept in relation to CFA.

CFA and Entity Allocations

Lee (1972. p.31) has suggested the production of CFA statements on a segmented basis. Rutherford (1981, pp.5-9) rightly points out the possibility of allocations in such proposals due to transfer pricing and joint cost problems. In fact, he concludes (p.9) that economic interaction makes segmented CFA statements difficult to construct and interpret.

These charges against what have been previously defined as entity allocations are serious ones and have to be answered. First, they are not exclusive to CFA — they could exist in all systems of reporting where more than one entity is being reported on, and where certain transactions affect more than one of the individual entities concerned. Thus, this is a fundamental problem of accounting when the reporting emphasis is on disaggregated data. Second, the proponents of CFA, as stated in an earlier section of this paper, have recognised the problem and commented on it. Indeed, one writer, Thomas (1980, pp.221-3), has gone so far as to state (after a lengthy and exhaustive study of transfer pricing and similar problems) that, at best, all that can be done is to live with the problem — that is in terms of deciding what one can put up with in order to get usable if imperfect information.

Within the context of external financial reporting, Thomas' advice is somewhat permissive in the sense that it may not be necessary to live with arbitrary entity allocations. What he appeared to ignore in his analysis is the entity concept — the need to define adequately the entity about which the reporting is to take place, and about which potential report users require credible information. In this way, internal management accounting proposals of Lawson (1971a, p.150) take on a new significance for external financial reporting. He suggested that divisional performance on a CFA basis should only be measured if the division was independent — that is, if the following conditions were met:

'A division is a truly separate part of the organisation and fulfills a role provided by competitors;

The price-elasticity of demand for the division's products is independent of the price-elasticity of demand for the company's other products;

Organisational and operating costs are wholly and exclusively ascribable to the division on an operationally measurable incremental basis, i.e. there is no cost interdependence between the company and division or allocation of costs between the two which are a joint cost of company and division'.

In other words, extending this to separable companies within a group, and assuming the separation reveals independent managers and segments with their own cash resources, they could then be treated as if they were separate entities for external reporting purposes. Each would be an autonomous unit which, if terminated, would not lead to the demise of the total organisation. In this way, the identified entity could be reported on without involving any arbitrary cost and revenue allocations. The separate cash flow reported would be that of the defined entity, and could therefore be seen as a flow which would be 'lost' to the organisation as a whole if the independent segment were no longer part of it. This is an important point for would-be users of external financial reports — they ought to be interested in having information (in CFA and other terms) about the contributions which independent segments are making to the overall cash flow, profitability etc. of the total organisation.

What potential report users do not appear to need is information which has been prepared on the basis of arbitrary allocations of revenues and costs. In CFA terms, these cannot give anything other than a misleading portrayal of segmental cash flows — being capable of 'manipulation' by management, depending on what arbitrary judgments are made by it regarding interactive transactions such as intersegmental sales and centralised administrative costs. In other words, if the defined entity is not independent in a business and financial sense (such as a company in a conglomerate group), then it is imprudent to attempt to report on it. If arbitrary allocations are being considered in order to complete such a reporting, commonsense suggests the exercise should not be undertaken.

This part of the analysis of CFA and the allocation problem draws attention to the entity concept in financial reporting. When producing segmental data on a CFA (or any other) basis, the segment must be adequately defined as an autonomous entity for which a credible reporting can be made for potential report users. In CFA terms, if this defining is undertaken, there ought not to be any inter-entity allocations in the CFA statements. Rutherford is therefore correct in his attention to the problem. But it can be avoided.

CFA and Classificatory Allocations

Rutherford (1981, pp.9-13) has also criticised the CFA proposals for their possible inclusion of three further types of allocation. These relate to capital/revenue, recurrent/non-recurrent and operating/financing distinctions. As these have been defined as essentially accounting classifications, they have been labelled for the purposes of this paper as classificatory allocations.

The first such problem concerns the need to differentiate between capital and revenue expenditure — the former having been recommended in the past for separate disclosure in CFA statements (Lawson, 1971b, p.46; and Lee, 1972, p.31). Before proceeding with the importance of such a recommendation, it is necessary to define the terms concerned – they are usually used in accounting without definition, and to define them may provide a clue as to the significance of any such distinction made in CFA proposals.

It is almost impossible to find a modern accounting definition – contemporary writers appear to disregard the distinction; it is apparently taken for granted that reporting accountants do not need guidance on such a matter. However, definitions made in an audit context could be of use (for example, Bigg, 1969, p.146):

> 'Capital expenditure may be said to be all expenditure incurred for the purpose of acquiring, extending or improving assets of a permanent nature, by means of which to carry on the business, or for the purpose of increasing the earning capacity of the business.
>
> Revenue expenditure is all expenditure incurred in the actual running of the business, and in maintaining the capital assets in a state of efficiency'.

Thus, although the above definition may be argued over in relation to its use of particular words (for example, 'permanent nature' and 'efficiency'), it is reasonably clear that the basic distinction is between expenditure on assets of a long-lived nature (usually classified as fixed assets for reporting purposes) and expenditure to aid the day-to-day operations and running of the business (some of which will be matched against revenues in the period in which it was incurred, with the remainder being carried forward under current assets for reporting purposes). But the distinction is far from clear, and appears to have been relatively neglected for years. It obviously affects the composition of income statements and balance sheets because of its influence on the determination of matched costs and asset valuations, but in CFA the issue is entirely one of disclosure – a cash outflow being a cash outflow whatever the nature of the expenditure it represents. That is why the potential allocation has been described in this paper as classificatory.

What has been argued for by CFA advocates is a disclosure of expenditure of a long-lived nature separate from that concerned with the day-to-day operations of the entity. Hopefully, this would provide potential report users with information about expenditure incurred to maintain existing activities and expenditure to ensure their continuity in the future. Given the difficulties of making a separation between capital and revenue expenditure, however, this recommendation is inadequate, and the solution may be *not* to treat them as essentially different (as has been recommended in most past CFA proposals), but instead to regard all such expenditure as if it were necessary to the short-term maintenance and long-term continuity of the entity – that is, to deduct all expenditure as one item (other than financial and fiscal outflows such as interest, taxation and dividends) from sales revenue, and to ensure there are adequate supporting descriptions and explanations of all major expenditure headings within it (for example, raw materials, wages, overheads, plant, vehicles, research and so on). This would avoid making spurious classificatory allocations in the form of separate deductions. The emphasis would be on disclosure for report users, to allow *them* to make judgments about the significance of the entity's expenditure. After all, it is the user who analyses, evaluates and decides. The reporting accountant ought to avoid anything in his disclosures which biases them towards a particular decision. The concept of reporting objectivity (or neutrality) has been one of the cornerstones of financial accounting for many years.

A similar conclusion could be reached in relation to any suggestion to separate out growth and replacement investment in CFA terms. Again, this would involve an arbitrary allocation problem unless the disclosure was merely limited to a single CFA deduction for expenditure supported by explanations of individual expenditure headings which incorporated a description of material items which had been incurred by the entity on new or increased facilities (for example, on increased stock levels or employee numbers, or additional plant and equipment).

The above arguments can be extended to cover distinctions between different types of cash inflows. Receipts from sales of long-lived assets can be separately disclosed in CFA systems without allocations being necessary (although they could be netted in the relevant statements against any expenditure on replacing them). Similarly, government grants and subsidies would appear to justify separate disclosure, as does the capital funding distinction between net cash flows from operations (an internal source of funding) and those from external sources (for example, banks and similar institutions). These separations of cash inflows should be made by adequate presentation and explanation rather than some form of 'rule-of-thumb' allocation. Equally, capital transactions which involve cash flow in part only (for example, a takeover or merger of an organisation satisfied by cash and shares and/or loans) need not involve any arbitrary allocation if the total cash outflow is adequately disclosed in the CFA statements, and supported by descriptions and explanations of the individual details of the complete transaction (Lee, 1972, pp.31-2).

What is therefore being advocated is an avoidance of unnecessary classificatory allocations by the substitution of simple cash flow additions or deductions with adequate disclosure and explanation — yet another example in this paper of the need to return to the fundamental concepts of accounting; in this case, to adequate disclosure (without the encumbrance of dubious allocations). By complying with this concept, CFA statements would provide report users with sufficient information to enable them to make judgments of the reporting entity as a basis to their decisions. The lack of classificatory allocations between capital and revenue receipts and expenditure in CFA would leave all cash inflows as inflows required to fund the cash commitments of the reporting entity; and all cash outflows as outflows (eventually to be recovered in future cash flows which should be reflected in published CFA forecasts — see, for example, Lawson (1969, pp.9-10) and Lee (1972, p.30) for such recommendations). There would be no need to make such complex classifications if adequate disclosure of all receipts and expenditure items were made, coupled with explanations of proportions of such items which can be attributed to changes in the nature and size of the entity's business activities. In other words, the recommended approach is not to classify capital and revenue items as apparently different additions or deductions in CFA statements; but instead to treat them as essentially cash inflows or outflows, with an adequate note to the statements of their nature and composition.

Finally, in relation to capital and revenue distinctions, it must be said that the foregoing comments are applicable to CFA statements only. In relation to statements of financial position, it must remain the case that the classificatory allocations of capital from revenue receipts and expenditure will determine what are matched as costs against sales revenues in determining income, and what are regarded as assets and liabilities for balance sheet purposes. In other words, any balance sheet is to some extent or other influenced by these allocations, even if valuations are used which avoid time-period allocations (such as is the case with net realisable values).

The remaining example of significant classificatory allocation (which might affect CFA) concerns the distinction between recurrent and non-recurrent transactions, and could be extended to include the distinction between ordinary and extra-ordinary items (the latter being required in the UK to be disclosed separately — Accounting Standards Committee (1974)). (Lee, (1972) for example, has advocated such distinctions when making CFA proposals). The problem in this case appears to be entirely similar to that of capital and revenue transactions. The distinction, if required, has to be made in the form of a subjective judgment unless some arbitrary rule is prescribed — and both approaches are unsatisfactory. But the allocations need not be made in CFA systems if there is adequate disclosure of the items concerned, including full explanations of the circumstances surrounding them. In other words, instead of having separate deductions and/or additions in CFA statements labelled as recurrent or non-recurrent or ordinary or extra-ordinary, it would appear more sensible to identify them in any relevant supporting explanation of disclosed figures, if they are regarded as material.

The latter point is a good introduction to a summary of the discussion on classificatory allocations. That there is potential for them, there is no doubt. That they exist, and that subjective and presumably arbitrary judgments are made, is equally not in doubt. That they can be avoided without harming the interests of report users is feasible. The approach ought to be to make adequate disclosure and explanation of *any* cash inflow or outflow that is material enough to be brought to the attention of users in order to satisfy the concept of full disclosure. However, it should not include the judgmental labelling of these items in a way that has prejudged the issue for the user — that is, describing the data as capital (or revenue), extra-ordinary (or ordinary), or non-recurrent (or recurrent). For who is to say, what is capital, what is extra-ordinary, and what is non-recurrent? Surely these are matters which ought to be left to the report user to judge and build into his particular model — that is, the reporting accountant must act neutrally when presenting his financial statements. CFA in this context reminds accountants that their responsibilities concern the provision of relevant information. Classificatory allocations appear to go beyond this function — out of the area of the report producer into that of the user. To avoid them would require the application of the well-known concepts of adequate disclosure and materiality in a way that forces the reporting accountant back to one of the foundations of financial reporting — the need to satisfy various defined user groups. Unless this is done, the answers to the questions of what is adequate disclosure and what is material in CFA terms will never be obtained.

Conclusions

Criticism of CFA systems includes statements that they are not completely allocation-free. Possible allocations in CFA include those relating to time-periods, entities, and classifications. From an analysis of these allocations in relation to CFA, it is reasonable to conclude that they can be avoided in such a system. Time-period allocations involving the division of accounting numbers are specifically excluded in CFA (and cash flow manipulation can be guarded against — although it is not strictly an accounting problem); entity allocations are unnecessary if entities to be reported in CFA terms are defined as autonomous units; and classificatory allocations should not be made if report users are left to judge fully explained and disclosed data of a material nature.

A useful by-product of this analysis has been the discovery that these allocation problems do not apply to CFA systems if proper care and attention is paid to the basics of accounting — first, the need for a reporting period, the length of which is relevant to the business activities of the entity concerned; second, the requirement to define and report only on independent entities; and, third, to disclose and explain data in a way which does not make judgments on behalf of the report user.

Finally, arbitrary allocations cannot be avoided in certain financial statements (for example, the balance sheet). Therefore, it may be that Thomas is correct when he says they may have to be lived with. CFA statements, on the other hand, can avoid them, apparently without reduction of relevance to their users. Surely this is one of CFA's most positive advantages?

REFERENCES

Accounting Standards Committee (1974), 'Extraordinary Items and Prior Year Adjustments', *Statement of Standard Accounting Practice 6* (1974).

Bigg, W.W. (1969), *Practical Auditing*, HFL (1969).

Chambers, R.J. (1967), 'Continuously Contemporary Accounting — Additivity and Action', *The Accounting Review* (October 1967), pp.751-7.

Chambers, R.J. (1970), 'Second Thoughts on Continuously Contemporary Accounting', *Abacus* (September 1970), pp.39-55.

——— (1974), 'Third Thoughts', *Abacus* (December 1974), pp.129-37.

Glautier, M.W.E. and B. Underdown (1976), *Accounting Theory and Practice*, Pitman (1976).

Lawson, G.H. (1979), 'Profit Maximisation Via Financial Management', *Management Decision* (Winter 1969), pp.6-12.

─────── (1971a), 'Measuring Divisional Performance', *Management Accountant* (May 1971), pp.147-52.

─────── (1971b), 'Accounting for Financial Management – Some Tentative Proposals for a New Blueprint', in R. Shone (ed.), *Problems of Investment*, (Blackwell, 1971), pp.36-64.

Lee, T.A. (1971), 'Goodwill – an Example of Will-o'-the-Wisp Accounting', *Accounting and Business Research* (Autumn 1971), pp.318-28.

─────── (1972), 'A Case for Cash Flow Reporting', *Journal of Business Finance*, (Summer 1972), pp.27-36.

─────── (1980), 'The Accounting Entity Concept, Accounting Standards and Inflation Accounting', *Accounting and Business Research* (Spring 1980), pp.176-86.

─────── (1981a), 'Cash Flow Accounting and Corporate Financial Reporting', in M. Bromwich and A. Hopwood (Eds.), *Essays in British Accounting Research*, Pitman (1981), pp.63-78.

─────── (1981b), 'Reporting Cash Flows and Net Realisable Values', *Accounting and Business Research* (Spring 1981), pp.163-70.

Robertson, T. (1981), *Management and Technology in a Changing Environment*, University of Edinburgh (June 1981).

Rutherford, B.A. (1982), *The Interpretation of Cash Flow Reports and the Other Allocation Problem*, University of Kent at Canterbury, (to be published in *Abacus*, 1982).

Stamp, E. (1979), 'Financial Reports on an Entity: Ex Uno Plures', in R.R. Sterling and A.L. Thomas (eds.), *Accounting for a Simplified Firm Owning Depreciable Assets* (Scholars Book Co., 1979), pp.163-80.

─────── (1971), 'Useful Arbitrary Allocations', *The Accounting Review* (July 1971), pp.472-9.

─────── (1974), 'The Allocation Problem: Part Two', *Studies in Accounting Research 9*, American Accounting Association (1974).

Thomas, A.L. (1970), *A Behavioral Analysis of Joint-Cost Allocation and Transfer Pricing*, Stipes Publishing, (1970).

Cash Flow Accounting, Profit and Performance Measurement: A Response to a Challenge

T. A. Lee

In a recent paper, Egginton (1984) provides a detailed critique of cash flow based financial reporting proposals. He concentrates on the suggestion that cash flow statements could replace conventional profit statements as a major source of financial information about entity performance. Defining performance in the general terms of resource augmentation or depletion, Egginton states that profit is central to performance measurement, and cash flow data are not capable of assuming such an informational role. Indeed, he regards cash flow reporting as having a strictly limited function in the assessment of entity liquidity. In this respect, he further suggests a place for this within the context of funds flow reporting.

The nature and extent of these criticisms and counter-proposals constitute a challenge to the proponents of cash flow reporting, and this paper is an attempt to answer the concern of Egginton regarding the following points:

(a) Whether or not cash flow data can be used to assess entity performance.
(b) The lack of a statement of financial position in cash flow reporting proposals.
(c) The de-emphasising of ownership in cash flow based thinking.
(d) Whether or not cash flow reporting avoids the allocation problem.
(e) The relevance and feasibility of reporting cash flow forecasts.
(f) The significance of cash flow reporting proposals vis-à-vis the problem of changing prices.

These appear to be the main objects of Egginton's attention, and will be discussed separately.

General weaknesses in criticism

Before proceeding to a detailed analysis and discussion of each of the above points, it appears to be essential to point out to the reader a thread of weakness which runs through much of Egginton's paper. Although it is a critique of cash flow reporting proposals in general, it is essentially a criticism of the work of Lee (1972). As such, it is exceedingly selective—concentrating on early proposals which have since been modified in order to improve and extend the first thoughts which were published. Although a later work of Lee (1981a) is recognised and explained briefly, it is not used extensively by Egginton to counter the arguments he makes concerning the earlier work. This appears to weaken his case considerably, and tends to make the following sections somewhat repetitive as the selective use of the cash flow reporting literature by Egginton has created many of the problems of response in this paper.

Performance measures

It is open to considerable debate as to what is meant by entity performance, and Egginton's narrowing of it down to resource changes appears to be unduly restrictive. Indeed, as Kaplan (1983) has recently argued, the popularity of all-embracing measures of performance such as profit may well have caused entity management to under-estimate the importance of performance measures such as market domination, productivity, and quality of products and services. Certainly, Egginton would appear to wish to exclude liquidity matters from performance measurement.

The cash flow proponents, on the other hand, see liquidity assessment as a critical aspect of examining entity performance in the sense that cash flow and not profit is the end result of entity activity. Profit is an abstraction; cash is a physical resource. This is not to deny the importance of profit as a guide to entity behaviour, but its nature ought not to be ignored.

Indeed, the later works of Lee (1981a, 1981b and 1984) reflect his concern over the avoidance of profit in his earlier papers. However, of particular importance to him in this respect is not so much profit *per se*, but the lack of recognition of unrealised cash flows in the reporting format. To recognise realised cash flows only appears to be stating half the story. The use of net realisable values (which are potential cash flows) appears to remedy the situation. They also allow for the measurement of realisable profit which, in Lee's system, is explained as a measure of total cash flow.

Thus, what Lee's system is attempting to provide is a means of assessing entity performance in cash flow terms which reflect actual and potential changes in its ability to command resources. This does not exclude the use of other means of assessing entity performance but it does suggest the considerable importance of cash flow as a reasonably objective measure of the latter. It further suggests that Egginton is wrong to state that cash flow reporting proposals are not concerned with entity performance.

This can perhaps be more clearly seen by means of an illustration using data provided by Egginton in Tables 1 and 2 of his paper. Egginton uses these figures in connection with his arguments regarding forecast and actual cash flows but, for the purposes of this section, only his actual data will be used:

	£
Sales receipts	400
Less: operating payments	270
	130
Less: taxation paid	40
	90
Less: dividend paid	40
Cash surplus	50

Egginton argues about the misleading nature of this cash flow signal, particularly relating to forecast cash flows, and actual and forecast profits (the operating surplus of £130 being considerably in excess of these other data).

In fact, part of the operating surplus has been due to working capital management, and Egginton further complains that this would not become apparent until the next period's cash flow results were reported—by which time the relevance of the information may be lost. This is an example of how Egginton has not applied the suggestions of Lee (1981a) to this problem, and has thus created a non-problem. A total cash flow approach would have produced the following statement:

	£	£
Realised operating cash flow (as above)		130
Unrealised cash flow:		
reduction in debtors	(25)	
increase in creditors	(20)	(45)
*Total cash flow from operations**		85
Less: taxation paid		40
		45
Less: dividend paid		40
Additional command over resources		5

*This figure is equal to realisable profit on a net realisable value basis and, due to the absence of non-monetary resources in the example, historic cost profit.

Thus, the total cash flow system reports on overall liquidity performance; and provides a measure of periodic profit should that be required. The reader is informed in this case that, although there has been a realisation of £130 of cash flow from operations, there has also been a decrease in working capital which has reduced potential cash flow by £45.

It is important to emphasise that, in Lee's system, the above statement is one of cash flow within which a profit measure is disclosed. It should not be interpreted as a profit statement containing cash flow data.

Finally, throughout his paper Egginton describes realised cash flow reporting in a format equivalent to that of a profit statement, and derived from an early paper of Lee (1972). Attention to later work of Lee in this respect would have evidenced that he has amended the format to that equivalent to a funds flow statement, and has used this in a number of analytical exercises (1982a, 1983a, 1983b, 1983c and 1984). The reason for adopting the funds approach is to avoid the suggestion in analyses of cash flow results of entities that taxation and distribution payments are being funded by borrowing. A more neutral formatting may well lead to the same conclusion, but puts the onus on the analyst rather than on the financial reporter. Indeed, Egginton uses the results of Royal Dutch Shell to criticise the profit-based format—dividends in only one year appearing to be covered by a cash flow surplus. This criticism would not have been necessary if he had adopted the formatting of Lee as follows (using the aggregate for seven years):

Egginton's format

	£b
Operating cash flow (after interest)	33.3
Less: capital payments	18.7
	14.6
Less: taxation payments	15.2
	(0.6)
Less: dividend payments	3.8
Additional borrowing	(4.4)

Lee's format

	£b	%
Operating cash flow	33.3	88
Additional borrowing	4.4	12
	37.7	100
Capital payments	18.7	50
Taxation payments	15.2	40
Dividend payments	3.8	10
	37.7	100

The first format could lead to the conclusion that the dividends had been funded by borrowing; the second format reveals that only 10% of available cash had been committed to dividends, and seven-eighths of the total cash had come from trading operations.

Statement of financial position

Egginton is correct when he complains of the lack of a position statement to complement a flow statement in the early cash flow reporting proposals. However, Lee (1978, 1979, 1981a, 1981b and 1984) has been a consistent advocate of such a position statement. Originally conceiving it as a net realisable value based appendage to cash flow statements (1978 and 1979), it is now conceived of as a fundamental part of the overall system of cash flow reporting (1981a, 1981b and 1984)—position data being compatible with those classifications used for flow data. Using the figures given in the previous section, and derived from Egginton's tables, the following statement of financial position would be reported:

	£	£
Realised asset:		
Cash		62
Readily-realised net assets:		
Debtors	158	
Less: creditors	90	68
Capital and retained profit		130

Thus, 48% of capital is in the form of cash, and the remaining 52% is in the form of near-cash resources.

Egginton devotes some time to examining the proposals of Lee regarding statements of financial position with respect to the problem of which net realisable value to use for reporting purposes. As he points out, there are essentially two values to use—a going concern value assuming an orderly liquidation (much favoured by Chambers (1966)), and an immediate liquidation value advocated by Sterling (Sterling 1979). Egginton assumes Lee utilises the Sterling approach because Lee's cash flow system does not assume the continuity of the activities of the entity (Lee 1981b). This is not the case (see Lee 1984). There is a distinction to be made regarding continuity of the entity and continuity of its activities. It would appear to be reasonable to assume changes in activity, and consequent realisation and non-identical replacement of assets. Except in extreme circumstances, it would not appear reasonable to assume the liquidation of the entity and, inevitably, its assets.

Thus, Lee's system does not assume continuity of activities currently undertaken but does assume continuity of the entity. Net realisable values used are those to be obtained in a normal sale of the assets concerned in their existing state. They should reflect expected proceeds at the time of reporting and according to the condition of the assets, and should not reflect the disposal intentions of management. In this sense, Egginton is correct in stating that these would reflect the best prices immediately obtainable; but wrong in suggesting that these are liquidation values to be achieved on the break-up of the entity.

De-emphasising ownership

Egginton states that cash flow reporting has been advocated as a means of de-emphasising the ownership orientation of the conventional profit statement, and doubts if the suggested cash flow statement presentations can do this. Certainly it is true that cash flow proposals have been made in the form of general purpose statements (see, for example, Lee 1979), and this would appear to reflect the growing awareness of accountants in recent years of the need to provide information to satisfy the needs of a variety of report users. In this respect, cash flow statements would appear to be particularly suited to a general purpose role because of the importance of liquidity matters to investors, lenders, creditors, employees and others.

The doubts of Egginton regarding the ability of cash flow presentations to de-emphasise the ownership orientation would appear to be directed at the earliest cash flow proposals in which a 'profit statement' presentation was adopted (Lee 1972). Once again, Egginton does not seem willing to use the evidence of later presentations in which a more neutral 'funds' format has been adopted. This can be seen in relation to the figures given in the section on performance measurement. These can be further explained as follows using the aggregate figures of Royal Dutch Shell:

Cash Inflows	£b	
Operating cash flow	33.3	The cash flow generated by Shell from its operations; the key to the long-term survival propspects of the entity, and of considerable concern to all interested parties.
Additional borrowing	4.4	The extent of external financing during the period, reflecting Shell's relatively small dependence on lenders and bankers.
	37.7	

Cash Outflows	£b	
Capital payments	18.7	The amount of cash flow ploughed back into Shell, and providing the basis for operating cash flows in the future; again, a matter of concern to most report users.
Taxation payments	15.2	A governmental share in the cash flow of Shell.
Dividend payments	3.8	The proportion of Shell's cash flow received by its shareholders as reward for their investment.
	37.7	

As the above brief descriptions evidence, no particular report user is emphasised by the data—unlike Egginton's 'profit' format which leads the reader downwards to dividend payments (£3.8b) funded by additional borrowings (£4.4b), thus emphasising debt-equity substitution.

The allocation problem

Egginton doubts the early claims of cash flow proponents that cash flow reporting avoids allocations. It must be agreed that these early claims were excessive if the definition of allocation is widened to include any partitioning or division in accounting. The debate on this issue can be read in Lee (1982b) and Rutherford (1982), and is commented on by Egginton. It is not intended to report the various arguments here but it is important to note the emphasis given by Egginton to the matching of costs with revenues in order to reflect the consumption of assets. This is consistent with his characterisation of profit measures as the central feature of entity performance assessment. Because cash flow accounting is concerned with the receipt and consumption of cash (a specific resource related to the entity's command over resources), it is wrong to compare it in any way with profit accounting (which is designed to reflect the receipt and consumption of all resources).

Cash flow forecasts

The early cash flow writings were very specific in their advocacy of reporting in actual and forecast terms (for example, Lee 1972). However, certainly from the point of view of Lee, the reporting of forecast cash flows is not an aspect of the overall system which has been developed. Indeed, as argued recently (Lee 1984), the problems of forecast reports are considerable. Egginton's comments are therefore very apt. But it ought to be noted that the recent proposals of Lee to combine his earlier proposals with net realisable value accounting in a total cash flow system evidence his primary concern to develop a relevant and feasible system of ex post reporting. However, if actual and forecast reports are to be produced then both can be prepared on the basis of Lee's total cash flow system. For example, taking Egginton's actual and forecast figures, the following comparative statement can be given:

	Forecast £	Actual £
Realised operating cash flow	90	130
Unrealised cash flow	5	(45)
	95	85
Less: taxation paid	40	40
	55	45
Less: dividends paid	25	40
Retained surplus	30	5

From these data, it is possible to examine the differences between forecast and actual figures in a way that meets much of Egginton's criticisms which are based only on realised cash data. The entity has achieved an operating surplus which is £40 in excess of forecast but this has been accompanied by a decrease in working capital which is £50 adrift from forecast. Thus, the overall cash flow performance has a £10 variance which has been further accentuated by a dividend which was £15 in excess of forecast.

Changing prices

Finally, Egginton complains of the ignoring of price changes by cash flow proponents. This criticism, as with others by him, has been answered in the overall system of cash flow reporting advocated by Lee (1981a). By using net realisable values as the basis for the system, it is possible to incorporate unrealised price changes in the various statements. As this has been demonstrated on several occasions in this paper, it is not intended to repeat the argument here.

Conclusions

The development of a system such as cash flow reporting is a long-lived affair which occupies many years of thinking, writing, testing and criticism. The bare bones of ideas are usually included in the earliest work, and this is then fleshed out in later writings. Often, early ideas are discarded in response to further thinking and criticism. Hopefully, the proponents of cash flow reporting are responding to their critics, and fine-tuning their ideas. The problem with Egginton's critique is that his arguments had already been answered in writings which he was obviously aware of. Nevertheless, he has given the opportunity for these arguments to be further refuted.

References

R. J. Chambers, *Accounting, Evaluation and Economic Behavior*, Prentice Hall, 1966.
D. A. Egginton, 'In Defence of Profit Measurement: Some Limitations of Cash Flow and Value Added as Performance Measures for External Reporting'. *Accounting and Business Research*, Spring 1984.
R. S. Kaplan, 'Measuring Manufacturing Performance: A New Challenge for Managerial Accounting Research', *The Accounting Review*, October 1983.
T. A. Lee, 'A Case for Cash Flow Reporting', *Journal of Business Finance*, Summer 1972.
T. A. Lee, 'The Cash Flow Accounting Alternative for Corporate Financial Reporting', in C. van Dam (ed.), *Trends in Managerial and Financial Accounting*, vol. 1., Martinus Nijhoff, 1978.
T. A. Lee, 'The Simplicity and Complexity of Accounting', in R. R. Sterling and A. L. Thomas (eds.), *Accounting for a Simplified Firm Owning Depreciable Assets*, Scholars Book Co., 1979.
T. A. Lee, 'Reporting Cash Flows and Net Realisable Values', *Accounting and Business Research*, Spring 1981a.
T. A. Lee, 'Reporting Cash Flows and Net Realisable Values', *Accountancy and Business Economics*, 1981b.
T. A. Lee, 'Laker Airways—The Cash Flow Truth'. *Accountancy*, June 1982a.
T. A. Lee, 'Cash Flow Accounting and the Allocation Problem', *Journal of Business Finance and Accounting*. Autumn 1982b.
T. A. Lee, 'Lonrho: Cash Flow and Borrowing'. *The Accountant*, 19 May 1983a.
T. A. Lee, 'Funds Statements and Cash Flow Analysis'. *The Investment Analyst*, July 1983b.
T. A. Lee, 'The Financial Statements and Cash Flow of the Hongkong and Shanghai Banking Corporation: 1865 to 1980', in F. H. H. King (ed.), *Eastern Banking: Essays in the History of The Hongkong and Shanghai Banking Corporation*, Athlone Press, 1983c.
T. A. Lee, *Cash Flow Accounting*, Van Nostrand Reinhold. 1984.
T. A. Lee and A. W. Stark, 'A Cash Flow Disclosure of Government-Supported Enterprises' Results', *Journal of Business Finance and Accounting*, Spring 1984.
B. A. Rutherford, 'The Interpretation of Cash Flow Reports and the Other Allocation Problem', *Abacus*, June 1982.
R. R. Sterling, *Toward a Science of Accounting*, Scholars Book Co., 1979.

Accounting Books Published by Garland

New Books

Ashton, Robert H., ed. *The Evolution of Behavioral Accounting Research: An Overview.* New York, 1984.

Ashton, Robert H., ed. *Some Early Contributions to the Study of Audit Judgment.* New York, 1984.

*Brief, Richard P., ed. *Corporate Financial Reporting and Analysis in the Early 1900s.* New York, 1986.

Brief, Richard P., ed. *Depreciation and Capital Maintenance.* New York, 1984.

*Brief, Richard P., ed. *Estimating the Economic Rate of Return from Accounting Data.* New York, 1986.

Brief, Richard P., ed. *Four Classics on the Theory of Double-Entry Bookkeeping.* New York, 1982.

*Chambers, R. J., and G. W. Dean, eds. *Chambers on Accounting.* New York, 1986.
Volume I: Accounting, Management and Finance.
Volume II: Accounting Practice and Education.
Volume III: Accounting Theory and Research.
Volume IV: Price Variation Accounting.
Volume V: Continuously Contemporary Accounting.

Clarke, F. L. *The Tangled Web of Price Variation Accounting: The Development of Ideas Underlying Professional Prescriptions in Six Countries.* New York, 1982.

Coopers & Lybrand. *The Early History of Coopers & Lybrand.* New York, 1984.

---

*Included in the Garland series Accounting Thought and Practice Through the Years.

*Craswell, Allen. *Audit Qualifications in Australia 1950 to 1979*. New York, 1986.

Dean, G. W., and M. C. Wells, eds. *The Case for Continuously Contemporary Accounting*. New York, 1984.

Dean, G. W., and M. C. Wells, eds. *Forerunners of Realizable Values Accounting in Financial Reporting*. New York, 1982.

Edey, Harold C. *Accounting Queries*. New York, 1982.

*Edwards, J. R., ed. *Legal Regulation of British Company Accounts 1836–1900*. New York, 1986.

*Edwards, J. R., ed. *Reporting Fixed Assets in Nineteenth-Century Company Accounts*. New York, 1986.

Edwards, J. R., ed. *Studies of Company Records: 1830–1974*. New York, 1984.

Fabricant, Solomon. *Studies in Social and Private Accounting*. New York, 1982.

Gaffikin, Michael, and Michael Aitken, eds. *The Development of Accounting Theory: Significant Contributors to Accounting Thought in the 20th Century*. New York, 1982.

Hawawini, Gabriel A., ed. *Bond Duration and Immunization: Early Developments and Recent Contributions*. New York, 1982.

Hawawini, Gabriel, and Pierre Michel, eds. *European Equity Markets: Risk, Return, and Efficiency*. New York, 1984.

*Hawawini, Gabriel, and Pierre A. Michel. *Mandatory Financial Information and Capital Market Equilibrium in Belgium*. New York, 1986.

*Hawkins, David F. *Corporate Financial Disclosure, 1900–1933: A Study of Management Inertia within a Rapidly Changing Environment*. New York, 1986.

*Johnson, H. Thomas. *A New Approach to Management Accounting History* New York, 1986.

*Kinney, William R., Jr., ed. *Fifty Years of Statistical Auditing*. New York, 1986.

Klemstine, Charles E., and Michael W. Maher. *Management Accounting Research: A Review and Annotated Bibliography.* New York, 1984.

*Lee, T. A., ed. *A Scottish Contribution to Accounting History.* New York, 1986.

*Lee, T. A. *Towards a Theory and Practice of Cash Flow Accounting.* New York, 1986.

Lee, Thomas A., ed. *Transactions of the Chartered Accountants Students' Societies of Edinburgh and Glasgow: A Selection of Writings, 1886–1958.* New York, 1984.

*McKinnon, Jill L. *The Historical Development and Operational Form of Corporate Reporting Regulation in Japan.* New York, 1986.

Nobes, Christopher, ed. *The Development of Double Entry: Selected Essays.* New York, 1984.

*Nobes, Christopher. *Issues in International Accounting.* New York, 1986.

*Parker, Lee D. *Developing Control Concepts in the 20th Century.* New York, 1986.

Parker, R. H. *Papers on Accounting History.* New York, 1984.

*Previts, Gary John, and Alfred R. Roberts, eds. *Federal Securities Law and Accounting 1933–1970; Selected Addresses.* New York, 1986.

*Reid, Jean Margo, ed. *Law and Accounting: Pre-1889 British Legal Cases.* New York, 1986.

Sheldahl, Terry K. *Beta Alpha Psi, from Alpha to Omega: Pursuing a Vision of Professional Education for Accountants, 1919–1945.* New York, 1982.

*Sheldahl, Terry K. *Beta Alpha Psi, from Omega to Zeta Omega: The Making of a Comprehensive Accounting Fraternity, 1946–1984.* New York, 1986.

Solomons, David. *Collected Papers on Accounting and Accounting Education. (in two volumes)* New York, 1984.

Sprague, Charles F. *The General Principles of the Science of Accounts and the Accountancy of Investment.* New York, 1984.

Stamp, Edward. *Selected Papers on Accounting, Auditing, and Professional Problems.* New York, 1984.

*Storrar, Colin, ed. *The Accountant's Magazine—An Anthology.* New York, 1986.

Tantral, Panadda. *Accounting Literature in Non-Accounting Journals: An Annotated Bibliography.* New York, 1984.

*Vangermeersch, Richard, ed. *The Contributions of Alexander Hamilton Church to Accounting and Management.* New York, 1986.

*Vangermeersch, Richard, ed. *Financial Accounting Milestones in the Annual Reports of United States Steel Corporation—The First Seven Decades.* New York, 1986.

Whitmore, John. *Factory Accounts.* New York, 1984.

Yamey, Basil S. *Further Essays on the History of Accounting.* New York, 1982.

Zeff, Stephen A., ed. *The Accounting Postulates and Principles Controversy of the 1960s.* New York, 1982.

Zeff, Stephen A., ed. *Accounting Principles Through the Years: The Views of Professional and Academic Leaders 1938–1954.* New York, 1982.

Zeff, Stephen A., and Maurice Moonitz, eds. *Sourcebook on Accounting Principles and Auditing Procedures: 1917–1953 (in two volumes).* New York, 1984.

Reprinted Titles

American Institute of Accountants. *Fiftieth Anniversary Celebration.* Chicago, 1937 (Garland reprint, 1982).

American Institute of Accountants. *Library Catalogue.* New York, 1919 (Garland reprint, 1982).

Arthur Andersen Company. *The First Fifty Years 1913–1963.* Chicago, 1963 (Garland reprint, 1984).

*Bevis, Herman W. *Corporate Financial Reporting in a Competitive Economy.* New York, 1965 (Garland reprint, 1986).

*Bonini, Charles P., Robert K. Jaedicke, and Harvey M. Wagner, eds. *Management Controls: New Directions in Basic Research.* New York, 1964 (Garland reprint, 1986).

Bray, F. Sewell. *Four Essays in Accounting Theory.* London, 1953. *Bound with* Institute of Chartered Accountants in England and Wales and the National Institute of Economic and Social Research. *Some Accounting Terms and Concepts.* Cambridge, 1951 (Garland reprint, 1982).

Brown, R. Gene, and Kenneth S. Johnston. *Paciolo on Accounting.* New York, 1963 (Garland reprint, 1984).

*Carey, John L., and William O. Doherty, eds. *Ethical Standards of the Accounting Profession.* New York, 1966 (Garland reprint, 1986).

Chambers, R. J. *Accounting in Disarray.* Melbourne, 1973 (Garland reprint, 1982).

Cooper, Ernest. *Fifty-seven Years in an Accountant's Office. See* Sir Russell Kettle.

Couchman, Charles B. *The Balance-Sheet.* New York, 1924 (Garland reprint, 1982).

Couper, Charles Tennant. *Report of the Trial . . . Against the Directors and Manager of the City of Glasgow Bank.* Edinburgh, 1879 (Garland reprint, 1984).

Cutforth, Arthur E. *Audits.* London, 1906 (Garland reprint, 1982).

Cutforth, Arthur E. *Methods of Amalgamation.* London, 1926 (Garland reprint, 1982).

Deinzer, Harvey T. *Development of Accounting Thought.* New York, 1965 (Garland reprint, 1984).

De Paula, F.R.M. *The Principles of Auditing.* London, 1915 (Garland reprint, 1984).

Dickerson, R. W. *Accountants and the Law of Negligence.* Toronto, 1966 (Garland reprint, 1982).

Dodson, James. *The Accountant, or, the Method of Bookkeeping Deduced from Clear Principles, and Illustrated by a Variety of Examples.* London, 1750 (Garland reprint, 1984).

Dyer, S. *A Common Sense Method of Double Entry Bookkeeping, on First Principles, as Suggested by De Morgan. Part I, Theoretical.* London, 1897 (Garland reprint, 1984).

*The Fifth International Congress on Accounting, 1938 {Kongress-Archiv 1938 des V. Internationalen Prüfungs- und Treuhand-Kongresses}. Berlin, 1938 (Garland reprint, 1986).

Finney, H. A. *Consolidated Statements*. New York, 1922 (Garland reprint, 1982).

Fisher, Irving. *The Rate of Interest*. New York, 1907 (Garland reprint, 1982).

Florence, P. Sargant. *Economics of Fatigue of Unrest and the Efficiency of Labour in English and American Industry*. London, 1923 (Garland reprint, 1984).

Fourth International Congress on Accounting 1933. London, 1933 (Garland reprint, 1982).

Foye, Arthur B. *Haskins & Sells: Our First Seventy-Five Years*. New York, 1970 (Garland reprint, 1984).

Garnsey, Sir Gilbert. *Holding Companies and Their Published Accounts*. London, 1923. Bound with Sir Gilbert Garnsey. *Limitations of a Balance Sheet*. London, 1928 (Garland reprint, 1982).

Garrett, A. A. *The History of the Society of Incorporated Accountants, 1885–1957*. Oxford, 1961 (Garland reprint, 1984).

Gilman, Stephen. *Accounting Concepts of Profit*. New York, 1939 (Garland reprint, 1982).

*Gordon, William. *The Universal Accountant, and Complete Merchant . . . [Volume II]*. Edinburgh, 1765 (Garland reprint, 1986).

*Green, Wilmer. *History and Survey of Accountancy*. Brooklyn, 1930 (Garland reprint, 1986).

Hamilton, Robert. *An Introduction to Merchandise, Parts IV and V (Italian Bookkeeping and Practical Bookkeeping)*. Edinburgh, 1788 (Garland reprint, 1982).

Hatton, Edward. *The Merchant's Magazine: or, Trades-man's Treasury*. London, 1695 (Garland reprint, 1982).

Hills, George S. *The Law of Accounting and Financial Statements*. Boston, 1957 (Garland reprint, 1982).

A History of Cooper Brothers & Co. 1854 to 1954. London, 1954 (Garland reprint, 1986).

Hofstede, Geert. *The Game of Budget Control.* Assen, 1967 (Garland reprint, 1984).

Howitt, Sir Harold. *The History of The Institute of Chartered Accountants in England and Wales 1880–1965, and of Its Founder Accountancy Bodies 1870–1880.* London, 1966 (Garland reprint, 1984).

Institute of Chartered Accountants in England and Wales and The National Institute of Economic and Social Research. *Some Accounting Terms and Concepts. See* F. Sewell Bray.

Institute of Chartered Accountants of Scotland. *History of the Chartered Accountants of Scotland from the Earliest Times to 1954.* Edinburgh, 1954 (Garland reprint, 1984).

International Congress on Accounting 1929. New York, 1930 (Garland reprint, 1982).

*Jaedicke, Robert K., Yuji Ijiri, and Oswald Nielsen, eds. *Research in Accounting Measurement.* American Accounting Association, 1966 (Garland reprint, 1986).

Keats, Charles. *Magnificent Masquerade.* New York, 1964 (Garland reprint, 1982).

Kettle, Sir Russell. *Deloitte & Co. 1845–1956.* Oxford, 1958. *Bound with* Ernest Cooper. *Fifty-seven Years in an Accountant's Office.* London, 1921 (Garland reprint, 1982).

Kitchen, J., and R. H. Parker. *Accounting Thought and Education: Six English Pioneers.* London, 1980 (Garland reprint, 1984).

Lacey, Kenneth. *Profit Measurement and Price Changes.* London, 1952 (Garland reprint, 1982).

Lee, Chauncey. *The American Accomptant.* Lansingburgh, 1797 (Garland reprint, 1982).

Lee, T. A., and R. H. Parker. *The Evolution of Corporate Financial Reporting.* Middlesex, 1979 (Garland reprint, 1984).

*Malcolm, Alexander. *A Treatise of Book-Keeping, or, Merchants Accounts; In *the Italian Method of Debtor and Creditor; Wherein the Fundamental Principles of That Curious and Approved Method Are Clearly and Fully Explained and Demonstrated . . . To Which Are Added, Instructions for Gentlemen of Land Estates, and Their Stewards or Factors: With Directions Also for Retailers, and Other More Private Persons.* London, 1731 (Garland reprint, 1986).

*Meij, J. L., ed. *Depreciation and Replacement Policy.* Chicago, 1961 (Garland reprint, 1986).

Newlove, George Hills. *Consolidated Balance Sheets.* New York, 1926 (Garland reprint, 1982).

*North, Roger. *The Gentleman Accomptant; or, An Essay to Unfold the Mystery of Accompts; By Way of Debtor and Creditor, Commonly Called Merchants Accompts, and Applying the Same to the Concerns of the Nobility and Gentry of England.* London, 1714 (Garland reprint, 1986).

Pryce-Jones, Janet E., and R. H. Parker. *Accounting in Scotland: A Historical Bibliography.* Edinburgh, 1976 (Garland reprint, 1984).

Robinson, H. W. *A History of Accountants in Ireland.* Dublin, 1964 (Garland reprint, 1984).

Robson, T. B. *Consolidated and Other Group Accounts.* London, 1950 (Garland reprint, 1982).

Rorem, C. Rufus. *Accounting Method.* Chicago, 1928 (Garland reprint, 1982).

*Saliers, Earl A., ed. *Accountants' Handbook.* New York, 1923 (Garland reprint, 1986).

Samuel, Horace B. *Shareholder's Money.* London, 1933 (Garland reprint, 1982).

The Securities and Exchange Commission in the Matter of McKesson & Robbins, Inc. Report on Investigation. Washington, D.C., 1940 (Garland reprint, 1982).

The Securities and Exchange Commission in the Matter of McKesson & Robbins, Inc. Testimony of Expert Witnesses. Washington, D.C., 1939 (Garland reprint, 1982).

*Shaplen, Robert. *Kreuger: Genius and Swindler.* New York, 1960 (Garland reprint, 1986).

Singer, H. W. *Standardized Accountancy in Germany. (With a new appendix.)* Cambridge, 1943 (Garland reprint, 1982).

The Sixth International Congress on Accounting. London, 1952 (Garland reprint, 1984).

*Stewart, Jas. C. (with a new introductory note by T. A. Lee). *Pioneers of a Profession: Chartered Accountants to 1879.* Edinburgh, 1977 (Garland reprint, 1986).

Thompson, Wardbaugh. *The Accomptant's Oracle: or, Key to Science, Being a Compleat Practical System of Book-keeping.* York, 1777 (Garland reprint, 1984).

*Vatter, William J. *Managerial Accounting.* New York, 1950 (Garland reprint, 1986).

*Woolf, Arthur H. *A Short History of Accountants and Accountancy.* London, 1912 (Garland reprint, 1986).

Yamey, B. S., H. C. Edey, and Hugh W. Thomson. *Accounting in England and Scotland: 1543–1800.* London, 1963 (Garland reprint, 1982).